The Official History of

WORCESTERSHIRE COUNTY CRICKET CLUB

THE CHRISTOPHER HELM
COUNTY CRICKET HISTORIES

Series Editors:
Peter Arnold and Peter Wynne-Thomas

GLAMORGAN
Andrew Hignell, with a personal view by Tony Lewis

HAMPSHIRE
Peter Wynne-Thomas, with a personal view by John Arlott

KENT
Dudley Moore, with a personal view by Derek Underwood

MIDDLESEX
David Lemmon, with a personal view by Denis Compton

The Official History of

WORCESTERSHIRE COUNTY CRICKET CLUB

David Lemmon

With a personal view by
BASIL D'OLIVEIRA

CHRISTOPHER HELM

London

© 1989 David Lemmon and Basil D'Oliveira
Christopher Helm (Publishers) Ltd, Imperial House,
21–25 North Street, Bromley, Kent BR1 1SD

ISBN 0-7470-2013-2

A CIP catalogue record for this book is available from the British Library

Typeset by Cotswold Typesetting Ltd, Gloucester
Printed and bound by Biddles Ltd, Guildford, Surrey

CONTENTS

A Personal View *Basil D'Oliveira*   I

1. Foley and a Family Affair   7
2. Fostershire   22
3. Hard Times   59
4. Out of the Trough   80
5. Middle of the Road   108
6. The Kenyon Years   141
7. Rise and Fall   173
8. Towards the Summit   204

Statistical Section   237

Select Bibliography   283

Acknowledgements   285

Index   285

A PERSONAL VIEW
Basil D'Oliveira

IN 1963 ON A CRICKET TOUR OF PAKISTAN with an Alf Gover Eleven, I approached my great friend Tom Graveney in the Hotel Metropole in Karachi and asked him whether he would give me his assessment of my ability as a player. He convinced me that I was good enough to play county cricket and indeed felt that I might even go further. This was genuine praise from a man and a player whom I have always admired.

I obviously had a few doubts whether I was capable of playing first-class cricket. Not having had any experience at that level and with only a few seasons of League cricket behind me made me feel a little apprehensive. So Tom's encouraging words were the spur I needed.

Tom had just left his home county, Gloucestershire, and joined up with Worcestershire. I had at that stage been approached by a number of counties. Strangely enough, after all the interviews and talks I was convinced by my discussions with Tom's brother, Ken, that Gloucestershire was the county for me. Tom felt that I would be very happy at Gloucester but felt equally sure that Worcestershire was the county I would be happiest at.

On my return to England Tom, after consulting with Don Kenyon, the Worcestershire captain, arranged an interview for me with the Worcestershire officials, namely the president, Sir George Dowty, the cricket committee chairman, the Hon. Richard Lygon, and the secretary, Joe Lister. After a very lengthy discussion I was still of the opinion that Gloucestershire was the county for me. However, Sir George Dowty, who up to that point had not said too much, then asked the other two to leave the room and spoke to me personally. He discovered my biggest fear was finding a home for my wife Naomi and my three-year-old son Damian.

Sir George then promised me that the Club would provide me with a house. It turned out to be a semi-detached which I am still living in today. The Club charged me £2.50 a week in rent. On the advice of Sir George I bought the house from the Club the following year at the original price.

This was in 1964 and started my first-class career with Worcestershire, which has blossomed from being a player to becoming the coach in 1980. A marvellously happy relationship that has now lasted 25 years. I still regard it as a great honour to walk through those gates at New Road as a member of Worcestershire County Cricket Club.

One point which I have to clear up is that I did tell a little 'white lie' to get the job. I made myself a lot younger than I was because I feared if my correct age was known I would never have got near those gates! Let's be fair—with only three seasons of League Cricket with Middleton CC in the Central Lancashire League, at my age no Club in its right mind was going to take a chance on signing me, a complete unknown. When my name was mentioned the public would say: 'Who?'

In my formative years all my cricket was played in South Africa on gravel pitches with coir matting. Not the ideal training ground for the hard graft of the professional English

I

game played on indifferent grass pitches. Having cleared the air I hope that in that great book in the sky I have now been forgiven for that little 'white lie'.

Whenever I did well for Worcester Sir George Dowty would come up to me and say: 'Well done'. He would also put £30 in my pocket and say: 'Buy the boys a drink'. A few years after he had retired I played in a Gillette Cup match at Hove against Sussex. I played well and was awarded the 'Man of the Match'. A week later I received a letter from Sir George. He had seen the game on TV and he wished to thank and congratulate me for doing so well for the County. Accompanying the letter was a cheque for £30 'to buy the boys a drink'. A lovely touch from a lovely man. The only problem now is the lads will be after me wanting to know when am I going to buy them a drink.

My first impression of Worcestershire was what a delightful and beautiful ground the County played on: a truly magnificent setting with the Cathedral rising in the background. It struck me how similar it was to Newlands, the Test Match ground in Cape Town, my home town in South Africa. The only difference is that in the background Worcester had the Cathedral and Newlands had Table Mountain and the brewery. The Committee, too, was made up of such nice and friendly people.

I was part of the big league, and it wasn't easy getting used to the fact that I was in a dressing room with full-time professional cricketers. Ever critical of our own, there were those who, after seeing me perform in the nets, thought I would never make it. Maybe in the early days I had my doubts too!

I had to qualify for one season, playing with Kidderminster CC in the Birmingham League and Second Eleven cricket. At first I wasn't happy with Second Eleven cricket and it showed in my performances. Eventually that grand old coach, Charlie Hallows, pulled me to one side and told me in a one-sided conversation a few home truths. He told me I was destroying the possibility of a first-class career even before it had started.

'Basil, you will have to perform in the second team before they will even consider you for the first', he said. In some very strong language he told me he was disgusted with my approach and performances. Today I realise how much I needed that telling off. Having always responded to all challenges, I was spurred on by his words to score hundreds just to show him I could play. Playing with much more determination and a greater awareness of the importance of Second Eleven cricket earned me rare praise from Charlie: 'You'll do for me, son!' He had achieved what he wanted.

I also learnt the importance of averages. I had never bothered in the past. I hardly ever knew or cared about my own averages. Players, personalities, great batting, fielding and bowling performances makes true sporting history to me. Even though I still feel the same I became aware how important averages were to others who had to judge and eventually pick me.

Worcestershire County Cricket Club celebrated its Centenary in 1965, my first full season with the Club. I had studied the first team and all its capped players. I had set my heart on fielding at first slip, to be the first change bowler and to bat at number five. Great, and at times seemingly impossible ambitions. As I quietly strived and achieved what I wanted I had another shock. I had not realised how jealously players guarded their places in the team. As I achieved my desires I was fast learning how to loose friends and make enemies. But I believed then as I do now that you need to set yourself certain goals and be single-minded in pursuing them. There were a lot of personal clashes in those days because the side was so talented: Kenyon, Horton, Headley, Richardson, Ormrod, Graveney, Fearnley, Standen, Gifford, Slade, Booth, Flavell, Coldwell, Brain, Carter, D'Oliveira, A fine squad of players.

Throughout the history of our Club star players have appeared and disappeared. To mention names would sometimes be an injustice to those not recorded but there are those players who are match-winners in their own right, individuals who will shine through and be identified as heroes and stars.

Don Kenyon, our current president and former captain and opening batsman, was probably one of the finest players of fast bowling in the country, at times a butcher with the bat and a superb back-foot player. Always a believer in watching great players, I copied a lot of my own back-foot play from him without falling into the trap of imitating him. He was a very astute captain who read his players very well. It has been said that a hallmark of all outstanding captains is that the team appears to captain itself. It was said of Worcestershire. Believe me nothing could be further from the truth. To captain such a talented side with a load of characters and personalities takes a certain kind of person. Don was the ideal man to lead and direct us into a happy and successful team.

Tom Graveney, that graceful batsman, was totally different to Don Kenyon. Tom played everything off the front foot. He was not the most exciting player I've seen (that accolade goes to the great Sir Garfield Sobers). But if I had to choose someone to play for me on all types of pitches day in and day out, Tom would be my man. To all us lesser mortals it was quite a revelation to see this master batsman work and work at his game. Practice will not make perfect but it will make permanent. Tom had a net every day and each was naturally a Test innings to him. He would revel in facing seamers, fast or spin bowling, on any sort of net pitches. It became a constant challenge to him.

Today as a coach I use Tom as an example to all our young players of how hard one needs to work to achieve success. There is no short cut. Every season I used to say to Tom that I was going to get more runs than him or top him in the averages. He would just smile, knowing full well I had little or no chance. But an old Aunt once said to me: 'Aim high—there is room up there for all.' Not a bad motto.

History has shown us that fast bowlers hunt in pairs. Never was this more true than with our two opening bowlers, Jack Flavell and Len Coldwell. Flavell was strong, oozing sheer aggression and pace, a great wicket-to-wicket bowler. I have seen some fantastic catches, taken off Flav's bowling but the only comment from Flav would be: 'What a purler', meaning what a great delivery he had just bowled. Whether or not the fielder had dived yards to right or left to make the catch did not really register with Flav. Coldwell, always the thinking in-swing bowler, applied intense concentration on where and how he wanted to put each delivery. He kept a mental picture of all batsmen's weaknesses and could produce a quicker ball that would take many players by surprise. I will always remember Len producing such a delivery to Colin Cowdrey at Worcester and hitting him a nasty blow in the face, knocking him over and onto his stumps!

Norman Gifford (left-arm) and Martin Horton (off-spin) were the spin twins. Giffy was the more attacking and aggressive bowler. He is a great believer in himself and in his ability to spin the ball. He also has a great sense of humour, with a witty and sharp tongue. Giffy's half-hour cabaret on the field is well-known throughout the game, always produced when things were not going too well. During a match with Gloucestershire at Worcester those two great Pakistani batsmen Sadiq Mohammed and Zaheer Abbas, on a flat pitch with the sun beating down, gave us some terrrible stick. Giffy was carrying the bulk of the attack. At the end of each over the batsmen would come together in the middle of the pitch to have a laugh and natter away in their own language. Giffy was getting redder and redder in the face and noticably building up to his 'half-hour'. Finally he cracked and, turning to the two batsmen he retorted: 'For Christ's sake, this is an English game—speak in English so we can all understand you.'

Martin Horton was more cunning and quiet both in his bowling and his humour, as on the occasion when Jack Flavell was lying on the table reading the newspaper and Martin sneaked up quietly without Flav noticing him and set fire to the edge of the paper. In no time at all Flav had a raging inferno on his hands. If ever Flav had caught Martin I think we might have been minus an off-spin bowler.

When you have match-winning bowlers like these in your side you need good catchers around the bat, because those quality bowlers will almost certainly create the chances. Here we were blessed with a more than capable wicket-keeper in Roy Booth and in Tom Graveney, Ron Headley and Dick Richardson, all fine and often brilliant close-to-the-wicket catchers. That to me is a big difference between an ordinary side and a good one. Those guys would take the half-chances.

In the 1970s we were joined by two great overseas players, namely, Glenn Turner (New Zealand) and Vanburn Holder (West Indies). Both gave sterling support to Worcestershire cricket. Glenn, on his record alone, was one of the great opening batsmen of our time. He was a very talented and gifted player, with an astute cricketing brain. Like all great players he worked hard and long at his game. Initially he could not hit the ball off the square! But after a while he became a superb strokemaker. At the finish I think Glenn had perfected his game to such an extent that he genuinely believed that the only way he could get out was by him making a mistake, not by being beaten by the bowler. It must be obvious to anyone reading this that there is no short cut to success, however gifted you might be. It is sheer bloody hard work.

Vanburn Holder was our overseas opening bowler and I believe in my time he was the best-loved of all the Worcestershire players. A man who carried his burden of work with a smile, his heart was as big as our County Ground. I rate him as one of the finest one-day bowlers I have ever seen. Besides his outstanding record as a County and Test match bowler, he had to bowl the last four or six overs of a game when the slog is on match after match, which takes some doing. He did it so well, while radiating all that is best in the game. All the other players also contributed their fair share to our success, but those international players were match-winners in their own right.

One player that I felt was unlucky not to play for England was Alan Ormrod (now coach at Lancashire). He became a fine opening batsman who played quick bowling so well. He never hooked or pulled or argued with anyone, particularly the fast bowlers. He just easily and simply swayed out of the way of those nasty lifting deliveries. Alas we were never to know whether his temperament would have stood up to the rigours of Test cricket.

But Worcestershire to me is also the Ladies Pavilion, which is reputed to produce the best teas in the game. The gatemen, the groundstaff, the office staff, these, too, are all part of one great family.

Well do I remember Dennis Philips, or 'Curly' as he is affectionately known to us, the score card seller with the sharpest tongue in Worcester, getting very emotional when the side wasn't doing too well. After winning the Championship in 1965 we were playing our old rivals Warwickshire at New Road the following year. We were having a very bad day and the Warwickshire supporters were giving Curly some terrible stick as he was going round the ground. Suddenly Curly looked up at the Championship pennant gently swaying in the breeze and pointing his finger at the pennant, he retorted: 'You Warwicks may well enjoy yourselves today, but you do not get that with Green Shield stamps.'

And there was Johnny O'Shea, the paper-seller: 'Excuse me, Sir, I have a cert for you in the 3.30.' He wasn't the greatest tipster in the world. Lovely characters, whom I will always remember.

To mind also comes the great times we have enjoyed, like winning the Championship in my first year of County Cricket in the final game of the season against Sussex at Hove. Dick Richardson and Roy Booth steered us home with an outstanding 50-run partnership for the sixth wicket. I never saw one ball of that partnership. Joe Lister (now secretary of Yorkshire) insisted that as this partnership got under way none of us was to move from our original places. As I was in the dressing room I was not allowed to leave. Joe Lister relayed the scores to us. Talk about being superstitious!

Winning the John Player League, as it was then known, in 1971 was another thrill. The statisticians had told us we needed to beat Warwickshire in our final game and score 232 in the allotted overs to go ahead of Essex in run-rate. However this did not come into it, as we bowled Warwickshire out for 126, so now we needed to get the runs in 17.5 overs. With a powerful innings from Ron Headley of 58 we got home with two balls to spare. A fitting way to win the League.

When winning the Championship in 1974 we went into the final game against Essex two points behind Hampshire. Fortunately for us we won the toss and on a wet wicket at Chelmsford put Essex in to bat. In ideal conditions for him, Norman Gifford took eight for 15. We got the much needed four points which put us two points ahead of Hampshire. Then we watched that lovely rain fall for three whole days. Hampshire never bowled a ball! Great Memories that I will always treasure.

We have at present as great a side as we have ever had. In terms of trophies, last season was the most productive in our history. Winning the Championship and the Refuge Assurance Sunday League, reaching the finals of the NatWest Trophy and the Refuge Assurance Cup and the quarter-final of the Benson and Hedges was truly a remarkable performance. To single out any individual would not be fair because all the players contributed in their own way to our success but I feel that everyone would agree that in Graeme Hick we have an exceptional talent. He is a player who I feel will thrill and entertain us with his batsmanship for years to come. Our members and supporters who have stood by us so loyally through the lean years when we were building our side can now enjoy with us our success and hopefully some entertaining and exciting cricket in the future.

To sum it all up I can truly say: 'To have come to work here for the last 26 years has been an absolute pleasure'.

FOLEY AND A FAMILY AFFAIR

IN HIS TWENTIETH-CENTURY EQUIVALENT to the Doomesday Book, *The Buildings of England*, Sir Nikolas Pevsner complained that Worcestershire had a scarcity of Roman ruins which was exceeded only by an almost total absence of Anglo-Saxon remains. It is a complaint that carries with it a hint of admiration, for the flat, fertile, heavily wooded garden fringed by hills that is the county of Worcestershire has little need of man-made remnants to assert its sense of timelessness. There is nothing to suggest that the Malvern Hills are any different now from what they were six hundred years ago when 'Long Will' Langland wandered over them and conjured his Vision of Piers Plowman wherein, between the high tower of truth and the deep dungeon of wrong, there was a 'fair field full of folk'.

Closer to our own time, the music of Edward Elgar, who was born when the great cathedral at Worcester was being restored and the idea of a county cricket club was forming in many minds, has made men dream dreams and see visions, and Elgar's fresh, wistful music had as its source and inspiration the county and the countryside which nurtured him. Elgar remained ever the child on the side of the Severn, and he would undoubtedly have agreed with what T. P. O'Connor said of Worcester and the Malvern country when he travelled through England in the years between the wars: 'I have never been in a place where the air is so delightful, where in so short a time you throw off weariness and anaemia, and all the fret and worries that come to you when your system is worn out.'

'It is,' said a traveller of more recent times, 'one of England's smaller counties with wonderfully illogical contours and little ugliness,' Such an assessment might well be applied to Worcestershire cricket.

The first evidence that we have that cricket was being played in Worcestershire in the early part of the nineteenth century is in an advertisement that appeared in the *Shrewsbury Chronicle* on 21 August 1829:

> 11 Gentlemen of the Shropshire C.C. will be happy to contend with the same number to be selected either from the Principality of North Wales or from any of the neighbouring Counties of Chester, Stafford, Worcester or Hereford, on the Cricket Ground at Atcham on any day or days this month or the next which may be agreed upon. All communications in answer to this friendly invitation to be addressed to the Secretary to the Shropshire Cricket Club, Atcham, near Shrewsbury.

Six years before this, Mr Powell, a resident barrister of Hereford, had gathered together ten friends and played a game of cricket against eleven junior members of the Oxford Circuit in a meadow near Hereford which belonged to Mr Powell. The Bar soundly defeated the Hereford side.

One must be wary of the county titles which were assumed by sides at this period and earlier, for it was common practice for eleven gentlemen to adopt the name of their county when gathered together for a game of cricket, so it would be hard to determine the representative nature of the Worcestershire County side which scored 72 and 96 and lost to the City of Worcester side at Powick Ham on 26 August 1830.

Powick, 'dairy farm of Pohha's people' a few miles south-west of Worcester, was a popular venue for cricket, and there were matches there and at Evesham in the years that followed the City–County match of 1830.

In August 1844, a Worcestershire county side lost twice to Shropshire. The home match was played at Hartlebury Common between Worcester and Kidderminster. That cricket thrived in the county at this time is apparent although records are scarce. What is known is that by 1847 a county club was in existence, for it was reported as having '58 members enrolled and a set of rules drawn up'. This county club co-existed with the City of Worcester club for the next eight years and helped to bring some of the great players of the day to appear in matches in the county.

In 1848, William Clarke's All England XI with Fuller Pilch, John Wisden, George Parr and Clarke himself overwhelmed Worcestershire at Powick Ham. Two years later, the county's home matches were played at Waresley, near Hartlebury, but when, in 1851, the All England XI again demolished Twenty-Two of Worcestershire, the match was played at a ground behind the Talbot Inn in the Tything. Humble as the playing standard of the men of Worcestershire may have been at the time, the year was a significant one for the county for it marked the first apperance of Lord Lyttelton in the side, so beginning an association between the distinguished Cobham family and the County Cricket Club which has lasted until the present day.

The Worcestershire County Club was essentially a gentlemen's club, amateur in spirit and aristocratic in outlook, but it changed radically in 1855 when on 5 May, at a meeting at the Star Hotel, Worcester, gentlemen interested in cricket formed a club by merging the existing City of Worcester and Worcestershire County clubs. The Reverend R. Peel was in the chair, and some fifty people were present. Mr E. A. H. Lechmere, twice High Sheriff of the County, was elected Chairman; Mr W. Bentley, Honorary Secretary; and Mr Martin Curtler, Treasurer. The subscription was fixed at half a guinea, but, liberally, the meeting decreed that mechanics (or factory workers) could become members of the Club for a fee of five shillings a year, and that for this sum they would be 'entitled to use bats and balls and the cricket ground on three nights a week and to have the privilege of playing cricket with the half-guinea members one night a week'. The new club was to play its matches at Pitchcroft, Worcestershire's racecourse, having obtained a piece of land stretching from the Paddock to the Centre Stand, but, over the next few years' matches were played at other grounds.

It seems that things did not go well for the new club, and, early in March 1857, it was reorganised, and then seemed to lapse. On 3 March 1865, the Star Hotel, Worcester, was again the scene of a meeting to form the Worcestershire County Cricket Club. *Berrow's Worcester Journal* reported the outcome of the meeting.

> Lord Lyttelton presided, and amongst the gentlemen present were Hon C. G. Lyttelton, Revs Dr Collis, C. J. Sale, T. King, T. H. Martin, A. H. Cocks, C.B., S. C. Allsopp, Willis Bund, and J. S. Isaac, Major Norbury, Captain Lavie, Mr W. Deighton (sec. pro. tem.), &c. It was announced that about eighty gentlemen had intimated their intention of becoming members of the club, and that some donations had been given towards the funds. A committee consisting of the following gentlemen was appointed to carry out the objects of the meeting: Lord Lyttelton (president), Earl Coventry, Hon C. G. Lyttelton, A. H. Cocks, Esq., C.B., Revs C. J. Sale and Walter B. Cherry, G. E. Martin, Esq., W. E. Dowdeswell, Esq., and Walter de Sodington Blount, Esq. J. S. Isaacs, Esq., was elected treasurer and Mr Deighton secretary (pro. tem.). A vote of thanks was passed to the noble Lord-Lieutenant for presiding. The meeting was adjourned to the 1st prox. The number of members has increased during the past week to nearly 100.

At the meeting on 1 April, it was announced that the field at Boughton Park was considered to be the most desirable for a home ground, and the committee was empowered to take it for the 1865 season. In fact, the Pleasure Gardens at Boughton Park, Worcester, were to remain as the County's home ground for thirty years. The ground was lent by J. S. Isaacs, the Honorary Treasurer, and the history of Worcestershire, like that of so many other county clubs, is testimony to the enthusiasm and generosity of a handful of pioneers. In Worcestershire's case, the energy and endeavours of three distinguished families, in particular, were to play a vital part in the formation and development of the Club.

In 1863, the Earl of Coventry had been president of the combined

City and County Club. He was then 25-years-old, had been a member of MCC since 1856 and was president in 1859 at the age of 21. He was to serve Worcestershire as player, administrator and patron all his long life. When he died, in 1930, at the age of 91, he was the 'Father' of the House of Lord's, having been a peer for 86 years, 10 months.

George William Coventry was a passionate cricketer, indeed he was an enthusiast in all that he did, and was known as 'a hard slashing hitter and slow lob bowler'. As well as assisting Worcestershire in their pre-first-class days, he played for MCC and I Zingari. He had a love of the turf that matched his zeal for cricket, and he was a member of the Jockey Club for 70 years. Two of his sons, Henry Thomas and Charles John, became noted cricketers and played for the County.

Henry Thomas Coventry was a right-handed batsman, slow right-arm bowler and outstanding fielder. He was educated at Eton and Oxford, but he did not appear in first-class cricket for the University. In fact, his only two first-class matches were against Oxford in 1888 when he scored 15 and 2 for MCC against them at Oxford and 0 and 11 in the return match at Lord's. He took his only first-class wicket in the first match. His brother, C.J., played his cricket for Worcestershire and was one of the five amateurs of good club standard that Major R. Gardner Warton invited to tour South Africa in 1888–89. The party was led by Sir C. Aubrey Smith, then a regular with Sussex, later a Hollywood film star, and included three Surrey professionals, Abel, Wood and J. M. Read, Briggs of Lancashire and Hearne of Kent. George Ulyett of Yorkshire joined the party later. The tour ended with, what are now regarded as, the first two Test matches between England and South Africa.

The Hon Charles John Coventry, 'a fair bat with a free style who can hit hard', played in these Test matches, and that was the extent of his first-class career. He batted at number ten and did not bowl in either match. England won the first game by eight wickets and the second by an innings. Charles Coventry had his moment as *Cricket* pointed out:

> It has been asserted that the English team has a tail, but on this occasion they nobly refuted the assertion, and came to the rescue like men, Coventry first with a dashing dozen.

To his 'dashing dozen' in the first Test, C.J. added 1 not out in the second, giving him a Test and first-class career record of 13 runs, average 13. He returned to South Africa in 1896 as a serving officer and took part in the Jameson Raid. He was reported killed in action, and arrangements were made in Worcestershire for a funeral service of commemoration. Shortly before the service was due to begin, news arrived that he was alive and well so the would-be mourners held a celebratory party on the village green instead; a celebration for one who was, arguably, Worcestershire's first England cricketer.

His nephew, John Bonynge Coventry, followed the family tradition in being educated at Eton and Oxford, and he was to give the County noble service in the 1920s and 1930s.

The other great family associated with the formation of Worcestershire County Cricket Club was, of course, the Lyttelton family. Lord Lyttelton, who presided at the inaugural meeting of the Club, played for Cambridge University against Oxford in 1838 and was out for a 'pair', having opened the innings. He had eight sons, all of whom were, at the least, highly competent cricketers. Indeed, six of them played first-class cricket, and all seem to have assisted Worcestershire at one time or another in the early days. The eldest, Charles George, was on the original committee of the County Club.

As well as assisting Worcestershire, the Lytteltons could field their own eleven, and, in 1867, the Lyttelton XI beat Bromsgrove School at Hagley, which remains the Lyttelton family home.

The most accomplished of the Lyttelton brothers was, undoubtedly, Alfred Lyttelton, the youngest of the eight. He won his cricket blue all four years at Cambridge, 1876–79, played for Middlesex from 1877 to 1887, appeared in four Tests against Australia and was President of MCC in 1898. He also played soccer, appearing for Old Etonians in the FA Cup Final of 1876 and for England against Scotland at The Oval. He was the best amateur tennis player of his day and excelled at racquets. Golf was said to be the only game of which he did not have total command.

His style as a batsman was bright and vigorous while he had no superior as a wicket-keeper in his day. In his last Test, at The Oval 1884, he watched from behind the stumps as Murdoch, 211, McDonnell, 103 and Scott, 102, savaged the England bowling. Then Lord Harris turned to Lyttelton and while Grace kept wicket he bowled lobs and took 4 for 19.

In a special tribute to him after his death in 1913, the Earl of Darnley wrote of him as:

> Tall, vigorous, muscular grace characteristic of every movement, the merriest eye, the most engaging smile that ever gladdened the heart of a friend—were ever so many brilliant and attractive qualities blended in one youthful person?

The merry eye and the engaging smile would appear to be traits of the Lyttelton family. Charles George became the Eighth Viscount Cobham in 1888, and his son, John Cavendish, Ninth Viscount Cobham, played for Worcestershire in 1924 and 1925. A fourth generation of the Lyttelton family first represented Worcestershire in

1932 when Charles John took the field against Gloucestershire at New Road at the end of June. He was to serve the County with fire and passion, and he certainly had a merry eye and an engaging smile.

His son, the present Lord Cobham, has maintained a close connection with the Club in the true traditions of the family.

In its formative years, the Worcestershire Club was essentially a gathering of aristocrats and gentlemen, and as well as the Lytteltons and the Coventrys, the name of the Marquis of Queensberry frequently appears in the batting order. Although more renowned in another sport, boxing, he was no mean cricketer and was often top scorer in the Worcestershire side although, in the late 1860s and early 1870s, this did not make him a prolific run-getter. In truth, Worcestershire were late starters. In 1864, the leading counties, Surrey, Yorkshire, Lancashire, Nottinghamshire, Middlesex, Kent and Sussex among them, were competing in an embryo form of the County Championship, and W. G. Grace was making his first appearance at Lord's. Worcestershire cricket was less ambitious.

In the years that immediately followed the foundation of the Club, the opponents were Malvern College, Bromsgrove School, Burton-on-Trent, Herefordshire, Cotswold Magpies, Breconshire, Shropshire and Incogniti, and the results did not suggest that the County was playing below its station or level of ability. In 1871, on 3, 4 and 5 August, Twenty-Two of Worcestershire met the United South of England XI and were beaten by four wickets. The home side made 132 and 149, and the great professional eleven hit 147 and 135 for six. Mr J. Raybould was Worcestershire's most successful bowler with six for 33 and three for 64 while the Reverend J. G. Crowdy hit 54 in the first innings and the Reverend Henry Foster 57 in the second.

Four years earlier, Mr H. Foster had appeared for Malvern College against the County. He was to spend his life at the school, and his seven sons were to receive their education there. All of them were to play first-class cricket for the County and to serve it with such affection and strength that for many years the terms Worcestershire and Fostershire became interchangeable in the public consciousness. They straddle the period at the end of the last century when the County attained first-class status, and the three eldest, Henry Knollys, Wilfred Lionel and Reginald Erskine, appeared for Worcestershire in the historic season of 1899.

In 1865, Worcestershire County Cricket Club had met and been soundly beaten by Warwickshire at Boughton Park, but the following year, had seen a famous victory for the new Club, mainly due to some excellent batting by Charles George and George Spencer Lyttelton and some good bowling by Walter Caldicott. Caldicott was also in the Worcestershire side which played the first Australian touring side at

Dudley in 1878. *Wisden* referred to the side as Worcestershire although other sources call it Eighteen of Dudley. The Australians were in some disarray at 35 for nine, but they finally made 59. The local side were bowled out for 33, and the tourists hit 223 for nine before rain ended play.

It should not be imagined, however, in spite of a victory over Warwickshire and matches against the Australian tourists, MCC and I. Zingari, that Worcestershire cricket was held in very high esteem at the time. Mention of matches in which Worcestershire appeared was rarely to be found in *Cricket*, the weekly record of the game which had room for much else, and *Wisden*, in 1888, reinforced the view that the matches in which Worcestershire took part were of little moment: 'The season of the Worcestershire Club was largely made up of matches which, though interesting enough in themselves, were not of sufficient general importance to enable us to find space for them in the pages of *Wisden's Almanack*.' The world of cricket, like the Victorian world in general, was moving quickly, changing fast, but Worcestershire defiantly maintained a more gentle, somnolent rhythm.

There was one man, however, who was restless to bring the County into the main stream of cricket activity, and if Worcestershire County Cricket Club can be said to owe their first-class status to one man, that man is Paul Henry Foley. A left-handed middle-order batsman and

Paul Foley, whose energy and enthusiasm drove Worcestershire to first-class status.

right-hand slow under-arm bowler, Foley first played for Worcester-shire in 1878. He stood 6ft 3in and had a commanding presence and personality which he used to good effect when he became Honorary Secretary of the Club. He appeared in only one first-class match, for MCC against Somerset in 1891 when he batted number eleven and scored 8 and 13, but he played regularly for Worcestershire. In 1895, when 38-years-old, he captained a Gentlemen of Worcestershire team to Holland and took eight wickets in an innings with his lobs in one of his matches.

A man of energy and vision, Paul Foley was ever eager to further the cause of Worcestershire cricket. He persuaded his cousin, Cyril Pelham Foley, a distinguished member of the Eton eleven, to assist the County in 1888 just after he had left school and just before he went up to Cambridge. However, Lt-Col Foley's main cricket was to be played with Middlesex and his life was to consist of much adventure outside the game. For more permanence, Worcestershire and Foley were to turn to the Foster family. By the beginning of the last decade of the nineteenth century, both H. K. and W. L. Foster, although still at Malvern School, were regular members of the County side, and they were already scoring heavily, but, as we have already seen, the County was struggling to keep pace with the developments in the game.

On 10 December 1889, at a private meeting at Lord's, representa-tives of Gloucestershire, Kent, Lancashire, Middlesex, Nottingham-shire, Surrey, Sussex and Yorkshire, the big eight, decided to regulate the method of deciding the County Championship. In effect, the County Championship as we know it today, however varied the system of points scoring, dates from the 1890 season. In May, 1894, the county captains agreed that Essex, Derbyshire, Leicestershire and Warwickshire should be allowed to compete in the Championship in 1895, and, in October 1894, Hampshire were added to that list.

Stoddart's team returned triumphant from Australia in the spring of 1895, and a new English cricket season, with fourteen counties competing for the championship, lay ahead (Somerset had been admitted in 1891). In nearly a century since Somerset joined, only three more counties, Glamorgan, Northamptonshire and Worcester-shire, have found their way into the competition.

Foley was quick to appreciate that the events that were taking place were significant to the future of the game and that Worcestershire and other less wealthy and influential counties would suffer in consequence if they did not keep pace with what was happening in the mainstream of cricket. He instigated a meeting at the Queen's Hotel, Birmingham, in March 1895, at which, as *Cricket* reported:

Following on the lines of the existing championship another

competition has been arranged for the minor counties, to be called the second-class championship. The inception is due to Mr P. H. Foley, the hon. sec. of the Worcestershire County C.C., which, with Bedfordshire, Durham, Norfolk, Oxfordshire and Staffordshire, represent the competition for the first year. The new movement is pretty sure to popularise county cricket outside the front rank. In any case it is pleasant to reflect that the younger counties generally are receiving increasing support within their own limits year by year.

The competition was neither reported nor mentioned in *Cricket* again until December 1895, when an account of a meeting of representatives of the minor county clubs was published. If this seems strange and the tone of the account of the inaugural meeting seems patronising, it must be remembered that the original minor county or second-class championship was not officially recognised. Official recognition was not granted until the competition was reorganised in 1901.

Hertfordshire joined the six counties listed as being represented at the inaugural meeting in Birmingham to compete in the championship in its first year as, uniquely, they have done ever since, but that initial competition was a somewhat haphazard affair. With the promotion of Essex, Derbyshire, Leicestershire, Warwickshire and Hampshire to the first-class championship, it had become evident, under Foley's prompting, that the remaining second-class counties needed some form of organisation if they were to survive, but only the seven counties we have mentioned were able to arrange the eight fixtures necessary for inclusion in the first season of the new competition. Strangely enough, matches with counties outside the competition were allowed to count in the competition, but this was an expediency forced upon the minor counties by the hastiness with which the tournament had been arranged.

At the December meeting of the seven counties, when Foley was again unanimously elected as honorary secretary and C. Pigg of Hertfordshire was in the chair, Durham withdrew their proposition that second elevens of first-class counties should be included in the competition and that only matches against counties actually competing should count. Durham, like the others, realised that 'the changes were not advisable in the present state of the organisation of the minor counties'. Foley proposed that neutral umpires should be appointed for each match, but his proposal was defeated because several counties felt themselves unable to incur the extra expenses for umpires' travel. The financial position of many of the minor counties, and several of the first-class ones, too, was not a healthy one.

One motion that was adopted was the one put forward by Mr Mallett of Durham, namely:

> That in the case of two or more counties in the competition being equal in points at the top of the competition on an unequal number of matches played, the MCC authorities shall be asked to decide which county is at the top of the competition.

There were some personal and heartfelt reasons for Durham putting forward this proposal, for the inaugural season had ended in some confusion. Under the system which had operated in the County Championship until the end of 1894, places were decided simply by deducting the number of matches lost from the number of matches won and ignoring the drawn games. This system was adopted for the new second-class competition although the restructured County Championship of 1895 was decided by a percentage system.

Lillywhite's Cricketers' Annual conceded that the Minor Counties' Competition had been something of an experiment, but added:

> That it will stimulate a new interest in the various districts most affected, even if it has not already had that effect to a considerable degree, there can be little doubt. Durham it was generally thought had a great chance for the first place, but it had to give way to Worcestershire, not altogether an inappropriate result when it it remembered that Mr P. H. Foley, the Worcestershire secretary, was responsible or had a good deal to do in the institution of the Championship.

The final table was as follows:

	P	W	L	D	Pts
Worcestershire	10	5	2	3	3
Norfolk	8	4	1	3	3
Durham	8	4	1	3	3
Oxfordshire	8	3	2	3	1
Bedfordshire	8	3	4	1	−1
Hertfordshire	8	2	4	2	−2
Staffordshire	8	−	4	4	−4

Although *Lillywhite's* awarded Worcestershire first place, no doubt on account of their greater number of victories, other sources placed them third behind Norfolk and Durham who had a better proportion of wins to defeats. Obviously, the counties themselves were in some confusion, which is why Durham forwarded their proposal. A triple tie is the generally accepted verdict today.

It is only fair to mention that all of Worcestershire's points were won or lost in matches against five of the other counties in the competition. They had victories over Staffordshire, twice, Cheshire, Durham and Hertfordshire, and lost the away fixtures to Durham and

Hertfordshire. There were two draws with Oxfordshire and one with Cheshire. Worcestershire and Norfolk did not meet. In gauging the strength of the side and of the competition, one should note that Worcestershire played several non-county matches in 1895 against such opponents as East Gloucestershire, Malvern College and Keble College, Oxford, and that they did not find this opposition too weak for them. Indeed, they were well beaten by Keble, yet the nucleus of the side that was to take them into first-class cricket was in existence, and ten of the team that were to take the field against Yorkshire in the first County Championship match of 1899 had already played for the County before the end of the 1895 season, and Wilson had joined Worcestershire in 1897.

Initially, the bowling seemed stronger than the batting, with Raynor taking 50 wickets at 13.43 runs each and Arnold 48 at 9.34 in the Minor Counties' Championship alone. Sam Raynor had played a few games for Derbyshire in 1891, but, unable to gain a regular place in the side, he joined Worcestershire as a professional although he did not appear after 1895. Edward George Arnold, on the other hand, was destined to become Worcestershire's first great all-round cricketer.

He was born in Exmouth and had come up from Devon to play for Worcestershire. He did not celebrate his nineteenth birthday until November 1895, but in that first season of the Minor Counties' Championship, he did sufficient to show his great potential, for, as well as being a fast-medium bowler with a beautiful high action, he was a very capable right-handed batsman, strong in defence and powerful in attack with a range of shots which increased with the years. He hit 214 runs, average 14.26, in 1895, which, meagre as it may sound today, was welcome in a side in which only two men averaged more than 20. Those two batsmen were E. P. Jobson and G. E. Bromley-Martin.

Edward Percy Jobson had been playing for Worcestershire over ten years and had hit a century against Warwickshire in 1881. Granville Edward Bromey-Martin, in contrast, had just left Eton where he had been captain in his last two years and was on his way to Oxford University where he was to gain his blue in 1897 and 1898. He was a free and stylish stroke-maker, very much in the character of the young Victorian amateur, and to him went the honour of scoring the only century hit for Worcestershire in the first season of the Minor Counties' Championship.

It should be mentioned, incidentally, that although Boughton Park was still officially Worcestershire's home ground, of the inter-county matches, only the game against Cheshire was played there. Staffordshire were entertained at Stourbridge, Durham at Kidderminster, Oxfordshire at Dudley, and Hertfordshire at Malvern. Foley himself

Worcestershire's first great all-rounder, E. G. Arnold.

conducted his activities from Stourbridge, but he had cast his eyes towards the county town. He saw, on the opposite bank of the Severn to the Cathedral, but still within the shadows of that still and noble building, an area of farmland. The land belonged to the Cathedral, and Foley, a man of immense vision, rented from the Dean and Chapter what is, in effect, the present county ground.

When Foley obtained the land, at a small rent, it was not a cricket ground, but three fields with a hedge through the middle of them and a hayrick. The new ground was celebrated by the winning of the Minor Counties' Championship in 1896. There was no debate this time. Neither Durham nor Norfolk was able to play the required number of matches, and whichever way the table was calculated, Worcestershire's six wins, two draws and one defeat was superior to

Buckinghamshire's four wins, one loss and three draws. Worcester-shire's only defeat came at the hands of Northamptonshire. H. K. Foster dominated the batting, and Arnold, whose batting was developing rapidly, was again the leading bowler.

Arnold's position as leading all-rounder was challenged by the advance of 'Dick' Burrows, five years his senior. Like Arnold, Burrows was tall, but, unlike Arnold, he was robust. He was born, and died, in Eastwood, near Nottingham, the town which claims D. H. Lawrence as its most famous son, and he had about him the vigour, strength and good humour of that mining area. He was essentially a quick bowler, strong in the shoulder, ample in the waist and behind, but in 1896, he also showed signs of becoming a more than useful batsman. His progress in both departments over the next two years was slow, but it mattered little, for Worcestershire took the Minor Counties' title in both 1897 and 1898 without losing a match. In the two season, they engaged in 18 competition matches and won 11 of them.

In 1898, Foley took another important and visionary step towards raising the level of cricket in Worcestershire and driving the County towards first-class status. He persuaded Fred Hunt, born in Berkshire, six matches for Kent, 23-years-old, to come to New Road as Head Groundsman and player. Hunt was a moderate all-rounder, a medium-pace bowler and useful batsman, but as a groundsman he has had no superior. He was to raise the standard of the wicket at Worcester to one of unparalleled excellence, and he was to become a rich adornment to the County for nearly half a century, a positive and colourful character. Much of his success was due to the fact that he was essentially a man of the soil. He farmed the land on the eastern side of the ground, and, in the early days, he and his staff found it neither a hardship nor strange to have to remove horses, sheep and cattle from the ground before play could begin. Hunt himself always insisted in using his horse in preparing the ground, but the horse has gone 50 years since and the land he farmed is now a petrol station.

The acquisition of Hunt was not Foley's only move towards furthering the Worcestershire cause. He was ever on the search for new players to strengthen the side. He approached Bill Wilmot, a noted wicket-keeper from Lancashire, but Wilmot could not come to an agreement with the County and his career ended after a few games for Derbyshire. In his approach to Wilmot, Foley had mentioned that he was confident that Worcestershire would soon be playing first-class cricket. This confidence was founded on the fact that Foley moved in high cricketing circles and had the ear of many influential men. Rather cruelly, Rowland Bowen was to write in his history of cricket that Worcestershire's elevation to first-class status was unmerited as it owed 'more to skilful lobbying than any feeling that they generally merited it'. Foley's lobbying, however, was backed by four years of success in the second-class competition.

In May, 1898, he wrote to the Clerk of the Dean and Chapter 'to formally ask for permission to erect a Pavilion on the County Cricket Ground'. He was sure of his request being granted, for he had already gained the consent of the Dean who had approved the plans. In October, 1898, Foley wrote to Derbyshire requesting fixtures for the following season and stating that he hoped Worcestershire would be playing in the County Championship in 1899. Derbyshire, like all other counties who granted Worcestershire fixtures in their first first-class season, demanded a guarantee of £50 per match. Sussex were still demanding this guarantee as late as 1902.

Foley drove on regardless of expense, and one wonders how much Worcestershire owes to him in financial terms as well as in the energy and effort he expended on behalf of the County to whom he so passionately dedicated his life. The Club was £300 in debt, and the erection of the pavilion and bringing the seating and fencing of the ground up to first-class needs was causing further expense. Always the visionary, Foley had high hopes that the new lady members would bring great financial benefit to the Club. By 1900, he was able to write proudly to the Dean: 'Our Ladies' Enclosure is becoming quite the Hyde Park of Worcester and tea there with the Cathedral in front and the match in progress is quite "the thing".' Eighty-nine years on, it still represents the greatest delight in county cricket.

The search for players continued. George Gaukrodger, a wicket-keeper, came from Belfast and had to serve a two-year residential qualification as did Dick Pearson. Pearson was born in Brixton and therefore qualified to play for Surrey, but the county of his birth made no moves to sign him and he began his residential qualification for Worcestershire in 1898 at the age of 18. After his move to Worcester, Surrey showed an interest in him and were indignant that Worcestershire had signed him, but their loss was one of the greatest of Worcestershire's gains.

By the end of 1898, Foley's efforts on his county's behalf had gained their total reward. He wrote to F. E. Lacey, Secretary of MCC, thanking him for his and his Committee's support and assistance in Worcestershire's gaining first-class status. This was now assured as Hampshire had granted them home and away fixtures so bringing them to the required minimum number of twelve in order to compete in the County Championship. All that remained now was to get all into order in time for the start of the 1899 season.

As late as February of that year, plans were still in operation for the erection of a grandstand, rows of seating, pay boxes and a press box. In

March, a request was made to the Postmaster for a telegraph office to be installed on the ground, and in April, only fourteen days before the opening match, there was a frantic plea to the builders that the Pavilion should be erected in time.

The days before that opening first-class fixture were hectic indeed, and it seems that the last nails were being banged into place just as the people began to come in through the turnstiles. The final image is of Paul Foley, wearing his customary brown bowler hat and boots, applying the last coat of paint to the sight-screen shortly before the County took the field as a first-class side for the first time. They were a young side, average age 25, and they could not have been asked to face more formidable opposition in their opening match, for they were confronted by Lord Hawke's Yorkshire, who were the Champion County and were just entering their golden period.

FOSTERSHIRE

FRANK MITCHELL, A TRIPLE BLUE AT CAMBRIDGE and a man who played cricket for both England and South Africa, was in his first full season for Yorkshire in 1899 and, as the only amateur in the side, led them in the opening encounter against Worcestershire in the absence of Lord Hawke. He had at his command a very strong side.

John Thomas Brown from Driffield had two triple centuries and eight England caps to his credit and is still regarded as having been one of the greatest of Yorkshire batsmen. The previous season, he and John Tunnicliffe had set up a world record with an opening stand of 554 against Derbyshire at Chesterfield. John Thomas Brown junior from Darfield was considered to be one of the fastest bowlers of his time and might well have played for England had not a dislocated shoulder ended his career abruptly in 1903. Hirst, Haigh and Wainwright were Test cricketers; Rhodes and Denton were soon to be similarly

Worcestershire v Yorkshire, 4, 5 and 6 May 1899, the occasion of Worcestershire's debut in first-class cricket. Back row (l to r): G. F. Wheldon, G. A. Wilson, P. H. Foley (secretary), E. G. Arnold, R. D. Burrows. Middle row: W. L. Foster, E. G. Bromley-Martin, H. K. Foster (capt.), R. E. Foster, G. E. Bromley-Martin. Front: T. Straw and A. Bird.

honoured. A sterner test could not have been devised for a young county taking its first hesitant steps in first-class cricket.

Mitchell won the toss and Henry Knollys Foster led his team onto the field. If they had any sense of inferiority, they did not show it, and they soon sent a shiver through the Yorkshire ranks. The great J. T. Brown was bowled by George Wilson for nought. It was not to be the end of Wilson's success. He bowled very quickly and was able to move the ball menacingly. Only Mitchell, elegantly, and Wainwright, somewhat fortuitously, offered any serious resistance. In two hours, Yorkshire were bowled out for 139. Wilson had bowled unchanged and taken eight wickets, the first eight batsmen on the score-card, for 70 runs. It was a magnificent performance with which to begin a first-class career.

Worcestershire began their innings in early afternoon, their supporters in buoyant mood. There was a quick shock when Granville Bromley-Martin was bowled by Schofield Haigh, but Arnold and H. K. Foster added 52 in an hour for the second wicket. Two silly run outs lost the home side some advantage, but Fred Wheldon batted with characteristic obduracy, and Worcestershire ended the first day at 176 for seven, an eminently satisfactory beginning to their first-class career.

Thirty-five more runs were added on the second morning before Wainwright bowled Straw and ended the innings. Worcestershire had a lead of 72. With J. T. Brown, Tunnicliffe, Denton, Mitchell and Moorhouse back in the pavilion, Yorkshire still trailed Worcestershire by five runs. Then came a decisive stand of 115 between Wainwright and the tenacious and tigerish George Hirst. The stand was broken by the slow bowling of Eliot Bromley-Martin, and he quickly finished the innings, the last five wickets going down for the addition of 23 runs. E. G. Bromley-Martin's 4 for 33 was to remain the best performance of his brief first-class career.

Wilfred Rhodes opened the Yorkshire bowling when Worcestershire began their search for the 134 runs they needed for victory, and he soon accounted for both openers, but Arnold again batted well, and he and R. E. Foster took the score to 54 for 2 at the close of the second day.

The Saturday dawned fair with Worcestershire seemingly set for an historic victory, and nothing in the early play suggested that Yorkshire could save the game, but then J. T. Brown of Darfield produced a spell of fearsome pace. The Worcestershire tail wilted, and Yorkshire won by 11 runs.

However disappointing the result, none could deny that Worcestershire had done more than enough to justify their elevation to first-class status. Of the side that played against Yorkshire, only H. K. and

23

R. E. Foster and G. E. Bromley-Martin had appeared in first-class cricket before.

Granville Bromley-Martin had been in the Oxford side in 1897 and 1898 and had scored 137 against Sussex at Hove in the first of those two seasons. His only century for Worcestershire was scored against Derbyshire at Worcester in August 1899. He hit 129 and shared a fourth wicket stand of 207 in two hours with H. K. Foster. His innings ended in bizarre fashion. He drove at a ball from Hancock, but a piece of his bat broke off and the ball went straight up in the air so that Wright was able to run in from point and take a simple catch.

Bromley-Martin's brother, Eliot, had been the principal bowler in the Eton side in 1884 and 1885, but, rather surprisingly, he had been unable to get into the Oxford Side. He played frequently for Worcestershire in the last decade of the nineteenth century and was Honorary Secretary of the Club before Foley assumed the duties. He was highly successful as a bowler in the second-class competition days, and, in 1897, he and Bird bowled unchanged to dismiss Hertfordshire for 75 and 116, but his first-class career was limited to twelve matches in the first two seasons of Worcestershire's elevation to the County Championship.

Like Eliot Bromley-Martin, Albert Bird was a slow off-break bowler. He was born in Moseley in 1868 and played for Warwickshire from 1887 until 1890 before joining Worcestershire as a professional in 1892. He was to take nearly 300 first-class wickets for the County, and his finest hour came at Southampton in 1901 when he took 14 wickets in the match.

Of Robert Dixon 'Dick' Burrows, we have already spoken. He, Arnold and Wilson did the lion's share of the bowling, and although he still batted low in the order, he played some useful innings. In many ways, Dick Burrows, an outstanding fielder in the old-fashioned point position, was something of a late maturer. He was, unquestionably, a great Club servant.

If George Alfred Wilson had a weakness, it was a lack of consistency. He had been born in Amersham in Buckinghamshire in 1877 and assisted the county of his birth and Staffordshire as well as Worcestershire. In eight first-class seasons with Worcestershire, he took 732 wickets at 24.06 runs each and gave yeoman service. C. B. Fry gave a fine assessment of him at the end of the first of those eight seasons:

In George Wilson, Worcestershire possesses a fast bowler of uncommon kind. He takes a short run, and has a swinging action, just above shoulder-high. He keeps a good length, and nips quickly from the pitch, but the peculiarity that makes him dangerous is in

WORCESTERSHIRE *v* YORKSHIRE

Played at New Road, Worcester on 4, 5 and 6 May 1899

YORKSHIRE WON BY 11 RUNS

YORKSHIRE	FIRST INNINGS		SECOND INNINGS	
J. T. Brown, sen.	b Wilson	0	c Straw b Burrows	29
J. Tunnicliffe	b Wilson	16	c Wheldon b Arnold	7
D. Denton	b Wilson	19	c Straw b Wilson	0
*F. Mitchell	b Wilson	32	run out	22
F. Moorhouse	b Wilson	2	b Burrows	7
E. Wainwright	c H. K. Foster b Wilson	35	c Arnold b E. Bromley-Martin	86
G. H. Hirst	c R. E. Foster b Wilson	14	c Wilson b E. Bromley-Martin	35
S. Haigh	b Wilson	1	c R. E. Foster b E. Bromley-Martin	4
W. Rhodes	b Arnold	4	c W. L. Foster b Wilson	1
†D. Hunter	not out	1	not out	7
J. T. Brown, jnr	c and b Arnold	9	c Wheldon b E. Bromley-Martin	2
Extras	b 4, lb 1, w 1	6	lb 4, w 1	5
Total		139		205

BOWLING	O	M	R	W	O	M	R	W
Wilson	25	6	70	8	31	11	69	2
Arnold	13	2	35	2	16	6	42	1
Burrows	12	2	28	0	12	2	29	2
Bird					8	1	27	0
E. G. Bromley-Martin					11.4	2	33	4

WORCESTERSHIRE	FIRST INNINGS		SECOND INNINGS	
*H. K. Foster	c Brown, sen. b Rhodes	38	b Rhodes	0
G. E. Bromley-Martin	b Haigh	0	c Tunnicliffe b Rhodes	12
E. G. Arnold	b Haigh	43	c Tunnicliffe b Hirst	33
R. E. Foster	run out	15	b Brown jnr	32
W. L. Foster	run out	0	b Haigh	22
G. F. Wheldon	not out	49	b Brown jnr	4
E. G. Bromley-Martin	b Haigh	0	c sub b Brown jnr	8
A. Bird	c Wainwright b Rhodes	14	c Mitchell b Brown jnr	0
R. D. Burrows	b Hirst	13	b Brown jnr	0
G. A. Wilson	c Mitchell b Hirst	9	b Brown jnr	2
†T. Straw	b Wainwright	9	not out	0
Extras	b 12, lb 6, w 1, nb 2	21	b 5, lb 4	9
Total		211		122

BOWLING	O	M	R	W	O	M	R	W
Hirst	31	12	65	2	11	4	23	1
Haigh	36	21	36	3	10.3	2	26	1
Rhodes	21	3	51	2	13	2	45	2
Wainwright	10.4	2	25	1				
J. T. Brown, jnr					9	4	19	6

Umpires: R. G. Barlow and W. Richards

Worcestershire's first County Championship match.

*Captain; †Wicket-keeper

the flight of his deliveries in the air. The ball from his hand comes not only much faster than you expect, but as it were gathers distance as it comes, just as a good long jumper urges himself a foot or so further than you would think possible as you see him rise in the air. But besides this Wilson sometimes has the power of making the ball swerve or curl in the air—a yard, his admirers aver. Like other bowlers with this peculiarity, he seems to be able to make the ball do more in the air when it is new and has not lost its shape or glaze, and when there is a wind blowing against him.

Yet, if Fry were enthusiastic about Wilson, the Worcestershire player who most caught his eye was Ted Arnold who had yet to come to his full flowering. Arnold had missed nearly all of the 1898 season through ill health, and indeed, this lean, clean-shaven, sharp-featured, intelligent cricketer was never robust. There was always the air of the artist about him, ever thinking, always creating. Fry was struck by him as soon as he entered first-class cricket, and he believed that Arnold had the potential to reach the highest level:

> He is tall, with the advantage of a long reach. His limbs are loose and pliant. His eye and timing faculty are excellent. His style is above reproach, as of one who has studied the elements of the game in a good school. He is an upstanding player, with that command over the bowling which belongs rather to batsmen who make the most of their height than to those who crouch or stoop. He seems to get a good sight of the ball, and to watch it carefully to the last moment. His defence is good, he plays at the ball, not at the bowler's arm, and he keeps his bat straight.
>
> He has strokes all round the wicket. On the off he plays forward strongly enough to force the ball to the boundary. He is a fine straight driver, running out without flurry, and hitting with a nice free swing. Quick of wrist and nimble of foot, he can hook a short ball. His leg-strokes are clever; any ball pitching just clear of the leg stump he can turn away for runs.
>
> He is a very fair medium-pace bowler, with an easy action. Though he usually keeps a good length, he does not confine himself to bowling over after over of mechanical precision, but tries to vary his pace and flight, and succeeds. On a bowler's wicket he can do a good deal with the ball; on hard wickets he is not so dangerous, but is always likely to secure a wicket, because he perceives there are other ways of doing this besides uprooting the middle stump.

Arnold was to take 72 wickets in 1900, 26 more than he took in 1899, but in 1901, he was again to be robbed of much cricket through ill health. Yet he came back the following season to complete the 'double' and he was to repeat the feat in the next three seasons. He was the first great Worcestershire all-rounder, and arguably the greatest.

Following his 'double' triumphs of 1902 and 1903, he was selected for the MCC side to tour Australia under Pelham Warner. In the first Test at Sydney, he opened the bowling with George Hirst. Duff and Trumper took singles in Hirst's over, and Trumper was left to face Arnold's first delivery in Test cricket. He offered a catch to R. E. Foster, who was also making his debut in Test cricket, and it was accepted. Then Arnold had Duff caught behind for three. He went on to take four for 76, and England won by five wickets. He missed the second Test, but his 18 wickets in the series played a vital part in England regaining the 'Ashes'. In all, he played ten Test matches and took 31 wickets, but he was less successful with the bat.

Before Arnold had won his first Test cap, Worcestershire had won another rather bizarre Test cap to add to those won by C. J. Coventry in March 1889. Among Lord Hawke's side that went to South Africa in 1898–99 was Alfred German Archer, a wicket-keeper who had been unable to find a place in the Haileybury side and had not played county cricket in England. Due to an injury to Bromley-Davenport, he was called into the England side for the second Test against South Africa at Newlands. He batted number ten and did not keep wicket. He was to play four matches for Worcestershire in two seasons, 1900 and 1901.

Worcestershire's regular wicket-keeper during the second-class competition days and in the early part of this century was Tom Straw. Born in Hucknall Torkard in Notts in 1870—he was to die in the same town 89 years later—he was one of Foley's acquisitions. He was an efficient, unfussy wicket-keeper and a dogged batsman. He won notoriety in the first championship season by being given out 'obstructing the field' in the first innings of the match against Warwickshire at Worcester in August. This might have gone unmentioned in cricket history had he not been given out in exactly the same way when the two counties met at Edgbaston in August 1901, two years later almost to the day. Straw was on the Worcestershire staff until 1907, but he appeared little after 1902 because of a hand injury.

His deputy and successor behind the stumps was Fred Wheldon although he was played for his batting rather than his wicket-keeping. Fred Wheldon was born in Langley Green, but first played for Warwickshire. His method of batting was simple in that he offered a solid defence to anything straight and was savage on anything outside the off stump, excelling in the square-drive and the cut. He could score runs quickly, but he did not prosper against leg side bowling. He was an excellent fielder as becomes one who was a noted professional footballer. As an inside-left, he was a member of the Aston Villa side

that won the 'double' in 1896–97, and he won two other
Championship medals and four caps for England.

We now turn to that nucleus of the first Worcestershire side, the
first three brothers of the Foster family.

The eldest of the seven brothers, Harry Foster lived a life of
leadership. H.K. was captain of the Malvern XI and a highly successful

H. K. Foster. (Allsport)

batsman, being in the side for four years. Illness slowed his progress at Oxford, but he gained his blue in 1894 and was in the side against Cambridge for three years. In his second season in the side, he produced one of the most brilliant and graceful displays of batting ever seen in the Varsity match. He had been yorked first ball in the first innings, but in the second, when Oxford had been set to make 331 to win, he hit 121 out of 159 in 125 minutes. His batting dwarfed everything else in the match although Oxford, all out for 196, lost by 134 runs. That innings was typical of Harry Foster at his best. Fry noted that 'when he gets the pace of the wicket and feels sure of himself he can force any bowling, however perfect its length, with marvellous brilliance'. His hitting was free and effortless, but he was brilliant rather than sound, a true Edwardian in spirit. He led Worcestershire in their first season in the County Championship, stepped aside for his brother, R.E., in 1900, but led the side again from 1901 to 1910 and in 1913. H.K. was a cheerful and capable captain who believed that the game was to be enjoyed.

Very strong on the off side, Harry Foster was one of the most attractive batsmen of his generation as befits a natural athlete who was the best racquets player of his time. His contribution to Worcestershire cricket was immense, and only Paul Foley gave more. He played his last three matches for Worcestershire in August 1925, only two months short of his 52nd birthday. He was a Test selector on several occasions, including the difficult year of 1921, and he acted as Paul Foley's Land Agent at Stoke Edith, Herefordshire, when he had given up full-time cricket.

Like his elder brother, Wilfred Lionel Foster was a fine racquets player, but he did not resemble Harry as a batsman, being sounder, more cautious, less fluent. Nevertheless, he was a fine player and topped the Worcestershire averages in that first Championship season with 894 runs at 42.57 an innings. Unfortunately, that was the only season in which he was able to play regularly. His 29 games for the County were stretched over a period of twelve years, for he had gone from Malvern College to the Royal Military Academy at Woolwich, and the army was to claim most of his time.

Second in the Worcestershire batting averages in 1899 was the third of the Foster brothers, Reginald Erskine, known as 'Tip'. He was the most talented of the seven brothers and the first truly great batsman to play for Worcestershire. He was a month past his 21st birthday when the County took the field against Yorkshire in the opening match of the 1899 season, and although he bore a close resemblance to his brother Harry in style and attitude, he was blessed with a touch of genius which is given to few. *Wisden* placed him alongside MacLaren, Fry, Jackson and Hayward.

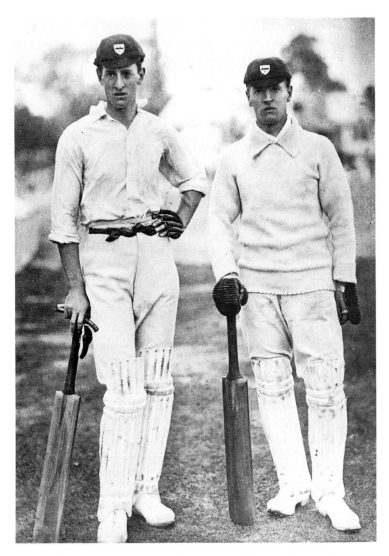

R. E. and W. L. Foster, record breakers in 1899 and batsmen of outstanding talent.

In 1900, his fourth year in the side at Oxford, he hit 171 against Cambridge at Lord's and ten days later, on the same ground, on the occasion of his debut for the Gentlemen against the Players, he hit 102 not out and 136. None before had ever scored a century on his debut for the Gentlemen. In the second innings, he scored 91 while C. B. Fry hit 19 at one time during their third wicket stand of 195, and 'Tip'

Foster's 136 came in 100 minutes with 24 fours. No wonder Fry wrote of him:

> Mr Foster, slimly built and clean-limbed, with a perfect eye and a classy pair of wrists, has great natural advantages; he is one of those cricketers who have all the faculties requisite for a batsman, and also, what does not necessarily follow, a graceful and elegant manner of using them. His pose at the wicket while awaiting the ball is alert and full of cricket; none but a run-getter would stand as he does. Mark the slight easing of the knees to gain a quick start at the ball. His strokes one and all are executed with decision and rapidity, and almost contemptuous ease.

This is praise indeed from one who was a fine judge and a stern assessor, and one should add to this Warner's comment that he could never remember seeing 'Tip' Foster drop a catch. He was the most noted slip-fielder of his day.

He took over the captaincy of Worcestershire in 1900, but thereafter he was never able to play regularly. He enjoyed two wonderful seasons at the beginning of the century and went to Australia with Warner's side in 1903–04. He made his Test debut at Sydney in the same match in which Ted Arnold first played for England, and hit 287. This remains the highest score hit by a batsman on his Test debut and the highest for England in Australia. He became the first batsman to share three century partnerships in a Test innings and his tenth wicket stand of 130 with Wilfred Rhodes remains a record in England–Australia Tests. He also hit 214 runs in a day, which no Englishman has bettered against Australia.

A. E. Knight, who was a member of the MCC party on that tour, noted that R. E. Foster, like all great batsmen, initially played back, trusting to the eye rather than the bat: 'His first seventy runs were obtained ere complete confidence had come to him, and in doubt he went back; only when, as it were, acknowledged master did he use his magnificent sweeping forward play.'

He played in the remaining four Tests of that series, although he was taken ill during the second, and he captained England in the three-match series against South Africa in 1907. That was the extent of the Test career of one of the greatest batsman of the 'Golden Age'.

Worcestershire's first victory in first-class cricket came against Oxford University in The Parks at the end of May 1899. R. E. Foster was in the Oxford side which also included Bosanquet. Ted Arnold hit 125 not out in the second innings, Worcestershire's first first-class century.

Arnold also played an important part in the County's first Championship victory, taking five for 70 in the second innings as Leicestershire were beaten by 122 runs at New Road. Put in to bat,

Worcestershire were bowled out for 206, R. E. Foster and Arnold holding the middle order together. Wilson, four for 41, and Burrows, three for 24, were the main reason why Leicestershire could only manage 126 in their first innings. Harry Foster and Wheldon played finely when Worcestershire batted again, and Leicestershire were left with the task of making 336 to win. For a time, with A. E. Knight, C. J. B. Wood and R. Joyce showing confidence, it looked as if they might do it, but Wilson and Arnold brought about a collapse, and Leicestershire were bowled out for 213.

This victory came in the first week in June, and the only other Championship victory recorded by Worcestershire in their first season was when Derbyshire were beaten by an innings at the end of August, but before then, the first centuries for Worcestershire in the County Championship had been recorded in historic circumstances.

On Thursday, Friday and Saturday, 27, 28 and 29 July, Hampshire were the visitors to Worcester. H. K. Foster won the toss and W.L. and Granville Bromley-Martin opened the batting. Two wickets had gone down and the hundred only just been reached when Reginald Foster joined his brother Wilfred. In 90 minutes, they added 161. Wilfred Foster batted just over three hours and hit 16 fours while 'Tip' hit 15 fours in his 134 which lasted for two and three-quarter hours. Eventually, Worcestershire were out for 428. Commendable bowling by Burrows, Arnold and Wilson gave Worcestershire a first innings lead of 75 after Barton and Major Poore had threatened to run riot. Robert Poore, 6ft. 4in and with a massive and powerful frame, was a formidable adversary. His 122 was one of his seven centuries in a season which saw him score 1,551 runs and finish top of the national averages with 91.23, Ranjitsinhji, Hayward and Abel, the next three in line, finishing nearly 30 runs an innings behind him.

When Worcestershire batted again Granville Bromley-Martin and Harry Foster went cheaply, but W.L. and R.E. again came together in a punishing stand. Both reached their second centuries of the match. Wilfred Foster's three first-class hundreds wer all scored in 1899, and his second innings 172 not out was the highest of the three.

This was the first occasion on which two brothers had both scored centuries in each innings of a first-class match, and the record stood unchallenged for 75 years. It was finally equalled by the Chappell brothers, Ian and Greg, who hit centuries in each innings for Australia against New Zealand at Wellington in March 1974.

Worcestershire, like Australia in 1974, could not force a victory. They bowled well and fielded valiantly, but the match against Hampshire was drawn. Had Simpson-Hayward been brought into the attack earlier, they may, perhaps, have had more success.

George Simpson-Hayward had been one of the two changes that

WORCESTERSHIRE *v* HAMPSHIRE

Played at New Road, Worcester on 27, 28 and 29 July 1899

MATCH DRAWN

WORCESTERSHIRE	FIRST INNINGS		SECOND INNINGS	
W. L. Foster	c Webb b Baldwin	140	not out	172
G. E. Bromley-Martin	b Steele	33	b Heseltine	21
★H. K. Foster	c Bennett b Baldwin	16	c Tate b Heseltine	10
R. E. Foster	lbw b Steele	134	not out	101
E. G. Arnold	b Hill	14		
G. F. Wheldon	b Hill	0		
G. H. Simpson-Hayward	lbw b Hill	8		
A. Bird	b Quinton	10		
R. D. Burrows	c Hill b Steele	35		
†T. Straw	not out	10		
G. A. Wilson	c Hill b Quinton	12		
Extras	b 11, lb 3, w 1, nb 1	16	b 1, lb 3	4
Total		428	(for 2 wkts dec)	308

BOWLING	O	M	R	W	O	M	R	W
Heseltine	16	1	66	0	32	4	100	2
Baldwin	34	10	0	2	18	3	50	0
Hill	27	4	80	3	15	1	50	0
Tate	30	7	66	0	11	1	37	0
Steele	22	2	62	3	8	1	41	0
Lee	1	0	16	0				
Quinton	9.2	0	32	2				
Webb	3	0	10	0				
Barton					5	0	26	0

HAMPSHIRE	FIRST INNINGS		SECOND INNINGS	
A. J. L. Hill	c Burrows b Wilson	0	b Burrows	19
V. A. Barton	c R. E. Foster b Burrows	62	b Arnold	36
Maj. R. M. Poore	c H. K. Foster b Burrows	122	lbw b Arnold	17
A. S. Webb	c and b Burrows	33	c R. E. Foster b Bird	20
★Capt F. W. D. Quinton	c H. K. Foster b Arnold	40	b Wilson	7
†R. A. Bennett	lbw b Burrows	0	b Simpson-Hayward	17
C. Heseltine	b Wilson	26	b Simpson-Hayward	31
E. C. Lee	b Arnold	31	not out	3
D. A. Steele	not out	10		
H. Baldwin	run out	9		
E. Tate	b Arnold	4		
Extras	b 2, lb 13, w 1	16	b 7	7
Total		353	(for 7 wkts)	157

BOWLING	O	M	R	W	O	M	R	W
Wilson	30	11	101	2	26	10	54	1
Burrows	29	7	73	4	10	4	22	1
Bird	33	11	79	0	16	6	27	1
Arnold	16.4	1	56	3	24	9	46	2
Simpson-Hayward	9	0	28	0	2.1	1	1	2

Umpires: J. Moss and W. Shrewsbury

The first of only two occasions in which brothers have scored centuries in each innings of a first-class match.

★Captain; †Wicket-keeper

Worcestershire had made for their second County match. He and Bowley had come in for E. Bromley-Martin and R. E. Foster, who was up at Oxford.

George Simpson-Hayward was an anachronism. Forty years after round-arm or over-arm bowling had been legalised and generally adopted, he was still bowling his lobs. He was born at Stoneleigh in Warwickshire, but his education at Malvern gave him his Worcestershire qualification. He did not get a blue at Cambridge, and he did not begin to play with any regularity for Worcestershire until 1902, yet he was amazingly successful. He took 68 wickets at 18.61 in 1908, and he went to South Africa with Leveson-Gower's side in 1909–10. In the first Test, he took six for 43 and two for 59, claiming a wicket, that of Zulch, with the fifth ball he bowled. He finished the series, his only Test matches, with 23 wickets at 18.26 runs each. He captained Worcestershire in 1911 and 1912.

It is difficult to assess how a spin bowler bowling under-arm could be so successful in an age which boasted a host of great bowlers, quick and slow. *Wisden* asserted that he seldom flighted the ball like the general run of lob bowlers and that he did not often turn the ball from leg. He relied on the speed with which he could make the ball turn from the off on a low trajectory, yet *Wisden* also credited him with exceptional powers of spinning the ball. Herbert Strudwick, the Surrey and England 'keeper, maintained that Simpson-Hayward was the only bowler he ever kept to who could 'twist the ball in his hand as though it were a billiard ball'.

Fred Bowley had been on the staff as a professional in the days before the County became first-class. He was born in Brecon, but had been brought up in Heanor and played for Derbyshire Colts when he was fourteen. He decided to adopt cricket as a profession, qualified for Worcestershire and played the first of his 396 games for them in May 1899, when he opened the innings and scored 4 and 4 against Sussex at Hove. He did not gain a regular place in the side until the following season.

Following the high-scoring match with Hampshire, Worcestershire drew at Derby where Arnold hit a century, and W. L. Foster hit his third and last hundred in the next match, a draw at home to Sussex. It was in the penultimate game of the season that the second victory was achieved.

The match was against Derbyshire who were to finish bottom of the table. W. L. and R. E. Foster went cheaply, and Arnold was out for nought, but Granville Bromley-Martin, 129, and Harry Foster, 162, put on 207 in two hours. Then W. W. Lowe hit 102 not out and added 87 in half an hour on the second morning with Burrows for the ninth wicket. Worcestershire reached what was then their highest score in first-class cricket, 557, and Wilson and Burrows were the main instruments in bowling them to an innings victory.

William Walter Lowe was a fine all-rounder, a quick and hard-hitting batsman, who could appear only infrequently for the County. He was yet another product of Malvern College, and the influence of the school's cricket on the early Worcestershire through the Fosters and their friends was most pronounced. Malvern excelled at cricket, racquets and soccer. Their cricketers were athletic fielders, and their batsmen bore the mark of freedom and wristy elegance in their stroke-play. They were a delight to watch, and they won the County the reputation of being an entertaining side, keen and happy. Other counties enjoyed playing against them.

Had Worcestershire beaten Yorkshire in the opening match of the first Championship season, they may well have gone on to do better than they ultimately did in finishing twelfth of the 15 counties. The record was a little disappointing, for they were 'at once looked upon to be a team fairly strong at all points' after the game with Yorkshire in May. They had some brilliant batsmen and some hard-working bowlers who promised much. Of Straw, it was said his 'wicket-keeping throughout the season has been of a very high standard'.

There was no need to despair. Much had been achieved, and the future looked bright. Even the grand old man, W. G. Grace himself, had played at New Road during the season, in a non-first-class fixture for his London County side. Inevitably, the champion had hit 175 not out and taken four for 64, but Arnold hit a hundred, and the match was drawn.

The Fosters could not be kept out of the news. In the close season, H.K. won the national racquets championship and W.L., who was acting as galloper or aide-de-camp for Lord Methuen in the Boer War, was reported as having had nine horses shot from under him in one day. In fact, he was invalided home from South Africa, but he did not venture into county cricket in 1900.

Although nominally captain and enjoying a wonderful season, R. E. Foster was able to play in only half the County's matches. He hit seven centuries, but none of them for Worcestershire, and of his 1,507 runs, only 556 were scored in the County Championship. He still finished top of the averages, but he was sorely missed in a county programme which had been extended to 22 matches.

The season began disastrously when Worcestershire went to Bradford and were bowled out for 43 and 51 and beaten by an innings. As *Cricket* explained:

After very heavy rain the wicket at the Park Avenue Ground was so greatly in favour of the bowlers that batsmen could do next to nothing with them. In such a case the side which has the best bowlers generally wins pretty easily, and this match was no exception to the rule. Rhodes and Haigh were irresistible; they bowled throughout the two Worcestershire innings.

Dr Grace followed this by taking a rather strong London County side to Worcester, and the home side suffered their second defeat. A third followed at Hove, and a fourth would surely have come at The Oval where Surrey hit 495 for five and Worcestershire were 30 for four when rain came to their rescue. In spite of a century by Harry Foster, there was another defeat at Old Trafford, yet amid this miserable run of failure, there were some sparks of comfort.

The opening match against Yorkshire had seen the debut of Arthur Bannister, a bowler capable of imparting considerable spin on the ball. He took five for 30 on his debut and finished the season with 65 wickets at 20.47 in all matches, which placed him high in the national averages, but he fell away in 1901 and passed from the scene, a talent unfulfilled.

More significantly, Fred Pearson made his debut in the match against London County and also played in the game against Oxford University and in the non–first-class match against the West Indian tourists. On these occasions, he opened the innings with Bowley who had won a regular place in the side and, after the first match of the season, became the regular opening batsman.

Fred Bowley was to be a pillar of Worcestershire cricket for 23 years. Tall, dark-haired, with a proud black moustache, he was all that was good and true in a county cricketer. He had a joy in playing the game which infected others. Against Hampshire, at Worcester, at the end of May 1900, he hit the first of his 38 centuries, and he batted as he always batted, with a technical surety and a stylishness that bore comparison with the Fosters. That he did not play in a Test match was because he lived and played in an age of abundant greatness in opening batsmen. He was contemporary with the younger Hobbs and the older Hayward, of Fry, MacLaren and Quaife. He had to be content with representing the Players against the Gentlemen, but it mattered little to him as long as he was playing cricket.

Wheldon also hit a maiden century, in the return match with Hampshire, which provided one of the three victories in a disappointing season. The other two wins were over Leicestershire at Worcester and Gloucestershire at Gloucester. In both of these games, George Wilson was outstanding, taking nine for 64 in the first and 12 for 144 in the second. He ended the season with 107 wickets in Championship matches and 119 in all matches, the first Worcestershire bowler to reach a hundred wickets in a season for the County.

One of Worcestershire's early favourites and prolific run-getters, Fred Bowley.

H. K. Foster, eminently consistent, became the first Worcestershire batsman to reach a thousand runs in the season in Championship matches, but he was closely chased by Arnold and Bowley, both of whom reached a thousand runs in all matches.

Arnold took 72 Championship wickets to confirm his standing as an all-rounder of immense potential, but Burrows lost all form and his place in the side, although he was to return with a vengeance in 1901.

The season 1900 had ended with Worcestershire again twelfth out of 15, and although they had won one more match than in the previous season, there was a great sense of disappointment. It seemed that they had gone backwards in spite of the deeds of Arnold, Bowley, Wilson, Harry Foster and R. E. Foster, whose performances at Oxford and elsewhere won wide acclaim.

The feeling of disappointment became stronger at the beginning of the following season when the first seven matches ended in defeat, three of them by an innings. One of the defeats was at the hands of Cambridge University at Fenner's. It was the first engagement with the University, and it provided Cambridge with their only win of the season.

These defeats were not without their moments of hope. Bowley played two fine innings in the match at Dewsbury where Worcestershire led Yorkshire by 13 runs on the first innings before going down by 90 runs. Another to shine in this game was W. H. W. Wilks who hit 109 in the first innings. It was to be the only century of a brief career. He was a talented amateur batsman who, like many others, could not give time to the game.

A greater glimmer of hope came in the seventh defeat when Leicestershire were the visitors to New Road. They were bowled out for 234, Burrows taking five wickets and Simpson-Hayward three. Burrows had won fame in the opening match of the season at Old Trafford when he bowled A. C. MacLaren and sent a bail 64 yards 6 inches. This constituted a record at the time, for such records were taken seriously in the early part of the century, and stood until 1911 when Burrows himself sent a bail 67 yards 6 inches.

There were other heroes in the Leicestershire game. Bowley and Pearson gave Worcestershire a scintillating start by putting on 147 of which Bowley, eagerly and joyfully, made 91. Pearson went on to reach a maiden first-class century.

Dick Pearson was to serve Worcestershire unstintingly until 1926, batting wherever required and bowling whenever and for however long he was needed. Totally committed to Worcestershire and cricket, he was one of the most popular of men, modest, unassuming and unselfish. He was the model professional, the backbone of the Club.

Thanks to Bowley and Pearson, Worcestershire led Leicestershire by 70 runs on the first innings, but the visitors hit 335 in their second, and, set to make 266 to win, Worcestershire fell apart and were bowled out for 186. Had it not been for a bold knock by skipper R. E. Foster, they would have been humiliated.

'Tip' Foster had now found his best form and he played a fine innings in the next match, at Bristol. He was ably supported by Arnold and Pearson who was reported as having 'played a great innings'. Foster scored 110, Pearson 90, Arnold 83, and defeat was avoided for the first time in the season.

The gloom had been lifted, and confidence was restored. R. E. Foster followed his century against Gloucestershire with 98 in the match against Derbyshire at Worcester. Arnold and Harry Foster hit fifties, Wilson had match figures of ten for 121 and Worcestershire won by an innings with more than a day to spare.

This proved to be just the inspiration that the County needed. They won six more matches during the season and moved up one place in the Championship table to finish eleventh. As well as the seven Championship victories, Worcestershire beat MCC at Lord's in spite of being dismissed for 77 in their first innings. The significant thing about this match was that it was the first occasion on which Worcestershire had taken the field in a first-class game without a member of the Foster family in the side.

It was in 1901, too, that Worcestershire engaged in the first tie in their history. They entertained the South African touring team at the County Ground on 15, 16 and 17 July. By the end of the first day, the tourists, having made 293, had reduced the County to 121 for six. On the second morning, the Worcestershire tail wagged well, and Arthur Bannister whose slow bowling had fallen away to such an extent that he had lost a regular place in the side and was not to be retained after 1902 hit 44, the highest score of his career, so that the South African lead was restricted to 69. With Wilson adding five for 39 to the five for 123 he had taken in the first innings, the home side bowled out the visitors for 140. This meant that Worcestershire had to score 210 to win on a wicket which was giving considerable assistance to the bowlers, and when they closed at 84 for five, hopes of victory were vanishing. On the last day, Simpson-Hayward, 12 not out overnight, played well and found an able ally in George Gaukrodger, the wicket-keeper who had arrived at Worcestershire via Yorkshire and Ireland. Gaukrodger was still fulfilling the necessary two-year residential qualification before he could appear in the Championship side, and he was to take over from Straw the following season. Simpson-Hayward was bowled by Kotze for 52, and Harry Wilson, a slow left-arm bowler whose six first-class matches were spread over six seasons, was soon out so that when Bannister arrived to join Gaukrodger 32 were needed with two wickets standing.

Gaukrodger was a stubborn batsman, who had hit 32 not out in the first innings, while Bannister tended to throw the bat. Again, Gaukrodger showed his tendency to 'get 'em in singles'. The pair added 23 before Gaukrodger was caught at slip. This brought in last man George Wilson with nine runs needed for victory.

Amidst scenes of great excitement, the last pair nudged closer and closer to the target, but, with the scores level, Wilson was stumped off Robert Graham, the medium-pace bowler, by Murray Bisset, and the match was tied. Wilson was Graham's eighth victim, and his wickets cost him 90 runs, a performance which he never bettered in his career, but followers of the game today will find it hard to comprehend how a batsman could allow himself to be stumped with only one run needed to win.

George Wilson redeemed himself in the next match when Worcestershire came close to beating the mighty Surrey side. Surrey began strongly and were 154 for one in the last over before lunch at which point Hayes fell to Wilson. Jephson was out immediately after the break, and two more wickets fell quickly so that five men were out for 209. George Wilson now bowled Walker, Dowson and Stedman with consecutive balls to become the first Worcestershire bowler to do the hat-trick in a Championship match. He had achieved the feat a year earlier in the game against London County, and he was to accomplish it again in 1904, against Leicestershire at Worcester. His record of three hat-tricks for the County was equalled by Roly Jenkins in 1949.

The last five Surrey wickets went down for ten runs, and Worcestershire took a first-innings lead of 44 thanks to a brilliant 135 by R. E. Foster whose 'innings was without fault and was, moreover, played at a time when failure would have probably meant disaster to his side'. Unfortunately for Worcestershire, Bobby Abel batted splendidly in Surrey's second innings and the visitors eventually won by 47 runs.

R. E. Foster enjoyed a marvellous season for Worcestershire, hitting five centuries in his 1957 runs, average 54.36, and gleaming in a golden age of batsmen. Unfortunately, the third son of the housemaster at Malvern College was never again able to give himself fully to cricket. He resigned the captaincy before the beginning of the following season, and Harry again took over.

The fourth Foster, Basil Samuel, made his debut for the County in 1902, but he was to play only seven matches for Worcestershire in nine years before appearing in a dozen matches for Middlesex, for whom he had obtained a residential qualification, in 1912. He was probably the least talented of the brotherhood, and his highest score, 86, was for MCC against the South Africans at Lord's in 1907. That was the year when he first appeared on the West End stage, for he was a talented actor of considerable charm who established himself in a series of successful musical comedies and later turned to management. He managed the Salisbury Playhouse until shortly before his death in 1959.

Ironically, the 1902 season opened without a Foster in the side, and although the County was to advance from eleventh to ninth in the Championship, it was not a successful season. The gap left by R. E. Foster, who played only eleven innings and scored 450 runs at an average of 50, was never adequately filled although Arnold, restored to full fitness, completed the 'double' in all matches, the first Worcestershire cricketer to achieve the feat.

The 1902 season also saw the first visit of an Australian touring side to New Road. The match started on 10 July, and the Australians were bowled out for 274 with Bird taking six for 69 with his off-breaks. Worcestershire came to within 72 of the visitors' score and then bowled them out for 199, but Armstrong and Jones wrought havoc among the home batsmen in the second innings and bowled the County out for 97 of which Bowley made 35.

After four seasons in first-class cricket Worcestershire were established as a middle of the table side. Their batting was attractive, their fielding keen and their bowling mostly honest. By 1902, membership had risen from 798, the total in the County's initial first-class season, to 1,153, but the Club was still in debt to the amount of more than £780, and that would have been larger but for a generous gift from Lord Dudley and the continuing efforts and unrecorded personal donations by Paul Foley.

For the time being, the precariousness of the financial position did not seem to concern people too greatly although, in 1903, a bazaar and a ballot for a bicycle helped to lessen the burden of debt. On the playing side, there was great optimism. After another wretched start Worcestershire again recovered and they rose to sixth in the table, the number of victories exceeding the number of defeats for the first time.

The fifth Foster, Geoffrey Norman, appeared in the side for the first time in 1903. He was fresh from school and went up to Oxford in 1905 and was to win his blue in all four years at the university. He was a gifted sportsman, representing England at soccer in an amateur international, and a talented batsman and brilliant fielder. Business took him to Kent for whom he appeared a few times in the 1920s. His son, Peter Geoffrey, played for Kent after the Second World War.

G. N. Foster was an eager hitter of the ball, and he and W. B. Burns put on 181 in 65 minutes against Hampshire at New Road in 1905. Like G. N. Foster, William Beaumont Burns first played for Worcestershire in 1903. A middle-order batsman capable of furious hitting and a bowler described by many as the fastest in England for his first five or six overs, Burns played several attractive innings for Staffordshire before beginning his residential qualification for Worcestershire. In 1903, he was able to play only in non-Championship matches, and he made his debut for the County against Oxford University in The Parks in May. He scored 3 and 35 and did not bowl.

Also making his debut for Worcestershire in that match was John Cuffe, the County's first overseas player. Born in Queensland, he had played for New South Wales before, following the example of Trott of Middlesex, he came to England to attempt to earn his living as a professional cricketer. A slow left-arm bowler and right-handed batsman, he qualified for Worcestershire and served the County

W. B. Burns, fast bowler and hard hitter.

splendidly as an all-round cricketer from 1905, by which time he was able to assist in Championship matches, until the outbreak of the First World War.

The all-round deeds of Burns and Cuffe lay in the future, but it must be said of Burns that, although he was never called for throwing, his action was viewed with the deepest suspicion in many quarters; for the present it was Arnold, George Wilson, Bird and John Keene, a left-arm slow-medium bowler who had played twice for Surrey in 1897, who bore the brunt of the bowling, and H. K. Foster, Bowley, Wheldon and Arnold who did most of the batting. Arnold took a hundred wickets in a season for the first time and produced some outstanding performances in what was an eccentric season.

The County beat Warwickshire twice, always a cause for satisfaction, and saved the home match with Yorkshire in remarkable manner. Yorkshire hit 518, and Worcestershire began the last day with two second innings wickets down and still 231 runs behind. Arnold, Wheldon and H. K. Foster, who made 120, batted with such resolution, however, that the game was drawn. Another hero of that match-saving second innings was Reginald Brinton who played only 13 matches, of which this was the first, in six years. He made 66 not out in dogged and defiant manner.

The return match with Yorkshire also ended in a draw, but fortune smiled on Worcestershire in this game. It was played on a wretched wicket at Huddersfield. No cricket was possible on the first day, only an hour and three quarters on the second and two hours on the last. In the three and three quarter hours that were possible, Hirst and Rhodes bowled out Worcestershire for 24 and reduced them to 27 for six in their second innings while Yorkshire declared at 76 for one.

Worcestershire's 24 remains the lowest score in their history. William Caldwell, who later went into the church, hit 11 of the 22 runs scored from the bat. Perversely, a fortnight before the debacle at Huddersfield, Worcestershire had scored 590, at the time the highest score they had ever made, against Somerset, whom they beat by an innings. Bowley, Wheldon and H. K. Foster all hit centuries, but Harry Foster's was the innings of the match. He hit 216 out of 338 made in the two and three quarter hours he was at the wicket. He hit 37 fours and scarcely made a false stroke. His off-side play was one of the delights of the age, and it was right that he should have the honour of scoring the County's first double century.

In the home match previous to this rout of Somerset, Worcestershire had entertained Hampshire, the weakest side in the Championship in 1903. Because of heavy overnight rain, play could not begin until 2.30 pm, on the Thursday, the first day, and Hampshire seemed to have the advantage in winning the toss in that they were able to bat on a wicket that was soft and slow and unlikely to give help to the bowlers. In 70 minutes, however, they were bowled out for 30, the lowest score ever made on the County Ground in a County match and the lowest score ever made against Worcestershire: 'Wilson, who maintained a tremendous pace, made the ball swerve in a way that made him irresistible, the batsmen being altogether unable to judge its flight.' By the close, Worcestershire were 223 for four. Bowley and H. K. Foster had put on 156 in 100 minutes for the first wicket to dispel any ideas that the pitch was treacherous.

Fred Bowley had a liking for Hampshire bowling and eight of his 38 centuries, including his first, were hit against that county. In an age dominated by the Fosters and the amateur spirit, Bowley bore comparison with the best. He allied a sound defence to a freedom of shot all round the wicket, and his driving was strong and elegant on both sides of the wicket. Why he never played for England will ever remain a mystery.

Worcestershire took their lead to 241 on the second morning, and by 3.45 pm, the game was over. As Sussex, a very strong batting side, were bowled out for 47 and beaten by an innings a month later, this was indeed a season of achievement. Wilson took ten wickets, Arnold nine, and Caldwell hit a career best 133 in this game, which produced the most noteworthy and surprising performance of the season. At their best, Worcestershire were a very fine side, but all too rarely could they put their best eleven in the field. R. E. Foster, for example, could play in only three matches, Simpson-Hayward in only five. It was the inevitable price to be paid for relying on so many talented amateurs. It is a fallacy to believe that the Edwardian Age was entirely peopled by wealthy men who had sufficient time and money to devote their summers to playing county cricket. Certainly the Fosters had to choose a profession by which they could earn their living, and cricket, though a passion, remained, for the most part, a hobby.

R. E. Foster triumphed on England's tour of Australia, 1903–04, as we have noted, but he was unable to assist Worcestershire in 1904 for business reasons. Arnold seemed a little jaded after his success in Australia, and the promise of 1903 was not sustained. Indeed, the County won only three matches in 1904, five in 1905 and two in 1906, yet these years were not without their moments of success.

At Oxford, in 1904, when a win was achieved against a rather weak university side, George Wilson took the first nine wickets to fall. Bird bowled the last man to rob him of all ten, as Reg Perks was to be robbed similarly in 1946. Wilson's nine for 75 was the best performance of his career, but this great-hearted bowler was already in decline, and his career ended in 1906. His problem was his lack of consistency. He took the third hat-trick of his career, against

WORCESTERSHIRE *v* HAMPSHIRE

Played at New Road, Worcester on 18 and 19 July 1903

WORCESTERSHIRE WON BY AN INNINGS AND 77 RUNS

HAMPSHIRE	FIRST INNINGS		SECOND INNINGS	
A. J. L. Hill	c Gaukrodger b Wilson	3	b Wilson	20
†J. Stone	b Wilson	4	c Bird b Arnold	3
*E. M. Sprot	c Simpson-Hayward b Wilson	13	b Arnold	47
A. S. Webb	c and b Arnold	5	b Arnold	16
C. B. Llewellyn	b Arnold	2	b Wilson	4
H. A. W. Bowell	b Arnold	0	b Wilson	0
F. H. Bacon	b Wilson	1	c Isaac b Keene	39
C. Heseltine	b Wilson	0	not out	10
H. G. Smoker	b Wilson	0	b Wilson	10
F. J. Kitchener	c Simpson-Hayward b Arnold	0	b Wilson	0
H. V. Hesketh-Prichard	not out	0	c B. S. Foster b Arnold	1
Extras	b 2	2	b 11, lb 3	14
Total		30		164

BOWLING	O	M	R	W	O	M	R	W
Arnold	11.1	4	13	4	26.1	7	64	4
Wilson	11	5	15	6	25	10	75	5
Simpson-Hayward					1	0	4	0
Keene					5	3	7	1

WORCESTERSHIRE	FIRST INNINGS	
*H. K. Foster	c Bowell b Webb	79
F. L. Bowley	c Smoker b Hill	102
E. G. Arnold	c Smoker b Sprot	7
G. F. Wheldon	b Llewellyn	21
†G. W. Gaukrodger	not out	34
G. H. T. Simpson-Hayward	lbw b Llewellyn	5
A. W. Isaac	c Webb b Llewellyn	0
B. S. Foster	b Hesketh-Pritchard	0
A. Bird	c Hill b Hesketh-Pritchard	0
G. A. Wilson	b Hesketh-Pritchard	13
J. W. Keene	c Kitchener b Hesketh-Pritchard	4
Extras	b 3, lb 1, w 2	6
Total		271

BOWLING	O	M	R	W
Llewellyn	30	3	108	3
Hesketh-Pritchard	16	2	56	4
Kitchener	5	2	19	0
Hill	7	0	26	1
Heseltine	3	0	17	0
Webb	6	0	21	1
Sprot	4	1	18	1

Umpires: C. E. Richardson and G. Porter

Hampshire's 30 is the lowest score made against Worcestershire.

*Captain; †Wicket-keeper

Leicestershire in 1904, and a year later, at Taunton, he became the first Worcestershire bowler to take 15 wickets in a match. He had one of his irresistible days, taking eight for 30 and seven for 112. He also bowled splendidly against the Australians in 1905, taking six for 80, but there were too many days when Worcestershire could not bowl sides out, and Wilson will always remain as one of those fast bowlers who never quite fulfilled all that had been expected of him.

John Keene, too, who had been able to turn the ball prodigiously in club cricket for Mitcham, did not realise expectations and left the County after the 1905 season. He later became coach at Loretto School.

On the credit side, Burrows, who had a benefit in 1905, Arnold and Bird soldiered on manfully while Cuffe and Burns, when available, had proved excellent acquisitions. The contribution of Ted Arnold at this time cannot be praised highly enough. In the four seasons, 1902 to 1905, he did the 'double' in all matches, and he was unflagging in enthusiasm and commitment. He made six scores of a hundred or more for the County in the depressing season of 1906, and, like Pearson and Bowley, would give whatever was asked of him. *Wisden* described his batting as the best feature of the Worcestershire season: 'He was not nearly so brilliant in his methods as Bowley, but he played several fine innings, and was the most dependable run-getter in the eleven.' Bowley, throughout the County's lean period, remained 'one of the most attractive professional batsmen now before the public'.

One new venture in 1905 was to play a county match away from New Road for the first time. In an effort to attract members from other parts of the county, the match with Leicestershire towards the end of June was scheduled for Amblecote, Stourbridge. It proved a triumph, for not only did Worcestershire win inside two days by an innings, but Arnold hit 134 and had match figures of nine for 112, while Fred Bowley hit 217 which remains the highest first-class score made on the ground.

Surprisingly, it was not the highest score made for Worcestershire in the 1905 season. That honour went to R. E. Foster, who appeared in the match against Kent and hit 246 not out in four and a half hours, with two sixes and 32 fours. What a talent—he was capable of picking up a bat for the first time in a year and playing as if he were in constant practice. He could spare only the second week in August for cricket in 1906, the matches against Warwickshire at Worcester and Somerset at Taunton. He hit 35 in the first match and 198 and 10 in the second. In the first innings at Taunton, he moved from 100 to 198 in just over the hour.

'Tip' Foster's first appearance of the season inspired other Worcestershire batsmen to great heights, for the game against

Warwickshire saw the County reach their highest score in first-class cricket, a record which withstood even the batterings of 1988. Remarkably, there were only two centuries on the Worcestershire side.

WORCESTERSHIRE v WARWICKSHIRE

Played at New Road, Worcester on 6, 7 and 8 August 1906

F. L. Bowley	c Lilley, b Santall	69
F. A. Pearson	lbw, b Hargreave	20
*H. K. Foster	b Charlesworth	124
J. A. Cuffe	c Hargreave b Santall	9
R. E. Foster	c Quaife b Charlesworth	35
W. E. C. Hutchings	b Byrne	67
W. B. Burns	c Kinneir b Moorhouse	125
G. A. Wilson	c Fishwick b Moorhouse	4
†G. F. Wheldon	not out	89
R. D. Burrows	c Devey b Moorhouse	43
A. Bird	c Santall b Hargreave	8
Extras	b 30, lb 7, w 3	40
Total		633

Warwickshire scored 335 and 223 for 4, and the match was drawn.

It was one of those paradoxes, or one of Worcestershire's 'wonderfully illogical contours', that the County should reach its record score in what was a very poor and uneventful season, yet *Wisden* sounded a note of hope: 'On paper there was an abundance of first-rate talent in Worcestershire, but the eleven never got in a winning vein.' The winning vein was to come in 1907.

In fact, it began in the opening match of the season when Worcestershire beat Yorkshire for the first time. The game was played at New Road in the middle of May. Harry Foster, Fred Bowley and 'Dick' Pearson gave the home county a fine start, and the amateurs, Burns and Swalwell, boosted the latter part of the innings so that Worcestershire reached a commendable 292. On the Friday, Yorkshire collapsed against Arnold and Cuffe, who bowled unchanged, and were all out for 119. Worcestershire, handicapped by the absence of the injured Bowley, struggled against Rhodes and Myers in their second innings. In spite of Harry Foster's 54, they were bowled out for 139 so that Yorkshire were left to make 313 to win. They batted with characteristic resolution, but they lost wickets regularly to Cuffe,

Arnold and Burrows and were never really in contention, so that Worcestershire won a memorable victory by 54 runs.

The return match with Yorkshire was played at Bradford in August when both sides were hit by Test calls. R. E. Foster, who was able to give himself more regularly to cricket this summer and led England against South Africa, Hirst and Rhodes were all engaged in the match at The Oval.

Worcestershire scored 155 on the first day, and this turned out to be the only three-figured score of the match. Twenty-two wickets fell on the second day while 142 runs were scored. The Yorkshire first innings ended at 62, and Worcestershire were then bowled out for 28. By coincidence, they were again without Bowley, who was called away on a personal matter.

It is remarkable that of the five occasions on which Worcestershire have been bowled out for under 30, three have been in Yorkshire, and this time they went on to win by 30 runs. Yorkshire, needing 122 to win, were 52 for three at the end of the second day, but the last seven wickets went down in 75 minutes on the last morning.

The hero of this famous victory was John Cuffe who, with Ted Arnold, bowled unchanged throughout the match. Arnold took six for 22 and one for 44 while Cuffe took four for 38, and nine for 38, a record once equalled and twice beaten for Worcestershire since that day in Bradford.

If one wishes to look for reasons for Worcestershire's meteoric rise in 1907, one need look no further than the advance made by the Australian all-rounder. Cuffe's batting was always resolute and reliable, and he averaged over 25 without the advantage of any large scores or many not outs, and in 18 Championship matches, he took 100 wickets at 18.91 runs each. This was an outstanding achievement, particularly when one considers that the New Road wicket was an enemy to bowlers at this time. Only three of the eight County matches played there ended in a result.

In many ways Cuffe's career anticipates Glenn Turner's in the resolve and determination that he showed to fulfil his ambition to become a professional cricketer. Born in Toowoomba, he did well enough as a young slow left-arm bowler on matting wickets against visiting English teams to win selection for Queensland in 1901–02. Queensland had not gained first-class status at that time, and Cuffe moved down to Sydney and played one game for New South Wales before setting sail for England and Worcestershire, to whom he gave yeoman service until the outbreak of the First World War. He later played in the Lancashire League and stood as a first-class umpire.

Arnold, if not the force of previous seasons, was still a very fine bowler, and Burrows thrived on the extra work he was given after the

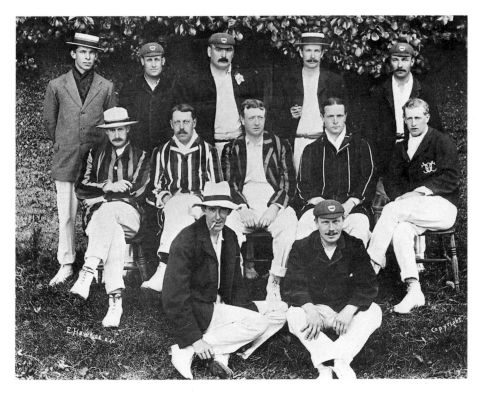

Worcestershire before the First World War, 1907. Back row (l to r):
J. A. Cuffe, F. A. Pearson, R. D. Burrows, F. L. Bowley and G. Gaukrodger.
Seated: R. E. Foster, G. H. Simpson-Hayward, H. K. Foster (capt.),
W. B. Burns, G. N. Foster. On ground: E. G. Arnold and A. Bird.

departure of Wilson. He also showed he could compensate for the retirement of Wheldon and, against Gloucestershire at Worcester, he hit the first of the two centuries of his career. He came in at number ten, was dropped in the deep field when 22, but then played a dashing innings, hitting 19 fours in his 112. Cuffe was at the other end, and the pair added 181 which remains a Worcestershire ninth wicket record. Cuffe finished with 81 not out, and Worcestershire went on to win by an innings and 109 runs.

Certainly Worcestershire's strength was in their batting, with G. N. Foster, who assisted the County after the term at Oxford, R. E. Foster and H. K. Foster filling the first three places in the averages. As *Wisden* remarked, one had to go back to the great days of Gloucestershire and the Graces to find a parallel.

Worcestershire won eight of their 18 matches and lost two, finishing in second place in the Championship, level with Yorkshire on 60 per cent. The title was decided on a percentage basis in those days with defeats subtracted from wins to give a number of points which were taken as a percentage of the matches in which a result was obtained. Neither Worcestershire nor Yorkshire seriously challenged the champions, Nottinghamshire, who won fifteen and were unbeaten so that they had 100 per cent. Worcestershire and Nottinghamshire did not meet, and, indeed, they did not come into contact until 1920 in championship matches.

The 1907 season was, in many ways, a boom time for Worcestershire. A second eleven was entered into the Second Class Counties Competition for the only time before the Second World War, and more people came to watch the Championship matches, but membership had fallen after the disasters of 1906 and debts increased. The debts were to continue, but the County was not to climb so high in the Championship table again until 1962.

There was no sudden decline, but there was a gradual slide which was arrested only by the outbreak of the First World War, by which time the Club's financial position had become precarious and the playing standard had fallen from the heights of 1907.

At the end of the 1908 season, the County was in trouble. *Wisden* reported:

> Worcestershire, like several other counties, have money troubles to deal with and at a special meeting in the autumn the committee, without going into details, put forward a scheme for adjusting the financial burden. There were rumours that the county matches at home would be shifted from Worcester to Dudley, but happily the report proved to be unfounded.

In fact, it would have been impractical to play first-class cricket at Dudley in 1909. The ground was relaid in 1910 and in the winter of 1911, but a long drought hindered the firm setting of the turf and large cracks appeared in the outfield. Matches due to be played at Dudley in May and June 1911, were switched to New Road and to Stourbridge, and it was not until the end of August 1911 that Worcestershire entertained Gloucestershire in the first county match at Tipton Road. It was a great festive occasion with a civic lunch at the Station Hotel marking the event.

There were great ambitions for the Dudley ground. A new pavilion, costing £1,000, was not quite ready in time for the Surrey fixture in 1912, but *The Daily Herald* spoke of dreams of splendour: 'Something like £5,000 has been spent to fashion the ground for first-class cricket and on completion of the pavilion, the whole area will be fully equipped and fit for even a Test match in due time.'

That was not to be, and such dreams in 1911 and 1912 were far removed from the realities of Worcestershire cricket. The crisis of 1908 was far more serious than anything that had gone before. The rise in gate receipts and the reduction in expenditure in 1907 had been offset by the loss of some 300 members. The Club's liabilities had risen to close to £4,500, and Lord Cobham stated that an 'intricate and delicate situation' had arisen when there was an attempt to meet these liabilities. It was no longer possible for a personal cheque from Paul Foley to meet the County's needs, and Foley himself resigned as secretary, believing, no doubt, that it was time for the burden of maintaining the existence of Worcestershire cricket to be spread more evenly. It was he who had brought a first-class club into being, and it was he who had assured its survival, but the task had become too great for one man. He was succeeded as secretary by G. F. Jones-Williams, but he continued to give the Club practical support.

The salvation of the County Club in 1908 was made possible by the efforts of several men. Lord Cobham, Lord Plymouth, Sir Charles Holcroft, Mr G. Holcroft and Mr Rowland Hill contributed £3,816 8s 6d between them. Foley gave £100 a year for three years, and, early in 1909, a bazaar yielded £1,018. There were further donations of £300 and calls upon guarantors so that the deficit was wiped out although, as we shall see, the crisis was not at an end.

From the outset, for financial reasons, it had been Worcestershire policy to play as many amateurs in the side as possible, but the quality and quantity had become thinner. Among the notable amateurs to make their debuts for the County in the years immediately before the First World War were J. B. Higgins, who was to blossom late in life, A. F. Lane, who was also to play for Warwickshire and was one of the best amateur cricketers in the Midlands, C. B. Ponsonby, a wicket-keeper who was to lead Worcestershire for a season, and Dr J. W. C. Turner; and there were also the last of the Fosters.

Maurice Kirshaw Foster appeared in two matches in 1908 when he was 19. He was to captain Worcestershire in the 1920s and to play for the County as late as 1934 so providing the last playing link between Worcestershire and the great family. The youngest of the seven brothers, Neville John Acland, played in three matches in 1914 and was to appear in five more in 1924, but, as he spent most of his life in Malaya, that was to be the extent of his first-class career in England. Surprisingly, he had failed to get into the eleven at Malvern, but he later captained the Federated Malay States.

The Fosters were still the heart of the Worcestershire side. R.E.'s presence in 1907 had helped lift the County to great heights; his absence the following season was one of the reasons for their decline. Harry Foster remained a tower of strength, hitting 215 against

Warwickshire at Worcester in 1908, when he finished top of the batting averages with G.N. second.

The other Fosters, when available, always contributed something of note, but their age of dominance was nearing its end. Their appearances were becoming less frequent, and nothing was seen of R.E. between the time he captained England against South Africa in 1907 and his appearance in the Worcestershire side against Yorkshire at Worcester in August 1910. He hit 133 in three and a quarter hours and was out for eight in the second innings. He did not play again during the season, at the end of which Harry Foster resigned the captaincy. He was 37-years-old, had led the Gentlemen against the Players at both The Oval and at Lord's in 1910 and was named as one of *Wisden*'s Five Cricketers of the Year, mainly for services rendered rather than recent achievement, for his run-getting had become less proficient. He maintained that he would not retire from the game even though he felt unable to give as much time to it as in the past.

G. H. Simpson-Hayward succeeded H. K. Foster as captain and led the side in 1911 and 1912 with H.K. taking over again for one season in 1913. From their debut as a first-class county in 1899 until the end of the 1910 season, Worcestershire were always captained by a Foster.

Throughout the difficult years which close the first part of Worcestershire's history as a first-class county, the band of professionals continued to give yeoman service. If Arnold was not quite the bowling force he had been in the early part of the century, he almost increased in stature as a batsman. In 1909, he hit 200 not out against Warwickshire and a year later he hit 210 against Oxford University.

The double century against Warwickshire came at Edgbaston over the August Bank Holiday when he and Burns put on a record 393 in four and a quarter hours. Burns was a ferocious hitter, and this remains one of the most remarkable feats of scoring in cricket history. Warwickshire had made 141 in their first innings, and Worcestershire declared at 578 for six. When Warwickshire batted again Arnold took seven for 44 to bring his match figures to ten for 114. Warwickshire were bowled out for 204 shortly after lunch on the last day. Arnold remains the only Worcestershire cricketer, and indeed one of a very select band of cricketers, who has scored a double century and taken ten wickets in a match.

By coincidence, both Burns and Arnold retired at the end of the 1913 season. Burns celebrated his last season with a hat-trick, but Arnold had a wretched final year. He was never blessed with good health and was certainly hampered in his last season, but nothing can detract from the achievements of the man and the honour and loyalty that he brought to Worcestershire. There was a time when, with his beautiful high action, he could extract life and lift from the most docile of pitches, for New Road was no friend to the bowler in the first decade of this century. He was a powerful batsman and a very fine fielder, especially in the slips, and 301 matches for the County, more than 15,000 runs and over 1,000 wickets in first-class cricket as well as 163 catches, confirm a very great all-round cricketer. He died in 1942 after a long illness from which he made periodic, but brief, recoveries.

Burns left at the end of the 1913 season to settle in Canada, but he returned to fight in the First World War and, serving as a Second Lieutenant in the Worcestershire Regiment, he fell at Contalmaison in July 1916.

The veteran Burrows took over the role of spearhead of the attack as Arnold declined and took a hundred wickets in both 1910 and 1913. He was 42 in 1913, but he appeared to have lost none of his speed and took 18 wickets against Middlesex and Somerset in the last week of the season to reach the hundred mark.

If Burrows was the spearhead of the attack, Cuffe had embraced Arnold's mantle of leading all-rounder. He did the hat-trick against Hampshire at Bournemouth in 1910 and completed the 'double' for the County in the following season. The First World War was to bring the Australian's first-class career to an end, but, as we have mentioned, he played in the Lancashire League after the war and was a first-class umpire for three seasons in the mid-1920s.

'Dick' Pearson was far from the end of his career. He reached 1,000 runs in 1909 and did the hat-trick against Surrey at Worcester in 1914, the season in which he also returned the best bowling figures of his career, nine for 41 for H. K. Foster's XI against Oxford University at Oxford. More notable, however, was his opening partnership of 306 with Bowley in three and a quarter hours against Gloucestershire at Worcester in 1913. Pearson hit nine fours in his 106 and was the first man out. Bowley batted only a quarter of an hour longer for his 201, playing 'extremely brilliant' cricket in what was batting of an 'exceptional character'.

Bowley was a gloriously vigorous cricketer and a year later, at Dudley, he hit 276 in ten minutes under five hours. For many years, it was to remain a record score for the County and it has been been bettered only twice since, by Turner and Hick. No higher score has ever been made by a Worcestershire player at Dudley, although F. R. Foster showed the quality of the wicket in that last season before the world went mad when he hit 305 not out for Warwickshire against Worcestershire in four hours twenty minutes, only three weeks before Bowley's great innings.

In one sense, Dudley has the saddest of memories for Worcestershire cricket. On 12, 13 and 14 August 1912, the County entertained the

Australian tourists at the ground in which there was much pride. Unusually for that time, there were three Fosters in the Worcestershire side, H.K., G.N. and R.E. Harry Foster was bowled for nought, but 'Tip' Foster and brother Geoffrey, who kept wicket, played bright and skilful cricket on a difficult wicket. R.E. was bowled by Macartney for 26 and G.N. was 62 not out when Worcestershire were bowled out for 143. The Australians made 407, but there was no play on the last day because of rain. That was the last time that R. E. Foster ever appeared in a Worcestershire side. The following year his health broke down and a visit to South Africa in an attempt to bring about a recovery had no lasting effect. On 13 May 1914, he died of diabetes. Arguably the greatest sportsman of his generation (he was an international soccer player), he was dead at the age of 36. *Wisden* suggested that: 'He had not reached the age at which, by means of rigid dieting, diabetes can sometimes be kept in check'. Unquestionably, had he been born 20 years later, medical science would have been able to extend his life.

The cricket world was shocked at the death of a pre-eminently great batsman. On Saturday, 16 May, when Worcestershire were playing Surrey at The Oval, the lunch interval was extended and players stood in a mark of respect to the great man whose funeral was taking place.

On the field, the Foster tradition was kept alive in 1914 by Maurice, who returned to the Worcestershire side after an absence of four years and hit more than 1,000 runs for the County with some brilliant batting. W. H. 'Bill' Taylor had taken over the captaincy, for Harry Foster could now give little time to cricket.

'Bill' Taylor had first played for Worcestershire against Oxford University at Oxford in 1909, a match in which another future Worcestershire captain, M. F. S. Jewell, made his debut for the County. Taylor was a moderate batsman and a quick bowler who led the County at a sad and troubled time, and one cannot help but feel that events off the field must have had some effect on performances on it, however brave the faces that were shown.

Apart from the old stalwarts, Pearson, Burrows, Bowley and the rest, there were younger talents emerging like Bale, Conway and Chester, yet Worcestershire finished bottom of the Championship in 1912, had only four counties below them in 1913 and only two in 1914.

Arthur Conway, a noted footballer with Aston Villa and Wolverhampton Wanderers, was a right-arm bowler of above medium pace who could never find consistency and played irregularly, but he stamped his name indelibly on the Worcestershire record book in June 1914. Against Gloucestershire at Moreton-in-Marsh, he took nine for 38 and six for 49. The match figures of 15 for 87 stand as a Worcestershire record to this day.

Like Herbert Strudwick, the Surrey and England wicket-keeper, Ernie Bale came from Mitcham. Seeing his way at Surrey blocked by the great Strudwick, Bale qualified for Worcestershire by residence and made his debut for them in 1908. He soon took over from Gaukrodger as the regular wicket-keeper, believed by many to have no superior in England save Strudwick himself. Certainly Bale's talents were recognised by the selectors for he was chosen to keep for the Rest of England in the prestigious match against the Champion County in 1910.

Bale's career was to continue after the First World War, but one may reflect what might have happened had A. G. Pawson not decided to make his career in the Sudan Civil Service. Pawson had been educated at Winchester and gone up to Oxford in October 1907. Druce Brandt, who had kept wicket in the Varsity match of 1907, was still in residence, and it seemed that Pawson had no chance of displacing him. Worcestershire arrived in The Parks to play Oxford University in June 1908, and announced that they had no wicket-keeper. The University suggested that they borrow Pawson for the match. He kept magnificently to the bowling of Simpson-Hayward, stumping three batsmen, including his rival Brandt, off the lob bowler in the first innings and taking a catch off Arnold in the second. It was to be the only County match in which he ever appeared. He took over from Brandt in the Oxford side and was awarded his blue in all four years at university. Whether or not Worcestershire ever approached him to play regularly we do not know, but Yorkshire certainly suggested to him that he might play for them (he was born in Bramley) with a view to taking over the captaincy. He decided, however, to follow his career abroad, and Worcestershire remained his only county.

Certainly the brightest young man to play for Worcestershire towards the close of the Foster era was Frank Chester. Born in Bushey in Hertfordshire, he lived in Worcestershire and joined the County staff in 1912. The following season he hit 703 runs, including three centuries, and took 44 wickets with his off-breaks. *Wisden* was in ecstasies about him!

> Nothing stood out more prominently than the remarkable development of Chester, the youngest professional regularly engaged in first-class cricket. Very few players in the history of cricket have shown such form at the age of seventeen and a half. Playing with a beautifully straight bat, he depended to a large extent to his watchfulness in defence. Increased hitting power will naturally come with time. He bowls with a high, easy action, and, commanding an accurate length, can get plenty of spin on the ball.

Frank Chester, a brilliant all-round cricketer who became the leading umpire after wounds in the war ended his career.

Having begun so well Chester should continue to improve, and it seems only reasonable to expect that when he has filled out and gained more strength he will be an England cricketer.'

In 1914, although his bowling fell away, there was nothing to suggest that that prophecy would not be realised. He hit 178 not out against Essex, taking four sixes off Johnny Douglas, and increased his aggregate of runs to 924. Then came the war, and while serving with the army in Salonika he lost his right arm just below the elbow, and the dream of playing for England on the cricket field was shattered.

Undaunted, determined to stay in the game, Chester turned to umpiring and joined the first-class list in 1922. He had two great qualities which raised him above the norm, youth and unflinching courage sharpened by adversity. In 1924, he stood in his first Test match, and for the next 30 years he was supreme among umpires, raising that taxing profession to a higher level than had ever been known in the history of cricket.

Chester's courage and determination to survive at a time when all looked lost mirrored the struggle for existence that the County whom he represented fought and won. In the summer of 1913, the financial position of the Club was such that it seemed that county cricket in Worcestershire must come to an end. How much money people like Foley, Lord Cobham and the other donors and guarantors had put in in an attempt to keep the Club in existence since the crisis of 1908 we shall never know, but by 1913, the position had again become critical. The efforts to spread cricket around the county in an attempt to stimulate interest had met with only limited success. As well as staging matches at Stourbridge and Dudley, a fixture had been allotted to Bournville in 1910. The opponents were Essex, whom Worcestershire were playing for the first time, but rain prevented play on the first and third days. The following year, Surrey were the visitors to Bournville, for the village, now in Warwickshire, was within the Worcestershire boundary at that time, but that was the last County game to be played there.

The 1913 crisis was of such magnitude that A. W. How, who had just succeeded Jones-Williams as secretary, had a breakdown in health which caused his resignation and the post was taken over by Cecil Ryder, a medium-pace bowler with Wednesbury who was to serve with the Gurkhas in the First World War. The wretched weather in 1912 had not only brought about a reduction in gate receipts, but the membership had continued to decline so that, in the middle of the 1913 season, the Club's liabilities were again in the region of £4,000. Lord Cobham and Judge Amphlett, ably supported by Lord Dudley and Lord Plymouth, launched an appeal which met with a ready response, so that £900 was raised in a few weeks. There was also considerable help from *Berrows Journal*, a long and faithful ally of the County Club, who organised a 'shilling fund' so that, according to *Wisden*, by the end of the season the deficit was wiped out and, it was believed, 'county cricket in Worcestershire will go on for certain for the next three years'.

This proved to be optimistic, for, by the middle of the 1914 season, the position was again critical. A special meeting of the members was called for 8 August when the committee forwarded the motion that the Club should be wound up. Inevitably, it was P. H. Foley who put forward the amendment that the Club should continue, and his amendment was carried with little opposition.

Foley announced that he had approached the first-class counties and had asked them to contribute £20 each for two years to enable Worcestershire to survive. Surrey, Kent, Yorkshire and Hampshire had immediately agreed their support, and Warwickshire and Derbyshire pledged contributions if the other counties would do the same. The meeting itself increased the guarantee fund from £850 to £1,160, and at another meeting in September when the decision to continue the Club was reaffirmed, Judge Amphlet stated that, if cricket proved to be impossible in 1915 because of the war, £350 would be needed, and £300 was promised before the meeting ended.

The professionals, too, played their part. Burrows, their spokesman, stated that they were prepared to play two matches in 1915 for nothing, and later they agreed to take winter pay for six months and to ask for no other remuneration unless county cricket went on as normal in 1915. At the end of the year, it was announced that the Club was free from debt, but by then the carnage in France had made the financial problems of Worcestershire County Cricket Club seem most insignificant.

On Monday, 3 August 1914, Germany had invaded Belgium, and Great Britain had declared war. At the time, Worcestershire were just beginning their drawn match with Warwickshire at Edgbaston. Although some counties cancelled a few of their remaining matches, Worcestershire did not, and the games with Surrey, Essex, Somerset, Kent, Sussex and Derbyshire went ahead after the outbreak of war.

The final match, against Derbyshire at New Road, was played on 29 and 31 August and 1 September. Maurice Foster hit 158, the highest score of his career, but Derbyshire won by five wickets. Of the Worcestershire side that took the field in that match, G. N. Foster, Chester and Harber, whose only first-class game this was, were never to appear for the County again, but by the time the others had reassembled much had changed.

HARD TIMES

EVEN AS WORCESTERSHIRE WERE LEAVING the field after their defeat by Derbyshire, the troops were massing for the Battle of the Marne. What had been the Golden Age of English cricket was to be separated from the rest of history, like so much else, by four years of suffering and violence. W. G. Grace died some 18 months after R. E. Foster, and the effective careers of men like Fry and MacLaren were at an end. Arnold Nesbitt, who had kept wicket for Worcestershire against Middlesex at Lord's early in 1914, was killed in the first few weeks of the war. J. E. V. Isaac fell in 1915 as did Lt-Col Cecil Palmer who, in 1904, had played for both Hampshire and Worcestershire. Palmer, a regular soldier, was killed at Gallipoli. Burns died two years later.

If the world was scarred and grieving and much changed in 1918, there was much in Worcestershire cricket that remained constant. Finance still presented a problem. At the Annual General Meeting in November 1917, Lord Cobham was pleased to announce that the Club was now solvent, and he paid a warm tribute to Judge Amphlett to whose energy the happier financial position, with a balance of £464, was due.

Richard Amphlett was Recorder at Worcester for 17 years and later became Judge of the County Court of Birmingham. He was an enthusiast to whom Worcestershire County Cricket Club owe a very great debt, for without him, and others like him who worked so hard and gave so generously, the Club would not have survived.

In 1917, Lord Cobham was optimistic and happy 'that the Committee has been able to keep things ready for the return of the young fellows from the front'. A year later, however, there was a distinct change of tone, as *Wisden* reported:

> At the Annual General Meeting it was announced that Worcester-
> shire would no longer be able to go in for County cricket on the old
> lines. As the Club had a balance of £500 in hand, the moment was
> considered favourable for retirement. At the same time it was
> hoped that the Club would arrange some friendly games, the idea
> being to have not more than two professionals in the eleven.

There appears to have been some change of policy after this meeting, for the County Secretaries Meeting at Lord's reported that Worcestershire had failed to qualify for the Championship. Presum-ably, it had been decided to enter the Championship after all, but it had been too late to obtain the necessary minimum of fixtures.

Worcestershire were well out of the two-day Championship debacle of 1919, but they did engage in nine first-class matches in which they used 26 players, only six of whom were professionals. Bale and Conway were the professionals most often used, and some of the amateurs, like Rupert Cave-Rogers, appeared in their one and only first-class match.

William Greenstock, who was in the side against H. K. Foster's XI at Worcester, was playing the last of his four games for the County at the age of 49. A master at Malvern, he first appeared for Worcestershire in 1899.

The first match against H. K. Foster's XI had been played at Hereford and was the first first-class fixture to be played on the Racecourse Ground. H. K. Foster's XI also met the Australian Imperial Forces team at Hereford immediately following the game against Worcestershire which had been played on 14 and 15 July and which Foster's XI won by four wickets. Worcestershire were also beaten by Somerset at Bath and by the AIF at Worcester, but the other six matches, like so many in 1919, were drawn.

Conway and Burrows both ended their careers in 1919. Burly, honest and likeable Dick Burrows was 48 years old and had been in the Worcestershire side since the County had attained first-class status. He ended on a good note, scoring 264 runs, average 33, hitting 82 against Warwickshire at Edgbaston, and taking 20 wickets at 17.80 runs each to finish high in the first-class averages. In 1923, he became a first-class umpire, and he and Frank Chester stood together in the Trent Bridge Test match of 1926 when the game between England and Australia saw only 50 minutes play possible. He was on the first-class list for nine seasons, and he always suggested a total joy in what he was doing as he had done during his playing days.

The friendly matches in which Worcestershire had taken part in 1919 had aroused little interest. The first match after the war, against Gloucestershire at Worcester, in June, had attracted barely 200 spectators, and the remaining matches were watched by only a few more people.

Major Beresford succeeded Ryder as secretary, and M. F. S. Jewell began the first of his three separate terms of office as captain as the Worcestershire Committee decided that the County would re-enter the County Championship in 1920.

In retrospect, it seems a hasty and unwise decision so complete and dismal was the failure, yet if Worcestershire were to continue to exist as a first-class county, what else could be done but play in the County Championship? It all began so promisingly. The season opened with a fixture against Hampshire at New Road. Pearson, Preece and W. H. Taylor bowled out the visitors for 176, and by the end of the first day, Worcestershire were only one run in arrears for the loss of Bowley, Cliff and Pearson.

Arthur Jewell, younger brother of the skipper, shared the wicket-keeping duties with Bale in 1920, and added to the lustre of his two stumpings and two catchings on the first day with a splendid century on the second so that Worcestershire took a first innings lead of 87. Alas, Hampshire then made 433 and went on to win by 220 runs.

That opening day of the season proved to be the falsest of dawns, for from that point onwards practically nothing went right for Worcestershire. Of 18 Championship matches, 16 were lost, most of them by considerable margins, and the only victory of the season came at Gloucester where the home county were beaten by 112 runs. A. N. Jewell was once again a hero, hitting 110 in the first innings, and W. E. Richardson, an amateur quick bowler, had match figures of nine for 103, which included a career best six for 48 in Gloucester-shire's second innings.

This proved to be the one ray of light in a miserable season. Apart from A. N. Jewell whose wicket-keeping earned much praise and won him a place in the Gentlemen's side at The Oval, only Bowley, Pearson and, when available, M. K. Foster did anything of note with the bat. H. K. Foster could play in only one match, but he was now 47, as was Bowley, while Pearson was in his fortieth year.

The two centuries by Arthur Jewell and one each from Bowley and Pearson were the only three-figured innings played for Worcester-shire during the season, but if the batting was weak, the bowling was deplorable, and opposing batsmen plundered runs merrily against the County. Seventeen centuries were taken off the Worcestershire attack, and Preece's 42 wickets at 30.11 runs each placed him at the top of the averages.

A medium-pace bowler from Broadheath, Preece was to assist the County until 1927, after which he became groundsman at Chance Brothers in Smethwick. He had to have a leg amputated in 1967, but *Wisden* published his obituary that year, confusing him with Cecil Preece who had died in November 1966. In fact, Charles Preece did not die until February 1976, two months after his 88th birthday.

It was little wonder that an attack, bereft of Burrows, Cuffe, Conway, Chester and Burns, should struggle, but the fielding, too, was of a very poor standard. Only Bale and the Jewell brothers escaped with much honour.

For financial reasons, as had been indicated in 1917 and, indeed, as long ago as 1899, the side was a predominantly amateur one. Pearson, Bowley and Preece were the only professionals to appear regularly, and groundsman Fred Hunt, one match, and Bale, three matches, were the only others to play. Twenty-seven amateurs took part in the 18 matches.

Bale retired at the end of the season, and, sadly, Arthur Jewell was

M. K. Foster.

never to play again. Born in Chile, educated at Felsted, he and his younger brother, J.E., played for Orange Free State in South Africa in the years before the First World War. Arthur Jewell served as a major in the war and showed immense promise as a wicket-keeper and opening batsman in a few matches in 1919 and for the County in 1920, but he suffered a long and wasting period of ill-health and died in 1922 at the age of 34.

His elder brother, Maurice, led Worcestershire with great determination and courage at what must have been a disheartening time, for the resources available to him were very limited indeed. Surprisingly, Worcestershire did not finish bottom of the table in 1920. Derbyshire, whom Worcestershire did not meet and who were without a victory, finished below them, but throughout the 1920s, the County were never out of the bottom four and on four occasions they finished last.

That the County improved in 1921 to win five matches and suffer 15 defeats and to finish higher than Essex, Warwickshire and the newly elected Glamorgan, was due, in the main, to some new arrivals. Harry Higgins had been severely wounded in the war, but he had recovered sufficiently to appear occasionally in 1920 and, more regularly available in 1921 and 1922, he hit 1,000 runs in each of those seasons.

Another amateur, H. A. 'Barmy' Gilbert, joined the County in 1921 and, with his fast-medium bowling, gave a fillip to the attack which, otherwise, remained weak. Humphrey Gilbert, a barrister by profession, had won a blue at Oxford and played four times for the Gentlemen in the years before the war. He had also been asked to attend the first Test at Edgbaston in 1909 in case he was needed to play for England against Australia, but that was the nearest he got to Test selection. He certainly added much to the Worcestershire attack in the early 1920s, taking 84 wickets at 23.69 in his first season.

Worcestershire after the First World War, 1921. Back row (l to r): Fred Hunt (groundsman), Maj. C. V. Beresford (secretary) A. J. Powell, C. V. Tarbox, A. M. Carr, H. O. Hopkins, J. F. Toppin. Seated: H. L. Higgins, Col. W. H. Taylor, F. Pearson, Maj. M. F. S. Jewell (capt.), F. L. Bowley, H. A. Gilbert, M. K. Foster. On ground: C. A. Preece.

The Higgins brothers, H.L. and J.B.

With Pearson's bowling showing considerable improvement and a young all-rounder, Charles Tarbox, making a promising start with 629 runs and 56 wickets, there was a ray of hope for Worcestershire, but the greatest hope remained almost hidden in 1921.

When Worcestershire took the field against Lancashire at Old Trafford on 29 June, they included in their eleven F. Root. He scored 2 and 1 and took two moderate wickets for 65 runs. He had three more games, picked up six more wickets and scored another 31 runs. He was 31 years old, and he was not new to first-class cricket, having played for Derbyshire from 1910 until the war and having been on the Leicestershire ground staff just after leaving school.

He was wounded while serving with the army in France in 1916 and was invalided home and taken to St Luke's Hospital in Bradford. While convalescing he was persuaded to play for Bowling Old Lane in the Bradford League. He enjoyed his league cricket, but he was anxious to get back to the county game, and Worcestershire, with bowling so depleted, needed and wanted him. Under the existing rules, he was forced to qualify for Worcestershire by residence so he moved to Dudley in the Birmingham League, which has been a wonderful nursery for Worcestershire and Warwickshire cricketers, and provided stimulating competition for men like Fred Root who were serving a necessary qualification period.

Root's impact with Worcestershire was not immediate, but within two years he was to become a great force in the land. His opportunities initially were limited, for the County policy of relying heavily on amateurs prevailed. Thirty players were used in 1921, and of the six professionals, only four played with any regularity.

That this policy was still necessary can be seen from the fact that although Worcestershire survived the season successfully from the financial point of view, they were warned at the end of 1921 that the healthy balance sheet was largely due to the share that they derived from Test match profits and that such income would not be forthcoming every year.

Maurice Jewell resigned as captain at the end of the season and W. H. Taylor was persuaded to take over again. Once more the problem that faced any captain was the lack of resources and the

Fred Root, who carried the Worcestershire bowling on his own shoulders throughout the 1920s.

Lt Col W. H. Taylor, captain of the County before and after the First World War.

constantly changing structure of his side. No fewer than 37 players were called upon in 1922, and Taylor is quoted as having said on one occasion, when he was skippering the side, that he had to be introduced to seven of his team by the senior professional.

Some of the amateurs passed by only once; others would have been used more often had they been more readily available. The most notable example is Gilbert Ashton, who played for Worcestershire from 1922 until 1936, yet appeared in only 27 matches. The eldest of the three brothers who were all outstanding sportsmen and who captained Cambridge University in three successive seasons, so emulating the Studd brothers, Gilbert Ashton won the Military Cross during the war and was later wounded, losing his left thumb, which did not seem to hinder his cricketing prowess. He led Cambridge in 1921 when they were spoken of as one of the very greatest of university sides and first played for Worcestershire the following season by which time he had taken over as Headmaster of Abberley Hall Preparatory School and was, therefore, resident in the county. A

A stalwart of the twenties and after, G. Ashton.

batsman in the classical mould, he hit 125 and 84 against Northamptonshire in his second match and finished second in the averages to Leonard Crawley.

Like Ashton, L. G. Crawley was a member of a great sporting family; like Ashton, too, his appearances for Worcestershire were to be very limited, but for very different reasons. Crawley played six times for Worcestershire in the space of two seasons, 1922 and 1923, hit 601 runs and topped the batting averages in both years, averaging 86 in the second season. Lord Harris, the great custodian of cricket's laws and morals, discovered, however, that Leonard Crawley was not properly qualified for Worcestershire, and MCC decreed him ineligible. This led to the famous angry scene in the Long Room at Lord's between Lord Harris and Lord Deerhurst, the Worcestershire President from 1921 to 1923, when the two eminent men became very heated indeed.

As Leonard Crawley, a highly talented player, was never able to give much time to the game even after he had moved to Essex, it cannot be said that he was the greatest loss to Worcestershire, but Lord Harris had also linked him with the professional William Fox.

Fox, who was born in Yorkshire, was just the type of batsman that Worcestershire needed, particularly after the retirement of Bowley, and he scored an encouraging 981 runs in 1923, his first season, but Lord Harris and MCC decided that he was not properly qualified, and he could not appear in the Championship again until 1926.

Bowley's long and lovely career had ended in 1922, and he hit 130 against Hampshire at Southampton in one of his last matches. It was one of the bright spots of a bleak season, in which the County finished bottom of the table with a solitary win over Glamorgan to their credit.

Another change in leadership saw Maurice Foster take over in 1923. He maintained the family tradition with some brilliant stroke-play. Tall, muscular, with wrists of steel which were used to telling effect, he was the last of the great line and linked the County to its roots. He could not hope, however, to work miracles, and neither Taylor nor Jewell had failed in their task as captain. There were, however, some sparks of encouragement for Worcestershire supporters.

At the age of 43, 'Dick' Pearson accomplished the 'double' for the first and only time in his career. It was a truly wonderful achievement by one of cricket's good and faithful servants. If one doubts the contribution that Pearson made to Worcestershire cricket or to the quality of the man, then one needs to reflect on the words of his team-mate Fred Root:

> I went to Worcester more or less as a rival for Dick's position as utility man, yet he helped me tremendously. He was the ideal

True and faithful servant, Dick Pearson.

professional cricketer. Selfishness was unknown to him, averages his abomination. His team always came first.

He sacrificed many years of his career for the benefit of the younger members of the side. If a young player fancied himself to go in first, Dick would bat lower down. If a young bowler thought the new ball would be helpful to him, Pearson at once became a change bowler. If a nasty half-hour before an interval had to be got over, he was ever ready to save another player.

But for Pearson there would have been no Worcestershire

County Cricket Club now. He played for Worcestershire with a fanaticism associated with the knights of the religious wars. Cricket was, in that sense, his religion, Worcestershire his god. If there was no money for wages it was Dick who did the waiting. He thought it an honour to wait.

Pearson and Root virtually carried the Worcestershire attack. In Pearson's 'double' year, 1923, for instance, they captured 270 wickets between them while 19 other bowlers used could not amass a hundred between them. Pearson ended his career in 1926, and it was typical of the man that, in his last home match for Worcestershire, against Hampshire, he scored 58 and in his last match, against Middlesex at Lord's when Worcestershire did not bat because of rain, he took three for 56.

As Pearson's career was drawing to its close, that of Fred Root, the man who admired him so greatly, was reaching a height that few had expected. Rejected by Leicestershire and by Derbyshire, his eight wickets for Worcestershire in 1921, followed by 41 in 1922, seemed only to confirm the view that these counties had of his ability. From 1923 to 1931, however, he never failed to take 100 wickets in the season for Worcestershire alone, and in 1928, he also scored 1,000 runs to complete the 'double'. The number of wickets that he took during those seasons, bowling for the most part with little assistance and fielding that was not always of a high quality, make astonishing reading:

1923	168
1924	152
1925	207
1926	103
1927	145
1928	118
1929	148
1930	131
1931	126

In matches outside the County Championship, he took another 37 wickets during this time. His 207 wickets in 1925 is a record which, one can safely say, will never be beaten.

Root had long held a desire to persevere with his leg-theory bowling which he had practised assiduously and had used at both Derbyshire and in the leagues. As Pelham Warner was quick to point out some years later, Root's leg-theory, often cited as the precursor of body-line, was not the same as the method employed on England's tour of Australia, 1932–33, although there were similarities. Root never attempted to intimidate or bowl short of a length. With his rather open-chested action, he bowled perfectly pitched in-swingers on or around the leg stump to a field which included from four to six leg slips. He was relentlessly accurate, swung the ball late and had the quality of variety.

He told how, having become established in the Worcestershire side, he asked Maurice Foster if he could try to develop the theory which had been fermenting in his mind for a decade, but which he had never been allowed to test to the full. Foster's reply was shaped by the results of the time: 'Bowl how and what you like, Freddie, so long as you stop the opposing teams getting 500 runs every time they bat against us.'

Foster was of great assistance, conferring with Root on the strengths of the method and as to how the bad features could be eliminated. He also advised Root to develop his out-swinger so as to use it as an alternative and an element of surprise. Root insists that it was the out-swinger which brought him hundreds of wickets.

In spite of Pearson and Root and the bravery and endeavour of others, Worcestershire's position in the Championship table rarely fluctuated. In 1925, the year that Root took 207 wickets, they were 16th, and for the next three years they finished 17th out of 17. In one area they always seemed to be well served, for Maclean, Ponsonby and Abell, who shared the wicket-keeping duties for most of the 1920s, were all most capable performers.

Maurice Foster, too, could always be relied upon behind the stumps when no one else was available, but this must have added to his worries when, as captain, he scarcely knew where the next eleven would come from or who would be in it. The reliance on the occasional amateur produced some bizarre occurrences.

In May 1925, Worcestershire called upon the Reverend Reginald Heber Moss, resident in the county. Moss, a medium-pace bowler in his youth, had won a blue at Oxford in 1889 and his last first-class match had been for Liverpool and District against the Australians in 1893, 32 years before Worcestershire called upon him for his one and only game for them at the age of 57. Remarkably, the veteran clergyman, who scored 2 and 0, bowled three overs in the second innings of this match for Worcestershire against Gloucestershire and took one for 5. His victim was Major M. A. Green, destined to become secretary of Worcestershire in 1946.

With an unending series of disastrous results and with the Club always on the brink of extinction because of financial problems, how did Worcestershire survive these years? Fred Root, who lived through those hard times, points to Pearson and 'two or three amateur players, including Major M. F. S. Jewell, M. K. Foster, and Major W. H. Taylor, coupled with never-despairing committee men', as to the reason for survival. It is worth considering what those men did so that Worcestershire cricket might survive.

After three years as captain Maurice Foster felt that he had had enough and resigned although he was to continue to play regularly. He had done a fine job at a most taxing time, but he felt that the burden of leading a side, the composition of which was constantly changing, could be carried no longer. Maurice Jewell again took over. He had first appeared for Worcestershire in 1909, but he had played for Sussex in 1914 and 1919, a season in which he had also appeared five times for Worcestershire so that he remains one of the few cricketers this century to have played for two counties in one season.

He was an aggressive middle-order batsman and a slow left-arm bowler of moderate accomplishment, but the contribution that M. F. S. Jewell made to Worcestershire cricket cannot be judged by figures. When he died, in 1978 at the age of 92, *Wisden* carrried an obituary of him that ranks among the most memorable pieces of writing from that august publication. The opening sentences of Jewell's obituary define clearly the role of the amateur in the 1930s and should warn us not to judge history in the light of modern customs and social practices. They show, too, the greatness of Maurice Jewell and of others around him:

> Those whose memories start in 1946 or later have no conception how much some counties at the bottom of the Championship before 1914 and between the Wars owed to certain amateurs, often only moderate players who could never have kept a place in a good county side, but who year after year gave up their summer to keeping their county going, captaining it themselves and somehow collecting an XI for each match, being rewarded at the end with perhaps two or three wins, perhaps less. It was largely due to the devoted labours of such as these that no first-class county ever had to pack up, though some in those days came pretty near it. In this category Jewell stood high.

Not only was Maurice Jewell a shrewd captain and a strong disciplinarian admired and respected by men like Root and Pearson, he was passionate about the Worcestershire Club, and he was unrelenting in his efforts to raise money and place the Club on a sound financial footing.

Money was the constant problem. The biggest amount given to a Worcestershire professional in those days was the £500 given to Fred Root to induce him to sign a new three-year contract in 1928. He had been offered £600 by a Lancashire League club, but his heart was with Worcestershire. The Club offered him £250 and stated that they would have to work very hard to get that, but they finally agreed to

M. F. S. Jewell (centre). No man did more to keep the Club alive in difficult times.

the £500, not quite knowing where they would get the money from. Root's comment is again revealing of the efforts of men like Jewell and Lord Coventry:

> Everybody at Worcester worked like a Trojan in an effort to reach the goal of £500 for my benefit. Whether it was ever obtained I do not know to this day, but I received that sum from the club.

Root was held in such affection by the people of Worcestershire, often accused of apathy, particularly in the county town itself, that public subscription raised enough money for a gold watch and chain, a bond for £100 and a unique piece of porcelain to honour his 207 wickets in 1925.

Lord Coventry and his son, Lord Deerhurst, were among those who worked feverishly behind the scenes to ensure that Worcestershire cricket would continue. They cherished no dreams of winning the Championship. Their joy was in the survival and ultimate prosperity of Worcestershire cricket. Their happiness came from the occasional surprise victory like the sensational win over Notts at Worcester in 1921 when Gilbert took 13 wickets and H. L. Higgins hit 50 in each innings.

'To see his rugged face light up with pleasure when he saw hope for the future of Worcestershire cricket,' said Root of Lord Coventry, 'was inspiration enough to face any odds.'

The important thing was that Worcestershire maintained the Foster-Malvern tradition and always tried to play attractive cricket. Even when, in 1926 under Jewell, they dropped to last in the table, there was praise for them. In spite of the Championship wooden spoon, they were shaping as a better side with a stronger backbone of eight professionals—Root, Pearson, Fox, Wright, Tarbox, Bowles, Rogers and Wilson. This made life considerably easier for Jewell, for only 24 players were called upon as opposed to the 39 of the previous season when Foster had felt the strain so heavily.

Jewell enjoyed his best season, hitting the only two centuries of his career, both against Hampshire, and taking 22 wickets at low cost which brought him second to Root in the bowling averages. Fox, a talented professional footballer, and Foster both reached 1,000 runs. Bowles, a slow left-arm bowler who had played for Gloucestershire, Wilson, medium pace, and Rogers, an all-rounder, were honest professionals who never quite reached the standard that had been expected of them. Leslie Wright from Durham was the professional with Stourbridge. He hit his maiden first-class century in the match at Portsmouth in 1926 when Maurice Jewell also reached three figures for the first time. The pair put on 181 for the first wicket, but Worcestershire were still beaten by nine wickets. Wright played until 1933, initially carrying much responsibility in the County's batting.

Root's form for Worcestershire was at last honoured by the England selectors. In 1926, he was chosen for the first Test against Australia, the first Worcestershire player selected for England since the war, but the match was ruined by rain and he never took the field. In the second test, at Lord's he bowled Collins in his first over and finished with match figures of four for 110. He did not play in the third Test, but he was England's most successful bowler in another rain-ruined game at Old Trafford, taking four for 84 in the 57 overs he bowled while Australia made 335. In spite of this performance, he was not chosen for the deciding Test at The Oval, and he never played for England again.

If England could do without Root's services, Worcestershire certainly could not. Jewell felt unable to give so much time to the game and relinquished the captaincy after the 1926 season. He was succeeded by Cecil Ponsonby.

The optimism of the previous season soon evaporated. Ponsonby was a capable wicket-keeper and a plucky captain, but he lacked the authority of Jewell or Foster, and once more the personnel of the side changed from match to match. Thirty-three players were called upon, and a solitary, surprise, victory over Middlesex at Worcester, with Root inevitably the hero, was all there was to show for the endeavour.

The poor record coupled with bad weather took its toll of the Club's finances. Match receipts fell by £1,086, a huge amount for the County to lose, and the deficit on the year was £812 which was underwritten by the guarantors. Yet amid this gloom, there were some significant stirrings.

A young Devonian, serving on the Lord's ground staff and seeing little hope of gaining a place in the Middlesex side, moved to Worcestershire and played as professional for Dudley in the Birmingham League while fulfilling his residential qualification. On 8 June 1927, the young man arrived at New Road to play his first game for Worcestershire, against the New Zealand tourists. He was carrying his cricket clothes in a little black bag, and it earned him the nickname of 'Doc'. *Wisden* lamented that, with neither Jewell nor M. K. Foster regularly available and Pearson retired, class batting was the County's dire need. That call was to be answered by Harold 'Doc' Gibbons. In the last game of the season, against Gloucestershire, he hit 86 in three hours. He displayed style, patience and an equable temperament. He was still short of his 23rd birthday, and he had a bonus of which Worcestershire was also desperately in need, he was a brilliant fielder.

There was another move at the end of the 1927 season when J. B. Payne relinquished his post as secretary in favour of C. F. Walters, who had shown classical batting promise with Glamorgan that was to augur well for the future. The present continued disastrously.

Louis Serrurier who had appeared in seven matches after the end of term at Oxford and had hit 110 against Gloucestershire at Bristol and topped the averages returned to South Africa where the rest of his cricket was to be played. The wicket-keeping and batting talents of George Abell, too, were to be for the most part lost as he went to India in the Civil Service after leaving Oxford in 1927. In India, he played for the Europeans and for Northern India, hitting 210 on his Ranji Trophy debut in 1934–35. His career for Worcestershire spread over

16 years, but he played only 34 times and not at all between 1928 and 1935.

Ponsonby's reign as captain ended after just one year. He played once in 1928 and then no more. His place behind the stumps was taken initially by Francis Summers who played with Astwood Bank and on one occasion for them disposed of the first five opponents from behind the wicket and then took off his pads and bowled the remaining five. There was no such joy for Worcestershire who, with Jewell taking over as captain for the third time, went through 1928 without a win.

One of the main problems was that the captain himself was able to play in only three matches so that the County was led by whichever senior amateur was in the side. J. B. Higgins and Captain Hill, a quick bowler, were the most regular of the 18 amateurs used. Other reasons for Worcestershire's decline to the lowest point that they had experienced since becoming a first-class county are harder to determine.

Root, a rough and ready batsman who liked to drive hard and high, did the 'double' for the first and only time in his career and hit the one and only century of his career, 107 against Kent at New Road. There were nine other centuries in the Championship, three to Fox and three to Gibbons who, like Higgins and Quaife, passed 1,000 runs in the Championship alone. Gibbons also hit his double century in the match against the West Indian tourists in which Fox hit 104 not out, Walters made his debut for Worcestershire but did not bat, and a young man making his first appearance in first-class cricket, Maurice Nichol, hit 104.

Nichol had played for Durham and had had a trial with Surrey before beginning his qualification for Worcestershire. He was to live up to the promise of that exciting start, but his career was to be cut short most tragically.

Gibbons' talent gained recognition when he was chosen for the Players against the Gentlemen at The Oval. He hit a polished 84, but, with twelve counties engaged in Championship matches, the sides were not fully representative. Amazingly, this was to be the only honour that Gibbons received although his name was often mentioned as an England candidate.

With Bernard Quaife (formerly of Warwickshire for whom he had played alongside his father, the famous William Quaife) now qualified and, as an amateur, lending solidity to the side, the Worcestershire batting was appreciably stronger than it had been for many years. The reason for the disasters then had to lie with the bowling, and with the lack of a regular leader.

A glance at the averages will show that Root, although still top of the bowling, was more expensive than in previous seasons, but it also

'Doc' Gibbons, record-breaker, record-holder and a batsman of style and equable temperament.

reveals that he virtually bowled unchanged from one end throughout the year, so inadequate was the support. The inconsistent Tarbox took 78 wickets, but they cost him nearly 40 runs apiece. Root was an eager and honest toiler with a powerful physique, but he was turned 38, and the wear and tear had to begin to take their toll, although as yet there was no sign that they were doing so and Worcestershire were eager to sign him for another three years as we have indicated.

The County's need for him and reliance on him was greater than ever, and in 1929, when he took 146 Championship wickets at 21.72 runs each, the other 15 bowlers used mustered only 180 wickets, with Gilbert's 43 at 31.11 placing him second to Root in the averages. Such bowling was hardly likely to aid Worcestershire in their attempt to find better results, but, in 1929, they climbed off the bottom for the first time in four years, a welcome event even if it was only by one place, with Glamorgan below them.

Again the captaincy presented a problem. Jewell was asked to continue, but he could find neither form nor fitness and resigned in mid-season after eleven matches. The Hon John Coventry took over for the last two months of the season and performed nobly in a very awkward situation.

The season began by Worcestershire entertaining the South Africans for the first match of their tour. The 'big six' had made it quite plain that they did not wish to meet the tourists in the opening fixture, and Worcestershire eagerly accepted the chance to host the initial game. It proved to be a highly successful move and established a popular tradition which, sadly, has been broken in recent years.

Overshadowing the tourist's match, however, was Worcestershire's visit to Leyton to meet Essex on 18, 20 and 21 May. Jewell won the toss and Worcestershire batted, but the captain immediately fell to Nichols. Higgins, Nichols, Gibbons, immaculate in style and totally calm, and Fox all gave the innings some substance, but, with eight wickets down, Worcestershire had just passed 200 and a familiar pattern seemed to be developing. Then came a most remarkable innings. The incoming batsman was Albert Frederick Lane, an off-break bowler and well-known Midlands cricketer who had played for Worcestershire before the war and then appeared occasionally for Warwickshire before returning to Worcestershire in 1927. A good club cricketer, he also played for Staffordshire and was 44 years old. *The Cricketer* tells the story of the match at Leyton:

> Those who were present at Leyton on Saturday last saw some cricket of an unusual nature, when, in Worcestershire's first innings, A. F. Lane went in, tenth man, and partnered Root. To that point the score was by no means large, but the newcomer was

at his best, and, whilst he was making runs, his partner was content merely to keep his wicket intact. The policy proved sound, for it was a fortunate thing that Lane had someone to keep him company. For 33 minutes Root did not make a run, and during that period, the amateur, hitting seven fours, scored 44 off the reel; altogether, he obtained his 70 in 65 minutes, whilst only seven other runs were being made. He brought off many powerful strokes all round the wicket, the most remunerative of them being eleven fours. His second innings on Monday was equally meritorious. Undefeated with 60 to his credit, he made his runs out of 70 in fifty minutes.'

The main feature of Lane's hitting was his bold driving and, once he knocked the bowlers off their length, he cut and pulled ferociously. He was last out, having seen the score rise from 207 for eight to 284, and Tarbox, who was not retained after this season, soon dismissed both Essex openers. Root then ate away at the middle order, and Worcestershire had a first innings lead of 84.

It is not often that a batsman can produce two violent displays of hitting in one match but, as *The Cricketer* related, Lane did. Going in at 127 for eight, he saw his side reach 197 and leave Essex the task of scoring 282 to win which, on a wicket that was improving, was, nevertheless, not going to be easy.

Charles Bray batted valiantly, but Root and, ultimately, Gilbert gave Worcestershire victory by 42 runs. It was their first victory since June 1927, and it ended a barren period of nearly two years, the bleakest time in the County's history.

Lane was never again to emulate his feats at Leyton and returned to his club at Cradley Heath, reappearing only briefly after 1929 for one match in the 1932 season.

Worcestershire beat Glamorgan at New Road a month later and so recorded their second win in 1929. There was at last a silver lining to the dark cloud that had hung over them. Gibbons had confirmed the early impression that here was a batsman of very high quality. Fox was dependable, and if Quaife, who had taken over the wicket-keeping duties for the first time and who was to prove at least adequate as he improved season by season, had disappointed as a batsman, the star of Maurice Nichol shone brightly and excitingly, for, in his first full season, he hit 1,442 Championship runs and was recognised as one of the most talented young batsmen in England.

If there was continued optimism over the improved standard of the batting, there was the ever-present gloom over finance and the bowling.

The distressing year of 1928 had ended with a loss of £906. The following year saw them lose £985, but their share of the profits from the MCC tour of Australia, fund-raising, donations and the faithful guarantors enabled them to reduce their debit balance to £160. Worcestershire cricket still breathed, but what of the bowling? Where was support for the willing, excellent, but ageing Root to come from? *Wisden* had a note that, in 1930, 'Perks (fast-medium) will have qualified for the county.'

ESSEX *v* WORCESTERSHIRE

Played at the County Ground, Leyton on 18, 20 and 21 May 1929

WORCESTERSHIRE WON BY 42 RUNS

WORCESTERSHIRE	FIRST INNINGS		SECOND INNINGS	
†M. F. S. Jewell	c Hayzelden b Nichols	0	lbw b Palmer	3
J. B. Higgins	lbw b Palmer	36	lbw b Nicholls	47
M. Nichol	lbw b Hipkin	27	c Hipkin b Palmer	19
H. H. I. Gibbons	c Bray b Nichols	64	b Palmer	8
W. V. Fox	c G. Eastman b O'Connor	24	b Hipkin	3
L. Wright	lbw b O'Connor	7	lbw b Hipkin	5
†B. W. Quaife	c G. Eastman b Nichols	7	b Hayzelden	6
C. V. Tarbox	b Hipkin	23	b Palmer	11
C. F. Root	run out	18	c Bray b Nichols	16
A. F. Lane	b Nichols	70	not out	60
H. A. Gilbert	not out	4	c Hayzelden b Hipkin	6
Extras	b 2, lb 1, w 1	4	b 6, lb 6, nb 1	13
Total		284		197

BOWLING	O	M	R	W	O	M	R	W
Nichols	21.4	3	80	4	18	2	61	2
Hayzelden	11	0	39	0	8	2	15	1
L. C. Eastman	11	4	27	0				
Palmer	16	3	47	1	18	5	45	4
Hipkin	19	2	41	2	16.5	7	27	3
Raison	4	1	13	—				
O'Connor	10	1	33	2	15	1	36	0

ESSEX	FIRST INNINGS		SECOND INNINGS	
C. J. Bray	c Root b Tarbox	8	c Quaife b Root	73
J. A. Cutmore	b Tarbox	8	run out	15
J. O'Connor	b Root	28	b Root	40
L. C. Eastman	lbw b Gilbert	69	b Root	22
M. S. Nichols	b Root	0	b Gilbert	5
*H. M. Morris	b Root	0	b Root	16
A. B. Hipkin	b Jewell	19	c Quaife b Gilbert	20
M. Raison	lbw b Gilbert	29	lbw b Gilbert	3
H. J. Palmer	b Root	13	b Root	4
†G. F. Eastman	not out	9	lbw b Gilbert	10
A. F. G. Hayzelden	b Gilbert	1	not out	4
Extras	b 7, lb 9	16	b 9, lb 17, w 1	27
Total		200		239

BOWLING	O	M	R	W	O	M	R	W
Root	29	9	59	4	47	13	77	5
Tarbox	14	3	53	2	11	4	29	0
Gilbert	13.2	1	44	3	41.1	16	73	4
Jewell	13	2	28	1	12	5	17	0
Wright					6	1	6	0
Nichol					6	2	10	0

Umpires: W. A. Buswell and W. Phillips

The match in which Lane played his two hard-hitting innings.

*Captain; †Wicket-keeper

OUT OF THE TROUGH

REG PERKS WAS BORN IN HEREFORD which, as Hereford was then outside the county of Worcestershire, meant that he had to serve a period of residential qualification once Worcestershire County Cricket Club showed interest in signing him. That interest was roused in a most unusual manner.

In 1927, when Perks was fifteen, the Gentlemen of Worcestershire arrived at the Racecourse Ground, Hereford, to play the Gentlemen of Herefordshire and found themselves one short. Perks, the son of the head groundsman at the Racecourse Ground, was allowed to miss school for the day to make up the numbers for the visitors. From that moment, he was marked down as a Worcestershire player.

Originally a poor batsman, he was seen as a bowler, above medium pace, of top quality, with his powerful run to the wicket and his lovely high action. He used his height to good effect and could swing the ball both ways, but he had more than technical capability. He had qualities which are not given to all quick bowlers, a perpetual zest for the game and great stamina. When Root and Perks were in harness, for all too short a period, Worcestershire had two men who wanted to bowl all the time. It was a luxury that the County had not often enjoyed, and its effect on the team was immediate.

In four years, Worcestershire had won only six matches and had met with 64 defeats, and suddenly, in 1930, they won five matches and were beaten only nine times. It may not sound an impressive record today, but to a side who had been floundering for a decade, it was a remarkable transformation, and they leapt to tenth in the table, their highest position since 1911.

As New Road now provided the venue for the tourists' opening match, Worcestershire were in the public eye from the start of the season, being the first to feel the power of Bradman's bat. Worcestershire batted first on Wednesday 30 April, Jewell having won the toss. The Australian players were muffled against a chilly breeze, but they bowled the home side out for 131, and Bradman was at the crease before the end of the day.

On the Thursday, Bradman announced his arrival as the *Sydney Sun* proclaimed:

Don Bradman made cricket history to-day in the match against Worcester. This young record-breaker in his first innings in England astonished the critics by the manner in which he flogged the bowling to every point of the field, and in 280 minutes he rattled up a brilliant 236, the highest score by an Australian against Worcester.

It was a wonderful display, and the crowd cheered and cheered him on his way to the pavilion.

It was, in fact, the highest score by a player making his first appearance in England and established an affection that Worcester was to have for Bradman, and Bradman for Worcester.

Woodfull, who also hit a century, declared at 492 for eight, and the Australians went on to win by an innings and 165 runs. Bradman offered only one chance, a hard return catch to Brook when he had made 215. Brook, who took four for 148, finally had him caught by Walters.

George Brook was playing his first game for Worcestershire although he was approaching his 42nd birthday. A slow left-arm leg-break bowler, Brook was associated with the Kidderminster Club and had had considerable experience in the Lancashire League. In his first season with the County, he took 128 inexpensive county wickets, and although he did not quite reach those heights again, he was a consistent wicket-taker for the next four seasons, finally dropping out of the side in 1935 and returning to his native Yorkshire to play for Keighley.

Brook is one of those cricketers about whom there has been some confusion, especially with regard to his age. For years it was accepted that he was 35 when he first played for Worcestershire, and it may well be that that was what the County believed, but research by the Association of Cricket Statisticians revealed that he was, in fact, born in 1888. The mistake may have arisen from *Wisden's* initial reference to him as being 'the wrong side of thirty-five'.

Reg Perks did not play against the Australians. His debut came in the opening Championship match, against Surrey at The Oval. Worcestershire were bowled out for 40, the lowest score of the season, and 182 and were beaten by an innings and 224 runs. Replying to Worcestershire's 40, Hobbs and Sandham began with a stand of 122 on what was a dead wicket, but the partnership was broken by Perks who had an illustrious first wicket, the great Jack Hobbs, and followed this by having Sandham caught behind by Styler shortly after. He claimed Fender on the Monday to finish with three for 106, a creditable start.

A strain was to keep Perks out of the side for eight matches, but he took 59 wickets in his shortened first season, including seven for 20 against Leicestershire. At last Root had support and was better for it, celebrating with his second nine-wicket haul for the Club, against Kent at Tunbridge Wells.

If the bowling was stronger, the batting, too, had a more assured look about it. Maurice Nichol was sending shivers of delight through the cricketing world. 'Few batsmen of the younger school have come to the front with more startling rapidity,' wrote Frank Thorogood of the *News Chronicle*. He hit more than 1,500 runs in the season and against Hampshire, at Bournemouth, made 262 not out, a score which had been bettered for Worcestershire only by Bowley 16 years earlier. Nichol hit 33 fours in what was his fifth and final hundred of the summer. *The Cricketer*, ever prone to conservatism, commented:

> In him Worcestershire certainly appear to possess a player of very great possibilities indeed, though whether he is a potential England batsman is yet too early to predict.

Had he played a half century later, Nichol, like Gibbons, would surely have won an England cap.

Gibbons himself did not quite live up to his form of the previous season, and Victor Fox fell away to such an extent that he was not retained although he reappeared briefly two seasons later. To compensate for this Wright and Walters, in his first season, both passed 1,000 runs, and Walters, as much as Nichol and Gibbons, had the look of an England player about him. He captained the side on several occasions.

Maurice Jewell, captain in the opening match against the Australians, did not play again during the season. 'Worcestershire's position being so much improved,' wrote *Wisden*, 'stalwarts in J. B. Higgins, H. A. Gilbert and M. F. S. Jewell, who rendered fine service in the lean years, seized the opportunity to drop out of the county ranks.'

H. L. Higgins, the younger of the two brothers who had been severely wounded in the war, had dropped out after the 1927 season, but J.B. played until 1930 when he was 45. He was employed by Cadbury's in India and took his leave in the summer months to play cricket in England. In the strangest circumstances he joined Worcestershire's impressive list of Test umpires when Jardine's side toured India in 1933–34. Hitch and Tarrant were supposed to stand in all three Tests, but a disagreement between Jardine and his opposite number, C. K. Nayudu, led to Higgins standing in place of Tarrant in the final Test at Madras.

Jewell, who was the brother-in-law of W. H. Taylor, was to play once in 1931 and twice in 1933 when he finished his career with 55 against Oxford University. His work for Worcestershire cricket continued. He was to become chairman, a trustee and eventually president of the Club. In the 1920s, he had formed his own concert party which travelled around Worcestershire giving performances and raising money for the County Club, and in September 1933, when the auditors reported a probable deficit of £2,247 17s 3d, the minutes of the committee meeting showed that 'Major Jewell offered to arrange a Pierrot Show during the winter months' in an attempt to reduce the debt. The love he had for the Club, and the affection in which he was held by all connected with it, became manifest in 1956 when he was elected an Honorary Life Member of the County Cricket Club.

'Barmy' Gilbert played one game in 1930 and that his last for the County. An enthusiastic and modest cricketer, H. A. Gilbert was an intelligent pace bowler who gave noble service to the County and may well have reached international level had he been able to spare more time from his work in the legal profession.

The Hon John Coventry, nominally the captain, played little in 1930 and Cyril Walters combined the posts of secretary and captain from 1931 until the end of the 1935 season. The side did not make the advance during these years that had been expected. They were young and talented, but there was never quite the balance to turn them into a top-class side. Some promise was not fulfilled, others were cut short, and availability and, above all, finance, remained a pressing problem. With the need to cut expenses in order to survive, it was inevitable that results should suffer, and when results suffered so did income. The County was caught in an unenviable spiral, but they never sank again to the depths of 1928. Nevertheless, there were some dreadful moments.

At the committee meeting at The Star Hotel on 5 February 1932, it was announced that there was an overdraft of £652, and 'Major Taylor referred to the payments paid to the professionals and their expenses, and said that in his opinion their wages should be reduced or their incidentals.' The matter was referred to the Finance Committee who were asked to write to Hampshire for information on cuts that that county had made in professionals' wages.

While concerned with finance the committee also had to be concerned with playing strength, and although they rejected an overture from Liddell of Northamptonshire, who was looking for a club, they were impresssed by a recommendation from A. T. Richardson of Kimberley that they should acquire the services of the Western Australian, E. H. Bromley. Worcestershire were one of the leaders in the quest for overseas players and already had the services of the South African Frank Ahl, but he proved to be a big disappointment and was not re-engaged after 1933.

Worcestershire cabled Bromley that Stourbridge Cricket Club would offer him £90 a year for the two year period when he would be serving his residential qualification for the Club. By the Annual General Meeting on 4 March, he had not replied. At the AGM, it was revealed that the overdraft was now £834 6s 1d, and 'After discussion it was agreed that the professionals be invited to consent to a voluntary reduction in wages.' On top of this, it was agreed that there should be neither trials for new players, nor any additions to the ground staff. The only item of expenditure approved was 25 shillings for a wheelbarrow to aid in repairs that were necessary to the roof of the pavilion and elsewhere.

At the General Committee Meeting on 14 April 1932, Lord Doverdale, the chairman, reported that Bromley had decided to remain in Australia. In fact, Bromley moved to Melbourne and played for Australia against Jardine's side later that year. He came to England with the 1934 side, but he did not fulfil the hopes that were held for him.

Worcestershire had more pressing problems. Fred Root had asked for payment of his train fares from his home in Dudley to Worcester to attend practice, and he also wanted £164 for his winter pay. The matter was referred to the Finance Committee, but it was apparent that Root's time with Worcestershire was drawing to a close.

By 26 May, the County's overdraft had increased to £976 14s 11d. Two months later, it was decided that Root should not be re-engaged. Root had pre-empted the situation by writing to ask what was to happen after 1932 when the professionals were told that they were being deprived of their baggage allowance and extras, and he was now 42 and showing signs of decline.

That decline had not been apparent in 1931 when he took 123 Championship wickets at under 16 runs each and established a County record in the great victory over Lancashire at New Road.

Walters won the toss, and Worcestershire made a moderate 169 after which rain ended play for the day. No play was possible until 2.30 pm on the Monday, and Lancashire were caught on a damp pitch drying under a hot sun. So difficult did the batsmen find the conditions that it took Lancashire two hours to reach 50 for the loss of five wickets. After tea, they lost their last five wickets for 16 runs. Perks and Root had proved devastating, and now Worcestershire struggled against the leg-spin of Richard Tyldesley. Only the solid Quaife and the cultured Nichol offered serious resistance, but Lancashire were left the daunting task of having to score 212 to win on a wicket which had encouraged the bowlers from the start. It was a task that they never looked like accomplishing and but for a ninth wicket stand of 40 between Paynter and Tyldesley, they would have been totally humiliated. Root's second innings nine for 23 remains a record for a Worcestershire bowler.

The following year, however, his decline was rapid. Following the decision not to retain him, he unwisely wrote a letter to a national newspaper which caused something of a scandal. The committee

WORCESTERSHIRE *v* LANCASHIRE

Played at New Road, Worcester on 16, 18 and 19 May 1931

WORCESTERSHIRE WON BY 126 RUNS

WORCESTERSHIRE	FIRST INNINGS		SECOND INNINGS	
L. Wright	lbw b R. Tyldesley	9	b McDonald	3
B. W. Quaife	c Duckworth, b Sibbles	5	c and b Sibbles	38
M. Nichol	b R. Tyldesley	40	b Sibbles	25
H. H. I. Gibbons	c Hopwood b R. Tyldesley	28	lbw b R. Tyldesley	2
*C. F. Walters	lbw b R. Tyldesley	6	lbw b R. Tyldesley	2
T. L. Winwood	c Duckworth b McDonald	30	lbw b R. Tyldesley	5
C. F. Root	b Sibbles	18	c Hopwood b Sibbles	0
†S. W. Styler	lbw b Sibbles	3	b R. Tyldesley	2
G. W. Brook	c and b R. Tyldesley	21	c Hopwood b R. Tyldesley	15
R. T. D. Perks	b Sibbles	1	st Duckworth b R. Tyldesley	9
P. F. Jackson	not out	0	not out	2
Extras	b 1, lb 5, nb 2	8	b 4, lb 7, nb 3	14
Total		169		117

BOWLING	O	M	R	W	O	M	R	W
McDonald	28	8	74	1	15	5	26	1
Sibbles	29	8	43	4	22	5	49	3
R. Tyldesley	21.5	10	31	5	24.2	13	28	6
Hopwood	14	6	13	0				

LANCASHIRE	FIRST INNINGS		SECOND INNINGS	
F. B. Watson	b Perks	7	b Root	0
C. Hallows	c Wright b Prks	12	b Root	12
G. E. Tyldesley	c Root b Perks	0	c Brook b Root	3
J. Iddon	c Nichol b Root	25	b Root	6
J. L. Hopwood	b Jackson	14	c Styler b Perks	0
E. Paynter	c Quaife b Brook	1	lbw b Root	24
*P. T. Eckersley	b Root	7	c Styler b Root	4
F. M. Sibbles	c Styler b Root	0	c Jackson b Root	8
†G. Duckworth	c Styler b Perks	3	b Root	0
E. A. McDonald	b Perks	0	(11) c and b Root	0
R. K. Tyldesley	not out	0	(10) not out	19
Extras	b 6	6	b 7, lb 2	9
Total		75		85

BOWLING	O	M	R	W	O	M	R	W
Root	19	8	27	3	18.4	7	23	9
Perks	15.5	4	19	5	12	2	25	1
Brook	9	2	12	1	4	0	22	0
Jackson	6	1	11	1	2	0	6	0

Umpires: E. J. Smith and W. R. Parry

Root's second-innings analysis is the best by a Worcestershire bowler.

*Captain; †Wicket-keeper

decided not to reply to his open letter and so prolong an unfortunate episode, but they did vote 10 to 3 against giving him another testimonial.

It must not be thought, however, that Root and Worcestershire parted acrimoniously. The County remained ever grateful for his services, and his memory is revered. For his part, Root never hid his affection for the county that took him in after the war when, having served as a dispatch rider and being hit in the chest by a bullet, all had seemed bleak:

> I was asked, after I had entered into the 'fat and forty' stage, to bowl off-spinners round the wicket. I expressed my inability to master that method of attack at such an advanced period of my career, and had no alternative but to sever a long association with Worcestershire which had been fairly successful, extremely happy, but not very remunerative.

He went to Todmorden in the Lancashire League for a few seasons, became a very good journalist, wrote a book called *A Cricket Pro's Lot* from which we have quoted heavily and which conveys vividly the life of the professional cricketer in the years between the wars. He was a good, honest and happy man.

As Root departed, Perks continued to advance, and, in 1931, he had the considerable honour of reprsenting the Players against the Gentlemen at Lord's. Nichol was also chosen as England's twelfth man for the Test match against New Zealand. If the batting lacked consistency, it had the merit of attraction with Gibbons, Nichol and Walters in the first four, yet dark clouds were looming.

The Nawab of Pataudi, so brilliantly successful at Oxford, made his first apperances for Worcestershire after the Varsity match but could barely muster a run, and only in 1933, after his sensational debut for

Worcestershire, 1932.

Reg Perks.

England, was he regularly available for the County. Montague White, a fast bowler from the Lord's ground staff, showed promise at first, but it was never realised. More disturbingly, Maurice Nichol missed much of the 1932 season through illness.

Nichol had been taken to Sunderland Royal Infirmary in the winter of 1931–32 suffering from pneumonia, and his recovery had been slow so that, although he performed capably enough in 1932, he never seemed fully fit on the occasions when he took his place in the side. The illness placed a strain on Nichol and on the finances of the Club, for this was before the days of the National Health Service or of county medical schemes for their staff. Nichol asked for financial support for the illness which had cost him £110, but the County could only grant him a sum of £20 and a loan of £30 which was to be deducted at £1 a week from his wages. He, along with Gibbons, Wright, Perks, Jackson, Martin and Bull were the only professionals that the County agreed to retain on a full-time basis at the end of the 1932 season, and Dudley, Stourbridge and Kidderminster cricket clubs were asked to supply at least one amateur for each county match in 1933.

We should, perhaps, pause to consider what wage a Worcestershire professional was earning in 1932. He was paid £2 a week all the year round, plus £4 for each home match and £7 for an away match with £2 bonus for a win.

Of the professionals engaged for 1933, there are three to whom we have as yet made no reference, Jackson, Bull and Martin.

Charles Bull played four times for Kent before joining Worcestershire in 1931. He developed into a sound opening batsman and scored 1,000 runs each season between 1934 and 1937. In 1938, in the opening match of the season against the Australian tourists, when Bradman hit his third double century in three matches against Worcestershire, Bull was hit on the head and also suffered a broken finger which not only kept him out of the game for some weeks but caused a total loss of confidence. His career was tragically cut short the following season.

Peter Jackson's career with the County lasted for 21 years, and he seemed to get better as he got older. He bowled medium pace or off-breaks, but it was as an off-spinner that he was most effective and good enough to draw favourable comment from Bradman. His career transcended the Second World War to which, like so many others, what were possibly his best years were lost. A most genial and gentle man, much respected by friends and foes, he was never as confident of his own ability as others were. Broad-shouldered and fair-headed, he was a magnificent leg slip, and he gave valuable assistance to Reg Perks in that position. His career straddled the downs and ups of Worcestershire cricket.

Sid Martin was another of Worcestershire's overseas imports. He began his career with Natal in 1925 and ended with Rhodesia in 1950. In between he gave eight seasons of splendid all-round cricket to Worcestershire, completing the 'double' on two occasions with his medium-pace bowling and strongly aggressive batting.

That the County needed to keep strict control on the number of professionals employed and the amount of money they were paid can be seen from the fact that, by January 1933, the overdraft had risen to £1,746, and Lord Doverdale and Lord Cobham were called upon to guarantee £1,000 while guarantees were named for the rest of the money. Within the next two months, the overdraft had leapt to £2,065, which again had to be guaranteed, but it was decided that the professionals must be interviewed regarding a lower rate of wages. On

19 April, the committee agreed. 'That the professionals be asked to consent to a reduction of 5 per cent in their wages to the end of the season.' It was also agreed that £10 was the maximum amount of talent money that would be paid. The Club was forced to spend money on an absorbent roller.

With only two Championship matches won in 1933, the County did not have any great worries over talent money. Other worries were developing. Jackson, Perks and Brook were the only bowlers to meet with success, and they were expensive, while, although Walters, Nichol, a wonderful player of spin, Martin and, in 19 matches, the Nawab of Pataudi batted in great style, Gibbons was inconsistent and appeared to have lost much of his panache. It was to prove temporary, but there was an event in 1933 which, although not taken too seriously at the time, was to prove of deep significance.

Worcestershire travelled to Leyton at the beginning of June to meet Essex. Nichol was out for nought on the Saturday, and on the Sunday evening collapsed at Stratford station and took no further part in the match. It was reported that he was suffering from heart palpitations. He missed the next match, but he returned for the game against Yorkshire and went on to complete his 2,000 runs for the season with his customary ease and elegance. He hit eight centuries in the season and was thought by many to be the most brilliant batsman in the country. His eight centuries would have been a County record but for Walters's nine.

E. W. Swanton has written that 'the Worcester ground, with its perfect wicket, the velvet out-field, upon which the bowls players used to bring out the woods and the jacks when stumps were drawn, and the beautiful cathedral background formed a proper setting' for Walters's style. It is a typically perceptive comment, for Cyril Walters was an artist in all that he did with a bat in his hand. There are some who are blessed with that fluidity of movement that makes their every physical gesture a delight to the eye. Such a man was Cyril Walters. 'For a fleeting moment, for what proved to be only six summers, whilst the swifts and swallows flew low over that lovely ground at Worcester,' said Roy Genders, 'Cyril Walters was to brighten the canvas with all those strokes which reveal the true artist.'

Immaculate in appearance, his jet black hair always in place, Walters possessed the strength of wrist and flexibility that made his driving bring gasps of joy so classical in execution was it. He batted as the ancients batted, or as we like to believe that they batted, upright and true, and for the older followers of Worcestershire, he evoked memories of the Fosters. He had re-learned his game when he came to Worcester, finding the basis of his style in the resources of his own personality. It was as if he threw off some shackles of rigid coaching

Cyril Walters, a batsman of rare grace.

that had been imposed upon him in his early days and expressed his own inherent charm through his batting.

England claimed him. He opened in all three Tests against West Indies in 1933 and was hailed as a natural successor to Hobbs or Sutcliffe. Said *Wisden*:

> If somewhat slightly built, Walters showed both at Lord's and Old Trafford that he not only possessed a good eye but a flexible pair of wrists. Also, his footwork was excellent. Essentially a stylist, Walters, as a rule, drives with great power and correct placing of the ball, while on the leg side he can turn it with the utmost delicacy. Everyone who saw the match agreed that when he and Hammond were in together against the West Indies at Lord's the batting of the two men, for sheer grace of style and beauty of execution, could not have been bettered.

He went to India with Jardine's side, played in all three Tests and hit 102 in the third, at Madras, the game which J. B. Higgins umpired. When the Australians arrived in 1934 he appeared in all five Tests against them and averaged more than 50. In the first Test, at Trent Bridge, Wyatt withdrew from the England side with a broken thumb and Walters became captain. His status as an amateur, of course, won him the captaincy ahead of the more experienced professionals, Sutcliffe, Hendren and Hammond. Those eleven Test matches in which he scarcely tasted failure were to constitute Walters' international career.

As Major Jewell pointed out at the end of 1933, Worcestershire, with Walters, Gibbons, Bull, Nichol and Pataudi, had batting resources galore; what they needed were bowlers and an improvement in the fielding. In July 1933 the committee reported that 'a young Australian' had been down for a trial and was to be offered £350 a year. Presumably, the 'young Australian' was the 26–year-old Frank Warne who had played for Victoria and was also to play in India and South Africa. He was a left-handed batsman and an off-break bowler who, with his first ball for Worcestershire, against Sussex at Hastings in August 1934, had John Langridge caught by Singleton at mid-on. Spectacular as this start was and pleasing as was the fact that he hit 1,000 runs the following season, Warne was not to prove the answer to Worcestershire's problems and left the County after 1938.

By August, 1933, the committee were anticipating a deficit of £2,186 on the year, yet in December they were expressing confidence in the financial future, having budgetted for the overdraft. More importantly, on the playing side, there was talk of a young all-rounder, Howorth, who had made one appearance in 1933, 'being groomed'. There was also hope that the former Cambridge batsman

Roger Human would be able to assist the County, which, in fact, he did until the outbreak of the Second World War, but, like so many talented amateurs of the time, only on an irregular basis.

The increased financial confidence of the Club became manifest in that, in January 1934, they felt able to buy a typewriter for office use for the first time, and there was a greater sense of urgency all round. There was annoyance that delay had lost Worcestershire the opportunity of signing a cricketer named Bird, and it was decided that action must be taken quickly to sign Joseph Horton, elder brother of Henry Horton who assisted the County after the Second World War before moving on to Hampshire. Joseph Horton was signed at £1 a week and spent five seasons with Worcestershire. There was also concern that Howorth had not received bowling coaching as was intended, but it was reported that he had been unwell. Above all, it was stated that the County was desperately in need of a good wicket-keeper.

The optimism and total confidence that the committee had in the batting proved to be misguided although they were not to forsee the tragic event that lay in store. The season of 1934 began in fine style, for although the County were heavily beaten by the Australians, for whom Bradman made his customary double century, the match realised a profit of £1,000. After a draw with Oxford University, the Championship programme opened with the crushing defeat of Northamptonshire at Northampton.

The home side led by 25 on the first innings, and Worcestershire were set to make 268 on the last day on a wicket on which batsmen had found run-scoring difficult. In just over three hours, Walters and Gibbons put on 215 for the first wicket. It was a brilliant performance, and Walters went on to make 159 not out in under four hours to take his side to a nine-wicket victory.

There was a week's gap before the side were engaged in the next Championship match, against Essex at Chelmsford over the Whitsun week-end. Pearce won the toss and Essex scored heavily on a perfect wicket, the captain adding 210 in three and a quarter hours with the all-rounder Nichols. Essex were to reach 469. On the Sunday, the Worcestershire players relaxed by playing golf, and then, in the evening, they engaged in some light-hearted wrestling matches before going to bed around midnight. Maurice Nichol had been among the party playing golf and wrestling and he seemed quite well as he smoked a pipe and read before finally retiring. He died in his sleep. It was later stated that death was caused by an enlarged heart. He was 29 years old. The shock to Worcestershire was great; the loss irreparable.

A large Bank Holiday crowd had gathered at Chelmsford on the Monday and were stunned by the news. A few minutes before

11.30 am Walters led out the Worcestershire side followed by the not out batsmen Eastman and Bray. All were wearing black arm bands. The crowd stood bare-headed and silent for two minutes as the Essex team, too, stood in front of the pavilion before the bell sounded for play to recommence.

Remarkably, however shaken Walters and his side were, they put on an outstanding performance. Walters and Gibbons followed their partnership at Northampton with 279 together in three hours, ten minutes. Walters hit 178, Gibbons 104, and Pataudi and Martin followed with 97 and 72 respectively. Worcestershire made 515 and took first innings points.

Good as that Worcestershire performance was, particularly in the prevailing circumstances, it also highlighted what was to be the County's problem throughout the season. The first five batsmen scored 480 runs between them; the next five 17. *Wisden* pointed to the lack of seasoned batsmen as the reason for Worcestershire's failure to win more than three matches: 'Often the "tail" began at the fall of the second or third wicket, and considering the number of times Walters and Gibbons set an example with a fine opening partnership, the batting failures were deplorable.'

There were mitigating circumstances other than the tragic death of Nichol. Walters was away on Test duty for much of the summer. Pataudi fell ill and played in only six matches, Quaife was solid, but not prolific, and, apart from the openers, only Bull and Martin reached 1,000 runs. The committee believed that a good coach was urgently required and engaged E. J. 'Tiger' Smith for April 1935, at a salary of £40. They also felt that they had found a wicket-keeper to take over from the adequate, but not brilliant, Quaife who, in any case, had only taken on the job to assist the Club after Styler had left the game through ill health and there was no other keeper on the staff. The man the committee settled on was J. S. Buller of Yorkshire second eleven. He was offered £250 a year for three years and told to get to Worcester as soon as possible.

While the batting generally disappointed, with the exception of Walters and Gibbons to whom we shall return later, the bowling also left much to be desired, nor was it helped by poor slip catching which resulted in Walters moving himself and Gibbons to that position although both were outstanding out-fielders. Perks was the main sufferer, yet, for the first time, he took 100 wickets in the season, a feat he was to accomplish every season from then on until the end of his career 21 years in the future. He had also decided that he could wallop the ball, and his left-handed batting began to be more profitable and to send the ball further into the distance than it had done in the past.

The vagaries or necessities of selection also could not have helped the Worcestershire cause. Teams were chosen for three or four matches in advance so that they need not bear any relation to current form. Therefore we read in the Selection Committee minutes of 13 July 1934:

> Team chosen v Somerset 18/7/34. Include Mr A. P. Singleton instead of Mr Humphries. Mr Quaife to Captain. Otherwise same as v Lancs. Drop Howorth to 12th Man if Lyttelton can play.

Then at the next meeting of the Selection Committee:

> Team v Gloucestershire 28/7/34. Mr Walters, Gibbons, Bull, Martin, Mr Lyttelton, Perks, Mr Singleton, Mr Quaife, Brook, Howorth, Mr Baker. 12th Man Jackson.
> Team v Leicestershire 1/8/34. Same as before but Warne for Howorth if available.

As Howorth took two wickets and hit 31 and 70 against Gloucestershire, it was, perhaps, as well that Warne was not available for the Leicestershire match.

To lose Pataudi through illness following the death of Nichol was a great blow. He was laid low shortly after hitting a brilliant 214 against Glamorgan in the first home match of the season when he and Gibbons put on 274 for the second wicket, but he averaged over 90 from his six matches. He appeared again briefly in 1937 and 1938, but, effectively, his days with Worcestershire were over. So too, at last, were those of M. K. Foster.

At the age of 45, Foster played in four matches and it was a thoughtful gesture that when Worcestershire needed only 23 runs to beat Somerset at Worcester in June he was sent in with Gibbons to get them. His final appearances marked the end of the playing link between the great Malvern family and the Club that they had done so much to create.

'Doc' Gibbons was to play with consistency and style until the outbreak of war. He was to earn the title of the best batsman of his time who failed to get a cap for England. From this distance it is difficult to understand how the honour could have been denied him, for he was a possessor of the calmest of temperaments, and his record speaks for itself. When one thinks of how England struggled for an opening batsman on the 1936–37 tour of Australia it is hard to know why Gibbons was left behind. In 1934, he hit 2,654 runs for Worcestershire at an average of 52.03. It is a record that has stood, approached but unbeaten, to this day. He hit eight centuries, and he and Walters ended a remarkable season by sharing an unbeaten partnership of 278 against Leicestershire.

In spite of the disappointing results, it had been a successful season financially for Worcestershire. Gate receipts had increased by £1,300, and for the first time since their admission to the Championship the Club had made a profit. On 12 September, they had £225 in the bank. By the end of the year, a profit of £253 19s 7d was announced as opposed to a loss of nearly £290 a year earlier. The improvement in the financial position had been brought about in part by an increase in membership of 500. The re-awakened interest in the County, however, brought with it added responsibilities. Suddenly, there was agitation and demand for more success.

The committee were aware of this and were determined to strengthen the side. They gave a contract of £150 a year to Phil King, a bespectacled batsman of aggressive tendencies who could also keep wicket. He proved a useful acquisition, and, in 1938, when he reached 1,000 for the first time, he hit a century before lunch against Hampshire. He was to move to Lancashire after the war, but not before he made Worcestershire an offer that they did refuse.

There was also a feeling that the Club needed to be put on a more professional basis, and that there were ends that needed tidying up. Gibbons, Martin and Perks were all given better salaries. Walters was paid £400 a year as secretary, and Joe Horton was offered 30 shillings a week, but his 'lack of keenness in the field' was remarked upon. There were several suggestions of rules and punishments that could be imposed for slackness, but Lord Cobham, with a wisdom that would be welcome among today's top administrators, commented that one could not legislate for attitudes.

The one area in which the committee always seemed to tread carefully was in their dealings with Fred Hunt who, by 1935, had been groundsman at Worcester for 37 years. He had created what was arguably the finest batting wicket in England and tended with pride the most beautiful of grounds where, so smooth was the outfield, it was used for bowls. Fred Hunt was his own man, set in his ways, adhering strictly to the traditions in which he had been reared and ensuring that he earned a comfortable wage at the same time. He stuck rigidly to his horse-drawn roller in the face of technological advances. It must be said that he had negotiated rather good terms for himself. He received £310 a year, plus the expenses of maintaining the horse, and another £15 for the bowling club square. The Club met all expenses for seeds, turf, marl and for repairs to the horse's harness, etc. Fred also received 6d for every car parked on his land adjoining the ground. He was a shrewd businessman.

The County Club received the offer of a motor roller at a very reasonable price, and they met in October 1934, to discuss how best to broach the matter with Fred Hunt. It was reported that the expense of keeping the horse with repairs to harness, etc was about £40 per annum:

> After much discussion the general feeling was that, if Mr Hunt would realise that the purchase of a motor roller would relieve him of much time and two men's labour and if he would accordingly agree to a reduction of his yearly emolument by some £25, it would be good to buy the motor roller on the very reasonable terms offered. But that if Mr Hunt would not agree to such a reduction, the roller shall not be bought.

Hunt gave no written reply to the request, but over a year later, the problem had been resolved in that the committee minuted: 'Our horse (34 years old) has had to be destroyed.' Fred, however, still preferred to rely on manual labour.

While dealing delicately with Fred Hunt the committee also had to show concern for their players. Dick Howorth had come from the Lancashire League, and those responsible for the running of Worcestershire County Cricket Club saw in him a great all-rounder, even though there were comments from within the Club that he was far from impressive in his first season. First he had to be found winter employment and then it was decided that he, Jackson and Perks were in need of coaching, for bowling was still the most troubled area. They went for ten bowling lessons to Fairfax's School, and Lord Doverdale, the President of the Club, paid for the lessons. It was to be almost his last act of generosity towards the Club he served so earnestly, for he died shortly before the beginning of the season in April 1935.

Had he lived, Lord Doverdale would have been well pleased with his investment, for Howorth and Perks both reached 100 wickets in Championship matches alone and Jackson was not far behind them with 88 wickets in the Championship. Such an improvement in the bowling was bound to bring the better results that had been hoped for, even though the batting was steady rather than brilliant. Gibbons had one of his poorer seasons, but Martin thrived while Quaife and Bull had several solid performances to their credit and batted consistently to reach 1,000 runs. The fielding, too, so long a weakness, improved dramatically, and there was a new zest about the side.

This may have been due, in part, to the man who captained the side for much of the season, the Hon Charles John Lyttelton. Walters strained a tendon in his left hand in May and was later reported to have broken down in health so that he played in only two matches after early June. He still hit more than 800 runs and topped the batting averages, but, in August, he resigned as secretary and captain, and the career of one of the most aesthetically pleasing batsmen ever to have represented England was over at the age of 30. His early retirement

Hon C. J. Lyttleton hits out. A cricketer in the cavalier style and an inspiring leader, he helped revive Worcestershire's fortunes just before the outbreak of the Second World War.

came as a great shock and disappointment, and it has never been fully explained. Certainly, it was not entirely due to health reasons, for he remains fit and well and is a keen follower of the deeds of the county he once graced. More likely, recently married, he wished to pursue a career outside cricket or he may simply have lost his appetite for playing the game every day as others have done.

C. J. Lyttelton led the side when Walters was not playing and took over the captaincy completely in 1936. His approach was very different from that of Walters, who tended to be over cautious in delaying declarations, but influenced, no doubt, by his knowledge of the fallibilities of his side. Charles Lyttelton was the eighth member of the illustrious family to assist the County. His father, the ninth Viscount Cobham, played occasionally in 1924 and 1925 and became president of the Club on the death of Lord Doverdale. He held the position until his own death in 1949 at which time he was also treasurer of MCC. As he was also Lord Lieutenant of Worcestershire and of the City of Worcester for the last 26 years of his life, his commitment to the county was total. Indeed, the characteristic that marked the Lytteltons was their lust for life. They did nothing in half measures.

Charles Lyttelton was an enthusiast, an inspiring leader who was held in the greatest affection by those he led and who referred to him as the 'Honourable Charles' and 'Skip'. Like Robins and Sellers of the same era, he was able to convince each man in his side of his own worth and to draw from him the best. Then the individual contributions were fused into a team effort that made Worcestershire a vital, attractive and happy side.

He had been a cricketer of most modest standard when he was at Eton and was nowhere near winning a place in the school side, but he was keen and eager. He studied the game, thought about it and turned himself first into a good club cricketer and then into a county player who, but for the war, may well have gone on to captain England. He would have been an immensely popular choice. If his game had a fault, it was that he was by nature a tremendous hitter who sometimes squandered those natural powers in search of theory, but happily not often.

He was no respecter of persons, holding the philosophy that great bowlers could be hit as far as ordinary ones and, in any case, it upset them much more. Assessing that Mitchell, the Derbyshire and England leg-spinner, always tried a googly for the first ball he bowled to an amateur, Lyttelton played for it and hit it a long way out of the ground. He would spend every available minute with Perks, Jackson and other senior professionals demonstrating his theories on batting and questioning them on how he could improve. He was a far better cricketer than he gave himself credit for being, perhaps because he had been a late starter or perhaps because, glorious extrovert that he was, he was such a modest and kindly man.

When his first century came it was in typically breath-taking style. Facing a total of 269 against Leicestershire at Loughborough in July 1938, Worcestershire were 0 for two when they resumed on the Monday. Cooper and Bull put on 113, and Lyttelton, at number six, hit 162, with four sixes and 16 fours. He and Palmer put on 99 in 40 minutes for the sixth wicket, and Lyttelton then shared a scintillating eighth-wicket partnership of 113 with Buller. After that he opened the attack, bowling two overs before handing over to Howorth and having captured the wicket of Les Berry. The *Worcestershire Year Book* once wrote of him that 'he might with advantage have bowled more frequently'.

It was said that he was well supported by a group of young ladies who were not only attracted by the skipper's debonair looks, but were amused by his somewhat colourful language. Reg Perks tells how:

> On one occasion the Hon Charles threw away his bat in disgust as not being fit for use—after a mishit from which he was caught on the boundary—and declared that any so-and-so could have it,

whereupon Perks himself took possession of the bat and used it for the rest of his days!

There were times when his hitting powers, the accumulation of a very brisk 30 or 40, were more effective than the more orthodox or stylish methods of the other members of his team. On occasions, he would try to convince them that his methods would be more effective in the prevailing conditions, never more memorably than at Stourbridge at 1936, the first year of his captaincy.

Worcestershire's opponents were Yorkshire who were then at the height of their powers, being in the middle of the period when they won the Championship seven times in nine seasons. Worcestershire had not beaten them since 1909.

Only four hours' play was possible on the Saturday when, to the surprise of all, Lyttelton chose to bat first on a wicket which had been afflicted by a thunderstorm and which was drying under a hot sun. The surprise was understandable in that Yorkshire possessed an attack which made them regarded as invincible on a turning wicket, for in Verity they had the best slow left-arm bowler in the world and one of the greatest of all time.

Lyttelton impressed upon his side that if they played their normal game or adopted a cautious approach, they were doomed, and he encouraged them to throw their bats at the ball. They responded, and the Worcestershire first innings of 148 contained 11 sixes. Lyttelton himself set the example. When he was joined by the left-handed Warne he told him to keep at Verity's end while he attacked Robinson, the off-spinner. In 35 minutes, Lyttelton hit 48 which included four sixes and four fours. As soon as he had to play the left-arm spin of Verity he was out.

On the Monday, 20 wickets fell while 217 runs were scored, and the day ended with Yorkshire needing 55 to win with eight wickets in hand. In spite of Leyland batting resolutely for an hour, they failed in their task, routed by the Worcestershire spin pair, Jackson and Howorth. Lyttelton had inspired his side to a famous victory.

Unfortunately, Warne, who began the season well, suffered an injury in June, had to undergo a hernia operation and could not play again, for he was still unwell in a nursing home after the season ended. Gibbons, however, recaptured all his old form, and Perks, Howorth and Jackson all took 100 wickets in Championship matches alone. At last Worcestershire had an attack, and it was young and virile.

The club was again in the red by the end of 1936, and although the financial position was better the following year, a deterioration in the state of affairs continued until 1939.

The 1936 season also saw an advance in Worcestershire's efforts to

WORCESTERSHIRE *v* YORKSHIRE

Played at Stourbridge on 16, 18 and 19 May 1936

WORCESTERSHIRE WON BY 11 RUNS

WORCESTERSHIRE	FIRST INNINGS		SECOND INNINGS	
H. H. I. Gibbons	c Hutton b Verity	13	lbw b Verity	10
C. H. Bull	c and b Turner	1	c Mitchell b Leyland	24
S. H. Martin	hit wkt b Robinson	20	lbw b Verity	2
★Hon C. J. Lyttelton	c and b Verity	48	c Leyland b Verity	2
†B. W. Quaife	c Sellers b Verity	0	not out	28
R. Howorth	c Sellers b Verity	14	c Hutton b Leyland	4
B. P. King	st Wood b Verity	13	c Mitchell b Verity	4
F. B. Warne	c Leyland b Robinson	8	c Mitchell b Verity	0
S. G. Shepherd	lbw b Robinson	9	c Barber b Verity	0
R. T. D. Perks	st Wood b Robinson	12	lbw b Verity	8
P. F. Jackson	not out	0	st Wood b Verity	0
Extras	b 9, lb 1	10	b 9, nb 1	10
Total		148		92

BOWLING	O	M	R	W	O	M	R	W
Rawlin	1	0	2	0	4	0	9	0
Turner	3	2	7	1	3	1	2	0
Verity	14	4	48	5	26.4	15	40	8
Robinson	11.3	1	81	4	6	2	12	0
Leyland					15	6	19	2

YORKSHIRE	FIRST INNINGS		SECOND INNINGS	
H. Sutcliffe	c Lyttelton b Perks	7	lbw b Jackson	29
A. Mitchell	c Warne b Martin	34	lbw b Jackson	17
W. Barber	c Quaife b Jackson	9	st Quaife b Howarth	5
M. Leyland	c Warne b Martin	20	lbw b Howorth	35
L. Hutton	run out	0	lbw b Jackson	0
C. Turner	c Martin b Jackson	27	b Jackson	0
†A. Wood	c Warne b Martin	3	lbw b Howorth	8
★A. B. Sellers	c and b Martin	4	c Martin b Howorth	2
H. Verity	not out	11	not out	6
E. P. Robinson	c Lyttelton b Jckson	0	c Lyttelton b Howorth	0
E. R. Rawlin	b Jackson	1	lbw b Jackson	4
Extras	b 2, lb 5	7		0
Total		123		106

BOWLING	O	M	R	W	O	M	R	W
Perks	19	6	35	1	6	2	15	0
Shepherd	2	1	4	0				
Howorth	9	1	25	0	15	7	21	5
Jackson	16	6	18	4	18.3	8	66	5
Martin	13	4	34	4	2	0	4	0

Umpires: A. Skelding and C. N. Woolley

The match in which Worcestershire hit their way to a surprising victory.

★Captain; †Wicket-keeper

encourage young and emerging talent in that a nursery was set up under the guidance of A. F. Lane and friendly matches were arranged against neighbouring second elevens. Not all young players reach the top, of course, but it is interesting to note when one reflects on the famous victory over Yorkshire at Stourbridge that Syd Shepherd, a 25-year-old medium pace bowler who also played for Cheshire, appeared in his one and only first-class match on that occasion.

New players were forcing their way into the side, however, several of them imported. Buller was qualified before the end of the 1936 season and took over the wicket-keeping duties from Quaife who continued to serve as a batsman. The reputation that Syd Buller won later as a fearless and most honourable umpire, linked by most observers of the game as, along with Chester, the finest we have known, has tended to obscure his worth as a wicket-keeper. He displayed the same characteristics in both jobs, a quiet efficiency that had no need of flamboyance or the need to assert a belligerence of character. He was unfussy behind the stumps and appealed only when he was convinced that the batsman was out. He was a determined and resolute cricketer, and he played an invaluable part in the rise in Worcestershire's fortunes.

Buller was joined in 1937 by another import from the north, Edwin Cooper who had played for his home town club Bacup in the Lancashire League. Eventually becoming an opening batsman, Eddie Cooper had a good first season and scored 1,000 runs. Tall and right-handed, with a sound defence, he appeared to be easy on his feet, comfortable in his stance and correct in his timing even if he seemed a little shy and lacking in confidence. He learned much in that first season, however, and in 1938 he was recognised as an attractive batsman of high quality who used his height to the full in getting to the pitch of the ball and whose high back lift enabled him to hit the ball with great power.

Another to join the side, although only for a season, was R. C. M. Kimpton, an Australian who had won a high reputation at Oxford. He hit 1,000 runs in all matches in 1937, and he was a capable wicket-keeper and change bowler when required, who returned to play a few games after the war.

To add to the 'league of nations' side, as Worcestershire became known, was R. J. Crisp, a South African pace bowler of considerable merit. He had a successful tour of England in 1935 and became associated with Sir Julian Cahn's XI. He qualified for Worcestershire, but, after eight matches in 1938, he played no more because of injury.

In 1937, Martin, Perks, Howorth and Jackson took 421 Championship wickets between them, a record which no other county could approach. The first two took 100 wickets in Championship matches alone and Howorth and Jackson had 100 wickets each in all matches. Given more opportunity with the ball, Martin revelled in hard work and with more than 1,000 runs from his exuberant batting became the first Worcestershire player since Fred Root to do the 'double'.

This was as well, for, with Pataudi playing in only two matches, Gibbons, in his best form once more, Bull and Cooper carried the batting. The great loss was Lyttelton, who was seriously ill at the beginning of the season and, after playing against Kent and Derbyshire and hitting 124 runs in four innings, did not play again during the season. This was obviously a severe blow, and one from which the County never effectively recovered.

Lyttelton was back for the beginning of the 1938 season and immediately caused a rumpus in the cricket world. Worcestershire had been deprived of the honour of hosting the first game with the tourists in the previous season, but they were the first to take on the Australians and Bradman, 258 this time, in 1938. Lyttelton won the toss and, to the astonishment of all, put the Australians in to bat first on a perfect wicket in fine conditions. The visitors hit 474 for six on the opening day and reached 541, their highest score against Worcestershire, on the Monday. Lyttelton's reasoning for his eccentricity in putting them in on a true and easy pitch was that he thought that a holiday crowd would like to see the Australians bat. In the chill that has descended on international matches since those days, it is a warming memory. He showed his grit by opening the Worcestershire innings with Bull, withstanding the lightning no-balls of McCormick, driving O'Reilly with gusto and hitting nine fours in his 50.

The injury that Bull suffered in that match, and to which we alluded earlier, was to hamper him for the remainder of the season, but Gibbons, in his benefit year, was in mighty form, as stylish and as pleasing as ever, and in the course of a season in which he scored more than 2,000 runs he passed Bowley's record of 35 centuries made for the County. Gibbons was one of those rare players who could give delight in defence as well as in the fluency of his attack, for he maintained a dignity, composure and grace in all that he did, and he was a batsman of tremendous courage.

He was desperately unlucky with his benefit match in which there was little play after the first day because of rain. It was the match against Middlesex at Worcester in July, and, Martin, after bowling well to take six for 85, broke a finger while batting. The injury was to keep him out of several matches. Otherwise, he would almost certainly have completed the 'double' again.

As it was, Dick Howorth came closest, failing by only three runs to reach 1,000 to accompany his 108 wickets in all matches. Both men were to achieve the 'double' the following season. Howorth had been well groomed and had long since silenced those critics who had said that he was not good enough. Always in control of himself, with a gentleness of manner and lack of histrionics which concealed an unquenchable passion for the game, Dick Howorth must rate with Ted Arnold as Worcestershire's greatest all-round cricketer. Only perhaps in his jaunty walk to the wicket with his County cap pulled down over his right eye could one discern the man's eagerness and impatience to be playing the game. As a left-handed batsman and bowler, he would have won an England cap earlier than he did but for the presence of Verity. The game was fun to him and he was greatly helped by Lyttelton, who insisted always that he should flight the ball and pitch it up. As a batsman, like Pearson, he was prepared to bat anywhere in the order, and did.

Howorth, like Cooper, had the distinction of coming from Bacup, and both Lancastrians served their adopted county well in the years before the war. Cooper had a particular affection for the wicket at Dudley and, in 1938, hit 111 against Lancashire there in June when he and Gibbons put on 207 for the third wicket and followed this with 216 not out against Warwickshire on the same ground two months later. He batted for six and a half hours and hit 22 fours in what was to be the only double century of his career. Martin hit 136 in the same match and he and Cooper put on 245 in three hours ten minutes for the fourth wicket.

Unfortunately, in the first match at Dudley, against Lancashire, Jackson sustained a back injury which was to keep him out for many matches and to hamper his effectiveness for the remainder of the season. Phillipson, the Lancashire all-rounder, attempted a short single off a no-ball and collided with Jackson who was trying to throw down the wicket. Phillipson broke a collar bone, and Jackson hurt his back.

Jackson, like Root before him, faced the fact that remuneration from county cricket was barely enough on which to live and he fell to the lure of the league, deciding to play for Old Hill on Saturdays in 1939 and to assist Worcestershire in mid-week matches, but his career with the County was far from over.

As well as the injury to Jackson, Worcestershire were not helped by the fact that Lyttelton, still recuperating from his illness, was forced to rest on occasions and was claimed by Territorial Army calls in August. This was a time of intense international crisis, and his father, Lord Cobham, was very active in the TA. In spite of all these difficulties, the County enjoyed their best season for 27 years, and in 1939, in spite of another tragedy befalling them, they did even better.

The year began with concern that the County Ground had been so waterlogged that there had been no hockey played there. Photographs of the Worcester ground turned into a lake by the River Severn a few

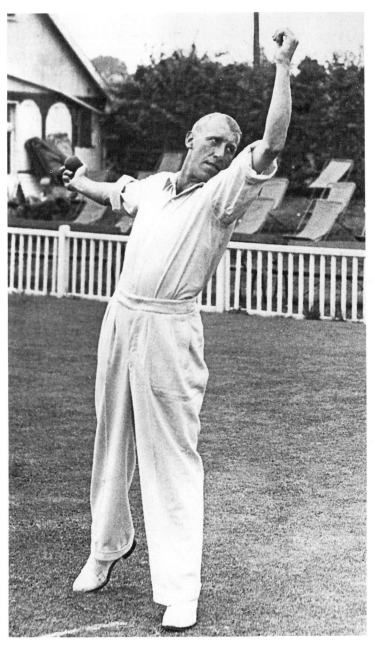

P. F. Jackson.

weeks before the cricket season is due to begin have become common, and some aver that this flooding is a reason for the wickets and outfield at New Road maintaining such a consistently high standard over the years. In fact, it is the backwaters which feed the Severn that cause the flooding. When the Severn itself rises, usually early in the year, these backwaters are filled to overflowing and spill over the ground. In the pavilion at Worcester, there is a brass plaque some 3ft 6in above the level of the floor which indicates the height to which the waters rose in the floods of 1947. The pavilion floor itself is several feet above the level of the ground. This height has not been reached since, but the ground is flooded nearly every year.

Fred Root had a tale that a 45 lb salmon had been caught on the Worcester ground when it was flooded, and he also said that so well was the ground tended and so rich after the flooding that Fred Hunt used to offer £1 to anyone who found a dandelion within the rails and never had to pay up.

The floods had subsided by the beginning of the 1939 season, and West Indies were thrashed in the opening match with Reg Perks taking eleven wickets. There were defeats at The Oval and at Bristol, but Kent were beaten at Gillingham, with fourteen wickets to Martin, and Hampshire were crushed at Worcester in a most thrilling game which saw some notable individual performances.

With Arnold making 179 not out, Hampshire reached 319 in their first innings. Gibbons countered with a magnificent 111 not out and took his side to within 57 of the Hampshire score. An inspired spell of bowling by Perks, who took eight for 59, brought about the downfall of Hampshire's second innings, which realised 197. Perks's performance was all the more remarkable when one considers that he did not have the help of Martin who was unable to bowl or field because of a torn thigh muscle.

Needing 255 to win, Worcestershire lost four men for 48 runs. It had been intended that Martin should not bat, but, in the face of a crisis, he insisted on batting with his thigh strapped and although he showed signs of being in considerable pain and discomfort, he joined Gibbons in an unbroken stand of 207 which gave Worcestershire a memorable victory. Gibbons hit his second not out century of the match, exactly 100, and Martin hit Bailey for the four which won the match and took his score to 102.

In joyful mood, Worcestershire travelled to Chelmsford for the traditional Whitsuntide match with Essex. The home side made 271 in their first innings on the Saturday, and on the Sunday evening, Bull and Buller were involved in a serious motor accident in Margaretting in between Billericay and Chelmsford. Bull was killed and Buller seriously injured. Chillingly and almost unbelievably, Worcestershire had lost a second most promising batsman during a match with Essex at Chelmsford and close on five years to the day after the tragic death of Nichol. Buller was out of the side until the closing weeks of the season, and in the second innings, Yarnold, the Worcestershire twelfth man, was allowed to keep wicket, an uncommon occurrence at the time. Two men short, Worcestershire put up a plucky display but lost by 295 runs.

For some weeks afterwards the team, not unnaturally, was in something of a state of shock, but they rallied splendidly to take seventh place in the table and to excite with promise of great things to come.

Howorth moved up to open the innings to fill the gap left by Bull's death, and Roly Jenkins, a young leg-spinner who had made a brief appearance the previous season, bowled very impressively on occasions. Another who had played the year before and who now showed a great talent was Charles Palmer, an amateur from Old Hill, who hit centuries against Northamptonshire, Glamorgan and Nottinghamshire and failed by only seven runs to reach 1,000 for the season. Gibbons, Cooper, Martin and Howorth all batted splendidly, and, indeed, there was consistency throughout the order. The 'double' men, Martin and Howorth, and Perks bore the brunt of the bowling, and for all three it was a memorable season.

Perks, with 143 Championship wickets, who had won his first Test cap against South Africa in Durban earlier in the year, was chosen for the third Test against West Indies at The Oval in August. He took five wickets in an innings as he had done in Durban, but he was never to play Test cricket again.

As the storm clouds of war were gathering to bring to a close the second phase of Worcestershire's history, and much else of more moment, the County played some of the most joyful cricket of its 40-year life. At Kidderminster in July, Somerset were the visitors. The County had played at Kidderminster since 1921, and were to play there until 1973 after which the venue was abandoned, only to be readopted in recent years.

In the 1939 match, no play was possible on the first day, and when the match started on the Monday, the damp pitch was responsive to spin so that Wellard quickly jettisoned his medium pace for off-breaks. Cooper batted with customary grace and style, but the last seven wickets fell for 18 runs, and Worcestershire were bowled out for 130. Somerset took a one-run lead, mainly through the efforts of their last pair, Horace Hazell and Sam Weaver, more famous as the Newcastle United, Chelsea and England wing-half with a long throw-in. It was this pair who were to provide the drama in the second innings, for when they came together Somerset needed just six runs to win.

Howorth bowled the last over of extra time (overs were eight-ball in 1939) and with his fourth ball he beat Hazell and bowled him. The scores were level so that Worcestershire had tied for the first time in their history.

Perhaps Howorth had a feeling for the dramatic, for, on 31 August, he had Butler of Notts caught by Lyttelton to bring Worcestershire victory by an innings and to complete the 'double' for himself. Three days later the Second World War began.

WORCESTERSHIRE *v* SOMERSET

Played at Kidderminster on 8, 10 and 11 July 1939

MATCH TIED

WORCESTERSHIRE	FIRST INNINGS		SECOND INNINGS	
R. Howorth	c Luckes b Wellard	16	b Buse	45
E. Cooper	lbw b Wellard	69	c Hazell b Buse	21
†B. P. King	c Weaver b Buse	3	lbw b Buse	17
H. H. I. Gibbons	c Priddy b Hazell	29	b Wellard	0
S. H. Martin	b Wellard	0	c Bennett b Hazell	25
C. H. Palmer	b Wellard	2	c and b Hazell	11
J. Stanning	c Priddy b Wellard	4	b Hazell	0
*Hon C. J. Lyttelton	c Lee b Wellard	1	c Gimblett b Hazell	0
E. H. Perry	st Lee b Wellard	0	run out	1
R. O. Jenkins	not out	1	not out	0
R. T. D. Perks	c Lee b Hazell	0	c Gimblett b Hazell	16
Extras	b 5	5	b 5, lb 1	6
Total		130		142

BOWLING	O	M	R	W	O	M	R	W
Wellard	16	1	45	7	16	1	62	1
Weaver	3	0	16	0	1	0	13	0
Buse	10	2	24	1	21	5	55	3
Hazell	11.7	2	40	2	5.7	1	6	5

SOMERSET	FIRST INNINGS		SECOND INNINGS	
F. S. Lee	b Perks	5	c Jenkins b Howorth	23
H. Gimblett	b Perks	0	b Perry	5
H. F. T. Buse	c King b Martin	26	b Perks	11
F. M. McRae	c King b Perry	1	st King b Jenkins	28
*E. F. Longrigg	c Howorth b Martin	13	c and b Howorth	1
J. Priddy	c Perks b Palmer	15	b Jenkins	13
†W. T. Luckes	b Perks	24	c Perks b Howorth	22
G. M. Bennett	b Perry	10	c Martin b Perks	16
A. W. Wellard	b Perks	0	b Perry	12
S. Weaver	b Jenkins	19	not out	3
H. L. Hazell	not out	13	b Howorth	4
Extras	lb 2, nb 3	5	lb 3	3
Total		131		141

BOWLING	O	M	R	W	O	M	R	W
Perks	13	1	40	4	10	2	34	2
Perry	12	2	31	2	10	1	43	2
Martin	11	1	26	2				
Howorth	4	1	18	0	9.4	1	27	4
Palmer	1	0	6	1				
Jenkins	2.5	0	5	1	10	1	34	2

Umpires: J. Smart and E. Cooke

Worcestershire's first tied match.

*Captain; †Wicket-keeper

MIDDLE OF THE ROAD

BY 1940, LYTTELTON, MORGANS, the County Secretary, R. H. C. Human, later killed in action, Cooper, Jenkins, King, Howorth, Jackson and Yarnold were all in the armed services. Perry, Buller, White, Perks and Singleton were soon to join them. At the beginning of the war an emergency committee was set up to manage the Club's affairs through the duration. G. W. Nicholls, the secretary, C. G. D. Smith and A. F. Lane bore the main burden. In 1941, Lane raised a side to play Warwickshire and paid all the expenses out of his own pocket. Cyril Smith served the county for nearly 50 years playing a major part in seeing it through crisis to success.

The two counties had met at Worcester on 5 August 1940, and 2,000 people saw Worcestershire win by 91 runs. Walters turned out for his old county and Gibbons hit 50. Mayer of Warwickshire took four wickets in an over, including the hat-trick, but Perks, seven for 40, and Howorth, three for 20, bowled unchanged to skittle out Warwickshire for 82. Lane had met all the costs of this game, too, and he must have been gratified that his side beat the old enemy on the two occasions that they met in the early years of the war. In 1942, when the game was played at Edgbaston and the sides were less representative, the result was a draw.

The County Ground was much used by the Worcester City Club and by schools. Indeed, in 1943 and 1944, Westminster School played all their home matches there. Fred Hunt, of course, kept the ground in good order although the stands fell into a state of disrepair. Players kept active in service games, in the Birmingham League, which was probably stronger than ever, and, from 1944 onwards, in G. O. J. Elliott's entertaining West of England XI. Gibbons batted with distinction on several occasions. He was a member of the Civil Defence.

The interest that these games aroused can be seen from the fact that when Worcestershire met the RAF at Worcester on 5 August 1944, 5,000 people attended and £387 was raised for the RAF Benevolent Fund. Spectators were well rewarded. Wally Hammond led a very strong RAF side and hit 117 before being bowled by Jackson. In spite of Perks's five wickets, Worcestershire were beaten by 97 runs.

Members supported the County nobly throughout the war so that the financial position improved considerably from what it had been in 1939, and when Brigadier M. A. Green arrived to take over as secretary in 1945 he was able to announce that the County was in credit and had a 'small but useful sum of money'. Green found that the

Club winter offices in the Caledonian Insurance Building had been closed in 1939 and not opened since so that when he came to work it was thick with dust. He was allowed a staff of one typist and chose a young lady in her teens, Grace Cook, who was to become a most vital part of the administration of the Club.

The committee remained much as it had been in 1939 as did the playing staff. At the outbreak of war Worcestershire had gathered together a side with an average age of 26 which was on the brink of great things. Of the side that beat Nottinghamshire in August 1939, Palmer and Jenkins were both under 21, Cooper was short of his 24th birthday, Singleton was 25 and Perks had just been launched on a promising Test career at the age of 28. In reserve were White, 24, Yarnold, 22 and Jackson, 28. By May 1946, seven years of non-first-class cricket had to be added to these ages. Cooper, King and Singleton were three who had lost the best years of their playing lives, while for Perks age had cut short his Test career before it began.

King was not re-engaged. He wrote to the County and asked to be re-registered, but the committee felt that there was no place for him. He wrote again saying that he would play as an amateur until he scored 1000 runs and then asked for £1 a run after 1,000. It was a novel and amusing offer, but it was refused. He moved to Lancashire and hit a century against his native Yorkshire and a century before lunch, a feat he had achieved for Worcestershire, against Gloucestershire. He retired after the 1947 season and became cricket and rugby league correspondent for the *People*.

Lyttelton, the pressure of public work crowding upon him, decided that he would not return to first-class cricket although he continued to play club cricket and maintained his passion for the game and the County all his life. He succeeded to the title on the death of his father in 1949 and, as tenth Viscount Cobham, was Governor-General of New Zealand from 1957 to 1962. He was named as president of the County Club in 1977, an honour in which he delighted, but which sadly he enjoyed all too briefly, for he died in March of that year. He had lived long enough to see the county into which he had breathed so much vitality repay his and other's efforts with honour.

It was written of C. J. Lyttelton, with total justification, that:

> No one ever enjoyed his cricket more or took more trouble to see that others enjoyed theirs and he amply repaid off the field the debt which he owed to the game.

Martin returned to South Africa where he played for Rhodesia, and Gibbons, who played three games as an amateur in 1946, quit the game at the age of 42, leaving an indelible impression of grace, resolution and honesty on all who saw him. He became director of a Fleet Street advertising agency, his name still firmly printed in the Worcestershire record books.

Alexander Parkinson 'Sandy' Singleton, an aggressive batsman and off-break bowler who had been at Oxford from 1934 to 1937, and captain in his last year, and who had assisted the County whenever possible in the late 1930s was an ideal choice to succeed Lyttelton as captain. He was a lively, joyful cricketer and an adventurous leader. Like his predecessor, he was immensely popular with his men. He also got off to a wonderful start in that first post-war season, scoring 475 runs at an average of nearly 70 in the first four matches. He could not quite keep that up, but he hit 1,773 runs in the season and took 43 wickets. He was very much the man of the time, exuberant, energetic, exuding the feeling that it was good to be alive. His very presence demanded entertaining cricket, but his reign was short, for he left England to settle in Rhodesia at the end of 1946. He teamed up with Martin for a few matches.

The rebirth of first-class cricket after the years of war brought with it an enthusiasm for the game which few could have anticipated. When the Indian tourists began their fixtures with the traditional match at Worcester a crowd of 8,000, one of the biggest ever seen at New Road, braved the chilly weather to see the first day's play.

Singleton, Howorth, Cooper, Gibbons, Jenkins, Perks and Buller remained from the Worcestershire side of August 1939, while White and Jackson, who also played much that year were also in the side. The newcomers were Martin Young and Ronald Bird, an adaptable batsman and fine close fielder who was to become County captain. Young stayed only three seasons before moving on to Gloucestershire. Brigadier Green asserted that Worcestershire were wrong in their treatment of Young and that the player left because he felt he was not being given a fair opportunity. He played 31 matches in three seasons, but won a regular place as an opener with Gloucestershire and had a fine record.

Worcestershire beat the Indians in the opening game of 1946 after trailing by one run on the first innings. Reg Perks took five for 53 in the first innings and went on to complete his 100 wickets for the season, although he could not play regularly because he was not demobilised until later in the summer. He produced a fine bowling performance which could have been even better when he took 14 for 96 in the local derby match with Gloucestershire at Cheltenham in August. Worcestershire led by five runs on the first innings, and Perks then produced an inspired spell of bowling which saw him take the first nine wickets to fall in Gloucestershire's second innings. With the last Gloucestershire pair, Scott and Goddard together, Perks bowled to C. J. Scott who swung and skied the ball to slip where Singleton, one of the surest of catchers, misjudged the spinning and whirling ball and dropped the catch. Scott then fell to Jackson to leave Perks with nine for 42 from 21 unchanged overs as the home side were out for 74. Worcestershire won by ten wickets, and no Worcestershire bowler has come as near to taking all ten wickets in a match.

Jackson, too, captured 100 wickets in the season and topped the County averages, but the outstanding player was Howorth who began with a century against the Indians and was the only man in the country, apart from India's Mankad, to complete the 'double'. He had been 30 in 1939 and what he might have achieved but for the war, one can only conjecture.

One newcomer to the Worcestershire side in 1946 was the 45-year-old former England captain R. E. S. Wyatt. Bob Wyatt had been conducting a running battle with the Warwickshire committee for about 15 years and although he had been prepared to return to them after the war, he sensed he would not be welcome and was happy to receive a warm invitation from Worcestershire. Initially, Warwickshire opposed his move, but Wyatt insisted, and as he already had a residential qualification, he made his debut for Worcestershire against Warwickshire at Dudley on 1 June. He was not immediately successful, but he ended the season in excellent style and topped the batting averages as well as taking 20 valuable wickets with his medium pace.

Jenkins, who showed great promise in batting, bowling and fielding, could have been given more work with his leg-spin, but his time was to come, as was that of George Dews, a noted soccer player, who appeared in a few matches and hit 78 against the RAF.

On 25 May, when Worcestershire entertained Surrey at New Road and Singleton was absent, Howorth opened with a young man who was still serving in the RAF, Don Kenyon. Kenyon was bowled by Parker for 15, and there was no play after the first day. A month later, playing for the RAF against Worcestershire, he was out for a 'pair', but he rectified this with 107 in two and a quarter hours for Combined Services against his own county at the beginning of August. Perks was also in the Services' side. Now available for the county side, Kenyon hit 90 against Middlesex at Worcester towards the end of the season, and it was recognised that here was an exciting talent, yet at that stage no-one could have foreseen how great would be his contribution to Worcestershire cricket.

The County survived the first post-war season well. Crowds flocked to watch cricket at Worcester though the team's form fell away a little as the season progressed. When Gloucestershire were beaten at New Road in July and Wyatt hit 150 not out, his second century in a fortnight, the attendance was the highest since the visit of

Bradman's Australians in 1938. The County faced a problem of increasing accommodation. Boundary boards were moved back, but the shortages of the age meant that there was a delay in erecting new seating because of the non-arrival of timber.

A Worcestershire institution had disappeared at the end of the Second World War when Fred Hunt finally retired. He was succeeded by George Platt, the former Surrey player, who had joined the County as coach in 1939. Platt was to return to coaching and was succeeded as groundsman by Syd Styler, the former wicket-keeper.

There were those whose attitudes remained as they had been before the war even though there was much that had changed. Certainly social barriers had begun to crumble a little. The County agreed, for example, to pay for the players' sweaters, which they had not done in the past, but then the County was financially more secure than it had been seven years earlier. Green was to argue some years after he had left the County that the conservatism and wariness on the part of the committee lost them the services of Washbrook and Hollies, and nearly cost them Kenyon as it had done Young. But then Green also said that the thing he loved most about Worcestershire was 'its purity, its unchanging simplicity, and its determined refusal to be modernized'. Perhaps you cannot have it both ways.

Green and Major Jewell came very close to capturing one bowler who was to have a distinguished career with his native county. Jewell had been impresssed with the boy when he played for an air force side against the Gentlemen of Worcestershire, and Green was instructed to track him down. This he did and found the lad a place on the Lord's ground staff in preparation for him to join Worcestershire. He found, however, that the young man had been born in Swansea so Green had to contact J. C. Clay to ask if Glamorgan would release him. Clay saw the youngster bowl and replied that he felt it would be better if Glamorgan kept him. The young man was Don Shepherd.

Most who lived through it remember the 1947 season with the greatest warmth and affection. It was the year of Compton and Edrich, of seemingly endless summer sun and of joyful cricket and happy crowds. It was also the year of Reg Perks' benefit and Dick Howorth's first Test cap, and, as we have already mentioned, the deepest flood on the County Ground.

Alan White took over the captaincy from Singleton. Like Wyatt, he had played for Warwickshire before joining Worcestershire, but he was a lesser technician and a more adventurous, some would say too adventurous, batsman than Wyatt. He captained Worcestershire for two seasons and shared the captaincy with Wyatt in 1949. During that time Worcestershire finished seventh, tenth and third in the Championship.

In the first of those seasons, Fred Cooper, who had played for Lancashire, joined his brother in the side and 'Laddie' Outschoorn made his first apperance. The second saw Michael Ainsworth, a naval officer and a fine bat, play the first of his few games for the County, and in the third we note the names of P. E. Richardson and J. Flavell for the first time.

White may not have been the greatest of tacticians or disciplinarians, but he had an infectious enthusiasm to which his side responded, and had there been someone to share the new ball with Reg Perks, Worcestershire might have done even better than they did. Charles Palmer was a master at Bromsgrove School and when he was able to play he emphasised what the County missed by his absence, but Kenyon was now regularly available and scored 1,000 Championship runs in his first full season, 1947, including two centuries at Dudley.

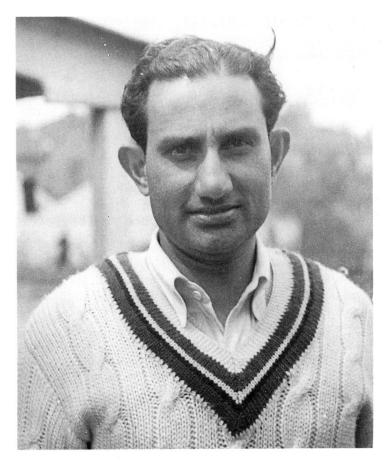

'Laddie' Outschoorn.

The first won the game against Warwickshire in June, for Worcestershire, trailing on the first innings, were set to make 271 in four and three quarter hours and were 22 for two before Kenyon hit 152 not out, his first Championship century, and, with Wyatt, won the game with 15 minutes to spare.

The second was against Nottinghamshire in August when he hit 102. Palmer hit 177 in the same innings, but this fine player was to be lost to Worcestershire in 1950 when he moved to Leicestershire as secretary/captain.

The great batting advance in 1947, a year in which while other counties' batsmen plundered runs, Worcestershire's did not score as heavily as one would have expected, came from Roly Jenkins. His leg-spin bowling was still greatly under-used, but he passed 1,000 runs in all matches.

Perks's benefit realised £2,950 and emphasised the amount of affection in which he was held by the people of Worcestershire, for, at the time, that sum was easily a record for the County. He had returned from the war, the black wavy hair turning grey, a little bulkier in weight and with perhaps something of the speed lost, but the heart was as big as ever even if the legs grew tired a little sooner. He deserved to be tired, for by the time he retired in 1955, he had taken a record 2,143 wickets for Worcestershire. He became an integral part of the County Ground, chatting to everyone, for everyone knew him, and enjoying a pint of bitter or two while he talked cricket after the game. All recognised him as a model professional, and for the people of Worcestershire he was a local hero and a man much loved.

Jackson continued to serve, pounding down both medium pace and off-breaks as required and capturing his 100 wickets regularly and economically, but in 1947, it was Dick Howorth who overshadowed all others, completing the 'double' in Championship matches alone. As he had proved himself to be the leading all-rounder in England, some might say the only all-rounder in England, at a time when the national side was in need of a quality spin bowler and left-handed batsman, it is hard to understand why he was not picked for his country sooner and more often, but again we must draw attention to the years lost to the war.

Sam Cook of Gloucestershire and Jack Young of Middlesex were left-arm spinners who played against South Africa in the Test series of 1947, and in the second and third Tests, England played two leg-spinners, Hollies and Wright. By the time the fifth Test arrived, England had won the rubber and Howorth's record could be ignored no longer so, to 'his mingled mirth and pleasure', he won his first Test cap at the age of 38.

England made 427. Mitchell and Dyer, the South African openers, played Copson and Gladwin without much bother and treated first change Wright with respect. Then Howorth was called up by Yardley. With his cap tilted over his right ear, Howorth made a gentle run to the stumps, flighted the ball in a tempting loop and pitched it outside off stump inviting the cover-drive. It was not quite as full a length as Dyer had anticipated and he hit the ball straight into the hands of Gladwin. Howorth had emulated Worcestershire's first great all-rounder, Ted Arnold, and taken a wicket with his first ball in Test cricket. He finished with three for 64 and three for 85, was far and away England's most impressive bowler, and hit 23 and 45 not out in the drawn match.

He was chosen for the tour of West Indies when the England side was led by 45-year-old 'Gubby' Allen. It was an unfortunate tour. Several of the leading players, Compton, Edrich, Bedser and Wright among them, did not make the trip, and some of those that did were not fully fit. The West Indies had been grossly under-estimated and Weekes, Worrell and the rest proved an unexpected and shattering experience. None came through the ordeal better than Howorth, who played in every match and always commanded respect. He took 13 wickets in the four Tests and 30 wickets on the tour. Johnny Wardle, who was on the trip, said later that he learned so much about variation in pace and flight from Howorth that was to stand him in good stead for the rest of his career. Howorth did not play Test cricket again.

Howorth was a wise cricketer. His bowling was artful in flight and accurate in length, and for all his humorous manner and languid air, he played the game hard. His batting was learned by experience and could be shaped to fit the occasion. He was also a man who would offer generous help to younger players and was ever ready to be of assistance to the skipper. 'Sandy' Singleton was quick to recall how much he owed to Howorth, Perks and Buller in his year as captain, for the amateur skipper of the 1930s and immediate post-war period was very dependent on his senior professionals, who could make life difficult for him if they chose to.

Buller had handed over the wicket-keeping gloves to Hugo Yarnold, quiet, unflappable, very underrated. Buller became county coach and helped with the second eleven that was established in 1948 and entered for the Minor Counties' Championship. Buller did a lot of bowling in Minor County matches. C. R. Maxwell, of whom so much had been expected with Notts and later Middlesex, but whose career was ruined by the war, played mainly in the seconds as wicket-keeper.

The 1948 season began with the Australians' visit to Worcester and with them, for the fourth and last time, Don Bradman. The great man hit only 107 this time, but it still left him with an average of over 200

Worcestershire, 1948. Back row (l to r): H. Yarnold, R. O. Jenkins, D. Kenyon, R. Howorth, E. Cooper and L. Outschoorn. Front row (l to r): P. F. Jackson, R. E. S. Wyatt, A. F. T. White, C. H. Palmer and R. T. D. Perks.

from his four innings at Worcester. Jackson bowled remarkably well to bowl Bradman and take five other wickets.

Outschoorn came to the fore with 1,178 Championship runs, and, of course, held some quite brilliant catches at slip or gully. He was born in Colombo, Ceylon, and had been taken prisoner of war by the Japanese at Singapore. He was a moody cricketer, but his engaging smile made him a popular one, and he was to score heavily for the County.

Wyatt was a splendid influence on the younger players with his sound technique and his willingness to converse on the science of the game. As a batsman, he was almost as good as he had been when a regular England player and, in many ways, more relaxed than in his Warwickshire days. He was an excellent model for a young batsman.

Eddie Cooper was as consistent as ever, and, like Palmer, he hit 50 against the Australians in the opening match, but Jenkins was the star of the year. In all matches he took 88 wickets and scored 1,356 runs. His memorable week came at the beginning of July. At Trent Bridge, he and Fred Cooper shared a stand of 170 and both men reached the

Worcester, 1948: Don Bradman and A. F. T. White, the captains, toss in front of the pavilion as the Australians begin their tour. Bradman hit 107 in this match, the only time in four visits that he failed to make a double century at New Road.

only century of their careers. From Nottingham, the team went to The Oval where Worcestershire won by eight wickets 'thanks largely to a brilliant all-round performance by Jenkins'. Surrey, not quite then the force they were to become a few years later, had moved smoothly past 200 in their first innings when Jenkins drew Constable forward and had him well stumped by Yarnold. Eric Bedser was bowled first ball, and Jenkins looked towards the pavilion to see who was coming

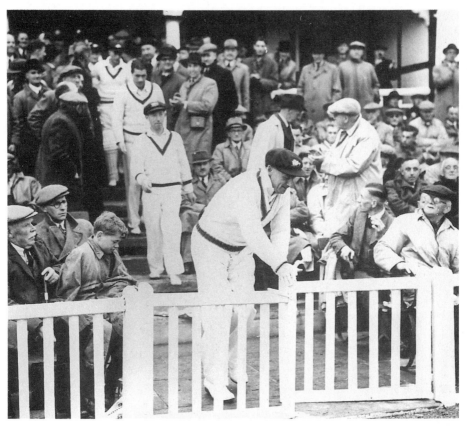

Bradman leads the Australians on to the field at Worcester, 1948.

in next. It was Stuart Surridge. Jenkins and Wyatt, who was leading Worcestershire that day, exchanged glances. Eddie Cooper was gestured to move to mid-on half-way back to the boundary. Jenkins, bowling from the pavilion end, tossed the ball up and Surridge, who could never resist a challenge, clouted it straight into Cooper's hands. Roly finished with six for 52, and then hit 81, but he was to have more in store for Surrey the following season.

He was picked to go to South Africa with George Mann's side, which was managed by the Worcestershire secretary, Brigadier M. A. Green. Jenkins was the outstanding bowler of the tour, for which he had been a late substitute for Eric Hollies. Reg Hayter's assessment of the England party drew special attention to the Worcestershire bowler:

> Chief cause for satisfaction was to be found in the rapid advance of Jenkins as a leg-break and googly bowler. Always ready to take

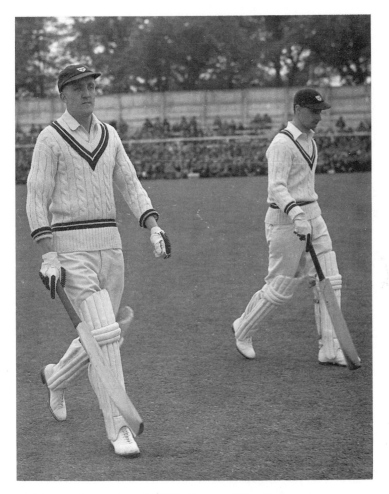

A Worcestershire opening pair: Eddie Cooper and Don Kenyon.

advice and learn from the experience of himself and of others, Jenkins quickly found the weakness of many South African batsmen against high-flighted and varied spin bowling.

Jenkins took an amazing 71 wickets on the tour, 16 of them in Test matches, a decisive contribution to England's series' victory. At Bulawayo, he encountered his old team-mates Martin and Singleton who were in the Rhodesian side.

Jenkins returned to England a better bowler and played a happy part in Worcestershire's joyful jubilee celebrations. His hat-trick against Surrey at The Oval in 1948 had been an appetiser for what was to come in 1949.

Charles Palmer and Eddie Cooper at New Road.

In July, Worcestershire lost to Surrey at The Oval, and it seemed that the return fixture at Worcester on 27, 29 and 30 August would follow the same pattern. The home side began disastrously, for in the first three quarters of an hour, Eddie Cooper, Kenyon, Outschoorn, Ainsworth and Bird were all back in the pavilion, the first four having been bowled by Surridge in the space of two overs. Palmer, who was also on the tour to South Africa and whose last season for Worcestershire this was, and Wyatt played steadily, but, after they had added 63, Wyatt was caught behind off Surridge. At 87 for six, Worcestershire were in deep trouble. Palmer was run out for 59. Reg Perks played a couple of lusty shots, but Alec Bedser took four wickets, and the home side were out for 142. By the close, Surrey were 140 for five, well in command, with Parker and McIntyre together.

McIntyre fell to Jenkins, caught by the incomparable Outschoorn early on the Monday morning, but the score advanced to 175, Parker and Laker unhurried, before there was a dramatic turn of events. Jenkins suddenly transformed the game. He had Parker caught behind, bowled Alec Bedser first ball and once more tempted Surridge into offering a catch to Perks and so complete his hat-trick. Jenkins then caught Laker off Howorth, and Surrey were all out for 180.

Worcestershire made 254 in their second innings, and this meant that Surrey needed 217 to win. At lunch on the last day, they were 82 for three.

At 93, Fishlock, who had been batting confidently, was caught by Bird off Jenkins. Fourteen runs later, Jenkins caught Barton off his own bowling, and in the next over, Howorth had Parker caught by Outschoorn. Jenkins had taken Barton's wicket with the last ball of the over, and with the first ball of the next, he dragged McIntyre forward and beat him to have him stumped by Yarnold. Alec Bedser came in and offered a return catch to give Jenkins his second hat-trick of the match. Laker became another Howorth-Outschoorn victim, and Jenkins ended the match when he caught and bowled Surridge. Surrey were out for 107, the last six wickets having fallen without a run being scored.

In 1949, Roly Jenkins hit 1,183 runs and took 183 wickets in all matches, 17 more than any other bowler, yet, in spite of this outstanding record and in spite of his success in South Africa, he played in none of the four Tests against New Zealand. He was, however, named as one of *Wisden's* 'Five Cricketers of the Year'.

The youngest of a family of ten, all of whom, the seven boys and three girls, were keen on sport, while father owned the winner of the Racing Pigeon Grand National of 1909, Roly Jenkins was recommended to the Worcestershire Club by one of its members, R. H. Williams, in 1936. He worked hard in second eleven and club and ground matches as well as gaining experience with Stourbridge in the Birmingham League before making his County debut against Essex in June 1938.

Roly Jenkins was such a fun cricketer that it is sometimes difficult to appreciate how much hard work went into making him the player he was. He was ever-ready to work, ever-ready to talk about the game and he was constantly thinking about it. There is a legend at Worcester that, on one occasion, when he was taking wickets regularly he insisted that all was not right and that he should be left out because he needed to practise and recapture his length and control. He went into the nets with a box of balls and bowled for hours on end, and those who passed by noted that he dropped every ball on the spot. Even in 1949, as the most prolific wicket-taker in the land, he went down to Maidstone to visit the great 'Tich' Freeman because he was afraid he was erring in basic technique. He would, and will, talk cricket all the time, and his wit and wisdom are a delight. To sit with him at a Test match at Edgbaston and listen to his comments on the lack of variety and adventure of what passes for spin bowling in recent England teams is often more rewarding than the game itself and certainly more entertaining.

Roly Jenkins.

He could never understand defensive bowling. When he took his two hat-tricks against Surrey he had figures of six for 112 in 27 overs and five for 54 in 15.3 overs. His run to the wicket was a short, fidgety roll, so appropriate of the name 'Roley' which was both a shortening of his Christian name and a nickname, and his delivery was almost round-arm, symbolically suggesting artfulness. He would toss the ball high in the air, but his command of flight, length and spin was always compounded by intelligent variety. He wanted to get a wicket every ball, and when you watched him you knew it.

Above all, he was an enjoyable cricketer. Once, at Cheltenham, George Emmett, the Gloucestershire batsman, hit him for four boundaries on the trot. As the home crowd roared approval, Jenkins looked down the wicket at Emmett and said: 'George, if you don't like me, say so—but for Christ's sake don't keep taking it out on the bloody ball!'

In an era when mass production was becoming the norm, people delighted in seeing a man of distinctive, humorous character. He was a favourite wherever he went.

Jenkins was not the only hero of Worcestershire's jubilee year. Eddie Cooper, Kenyon and Outschoorn, who hit 215 not out against Northants, scored 1,000 runs in Championship matches alone, and Howorth, in his benefit year, and Perks were as penetrative as ever. If Jackson took fewer wickets than in recent seasons, he was still an essential part of the attack and gave able support.

In the field, Worcestershire excelled. Outschoorn held a record 55 catches in the slip, gully and other close-to-the-wicket positions while Hugo Yarnold made history behind the stumps with 110 dismissals in all matches. This remains the third highest number of victims by a wicket-keeper in the history of the game, and he was only the fourth 'keeper after Ames, who did it three times, Huish, twice, and Duckworth to claim 100 dismissals in the season. What may seem remarkable to followers of the game today is that 47 of Yarnold's 110 victims were stumpings. Most of them came off Howorth and Jenkins, who were constantly beating or finding the outside edge as they turned the ball away from the bat. In recognition of his achievement, Hugo Yarnold was presented with a cheque for £100 by the Worcestershire Club.

For much of the season, Worcestershire were in contention for the title, but, in the end, they finished in third place, 20 points behind the joint champions Middlesex and Yorkshire. Undoubtedly, it was the two defeats at the hands of Middlesex which blighted Worcestershire's hopes. The first meeting of the two sides was at Worcester in July, when Jack Robertson hit 331 not out, his runs coming on the first day. A month later, in the return game at Lord's, Middlesex won by five wickets and ended Worcestershire's dreams of winning their first Championship.

One of the problems that Worcestershire had faced in 1949 was that neither Alan White nor Bob Wyatt could play regularly so that several of the leading amateurs captained the side during the season. White's career ended in 1949, and Wyatt was sole captain in 1950, or such was the intention, for Wyatt was a member of the Test selection committee and was able to play in only eleven Championship matches.

This could not have helped the side who still relied heavily on an ageing attack. Perks still took his 100 wickets and seemed as sharp as ever, presenting all sorts of problems for opposing batsmen, and Howorth, Jenkins and the durable and faithful Jackson were still formidable bowlers, but time was running out. Jenkins played in the famous Ramadhin and Valentine Test at Lord's and rivalled his West Indian adversaries with five for 116 and four for 174, but the age of the leg-spinner as an integral part of every side was drawing to its close although few realised it at the time.

The exciting arrival in attack was George Chesterton, a relentlessly accurate right-arm medium-pace bowler with a double Malvern connection in that he was both educated there and taught there. He was a tremendous asset to the County side, but he was able to assist only in the school holidays and his 47 matches for Worcestershire were spread over eight seasons.

Other young players to make their mark were Norman Whiting, a middle-order batsman, whose promise was not sustained, and George Dews who topped 1,000 runs and fielded magnificently in the outfield. He was to give wonderful service to the County in the Pearson tradition as was Bob Broadbent, who made his debut in the last match of the 1950 season. He hit a fine 77 as Worcestershire ran to 387 for nine against Leicestershire, but he suffered something of a trauma with his medium-pace bowling when Les Barry hit 18 off four balls. He caught Prentice, the Leicestershire opener, off Perks, and later held two more catches which set him on his way to the 298 he was to take for Worcestershire, who were gathering together a highly talented fielding side.

Worcestershire gained their seventh Championship win of the season in that final game at Leicester, and they owed much for the win not only to Dick Howorth, who took ten wickets, but to Don Kenyon, who hit 155. It was his sixth century of the season for the County and took him past 2,000 runs in Championship matches alone. He had now matured into a batsman of top quality and played in a Test trial and for the Players at Lord's. His defence was surer and that exquisite cover drive evoked memories of Wally Hammond at his best.

Kenyon's form was to remain consistent for the next 16 years. He was to become an England player, although he was never to do himself justice at international level, and he was to inspire Worcestershire to honours that years earlier had looked beyond their wildest dreams, but first there was to be a period of agony and reconstruction.

In 1951, Kenyon again passed 2,000 runs in first-class cricket and inspired the side to gloriously enterprising and entertaining batting. He was ably supported by Eddie Cooper, with whom he made an opening pair as good as any in the country, Broadbent, who had quickly developed into an attacking batsman, Outschoorn, sounder in defence, and the ebullient Dews. Jenkins also scored well as did Bird, and there were some useful contributions from Peter Richardson and Bob Wyatt.

At the age of 50, Wyatt was still captain, but he was in his last season and, with his other commitments, was able to play in less than half the games.

The attack was deprived of the dependable and hard-working Jackson, who had retired and whose off-breaks have never completely been replaced, but Howorth, Jenkins and Perks, still able to disturb most openers in the land, all took 100 wickets. There were more than 50 wickets, too, for the often wild Jack Flavell, who had taken 20 expensive wickets the previous season, but who was showing signs of being able to fill the place which Reg Perks must surely soon vacate.

The fielding was generally exhilarating, with Broadbent, Dews and Outschoorn outstanding, and the wicket-keeping of Hugo Yarnold as good as any in the country. He had followed his 110 victims of 1949 with 62 caught and 32 stumped in 1950. In 1951, he again topped the wicket-keepers' list with 58 caught and 37 stumped. In the match against Scotland at Broughty Ferry, he claimed seven victims in the second innings, including a world record six stumpings. He had had one stumping in the first innings. What was never appreciated by many who watched the calm, alert and skilful Yarnold was how much of the man's career was spent fighting against discomfort. Ultimately, he suffered the removal of both knee-caps and kept wicket in foam backed pads which gave added protection. Off the field, he wore a leg caliper to ease the strain. He retired in 1955, became an umpire and stood in a Test match. He was killed in a road accident in 1974 when he was returning from umpiring the game between Northants and Essex at Wellingborough.

The fielding, perhaps, reflected the exuberance of the batting in 1951. Worcestershire finished fourth in the table, the third best

Hugo Yarnold behind the stumps. Reg Perks is at slip.

performance in their first-class history, but their form came too late for them to be serious contenders for the title, which was won by neighbours Warwickshire. The last weeks of the season brought some memorable performances, however, none more memorable that the victory over Nottinghamshire at Worcester at the end of July.

Nottinghamshire made 300 in their first innings, Perks taking seven for 111. A century partnership for the second wicket between Kenyon, 70, and Outschoorn, 106, laid the foundation for Worcestershire's reply of 450 for nine declared, Broadbent, Bird and Jenkins all making useful contributions. J. D. Clay led Nottinghamshire's solid second innings with 96 out of 280 which was made at under three an over, Howorth bowling 30 overs and taking five for 42.

The Notts' second innings ended late on the last day, and Worcestershire were left ten minutes, plus an extra half an hour if desired, in which to score 131 if they wanted to win the match. The

Worcestershire, 1951. Back row (l to r): H. Yarnold, D. Kenyon,
G. H. Chesterton, N. H. Whiting, G. Dews, L. Outschoorn. Front row:
E. Cooper, R. E. Bird, R. E. S. Wyatt, R. T. D. Perks, R. Howorth.

expected pattern was ten minutes batting to fulfil the necessary time
requirement, and then the match agreed drawn, but Worcestershire
thought otherwise.

There was some surprise when Dews opened the innings with
Kenyon instead of Cooper, and Kenyon increased the surprise when
he opened the scoring by hooking Farr for six. When the normal span
of time was ended Worcestershire had scored 54 for 0 from five overs
and, seemingly intent on scoring at the required rate of 196 an hour,
they claimed the extra half hour. Kenyon was bowled by Smales after
he had hit 38 in 20 minutes, and Jenkins, who was sent in at number
three, ran all the way to the wicket and launched such a violent assault
on the bowling that he soon overtook Dews who, nevertheless, scored
43 in 35 minutes. Jenkins's 47 came in 15 minutes, and with the aid of a
bye, a leg-bye and a wide, Worcestershire reached their target with
five minutes to spare. They had scored 131 for 1 in 35 minutes. The
runs came off 12.1 overs, which, even in a Sunday League game to-day
would be a phenomenal rate of scoring.

Wisden remarked a year later that this was not only 'the best batting performance of the season, but one of the most notable in the whole history of cricket'. Yet it went almost unnoticed in the press and was not mentioned in *The Cricketer* until an angry letter from Peter Jackson of Surrey drew attention to the feat:

> Surely a comparable number of runs has *never* been scored more quickly in first-class cricket even late in an innings? But Worcestershire's feat was against fresh bowling. Why did it receive so little publicity? There have been many cases this season of a freakish scramble for points after nearly three days of unenterprising batting; but in this case runs had been scored at a good pace throughout the match.
>
> Apparently one reason for the lack of publicity was that no major 'daily' had a correspondent at the match; but I had hoped that *The Cricketer* might pay tribute to such a bold enterprise—the sort that can do cricket nothing but good—as well as to the sportsmanship of Simpson, the Nottinghamshire captain, who, in the words of almost the only daily paper to mention the affair, 'saw to it that no time was wasted.'
>
> It's an old gibe, I know, but one feels that such a welter of fours and sixes would have been bruited about much more if it had taken place at Lord's or The Oval.

The final comment was not made without justification. Worcestershire were not a fashionable team. They were homely and likeable, but the press did not see them as serious challengers for the Championship and ignored them accordingly, but at a time when there was growing concern about 'brighter cricket', it seems folly to have ignored such a performance. *The Cricketer* simply asked its readers for information regarding a 'better feast of quick scoring'.

Worcestershire's drama did not end with the victory over Nottinghamshire. A month later they visited Somerset at Taunton. This was a match of changing moods and fortunes and revolved around a confrontation between 'Laddie' Outschoorn and his skipper Bob Wyatt.

Outschoorn was, as we have said, a cricketer of varying moods who, according to Gerald Pawle, batted with such perversity at Worcester on one occasion, failing to hit the ball off the square, that Dick Howorth had said to him: 'You'll have us all out of work if you go on playing like that. We shan't have any members left by next season, and these people pay our wages!'

In the game at Taunton, splendid bowling by Roly Jenkins, who took seven for 81, saw Somerset dismissed for 231. Don Kenyon hit his third century in successive matches, passed 2,000 runs for the season and, with Bob Broadbent scoring an aggressive 91, Worcestershire took a first innings lead of 137 in spite of the fact that Outschoorn had retired hurt with an injured leg after scoring 37.

Worcestershire were in a commanding position, but Gimblett was dropped off Wyatt's bowling and went on to make 174 not out in 5 hours 40 minutes. Rogers declared at 350 for eight and left Worcestershire to make 214 in under two hours.

Wyatt asked Outschoorn how bad his leg was. Wyatt's biographer, Gerald Pawle, takes up the story:

> 'Oh, it's very bad,' said Outschoorn . . . 'very bad indeed.'
>
> 'You know we're batting last. Suppose we want about 10 to win . . . Will you go in to bat?'
>
> 'No!' said Laddie.
>
> He was told to pack his bag. Wyatt phoned the Worcestershire Secretary, Mike Green, and informed him that Outschoorn, fit or not, would not be required for the next match. He then borrowed a railway timetable and said to Laddie: 'There's your train. Report to Brigadier Green when you get back.' Many years later my informant, who was playing in the match, remarked admiringly: 'There was a good example of discipline for you. Bob, who had so often played on after suffering serious injury, had little sympathy for anyone who refused to make an effort in a crisis.'

Worcestershire kept pace with the clock in their search for 214 in under two hours, and Cooper, Howorth and Broadbent batted particularly well. Wyatt dropped down the order and came in when six wickets were down. The last ball of the match arrived with Buse bowling to Wyatt and six runs needed for a Worcestershire victory. Wyatt drove it high and hard straight into the pavilion, and a thrilling win had been achieved. There were two more matches, in the second of which Wyatt hit 59 and shared a third wicket stand of 104 with Broadbent, and that was the end of Wyatt's career with Worcestershire.

It was also the end of Dick Howorth's playing career. He had remained at the top of his form until the last, but, at the age of 43, he had decided to retire. His old skipper, now Lord Cobham, realising that Howorth still had a few good years left in him, asked him why he was retiring. 'Because it's not as much fun as it was,' was the all-rounder's reply.

A quiet, warm-hearted man, Dick Howorth remained somewhat disenchanted with the game for the rest of his life. A wonderfully determined and reliable cricketer, he was much respected and immensely popular, but, like many of us, he failed to accept the changes that were happening in the world and in cricket. He was not alone.

Dick Howorth.

Brigadier Green felt that the committee was unable to come to terms with the demands of the changing social attitudes. Green had twice managed MCC tours abroad and had paid the salary of scorer David Rabjohns who took over his job as secretary while away. This was not the custom at other counties, who were proud to see their secretary receive the honour of managing an England side abroad.

Green was a dynamic secretary whose energy and vision brought into existence the Worcestershire Supporters' Club Association in 1951. He enlisted the help of Jack Worrell and Tommy Jones of the Worcester *Evening News and Times* and persuaded Harold Morris, who had just ended his term of office as Mayor of Worcester, to be the first chariman of the association. It was an instant success and has raised vast sums of money for the County Club.

Major Jewell was a staunch supporter of Green, but Green felt that even he was fighting a losing battle and that the cautious and ultra conservative elements in the Club wer a hindrance to progress:

On my return from Australia, the annual general meeting was due to take place. The Chairman and committee were worried as the Club had lost about £1,400 in the 1950 season. This had been known before I left, and was not abnormal, but the accountants and bankers on the committee had been active on saving while I was away.

Two or three whose knowledge of cricket was not their strongest point started a general reduction in all directions.

It was a cautious policy which I knew would be fatal. At that time the playing staff had lost several older players and the new ones, young though they were, would have to come on at high salaries. One of these was Valentine, the West Indian, who did agree to play for Worcestershire but, when he heard he would lose his International status, he withdrew.

The pay for this player would have been more than the senior professionals were being given, therefore a general revision and increase would be essential. The prospect of long committee meetings, and also my leave to travel in future being restricted to a month, as the committee would never agree to a longer time again for another tour, bred in my mind the notion that I must seek my release. So I resigned as secretary to Worcestershire.

Green became rather bitter at what he saw as stagnation at Worcestershire and commented, when he visited New Road in 1954, that, in spite of the ground improvements brought about by the Supporters' Association, it was apparent that 'Worcestershire was becoming the paradise of the veteran player and discards from other counties.'

131

This is a harsh statement, but certainly the County had now entered a difficult period in their history. Not only did Howorth leave at the end of the 1951 season, but so, too, did Eddie Cooper who became coach and head groundsman at the Royal Naval College, Dartmouth.

Crisp, neat and fluent in style, Cooper was a very fine player, and an absolute delight to watch, but he was never quite the dominating force after the war that he had been in his three seasons before 1939. More than any, perhaps, his cricket suffered the loss of those seven years.

With Ronnie Bird, a sound batsman and a confident if unadventurous captain, now in charge, Worcestershire faced many problems. There was a desperate need for a slow left-arm bowler to replace Howorth and a seam bowler to assist the ever-green Perks, who still produced his 100 wickets a season. Jenkins completed the 'double' again in 1952, and there was promise from a young off-spinner named Martin Horton and from Ken Lobban, a fast bowler from Kidderminster. Lobban, Jamaican-born, took seven for 9 when Kidderminster bowled out Aston Unity for 19 in 1952, but he failed to sustain form at first-class level.

The batting was less of a worry with Outschoorn, very sound in defence but also capable of bold attack, Broadbent, a fine attacking player but a nervous starter, Bird, a young Peter Richardson and the incomparable Kenyon all doing well. Kenyon, indeed, scored 2,489 runs in 1952 and the following year, when he played for England against Australia, he became the first Worcestershire batsman to hit a century against the Australians. The tour opened at New Road, and Kenyon hit 122 before being bowled by Benaud. Broadbent hit Miller out of the ground, but Miller retaliated later with an innings of 220 not out.

Two players signed from Yorkshire, John Ashman and John Whitehead, played their first games for Worcestershire on that occasion. Ashman was a slow left-arm bowler whose trial was extended when Jenkins was injured, but he was not a success. The fast-medium pace Whitehead had had some experience with Yorkshire for a few seasons and did reasonably well with Worcestershire, but neither player proved to be the answer to the County's problems.

Kenyon continued to shine through all the adversities, as did Reg Perks, and Richardson, Dews, who had missed much of the 1952 season with injury, and Broadbent scored freely, but Richardson was on national service in 1954, Horton was rarely available, and two Australians, Hughes and Harkness, after showing some promise, decided to return to their native country. The most surprising acquisition for 1954 was Charles Grove, who had been released after 15 years with Warwickshire and was signed by Worcestershire to share the new ball with Perks. As Grove was 41 and Perks 42, it is

Martin Horton.

doubtful whether any county has ever fielded an older opening attack. Grove dropped out of the side in mid-July, and Flavell, young and inconsistent, shared the new ball with Perks who, in spite of suffering from a plethora of dropped catches, still claimed his 100 wickets in a dreadfully wet summer.

Kenyon remained a man for all weathers. He was the first cricketer in the country to reach 1,000 runs and the first to 2,000. Indeed, only

133

one other batsman, Livingston, the Australian who played for Northants, scored 2,000 runs, but he was 367 short of Kenyon's 2,636 in all matches. Kenyon hit six centuries, two of them double hundreds, but he was not chosen for a Test against Pakistan nor was he named in the party that went to Australia, although the fact that England used four different opening partners for Hutton on that tour suggests that he was very much needed.

The gradual reshaping of the Worcestershire Club was taking place. The new score-board, built through the fund-raising efforts of the Supporters' Association, was opened in 1954, and the secretary, Major Bayly, was given an assistant, Joe Lister. Lister played twice for Yorkshire in 1954, and then had the distinction of playing for Worcestershire against Cambridge University later in the season. Lister had, and has, an innate grasp of the needs of the game. He was a very hard-hitting batsman with a fine tactical sense and a business acumen and administrative ability that was to make him an outstanding secretary. He had the advantage of serving his apprentice-ship in the difficult years. He became joint secretary with Peter Richardson in 1956 and 1957 and took over sole responsibility in 1958, holding the post until 1971 when he left to take up a similar position with Yorkshire.

Worcestershire made a radical move in 1955 when they appointed Reg Perks as captain. For a Club which had thrived on the amateur tradition, it was a giant step and a tacit acknowledgement of the changing times. It was a most popular choice, for no man has served a county better or with such unswerving endeavour and loyalty.

The season began encouragingly with victory over the South African tourists. This was a strong South African side, and this was the only defeat that they suffered outside the Test series. The Worcester-shire victory was based on fine knocks from Kenyon and Outschoorn, and excellent bowling by Bob Berry, the former Lancashire and England slow left-arm bowler, who was making his debut for Worcestershire, the county against whom he had taken all ten wickets for Lancashire in 1953. Berry was to play 94 matches for Worcester-shire and to become a capped player with 250 wickets to his credit, but he moved to Derbyshire in 1959 and gained his third county cap. The lasting impression is of a talent not fully realised. His first bowling spell for Worcestershire, however, brought him five South African wickets for 60 and gave his county a first innings lead of 51. Resolute batting took the home side to 209 in their second innings and left the tourists a target of 261, and 220 minutes in which to get the runs.

Heavy showers had made the pitch wet, and . . .

when Perks moved Berry to the Diglis end he fortunately provided ideal conditions for Horton, who, bowling from the New Road end, so completely bewildered the opposition with his off-spinners that he finished the match with this analysis: 12.5 overs, 4 maidens, 25 runs, 8 wickets, taking nine for 56 in the innings—easily the best performance of his short career.

In fact, it was to remain the best performance of Horton's career, although many notable feats were to follow, and it heralded what was for him an outstanding first full season, for, at the age of 21, he completed the 'double' in all matches.

Unfortunately, the success against South Africa did not continue for the County, who had to wait until the beginning of July for their first Championship victory. There was a lack of substance in the batting and it was not until Lister and Dick Richardson, both aggressive players, came into the side late in the season that there was much sign of scoring power in the lower order. Kenyon, of course, took all the responsibility on his shoulders and once more topped 2,000 runs in all matches.

The bowling lacked consistency, particularly as Roly Jenkins missed the early matches through illness, but there were some notable performances. At Dover, in August, with Perks out of the side, Jack Flavell took nine Kent first-innings wickets for 30. This was to remain the best bowling performance of his career although he was, as yet, not the power he was to become a few seasons later. He seemed to have a taste for the Kent batting, for the first of his three hat-tricks had come against them at Kidderminster in 1951.

It was a disappointment for Worcestershire, for Perks and for many followers of the game that the County did not do better in what the great professional decided was to be his last season, his one and only of captaincy. He was 43 and decided that the time had come to say goodbye to county cricket, although he was to serve on the Club committee for some years.

He arrived at Bournemouth for the last match of the season with 95 wickets to his credit and soon made it 96 when he bowled his old team-mate Henry Horton. Rayment, Rogers, Barnard and Sainsbury all followed, without the help of a fielder, to give 100 wickets in a season. It was the 16th time that he had achieved the feat. Only Rhodes, Shackleton and Freeman have taken 100 wickets in a season on more occasions.

It was appropriate that Perks's career should end at Bournemouth, for it was there, 27 years earlier, when, as the twelfth man and scorer, he had had his first taste of county cricket with Worcestershire.

The words 'faithful', 'loyal', 'honest', 'true' tumble over each other when there is talk of Perks. His friend John Arlott will say of him simply: 'He was a lovely man'. The affection in which he was held can best be seen by the fact that, hearing he was unwell, his old captain,

Lord Cobham, drove 25 miles through snow and harsh weather to see Perks shortly before he died in 1977. The world was a lesser place for his parting.

To succeed Perks as captain, Worcestershire appointed Peter Richardson, the left-handed opening batsman who had come from the Cathedral School, Hereford, and who had scored 2,294 runs in 1953, his second full season in first-class cricket. He was 25-years-old and had initially been an attractive stroke-maker in the amateur tradition, but, as his career progressed, particularly after he became an England opener, he eschewed his back-lift and became a nudger and deflector and pusher so that it was said of him and his brother Dick, a more attractive but more vulnerable batsman, that 'Peter had five strokes but only played three while Dick had six and always played eight'. Whether that be true or not, Peter Richardson scored very many first-class runs and enjoyed a successful Test career.

With his experience of captaincy limited, Peter Richardson would obviously lean heavily on the senior players, and the position was not helped by the new captain becoming a regular England player during his first season of leadership. Peter Richardson was an enthusiast, however, and his enthusiasm was infectious, never more apparent than in the fielding which, in 1956, came close to its former standard of excellence with Dick Richardson, Dews and Broadbent all being high on the list of catchers in the country, and Roy Booth, following the Yorkshire tradition of wicket-keepers, proving to be an excellent successor to Yarnold, who had retired. Booth was so impressive that he was awarded his County cap after his first season.

It had been hoped that Flavell would take over the mantle of Perks, but he missed many matches through illness and it was Coldwell and Aldridge, both raw but full of pace and heart, who made the greater impression. The spin bowling was varied and penetrative, with Berry, Horton and the effervescent Jenkins performing consistently well.

Roly Jenkins was a fine senior professional, full of artistry, thought, endeavour, anecdotes and cheerful aggression. He was of tremendous value to the side in that he took over as captain when Richardson was on Test duty. Peter Richardson played in all five Tests against Australia in 1956 and hit a century at Old Trafford in the match in which Laker took 19 wickets.

Jenkins was captain when Yorkshire came to Kidderminster in July 1956. He won the toss and Worcestershire batted. Don Kenyon batted throughout the first day. Having taken 244 minutes to reach his first hundred, his second came in 119 minutes. When he arrived at the ground on the Thursday he found Roly Jenkins pacing up and down undecided as to what to do. The Yorkshire players had anticipated an overnight declaration, and some of the later order, Johnny Wardle

The Richardson brothers: Peter, Brian and Derek.

among them, had adjourned to a nearby hostelry to enjoy some pre-lunch refreshment. Kenyon began to put on his fielding flannels when Jenkins asked what he was doing. Kenyon looked surprised, but Roly announced that they were batting on. Wardle was not amused to be called hurriedly from his social engagement and showed his displeasure by bowling an opening over which, at the kindest, could only be described as mundane. Vic Wilson, the Yorkshire skipper, was furious, and Wardle was banished to the outfield. Don Kenyon seized on the situation to enjoy himself to finish with 259 in 7 hours 35 minutes. His innings, the highest of his career and the highest against Yorkshire this century, included a six and 31 fours. Jenkins declared when Kenyon was sixth out at 440.

In three and a quarter hours, Yorkshire were bowled out by the Worcestershire spinners for 163, and the game was over before lunch on the third day when, with Horton taking five for 64 and Jenkins four for 61, Yorkshire succumbed for 183.

The amount to which Worcestershire depended upon Jenkins and Kenyon became manifest in 1957 when Jenkins, so long the mainstay of the side's slow bowling, completely lost his form. His ability to spin the ball prodigiously was as constant as ever, but the 'mechanics' of flight, length and direction deserted him, and, in spite of hours of dedicated practice, they never returned sufficiently to satisfy Jenkins himself. He retired after a handful of matches in 1958 and a spark of fun in the game was extinguished.

With Peter Richardson on Test duty, and for one match brother Dick too, and Jenkins absent, there were constant changes of leadership and victories were few as the County dropped to 16th in the table, their lowest point for 23 years. There were some rays of hope, notably in the bowling of Jack Flavell, who took 101 wickets, 97 in the Championship, and of further promise from Coldwell, but it was the inability to bowl out opponents twice, the vital ingredient for a Championship-winning side, that was the blatant weakness. Even

Worcestershire, 1957. (L to r): D. W. Richardson, R. G. Broadbent, L. J. Coldwell, G. H. Chesterton, M. J. Horton, R. Booth, J. Flavell, P. E. Richardson, D. Kenyon, G. Dews and L. Outschoorn.

without Peter Richardson, there were plenty of runs from Kenyon, Dick Richardson, Broadbent, Dews and Horton. Booth, magnificent behind the stumps, Dews and Dick Richardson were among the leading fielders in the country.

Worcestershire played joyful cricket, but, as Don Kenyon, a tough competitor, has said since: 'We knew from the start of the season that we were never going to win anything. We just enjoyed playing.' They were good to watch, but the time was approaching when that would no longer be accepted as sufficient, for there were other interests and leisure pursuits and people no longer flocked to cricket as they had done in the years immediately after the war.

George Dews.

Thanks to the tremendous efforts of the Supporters' Association, the Club was no longer beset by financial problems, and the improvements that had been made to the ground never threatened its essential character.

Peter Richardson was relieved of his secretarial duties in an effort to allow him to concentrate his efforts on leading the side on the field, and Joe Lister became the senior administrator, the sole secretary.

In 1958, there were signs that these changes could bear fruit. More games were won, and the realisation that 17-year-old Doug Slade possessed great potential as a left-arm spinner as well as a competent batsman was heartening. Flavell was becoming established as successor to Perks in consistency and pace, and Pearson, whose action had once been under scrutiny, took 60 Championship wickets to make a good pace quartet with Aldridge, Flavell and Coldwell. Even an injury that kept Kenyon out of the side for several matches did not totally blight the side for whom Horton and Dews performed especially well with the bat. The fielding was good, and, day in day out, Booth had no superior behind the stumps anywhere in the country. The season ended with victory over Surrey at The Oval.

In fairness to Surrey, who had just won the Championship for the seventh year in succession, the game was ruined by rain and they declared 120 runs behind in order to keep the game alive, but for Worcestershire, it was some compensation for the defeat four years earlier when they had been bowled out for 25 and 40.

It was a cheering way to end the year, but clouds suddenly lowered over the Club in the following winter. Peter Richardson was troubled by personal problems, and it was decided that he should leave the County and move to Kent whom he was to serve with distinction.

Worcestershire suddenly found themselves in need of a captain. Jenkins had gone or he would have been the obvious choice. Where to turn? The committee decided to appoint Don Kenyon.

THE KENYON YEARS

DON KENYON COULD NEITHER HAVE anticipated nor coveted the captaincy of Worcestershire. Reared in the old tradition of the amateur skipper, he had been playing for the County since 1946 and was 35 years old. The circumstances in which he had taken over the captaincy were hardly encouraging, nor were the times themselves propitious.

Cricket was in a state of uncertainty and unhappiness. It was going through a period of dullness. Its social structure was being questioned, and it was wracked by controversy and self-questioning. England had returned from Australia where, not only had they lost the Test series by four matches to nil, but they had suffered a series of injuries, and the whole tour had been soured by the doubts over the legality of the actions of some of the Australian bowlers, notably Meckiff and Rorke.

These doubts were also cast on the legality of the actions of two Worcestershire bowlers. In the opening match of the 1959 season, against the Indian tourists, Kenyon's first game as captain, umpire Buller no-balled Pearson five times for throwing. Centuries by Dews and Broadbent could not dispel the worry over this incident, and the concern was compounded later in the season when Aldridge, too, was called for throwing.

Don Kenyon. A quarter of a century on, he remains the hero of Worcestershire.

Both men worked hard to rectify their faults, but both were called again the following season and left the game within a couple of years.

This was not the happiest of starts for the new skipper, and nothing in Kenyon's first season in the job suggested that there would be a resurgence in the fortunes of Worcestershire cricket. The worries over Pearson and Aldridge meant that Coldwell finally became settled as the ever-improving Flavell's opening partner, and Coldwell accepted his chance well, but the spin bowling department almost disappeared. Horton scored more than 2,000 runs and played twice for England, but his off-breaks had little success. With both bat and ball, Slade, so promising the year before and seen as Howorth's natural successor, failed completely. Ron Headley, a left-hander who had played twice in 1958 and excited much favourable comment, was also bitter disappointment, and with Broadbent and Outschoorn, in his benefit year, falling away, the County seemed in a state of retrogression rather than resurgence.

Kenyon shouldered responsibilities well and his batting did not suffer. Dews and Dick Richardson were pugnacious, and Roy Booth added 1,000 runs in the season to his handsome wicket-keeping, but there was little else to lighten the gloom.

A win at Bristol and at Dudley over Northants seemed only another false dawn as Worcestershire began the 1960 season, and the same old pattern was developing. There had been an emphasis on youth, but Martin Horton suffered a broken bone in a knee cap which kept him out for five weeks and deprived the side of the experience that was necessary to encourage the youth, although the thoughtful Horton himself was only 26.

With Kenyon absent, George Dews, in his benefit year, led the side for three matches in June, all of which were away fixtures, the last at Tunbridge Wells. It was decided to include a 20-year-old slow left-arm bowler for this match, Norman Gifford.

It is a reflection of the way in which cricket had changed that Gifford made his first-class debut in an all-professional side. Indeed, Alan Duff, the Oxford leg-spinner, played four games for Worcestershire late in the season, and he was the only amateur to appear for the County in 1960. The distinction between professionals and amateurs in cricket was soon to be abolished.

In the years that have elapsed since his first-class debut, Norman Gifford has often entertained dinner gatherings with the story of the game at Tunbridge Wells. It began so well when he bowled Phebey to claim his first-class wicket within an hour of play. He later took some stick from the left-handed Peter Jones, who hit 73 in 95 minutes with two sixes and nine fours, but Gifford took the last three wickets and ended with four for 63, a highly satisfactory debut.

The trouble was, as *Wisden* explained:

The pitch, grassless and soft at first, dried under a hot sun, leaving crusty edges on the indentations made when the ball dug in earlier. No two deliveries behaved alike; many rising sharply, some keeping low and nearly all deviating to an unaccustomed degree. Worcestershire, not the strongest of batting sides, floundered against Brown and Halfyard, both of whom needed to do little more than turn over their arms. The pitch did the rest.

Worcestershire began their first innings at 3.50 pm, and it ended at 5.25 pm. As there was a 20-minute tea break at 4.15 pm, the innings had lasted for 75 minutes. Six wickets had gone down for nine runs, and although the target was only 38, Worcestershire never looked likely to avoid the follow-on.

Mainly due to a stubborn innings by Broadbent, the second innings lasted 95 minutes, and the match was over ten minutes into the extra half hour which Cowdrey had claimed. An example of what the batsmen suffered can be seen from Booth's fate in the second innings. The ball flew off one of the many patches, caught the top of Booth's bat, shot up and hit him on the cheek from where it lobbed to the close field for a catch.

Excited at being in the Worcestershire side, delighted at his initial success, Gifford found himself on the way home at 8.00 pm on the first day of the match, the game completed. At least Worcestershire had been a part of cricket history, and this extraordinary match is worth recording.

The wisdom of playing two slow left-arm spinners was doubted in some quarters, but it paid dividends. From mid-July onwards, the side began to play positive cricket and earn points. Slade finished with 92 Championship wickets, and Gifford a most encouraging 31. Flavell was the spearhead of the attack, and the batting, 'not the strongest' earlier in the season, took on a firmer look as Headley grew in confidence and Richardson, Dews and Kenyon reached their best form. Suddenly, there was a note of cautious optimism, even though the County had remained low in the table.

To the discerning, it could be seen that Kenyon was shaping the side to his own beliefs and requirements. Outschoorn had retired after years of solid run-getting and blinding catches, and even Broadbent stood down at times as a younger, larger pool of players was given a taste of first team cricket. Much emphasis was placed on the quality of the fielding. In this respect, Roy Booth was an inspiration.

In all matches, in 1960, he hit 936 runs, took 85 catches and made 16 stumpings, so coming very close to the elusive wicket-keeper's 'double'. He had played for Yorkshire from 1951 to 1955, but the

KENT *v* WORCESTERSHIRE

Played at the Nevill Ground, Tunbridge Wells on 15 June 1960

KENT WON BY AN INNINGS AND 101 RUNS

KENT	**FIRST INNINGS**	
P. E. Richardson	b Flavell	23
A. H. Phebey	b Gifford	16
*M. C. Cowdrey	c Broadbent b Pearson	17
R. C. Wilson	c Headley b Flavell	0
S. E. Leary	st Booth b Slade	23
P. H. Jones	c Broadbent b Slade	73
A. L. Dixon	c Dews b Pearson	17
†A. W. Catt	st Booth b Gifford	0
D. J. Halfyard	st Booth b Gifford	0
A. Brown	b Gifford	1
P. A. Shenton	not out	7
Extras	b 7, lb 2, nb 1	10
Total		187

Fall: 1-41, 2-43, 3-43, 4-68, 5-104, 6-151, 7-154, 8-161, 9-179

BOWLING	**O**	**M**	**R**	**W**
Flavell	18	8	25	2
Pearson	16	7	35	2
Slade	18	5	54	2
Gifford	17	5	63	4

WORCESTERSHIRE	**FIRST INNINGS**		**SECOND INNINGS**	
R. G. A. Headley	b Halfyard	0	c Wilson b Halfyard	0
J. B. Sedgley	c Leary b Brown	7	c Richardson b Brown	2
A. H. Spencer	b Brown	0	c Leary b Brown	4
D. W. Richardson	b Brown	0	b Halfyard	2
R. G. Broadbent	b Halfyard	0	c Catt b Halfyard	22
*G. Dews	lbw b Brown	0	b Brown	0
†R. Booth	b Brown	2	c Shenton b Halfyard	7
D. N. F. Slade	b Halfyard	9	c Leary b Shenton	11
N. Gifford	not out	0	c Brown b Shenton	4
D. B. Pearson	b Halfyard	0	c Cowdrey b Halfyard	2
J. A. Flavell	b Brown	1	not out	0
Extras	b 1, lb 5	6	b 5, lb 1, w 1	7
Total		25		61

1st inns: 1-6, 2-7, 3-8, 4-9, 5-9, 6-9, 7-24, 8-24, 9-24
2nd inns: 1-0, 2-6, 3-7, 4-17, 5-18, 6-40, 7-51, 8-51, 9-61

BOWLING	**O**	**M**	**R**	**W**	**O**	**M**	**R**	**W**
Halfyard	9	4	7	4	13		20	5
Brown	8.5	1	12	6	8	2	22	3
Shenton					4.5	0	12	2

Umpires: T. J. Bartley and J. S. Buller

Worcestershire were defeated in one day.

*Captain; †Wicket-keeper

presence of Binks had stopped him from gaining a regular place, and so he followed the much-trodden wicket-keeping road from Yorkshire to Worcestershire, for whom he first played in 1956. Tall, slim, immaculate in dress and style, he exuded confidence without flamboyance, and for five or six seasons it is doubtful if he had a superior in the country. He was an intelligent, perceptive, determined and loyal cricketer and as such was of immense value to the skipper.

Kenyon knew what he wanted. A highly intelligent man, he was quick to see the changes that were taking place in the game and in the expectations of those who paid to watch it. In the importance he placed on fielding, he saw the need to adapt to the modern game, and he enforced changes. In all counties, for many years, it had been customary to place some of the older players in close-to-the-wicket positions so that they would be spared undue running in the outfield. Kenyon wanted his best fielders in the positions where catches were offered, and Gifford, Dick Richardson, Slade and Standen were the men who often clustered round the bat.

Jim Standen had first appeared for Worcestershire in 1960. The following year he played in 26 matches, a useful medium-pace bowler, valuable late order batsman and, as Kenyon will assert, a fielder without parallel. Standen was a goalkeeper with Arsenal and West Ham United with whom he won a Cup Winners' medal and a European Cup Winners' Cup medal. He was a superbly fit, happy and likeable extrovert, who could and did catch everything within his reach and much that was not. Kenyon recognised him as a cricketer of immense value even though his football commitments were to restrict his appearances. Kenyon knew, too, the importance of strength in depth which give the team the substance to meet any emergency.

The side was provided with the bonus of the late maturation of Flavell and Coldwell. Flavell was 32 when he won his first England cap in 1961, and Coldwell was 29 when he followed him in to the England side a year later. Jack Flavell, who had played soccer for Walsall, worked hard at his cricket. He had fire from the start, and he was always strong and whole-hearted, but he added accuracy and control through sheer perseverance. He made himself an England bowler, and a bowler whom many would do well to emulate for he maintained a relentless attack on the stumps, never allowing a batsman a moment's respite.

Like Jack Flavell, Len Coldwell was not well treated by injuries, but like Flavell, Coldwell had a big heart. He hailed from Devon and was recommended to the County by Eddie Cooper. He arrived for trial covered in cuts and bruises sustained in an accident on his way up from Devon, but he proceeded to give great discomfort to some of the senior batsmen. He fought his way through stern competition to

Jim Standen.

become Flavell's new ball partner, and he was the perfect complement
to the fiery, red-head (not only because he himself was thinning a little
on top). Coldwell relied much on the in-swinger and on variety of
pace. He moved the ball disconcertingly late and often surprised with
the away swinger. Like Flavell, he was relentlessly accurate so that, for
the batsman, there was no escape. Like all great quick bowlers, Flavell
and Coldwell hunted in pairs.

Gifford was given the slow left-arm spot, and with Horton
providing the off-breaks, Worcestershire had a perfectly balanced

Jack Flavell.

attack supported by wicket-keeping of the highest quality and dynamic fielding in the close catching positions. Mention has been made of Standen's abilities in this respect, but Dick Richardson, too, was a fielder of exceptional ability. He was a wonderfully free and happy cricketer who knew no fear, and, in 1961, he established a Worcestershire record with 65 catches.

As an enterprising batsman, Richardson continued to score prolifically. Horton, Dews, Kenyon, Broadbent and Booth were eminently reliable, and Ron Headley had begun to fulfil all the promise that he had shown when he first appeared for Worcestershire at the age of 19. Ron Headley carried the weight of being the son of the man who is considered by many to be the greatest West Indian batsman of all time. George Headley was a Jamaican who had come to play for Dudley in the Birmingham League, and Ron followed his father into the Dudley side, rattling up his centuries while still a teenager. Unlike his father, Ron Headley batted left-handed, but he shared the West Indian eagerness to attack the bowling, and his ferocious and elegant driving was a delight to the eye. He also fitted the Kenyon requirements in that he was an exceptionally fine fielder in any position, snapping up catches close to the wicket or attacking the batsman from the outfield with his feline grace.

Headley had a very fine season with the bat in 1961 when, in the early stages of the season, there seemed to be little difference from the previous season. It was discovered that Doug Slade, who had sustained an injury while playing football in the winter, was more seriously injured than had been realised, and after a couple of matches he was out for the rest of the season. But it was against such mishaps as this that Kenyon had planned and built his squad. He was ably supported off the field by coach Charlie Hallows, by the chairman of the cricket committee, the Hon Richard Lygon and, later, by the President Sir George Dowty, a man of vision and energy. There was a new sense of discipline and urgency in the Club, and there was competition for places, for, among those waiting in the wings, there was Tom Graveney, whose batting was sheer beauty and who had touched greatness.

Graveney had left Gloucestershire, with whom he had won an international reputation, after he had been deprived of the captaincy. He had been hurt by the decision, but Gloucestershire had opposed his departure, and he had to spend a year qualifying for the county across the border.

Graveney's time with Worcestershire lay in the future. For the present, the County got off to a moderate start and at the end of June 1961, they were eleventh in the table, so that it looked very much as if it would be business as usual.

Then came a transition. At the beginning of July, Warwickshire were beaten on a difficult wicket at New Road. Batting was slow and cautious, and Jack Flavell took five wickets on the last day. Later the same week, at Dudley, Headley and Kenyon shared a second wicket stand of 170, both reaching 150. On the last morning, Jack Flavell became the first bowler in the country to reach 100 wickets and Worcestershire beat Somerset by 233 runs.

Rain ruined the return local derby match with Warwickshire as it did the match with Gloucestershire at Worcester when Jack Flavell took seven for 24 and the visitors were bowled out for 83. The teams travelled from New Road to Bristol for the return game which went very much in favour of Gloucestershire. Flavell and Standen survived the last few hectic overs to save the game.

There was defeat at Somerset, but Leicestershire were beaten so that Worcestershire found themselves fifth at the end of July and being written of as Championship contenders.

Glamorgan, Northants, Essex, Middlesex and Lancashire were swept aside in quick succession, and the people of Worcestershire themselves even began to believe that the Championship could be possible. Hopes were dashed at Bradford. Yorkshire, always doughty opponents and nursing dreams of topping the table themselves, were faced by a Worcestershire side without Kenyon and Dews, ill, and Flavell, called up for the Test match. Yorkshire won by an innings and ended Worcestershire's Championship hopes, but the County clung on to fourth place, and there was a new look about all they did. They had bowled their overs faster than any other side in the country, and, in so doing, had emphasised their positive approach and given themselves more time in which to get wickets. Four bowlers, Flavell, Coldwell, Horton, who did the 'double', and Gifford had taken 100 wickets in all matches. Gifford had 118 Championship wickets and a county cap in his first full season.

George Dews retired at the end of the 1961 season, but, in spite of this loss, Worcestershire looked to be an even stronger side for the 1962 campaign. Tom Graveney, a middle-order batsman of world class, was available to bolster the batting. Slade was fit again, and Duncan Fearnley, Alan Ormrod, Bob Carter and Fred Rumsey were young men able to bring strength to the pool of players. Excitement was high. There were, however, to be disappointments.

Flavell began in tremendous form, but, after taking 89 wickets by the second week in July, he strained an Achilles tendon and was out for the rest of the season. This was a serious loss and played a significant part in what happened in August. On top of this, Headley broke his right wrist, and Horton, Coldwell and Broadbent were all unavailable at one time or another because of injury.

The season began wonderfully well. Rain robbed Worcestershire of victory in the opening match against Glamorgan at Worcester, but Middlesex, so long a bogey side, were beaten at Lord's, and Northamptonshire and Kent were also brushed aside. When Yorkshire came to New Road, Flavell and Coldwell proved more effective than Trueman and Platt, who nevertheless took ten wickets, in a match dominated by the seamers. Needing to get 229 to win in three hours, Yorkshire ended on 103 for 7 and were thankful that Illingworth and Vic Wilson had batted in stubborn fashion to save them from defeat. A victory at Trent Bridge and a draw in a high-scoring game with Middlesex, were followed by an innings victory over Essex at Romford. From there, Worcestershire travelled to Tunbridge Wells where the return game with Kent was drawn. Somerset, fresh from their victory over the Pakistan tourists, were the next visitors to New Road.

Kenyon won the toss, and he and Horton opened the batting against Ken Palmer and Bill Alley. Eight minutes before lunch, the first wicket fell when Kenyon was bowled by Palmer for 97. In 127 minutes, he and Horton had put on 167, and although Headley was run out without scoring, Worcestershire lunched at 172 for 2. In the afternoon session, Horton and Graveney completely dominated the bowling. They added a record 315 in under three hours for the third wicket. Horton reached his highest score in first-class cricket, 233, which was also the highest score made in 1962, while Graveney finished with 164 not out. Horton's runs were made out of 481 in 284 minutes and included 36 fours. Kenyon declared and left some 50 minutes batting for Somerset before the close during which they hit 72 for the loss of Atkinson.

Worcestershire's 520 for three declared was the highest county score for five years and had been scored at a phenomenal rate. The first hundred came in 73 minutes after which the timetable was as follows:

200 in 140 minutes
300 in 202 minutes
400 in 244 minutes
520 in 310 minutes

Somerset were unable to cope with the in-swing bowling of Len Coldwell and were out for 270, bolstered by an eighth wicket stand of 83 between Lomax and Langford. Horton bowled Langford and finished with three for 68. Under the existing rules, Worcestershire could not enforce the follow-on, but they had to bat again and plundered runs quickly so that Kenyon was able to declare and set Somerset to make 406 in 305 minutes. They lost two wickets for 26 before the close, and the game was over before lunch on the third day.

This was heady stuff from Worcestershire, who were now second in the table, undefeated, and, in the eyes of many, the best balanced and most accomplished side in the Championship.

Coldwell had taken seven for 74 in the match and had heard that he had been selected for England. Horton had added six for 119 to his 233. In an age of covered wickets when his side relied predominantly on a seam attack, Horton's bowling opportunities became fewer, but he and Gifford and Slade still turned several matches in Worcestershire's favour. Horton was a powerful batsman of even temperament. He could hit hard on both sides of the wicket, and his totally professional approach to the game made his partnership with Kenyon one of the most awesome and prolific in the country. If and when the opposition succeeded in breaking it, they still had Headley, Graveney, Richardson, Broadbent and Booth to contend with.

After the triumph against Somerset there was a draw at Old Trafford and an innings victory over Glamorgan at Neath. Northamptonshire, whose only defeat in the season had been at the hands of Worcestershire in May, were the visitors to Kidderminster on the last day of June. Tom Graveney hit 115, but Norman and Lightfoot scored heavily and with Crump taking ten wickets in the match, Northants won by eight wickets. This was Worcestershire's first defeat of the season, and it came on 3 July, leaving them unbeaten longer than any other county.

The defeat at Kidderminster had been a painful one, for it was in this match that Headley sustained a broken wrist which put him out for the rest of the season. Worse was to follow.

At Stourbridge, without Graveney and Coldwell who were on Test duty, Worcestershire trailed Lancashire by 63 on the first innings, but they were bowled back into the game by spinners Horton and Gifford and were left to score 184 to win. This was by no means an easy task on a pitch on which twenty wickets had fallen on the first day, but Horton, on top of his form, played a gem of an innings. He and Kenyon attacked the bowling from the start and runs came at more than four an over. Kenyon was lbw for 46 with the score on 85, and Fearnley who, if he never quite translated the dominance he showed in second team cricket to the first-class game, played a valuable innings for Worcestershire, batting with great sense, and giving the strike to Horton at every opportunity. Horton was in total command of the bowling. He hit two sixes, a five and 12 fours in his 111 not out in 143 minutes, and Worcestershire won by nine wickets in two days.

Warwickshire were the next visitors to New Road and were always on top in a low-scoring match. It was a game in which nothing went right for Worcestershire who, uncharacteristically, dropped several catches and were beaten in two days. Moreover, having bowled six overs in the second innings, Flavell hobbled from the field and from the Worcestershire side for the rest of the season.

There was an encouraging win over Somerset at Bath and a draw at Edgbaston, but Worcestershire travelled to Gloucester without Graveney and Gifford, playing in the last Gentlemen and Players fixture, Flavell, Headley and Coldwell, all injured. As often happens in such circumstances, the second team players who took the places of the regulars performed admirably, but some of the more established players did not do quite so well.

Bob Carter and Fred Rumsey, two big, genial men, bowled at a brisk pace and never allowed Gloucestershire to settle. The home side were all out for 221, Carter three for 75, Rumsey five for 37. This was an excellent start for Worcestershire, and Kenyon and Horton began purposefully enough in reply, but suddenly the innings fell apart, and five wickets were down for 59 runs. The slide was halted by Ormrod and Booth who added 42, but it was Slade and Ormrod who transformed the innings. Ormrod batted 200 minutes for his 58 while Slade unleashed a cascade of strokes to reach 99 in 210 minutes. His runs came out of 167 and he was left stranded one run short of his century when Carter was bowled by Windows.

Worcestershire led by 47 on the first innings, but from that point onwards, the game swung in favour of Gloucestershire who finally won by 30 runs with 15 minutes to spare, the contribution of David Allen being decisive, for he took five wickets, and brilliantly caught Kenyon and ran out Broadbent when those two batsmen looked as if they would win the game for Worcestershire.

The failure at Gloucester was only to take on giant proportions when the season was over, for it is always easy to look back and say that was the day where it all went wrong. Worcestershire did not lose another game for the rest of the season, but there were frustrations in plenty.

From 1 August to 24 August, the County played seven matches of which only one ended in victory while six were drawn. Rain robbed them of much cricket, and often of a win, such as in the match against Surrey at Worcester when, needing 148 in four and a quarter hours, they could only sit and watch the rain come down. The absence of Flavell and Coldwell was also a decisive factor, depriving them of the penetration that was needed to clinch matches.

The drought ended when Gloucestershire were trounced at New Road. Worcestershire took maximum points, 14, from this game and needed the same amount from their last match, at home to Nottinghamshire, if they were to go top of the table.

How success breeds interest and excitement! It seemed that the whole of Worcestershire was trying to pack into the County Ground on Saturday, 1 September 1962, and they had an instant reward when Len Coldwell had Norman Hill caught at slip by Tom Graveney without a run on the board. The success did not end there, for, in a spell of three for 7, Coldwell bowled both Winfield and Maurice Hill while Poole was run out and Bilbie bowled by Carter to reduce Notts to 32 for five. Opener Alan Gill had remained solid and at last found an ally in Carlton Forbes. They added 56, and although both fell within eight runs of each other, Millman and Corran gave Worcestershire further frustration with an eighth wicket stand of 84. Carter took the last two wickets, Cotton and 'Bomber' Wells, and Notts were all out for 193.

Worcestershire's anxiety was betrayed by the nervousness of their batting. They did not assert the expected authority, and, Richardson apart, there was a hesitancy in the early batting so that six men were out for 118. Contrary to common belief, it is not star batsmen or star bowlers that win cups and titles, but the bits and pieces men, those who can contribute something in all aspects of the game and do so when it is most needed. Standen was a 'bits and pieces' man, and so, to a great extent, was Doug Slade. They halted the Notts' advance, and at the end of the first day, Worcestershire were 171 for six.

Standen and Slade were both out quickly on the Monday morning. Each had scored 40, not a score likely to cause a stir in the record books, but often, as on this occasion, invaluable in the context of a match. The Worcestershire revival was not over as Gifford, 21, and Coldwell, 37, added a swashbuckling 63 for the ninth wicket. Coldwell's 37 was to remain the highest score of his career.

Worcestershire had a first innings lead of 60, and with Coldwell and Carter again in fine form, it looked as though they would win in two days. Corran and Millman again revived their side as they aded 85 for the eighth wicket and ensured that the game would go into a third day. When Coldwell bowled Wells some 15 minutes before the close Notts had made 251, and Worcestershire had just over a day in which to make 192. They ended the day on 2 for no wicket.

A heavy thunderstorm threatened the home side's success. The ground was left covered with pools of water, and a further downpour added to the woe. When the rain ceased players and spectators joined groundstaff in a massive mopping up operation and, miraculously, play was possible at mid-day. Kenyon had been dropped the night before, but in 75 minutes before lunch, 91 were scored for the loss of Horton and Richardson.

A crowd of 3,000 sat apprehensively as storm clouds again gathered. Kenyon and Graveney were aware that the race was against whatever time the weather would allow. They unleashed a stream of glorious strokes which took their stand to 145 in 95 minutes. Graveney finished with 62, and when Don Kenyon drove Poole for four it won the match for Worcestershire and brought him the 67th century of his career. He can rarely have batted better.

The crowd massed in front of the pavilion, and Kenyon led his team onto the balcony to receive their applause. Champagne flowed freely. Worcestershire were top of the table, and they could only be denied the Championship if Yorkshire gained an outright win over Glamorgan at Harrogate three days later.

In spite of the loss of the second day's play, this is just what Yorkshire did as Don Wilson, ten for 72, was mainly instrumental in bowling out the Welshmen for 65 and 101. Worcestershire were disappointed, but not surprised, and, importantly, they had experienced the sweet smell of success.

The second eleven had won the Second Eleven Championship to emphasise the strength in depth policy and to augur well for the future. A buoyant committee under chairman Gilbert Ashton, who a year earlier had had to make staff cuts for economy reasons, announced that all players were to be offered new contracts and that, as the County's finances had improved, they were seeking new players to strengthen the squad, for, on occasions, with injuries and Test calls, they had found it difficult to field two sides.

The new players did not materialise for the 1963 season, with the exception of Richard Devereux who played in a few matches, and neither did Worcestershire's hopes of success in the Championship. They did not win a Championship match until mid-July when struggling Derbyshire were beaten at New Road. Richardson had a poor season, Broadbent played in only seven matches in his last year before retirement and Standen, because of soccer commitments, played in only nine. Coldwell missed most of the season through injury, and his deputy, Bob Carter, found difficulties in coming to terms with the new front foot rule, yet poor as their Championship form was, Worcestershire still enjoyed a good season.

It was a time of great change for cricket. The amateur–professional distinction had been abolished and all were now 'cricketers'. There was the amendment to the no-ball law to which we have referred above, and, at last, the Championship was decided on a straightforward points basis without any recourse to averages or percentages. In an effort to halt the decline in interest in the game and to bring back the crowds, it was also decided to introduce a one-day knock-out competition, sponsored by Gillette.

The idea had long been mooted, but it had taken until 1963 and the need for radical remedies to the worsening financial crisis in the game to become implemented. The initial obstacle was that organisers could only conceive of the knock-out competition within a three-day framework, and it was not until the idea of a one-day, limited-over competition was accepted that the tournament came into being.

The first Gillette Cup was restricted to the 17 first-class counties and was played over 65 overs with no bowler allowed to bowl more than 15 overs. It was not until 1966 that the 60-over, 12-over quota for a bowler, format was adopted.

The first match in the new competition began at Old Trafford on 1 May 1963, but bad weather took it into a second day. Lancashire beat Leicestershire by 101 runs.

Worcestershire's first tie was played at New Road on 22 May. They began badly, but Headley and Graveney added 145 for the third wicket, and the County reached 229 for nine. Stewart and Edrich began Surrey's reply with a stand of 82. Thereafter, the side fell apart and were all out for 115. Jim Standen did the damage with five for 14 in 15 overs. He also caught Loader off Slade, and as he had hit 13 not out, he was the obvious man-of-the-match.

Tom Graveney took the individual award when Glamorgan were beaten by 46 runs at Neath. Graveney hit 93 as Worcestershire made 238 for eight. The opposition again collapsed, the last six Glamorgan wickets going down for 37 runs, five of them to Jack Flavell.

Jack followed his five for 43 at Neath with a devastating six for 14 in the semi-final against Lancashire at New Road. Four of his victims were lbw, a testimony to his relentless attack on the stumps, and Lancashire were bowled out for a miserable 59. As the weather was uncertain, Kenyon and Horton attacked the bowling from the start and hit 33 in 20 minutes. Kenyon played on to Higgs, but Headley helped Horton finish the job, and Worcestershire won by nine wickets, having hit 60 in 10.1 overs.

Sussex were Worcestershire's opponents in the first Gillette Cup Final, and although the weather was cold and damp, a capacity crowd of 25,000 not only enjoyed the game, but shaped the future of English cricket for the foreseeable future so intense was their delight in the new form of the instant game that they were offered.

Dexter won the toss for Sussex and chose to bat first on a wicket that was soft and not conducive to stroke-play. Nevertheless, Richard Langridge and Alan Oakman put on 62 for the first wicket. Just as it seemed that Sussex would run away with the game, Norman Gifford had Oakman caught and, five runs later, bowled Langridge.

From the start of the first limited-over tournament, counties and captains had adopted a predominantly seam plan, relegating spinners to the pavilion, but Worcestershire's attack consisted of two seamers and three spinners. Two of them, Gifford and Slade, were particularly effective, and Gifford's four wickets and 15 economical overs were to gain him the individual award.

Dexter was wonderfully caught at slip by Broadbent, so acrobatic off bat and pad that the batsman stood his ground either in query or disbelief. The innings of the day was played by Parks who hit a six and four fours and batted with a confidence that few others could muster. Sussex were bowled out with 4.4 of their overs unused.

There was an early disappointment in the Worcestershire innings when Tony Buss trapped Don Kenyon lbw, but at 80 for two, with Headley and Graveney looking set and making the pitch look easier, a Worcestershire victory looked most probable. Then the batting disintegrated, mainly through inexperience of the type of game in which the two teams were taking part.

Headley was very slow to accumulate runs, but with only 169 needed and overs to spare, this would not seem important today. Graveney, however, anxious for the clock, felt the occasion needed drastic measures, lashed at the accurate Oakman, who bowled an immaculate spell of gentle off-breaks, and was caught off a skier. Headley perished to Bates, and with the late middle-order contributing little and with Gifford and Flavell bowled by successive deliveries, Worcestershire arrived at 133 for nine and only Carter and Booth standing between them and defeat.

Roy Booth was magnificent, but a run a ball was needed, and Dexter had posted a ring of fielders round the boundary. Some called this 'superior tactics', but in other quarters, Dexter's action was loudly condemned, although he was doing nothing that was not within the rules of the time. Needing boundaries rather than singles, Booth found his way cut off, but the batsmen ran and scampered and 21 had been added when Carter, anxious to let his partner keep the strike, was run out attempting a second run. Sussex had won the first Gillette Cup by 14 runs.

The late Gordon Ross, who was the organiser of the competition for many years, admitted that he was 'a trifle sorry that Worcester's boldness in being prepared to throw in their spinners and play attacking cricket was not suitably rewarded. Dexter's seamers and his all-round boundary parade of fielders won the day.'

Ross was consoled by the fact that Gifford had won the individual award, a decision made by Sutcliffe and Woolley, who also paid tribute to Booth's gallant innings.

Kenyon and his side had played the game in the best possible spirit and had won many admirers although not the trophy itself. Once again they were the bridesmaids, but they had been at the feast enough times now, close to the top table, to make the prospect of being the bride all the more inviting. Yet it would need a positive and inspiring leader to pull the side together and to convince them that they were not always destined to be runners-up.

GILLETTE CUP FINAL
WORCESTERSHIRE *v* SUSSEX

Played at Lord's on 7 September 1963

SUSSEX WON BY 14 RUNS

SUSSEX

R. J. Langridge	b Gifford	34
A. S. M. Oakman	c Slade b Gifford	19
K. G. Suttle	b Gifford	9
*E. R. Dexter	c Broadbent b Horton	3
†J. M. Parks	b Slade	57
L. J. Lenham	c Booth b Gifford	7
G. C. Cooper	lbw b Slade	0
N. I. Thomson	lbw b Flavell	1
A. Buss	c Booth b Carter	3
J. A. Snow	b Flavell	10
D. L. Bates	not out	3
Extras	b 9, lb 10, nb 3	22
Total (60.2 overs)		168

Fall: 1-62, 2-67, 3-76, 4-98, 5-118, 6-123, 7-134, 8-142, 9-157

BOWLING	O	M	R	W
Flavell	14.2	3	31	2
Carter	12	1	39	1
Slade	11	2	23	2
Gifford	15	4	33	4
Horton	8	1	20	1

WORCESTERSHIRE

*D. Kenyon	lbw b Buss	1
M. J. Horton	c and b Buss	26
R. G. A. Headley	c Snow b Bates	25
T. W. Graveney	c Dexter b Oakman	29
D. W. Richardson	c Parks b Thomson	3
R. G. Broadbent	c Bates b Snow	13
†R. Booth	not out	33
D. N. F. Slade	b Buss	3
N. Gifford	b Snow	0
J. A. Flavell	b Snow	0
R. G. Carter	run out	2
Extras	b 8, lb 9, nb 2	19
Total (63.2 overs)		154

Fall: 1-7, 2-38, 3-80, 4-91, 5-103, 6-128, 7-132, 8-133, 9-133

BOWLING	O	M	R	W
Thomson	13.2	4	35	1
Buss	15	2	39	3
Oakman	13	4	17	1
Suttle	5	2	11	0
Bates	9	2	20	1
Snow	8	0	13	3

Man-of-the-Match: N. Gifford

Umpires: W. A. Buswell and W. Phillips

*Captain; †Wicket-keeper

The task of convincing the side became a shade harder when they went out in the first round of the Gillette Cup in 1964 on 25 April, before the season had properly begun. They were beaten by Glamorgan at Newport by one wicket. The home side reached the last over, bowled by Horton, with nine runs still needed, but three singles were followed by Shepherd hitting the ball into the crowd to win the game.

A draw with the Australians and victories at Old Trafford and Lord's soon put the side in good heart, and Glamorgan were trounced at Worcester. Broadbent's career had ended after the Gillette Cup Final, a game in which Standen did not play because of his football commitments. He was able to play in only eleven Championship matches in 1964, but his value to the side with the ball, in the field, sometimes with the bat and always with his presence was immense.

Flavell and Coldwell were in harness together again, at least temporarily, and Carter and new acquisition Brian Brain, who had first played in 1959, but who had left the staff in 1960 and had now returned, were excellent reserves on whom to fall back. Duncan Fearnley had taken over from Broadbent at number six.

A fourth Championship victory in succession followed, at Leicester. Rain thwarted Worcestershire in the match with Yorkshire, but Kent were overwhelmed at Dartford so that the end of May was reached with Worcestershire having gained 52 points from six matches, exactly the same record as neighbours Warwickshire with whom they were level at the top of the table.

The first match in June, against Sussex at Worcester, was totally ruined by rain, but the County next travelled to Chesterfield where they had to take on Derbyshire without Coldwell and Flavell who were bowling for England against Australia at Trent Bridge.

Jim Standen, however, was back in the Worcestershire side and opened the bowling with Carter. He quickly accounted for Hall and was to finish with five for 64, but Worcestershire endured a grim day as the home side took five and a half hours to make 203. Slade bowled 13 overs for 15 runs, and when Kenyon offered the occasional and tempting leg-breaks of Ron Headley the West Indian was treated with such respect that he took one for 3 in 7.4 overs, six of which were maidens.

Only an hour and a half's cricket was possible on the second day, and Kenyon, anxious to keep the game alive, declared at 90 for six, 113 behind, after Worcestershire had batted even more dourly than Derbyshire. Lee's declaration left Worcestershire under three hours in which to make 174, no easy task on a wicket on which the scoring rate throughout the match had been 1.7 an over.

Kenyon and Horton gave them a brisk start, but it was Graveney with 60 in as many minutes who made victory seem assured. Twice in four balls he lifted off-spinner Smith for six, but Morgan bowled his medium pace well for Derbyshire and nine wickets were down and eight runs needed when Carter joined Gifford with the rain falling steadily. It was here that Worcestershire showed their real mettle, and Carter hit the winning run with two balls remaining.

It was as well that Gifford and Carter managed that dramatic last-over victory, for Warwickshire won again and went ahead in the Championship race when, having beaten Glamorgan convincingly, Worcestershire took only one point for a tie on the first innings from the drawn game with Surrey at The Oval.

The first sign of tension arrived when the two leading sides met at New Road on 13, 15 and 16 June. More people attended the match than any game at Worcester since the visit of Bradman's Australians 16 years earlier. There were 13,000 present on the first day and the aggregate attendance was 24,500. Kenyon won the toss and batted. In a consistent though never exhilarating performance, Worcestershire reached 256. The visitors' innings followed a similar pattern, but when their ninth wicket went down they were still ten short of Worcestershire's total. Miller and Jack Bannister brought their side nearer and nearer to taking first innings points, but, with the score on 255, Flavell yorked Miller, and Worcestershire had a lead of one, and the points.

Kenyon hoped for brisk runs and a chance for his bowlers to bowl out the opposition without giving Worcestershire's closest rivals, in every sense, too much hope of victory. On the last morning, however, Ibadulla took three quick wickets, and Kenyon and Richardson had to rebuild the innings. Once they had done so there was no time for a declaration, neither could Warwickshire have expected a 'sporting' declaration on such an occasion, but the match ended amid barracking and protests. It died a lingering death.

A victory over Somerset separated matches against Cambridge and Oxford Universities. Basil D'Oliveira, who was qualifying for the County and who made his debut for them in the opening match of the season against the Australians, played in both of these games and, in the second, against Oxford at Worcester, he hit 101, his first century for Worcestershire and the shape of things to come.

Back on the Championship trail, with Coldwell, Carter and Standen in hostile mood, Worcestershire beat Derbyshire by 42 runs. They then went to Edgbaston for the return match with Warwick-shire.

The Championship was now a two-horse race with Warwickshire in front. Jack Bannister had chosen the Worcestershire match for his benefit, but, sadly, injury prevented him from playing. Worcester-shire welcomed back Gifford, who made his Test debut in the series against the Australians, but not Flavell, who had broken down with Achilles tendon trouble in the Headingley Test and was not to play for England again. Ironically, Flavell's place was taken by Fred Rumsey who, unable to win a regular place at Worcester, had moved on to Somerset where he met with great success.

Huge crowds again watched the struggle between the Championship contenders. Kenyon won the toss and batted, but it was soon apparent that the pitch was of uncertain character, described by journalist Ron Roberts as being unworthy of the teams' combined talents. The opening stand was worth 35 when Kenyon fell to Cartwright who, in combination with another medium-pacer, Dr Rudi Webster, ran through the rest of the Worcestershire batting so that the visitors were all out for 119. Graveney's sound technique and experience shone like a beacon from the wreckage as he finished on 32 not out.

Warwickshire struggled even more painfully than Worcestershire had done. Coldwell and Standen bowled unchanged for 42 overs, and Warwickshire were all out for 72. Standen had six for 45, part of what was for him a wonderful year. He had joined Worcestershire after he had kept goal for West Ham when they beat Preston in the FA Cup Final at Wembley, and although his appearances were limited, he finished top of the first-class bowling averages with 64 wickets at 13 runs each. Coldwell was second, and Flavell and Gifford, both of whom passed 100 wickets, finished in the top twelve.

When Worcestershire batted again Kenyon and Horton went quickly, but Graveney, 95, and Headley, 78, joined in a stand of 124. They were never able to display their rich range of strokes, but they revealed the utmost discipline and concentration, and Graveney, who had batted for more than two hours for his 32 in the first innings, was at the crease for nearly five hours in the second.

Kenyon declared at 258 for eight on the last morning, leaving Warwickshire the task of scoring 306 in five hours. Against bowling that was aggressive and fielding that was electric (Richardson took four catches), Warwickshire had no hope of survival. Horton, Coldwell and Gifford each took three wickets, and Warwickshire were out for 86. It was the first time that they had been dismissed for under 100 in both innings by Worcestershire.

Worcestershire now had a nine-point lead and games in hand, but they lost three of their next four amtches to send shudders of despair through their supporters. They surrendered their unbeaten record to Somerset at Worcester and lost to both Yorkshire and Hampshire. These defeats all came when the side was chasing victory and underlined Kenyon's positive approach to the game. When others might have weakened or lost their nerve he encouraged his side with the philosophy: 'At this stage, points are all-important. We must have results. If we lose when chasing reasonable prospects of victory, we are still doing the right thing.'

By the end of the first week in August when, following victory over Leicestershire, they drew with Northants, they had recaptured the lead from Warwickshire, who were busy beating the Australians.

In the drawn game with Northants at Worcester, Tom Graveney had hit his third century in six innings and the 100th of his illustrious career. Now the winning post was in sight, and, as others faltered, Worcestershire, driven on by Kenyon, chased victory for every ball of every match. Essex, Gloucestershire, Nottinghamshire and Middlesex were beaten in successive matches, three with ease, Nottinghamshire, at Trent Bridge, by one wicket when Flavell hit Gillhouley for two fours when nine were wanted from the last-wicket pair. When Gloucestershire arrived at Worcester on Saturday, 22 August for the return fixture Worcestershire knew that if they won and Warwickshire failed at Southampton, they would be Champions for the first time in the Club's history.

The crowds again flocked to New Road, and again there was delight when Kenyon won the toss and he and Horton came out to open the innings. They could not have given the County a better start, for they put on 187 in three and a half hours, Worcestershire's biggest stand of the summer for any wicket, before Kenyon was bowled by Mortimore. Kenyon's 114 included a six and 11 fours.

Horton went at 223, four short of his century, but the next 100 minutes produced 175 runs. Headley and Graveney shared a glorious partnership of 126, and Headley's 103, which included two sixes into the Ladies' Pavilion and 14 fours, occupied two and a half hours.

Kenyon declared, and there was immediate success for the Worcestershire bowlers. On a wicket freshened by rain, Flavell took three wickets for nine runs in four overs. Coldwell removed Nicholls, and Gloucestershire were 28 for four. There was some stiffer resistance from the late order, but Brain broke through, and Gifford began to turn the ball appreciably to trouble all batsmen. The last two Gloucestershire wickets added 97 runs, more than doubling the score, but the visitors followed on 206 runs in arrears.

The second Gloucestershire innings followed a pattern similar to the first. At 77 for six, they looked well beaten and excitement grew, but Allen and White were in no mood to capitulate without a fight and frustrated Worcestershire with a stand of 94. Allen was lbw to Gifford, and White was run out following some fine work by Booth, whose calm and authority behind the stumps was an inspiration to the fielders.

Allen was eighth out and Meyer ninth, but Bevan and Graveney

made a dogged stand. Ken Graveney, Tom's elder brother and father
of David, the recent Gloucestershire captain, was a better batsman
than number eleven would suggest and clumped Gifford for a couple
of fours, but then the left-arm spinner, as wily at 24 as he was when he
finished his career at the age of 48, tossed the ball into the air, drew
Graveney forward, beat the outside edge, and Roy Booth whipped
off the bails to accomplish the most famous and important stumping in
Worcestershire cricket history. It was one of nine stumpings credited
to Booth in 1964, when he also took 91 catches to bring him to the 100
mark for the second time and to place him 22 ahead of Arnold Long,
who finished in second place, in the list of the country's wicket-
keepers.

Worcestershire, had won by an innings and two runs at 3.12 pm on
the last day, 25 August. An excited crowd of more than 1,000 gathered
in front of the pavilion to await news from Southampton.

Mike Smith had asked Hampshire to bat first, and on the Saturday
the home side had reached 314 for six. A second wicket stand of 101
between Barber and Ibadulla, who reached a fine hundred, seemed to
set Warwickshire on the way to a good score, but their last eight
wickets fell for 54 runs, and they only narrowly avoided the follow-on
so that, by the end of the second day, Hampshire were well in charge
and Worcestershire were delighting in the news from the south coast.

Ingleby-Mackenzie eventually asked Warwickshire to make 314 at
a rate of 90 runs an hour, a most daunting task, yet one which they

*J. K. Graveney is stumped by the immaculate Roy Booth of the bowling of
Norman Gifford, 25 August 1964, and Worcestershire are County Champions for
the first time.*

WORCESTERSHIRE *v* GLOUCESTERSHIRE

Played at New Road, Worcester on 22, 24 and 25 August 1964

WORCESTERSHIRE WON BY AN INNINGS AND 2 RUNS

WORCESTERSHIRE	**FIRST INNINGS**	
*D. Kenyon	b Mortimore	114
M. J. Horton	c Meyer b Windows	96
R. G. A. Headley	not out	103
T. W. Graveney	c Windows b Mortimore	57
D. W. Richardson	not out	18
J. A. Ormrod		
†R. Booth		
N. Gifford		
B. M. Brain		
L. J. Coldwell		
J. A. Flavell		
Extras	b 6, lb 3, nb 1	10
Total	(for 3 wkts dec)	398

Fall: 1-187, 2-223, 3-349

BOWLING	**O**	**M**	**R**	**W**
A. S. Brown	29	3	121	0
Windows	15	2	58	1
Mortimore	39	10	89	2
Graveney	12	2	29	0
Allen	24	5	91	0

GLOUCESTERSHIRE	**FIRST INNINGS**		**SECOND INNINGS**	
R. B. Nicholls	c Ormrod b Coldwell	7	lbw b Flavell	22
†B. J. Meyer	c Headley b Brain	25	(10) c Booth b Flavell	5
D. M. Young	c Kenyon b Flavell	2	(2) c Booth b Gifford	10
D. Brown	c Headley b Flavell	0	(3) b Brain	0
J. M. Bevan	lbw b Flavell	0	(9) not out	8
A. S. Brown	c Horton b Gifford	21	(5) c Booth b Flavell	18
D. A. Allen	c Graveney b Gifford	22	lbw b Gifford	68
R. C. White	b Gifford	12	run out	21
J. B. Mortimore	c Graveney b Flavell	47	(6) b Gifford	9
A. R. Windows	b Brain	28	(4) c Richardson b Brain	1
*J. K. Graveney	not out	19	st Booth b Gifford	19
Extras	b 3, lb 5, nb 1	9	b 13, lb 7, nb 3	23
Total		192		204

1st inns: 1-22, 2-28, 3-28, 4-28, 5-50, 6-64, 7-86, 8-95, 9-148
2nd inns: 1-22, 2-23, 3-31, 4-56, 5-71, 6-77, 7-171, 8-172, 9-179

BOWLING	**O**	**M**	**R**	**W**	**O**	**M**	**R**	**W**
Flavell	20.3	5	44	4	26	3	69	3
Coldwell	20	11	14	1	6	4	9	0
Brain	17	4	52	2	12	0	32	2
Gifford	24	8	61	3	32.2	15	50	4
Horton	7	4	12	0	10	2	21	0

Umpires: W. E. Phillipson and F. Jakeman

This victory, with Warwickshire's defeat at Southampton, ensured Worcestershire their first Championship.

*Captain; †Wicket-keeper

came close to accomplishing. Barber, Stewart and Cartwright took them to a winning position, and, with 14 minutes and two wickets left, they needed 26 to win. Then Ingleby-Mackenzie rested his spinners, brought back Shackleton and White, and Warwickshire were beaten by 17 runs.

When the news reached Worcester there was great jubilation. Many years of hard work and the honesty and generosity of men long since dead like Foley and Harry Foster had made this moment possible as well as the magnificent efforts of a beautifully balanced side who played exciting cricket.

Two more victories followed before the end of the season, and Worcestershire's margin of 41 points over Warwickshire was far greater than had looked possible for most of the season. Their 18 wins and three defeats in 28 matches confirms the positivity of their cricket. None begrudged them their success.

Cardus, in *Playfair Cricket Monthly*, remembered the giants of the past, like H. K. Foster 'whom I last saw acting as steward in Worcester

Worcestershire, 1964, County Champions. Standing (l to r): W. Faithful (scorer), C. D. Fearnley, R. G. A. Headley, J. A. Ormrod, B. M. Brain, L. J. Coldwell, R. G. M. Carter, J. A. Standen, N. Gifford, D. N. F. Slade, C. Hallows (coach), W. B. Powell (masseur). Seated: T. W. Graveney, M. J. Horton, D. Kenyon (capt.), Sir George Dowty (President), J. A. Flavell, R. Booth, D. W. Richardson.

Cathedral, at the music festival one mellow September, when Elgar, white-haired and in his last years, conducted *The Dream of Gerontius*. In my mind music and cricket are inseparable when I think of Worcester. Can I make any compliment more handsome than that to Don Kenyon's champions, in this mellowing September of their ripe harvesting?'

The Championship success had been achieved a few months before the Club's centenary so that during the celebration year, 1965, the Championship Pennant flew over the County Ground. It certainly did not look as if it would stay there when only one win, over Lancashire, was recorded in May, and only one other Championship win, over Derbyshire in two days, was recorded in June. Glamorgan were beaten in a low-scoring match at the beginning of July, and then three drawn games followed in this wretched summer.

It was hard to find reasons for the poor form. Kenyon was now a Test selector and missed several matches, which did not help him to find consistency with the bat, but Graveney, who had taken over from Horton as vice-captain, led the side capably when called upon and was in prime form with the bat. Flavell, who worked for the Dudley GPO in winter so as to get regular exercise, had a season free from injury and Test calls and played in every match. He ended the season with 142 wickets at 14.78 runs each, an outstanding performance. He spent five weeks in mid-season without the assistance of Coldwell at the other end, for Coldwell was again troubled by a leg injury, so Flavell's performance was all the more meritorious.

Headley, too, was ever-present, and moved up to opening the innings in exhilarating fashion late in the season when Horton dropped out of the side. And Basil D'Oliveira was now qualified so that the side should have been stronger than it was the previous season.

Debarred by the apartheid laws of the time from playing first-class cricket in South Africa because he was a 'Cape Coloured', D'Oliveira, encouraged by John Arlott and Peter Walker and with the help of public subscription, came to England to play for Middleton in the Central Lancashire League. His all-round talent was soon evident, and when he toured with the Commonwealth side that included Graveney and Gifford in 1961–62 he was persuaded by them that he was capable of playing county cricket. Accordingly, he qualified for Worcestershire and made his Championship debut against Essex at Worcester in May 1965, hitting 106 and sharing a fourth wicket stand of 183 with Tom Graveney.

He was 33 years old when he began his full time career with Worcestershire, but a first season in which he scored 1,523 runs and took 35 wickets in Championship matches confirmed that he was a cricketer of exceptional ability. His stance was relaxed and sideways on, but his backlift was minimal, the legacy of the deplorable wickets on which he had learned his cricket in South Africa, yet he had such power in the forearms that he was a mighty hitter of the ball once he was settled. He bowled with a classic sideways on action and maintained an accuracy with his gentle medium pace and disconcerting 'wobble'.

If his talents as a cricketer were recognised from the start, his quality as a man became apparent to all in 1968 when, chosen as a replacement for the injured Cartwright for the England tour of South Africa, he was refused entry into the Republic. He had been a controversial omission from the original party for he had scored a century in the final Test at The Oval in 1968, yet throughout the wrangles and bickerings and recriminations which followed he maintained a dignity and a determination not to be drawn into tabloid press slanging matches that marked him as a man on whom lesser sportsmen in the public eye would do well to model themselves.

His joy was in playing cricket for Worcestershire, for it was the realisation of an ambition that he thought could never be realised, and he remains eternally grateful to the County. It was this quality of something like wonder at finding himself doing what he was doing that gave his cricket a passion that was recognisable by all. He became, and remains, an immensely popular figure, and if he has remained thankful for what Worcestershire County Cricket Club have given him, the Club itself has felt blessed to have had him as a member.

In spite of the magnificent start made by d'Oliveira and the excellent form of Graveney and Flavell, nothing seemed to go right for Worcestershire. A crowd of 10,000 at New Road saw them lose to Sussex in the second round of the Gillette Cup. At the end of May, they languished 14th in the Championship table. By the end of June, they were 12th. Midlesex, Glamorgan and Northamptonshire alternated in the lead in the Championship throughout July and August, and when Worcestershire entertained Kent at Dudley on 24, 26 and 27 July, they were still stranded in mid-table, seemingly their season over.

A D'Oliveira century and a stand of 131 in as many minutes with Graveney set up a nine-wicket win over Kent, and Sussex were beaten in the next game, at Worcester. Twenty wickets fell on the first day when conditions were very bad. The seam bowlers revelled in the encouragement given them, and Worcestershire, 106, trailed by four runs. It was D'Oliveira who perplexed Sussex in the second innings when they again made 110. Rain ended play with Worcestershire, needing 115 for victory, on 47 for two. The rain dampened the spite of the pitch, and on the last morning, Graveney, 63, and Horton, 46, took Worcestershire to an eight-wicket victory.

Derbyshire were beaten by an innings at Chesterfield, and Hampshire, set to make 157 in just over two hours, should have been beaten at Worcester. Jack Flavell took the first six wickets in ten overs, and Hampshire slumped to 62 for eight, but, amazingly, both White and Sainsbury were dropped off simple chances and survived to draw the game. As Kenyon admitted later, 'missed catches became a positive disease for a few matches'. Sad for a side which prided itself so much on its fielding.

Centuries by Graveney and D'Oliveira took the County to 410 for five declared against Leicestershire, and Flavell and Coldwell then bowled unchanged as the visitors were shot out for 52 in 16.2 overs to give Worcestershire an innings victory.

Flavell and Coldwell produced another match-winning performance against Somerset at Kidderminster. Worcestershire trailed by 39 on the first innings, having been bowled out by Rumsey and Alley for 91. Then Flavell and Coldwell again bowled unchanged, and in 30.2 overs, Somerset were bowled out for 89, Flavell taking seven for 29. On a wicket that was still troublesome, Kenyon opted for attack as Worcestershire went in search of 129 to win. Three times he hit Langford for six, and of his 12 fours, six were taken off Rumsey. He and Headley put on 110 for the first wicket, Worcestershire's first three-figured opening partnership of the season, and the County won by nine wickets, having reached their target in 110 minutes. Kenyon was out for 77.

More importantly, Northamptonshire's run of 12 matches without defeat was brought to an end at Worcester in mid-August when Doug Slade returned the remarkable figures of 14.4-7-16-5 in the second innings.

The last home game saw Surrey the visitors to New Road. The hero of this match was Len Coldwell who, at the most crucial of times, produced the best bowling performance of his career. He opened the bowling with Flavell and took the first eight wickets to fall at a personal cost of 11 runs. He was desperately unlucky not to take all ten, for both Arnold, first ball, and Harman were missed off him, and he finished with eight for 38 as Surrey were bowled out for 94. Worcestershire made 314 for eight and went on to win by an innings and 92 runs. Gifford took six for 33 in Surrey's second innings when Coldwell had two more wickets.

Northamptonshire, thwarted by the weather in their last fixture, had now completed their programme and led the table, 16 points ahead of Worcestershire and 20 points ahead of Glamorgan. Glamorgan faltered when they lost to Derbyshire which meant that Northants were champions unless Worcestershire won their two remaining matches.

Basil D'Oliveira hits a boundary off Pat Pocock, Surrey v Worcestertshire, The Oval, 1966. Arnold Long is the wicket-keeper.

The game at Bournemouth caused some debate, but Ingleby-Mackenzie argued that he played it just like any other match in a season which had been ravaged by rain. Worcestershire were admirably served by Headley and Graveney who, after two wickets had fallen for 71, added 173. Both men reached centuries, and Kenyon was in the happy position of being able to declare at 6.00 pm with 363 for nine on the board. Before the close, the dangerous Roy Marshall had been spectacularly caught by Headley so that Worcestershire were in a strong position.

Their hopes were dashed on the second day, however, when rain cut the playing time by half. This meant that Hampshire's first innings continued into the last morning when, as soon as they had saved the follow-on, Ingleby-Mackenzie declared.

Kenyon knew that anything less than victory was of no use to

Worcestershire and that defeat, in this context, was immaterial so, after one ball, bowled by the Hampshire captain, he declared at 0 for no wicket. This left Hampshire two hours forty minutes in which to score 147, a generous declaration. However, suddenly, the sun came out and the damp pitch began to dry under powerful sunshine. The wicket became a nightmare for batsmen. Flavell was unplayable, Coldwell a constant threat. The close-catching was dramatic, the fielders a perpetual menace to the batsman. Nobody in the Hampshire side reached double figures, and in 65 minutes they were all out for 31. Eight catches were taken close to the bat, and the bowling figures of the Worcestershire seamers were:

Flavell   8.3-4-9-5
Coldwell   8-2-22-5

The side travelled to Hove for the final match of the season with all to play for.

Sussex won the toss, which could have proved a great advantage, but Flavell was again in irrepressible form. The opening stand of 25 was the highest of the innings, and Sussex were all out before lunch on the opening day. Worcestershire were in sight of the Championship. It proved to be not quite so easily within their grasp as it seemed at lunch on that opening day, for Kenyon, Headley and Ormrod were all back in the pavilion with only 33 scored. A fourth wicket fell, D'Oliveira, at 68, but Graveney, Richardson and Booth ground Worcestershire into a lead of 94.

Sussex again began poorly, but Pataudi, displaying more strokes than anyone else in the match had done until this point, batted delightfully, and the late-middle order showed considerable determination. Eventually, Sussex were dismissed for 225, and Worcestershire needed 132 in four hours twenty minutes to win the match and the Championship.

If the feats of Graveney, Headley and D'Oliveira with the bat had taken Worcestershire to this point, it was to be the lesser mortals, the invaluable 'bits and pieces' players, who were now to come to the fore. Kenyon, Headley, Graveney, Ormrod and D'Oliveira were out for 70, and the target suddenly seemed a very long way away. Booth now joined Richardson. Neither man had enjoyed a good season with the bat.

In an innings which was totally against his natural inclinations, but which was of paramount importance to the side, Richardson batted for two and a half hours for 31 not out. Booth gave just the support that was needed, and with tension mounting and time running out, he lifted Oakman into the crowd for the bravest of sixes. Snow came back to have Booth caught behind for 38, but the score was now 121, and Slade helped Richardson to score the last eleven runs which kept the title at Worcester.

If one felt some sympathy for Northants, who were robbed of the Championship by four points with only seven minutes of the season remaining, one could also reflect that, to win the title, Worcestershire had won ten of their last eleven matches. Rarely can a county have put up such a storming finish to take the Championship. Kenyon was in no doubt as to why the title was won: 'Complete team spirit and effort and a happy side.' But this was no longer a side of exuberant youth. Graveney was 38, D'Oliveira 33, Flavell 36, Booth 39, Coldwell 32, and Kenyon himself 41. It could only be a very short time before the side broke up.

The signs of that break-up began to be seen in 1966 when the County, although well behind Yorkshire for much of the season, were not deprived of their title until the last match of the season when they lost to Sussex at New Road while Yorkshire were beating Kent in two days at Harrogate.

Although he was to play on and off until 1970, Jim Standen appeared very little in 1965 and 1966 while Martin Horton, having enjoyed a return to form in 1966, retired at the end of the season. He went to New Zealand where his coaching played a significant part in the great advance made in New Zealand cricket in the next few years.

Graveney and D'Oliveira were in the England side in 1966, and their batting, and that of Test selector Don Kenyon, was much missed on occasions, but Ormrod, with 1,000 runs and a County Cap, and Ted Hemsley, a newcomer, showed advances. The batsmen were not helped by a new rule which was introduced in 1966 which limited the first innings of each side to 65 overs in the first 12 matches played by each county on a home and away basis. It was a most unfortunate experiment.

The strength of the Worcestershire side was still apparent in that Tom Graveney finished top of the national batting averages while Jack Flavell was second only to Derek Underwood in the bowling. There were rain interruptions in countless matches, and no decision could be reached in the game with Essex at New Road at a crucial time of the season. Still, Worcestershire finished as runners-up to Yorkshire, 18 points in arrears, and ten years earlier such an achievement would have been greeted with wild celebrations.

The day after losing to Sussex in the final Championship match, Worcestershire trotted down to London to appear in their second Gillette Cup Final in four seasons. They had beaten Notts by 19 runs at Worcester in spite of an astonishing batting collapse and had overwhelmed Essex in the quarter-final. Thanks to a fine century by Martin Horton, they had also destroyed Hampshire in the semi-final although Coldwell's final spell of four for 6 had an influence on the outcome, too. Their opponents in the final were the old enemy, Warwickshire.

The competition had really captured the public imagination, and once again there was a capacity crowd for the final. The sun shone, and Kenyon won the toss. Kenyon and Horton began confidently enough, but Kenyon broke his own wicket in completing a shot off Webster. Cartwright then bowled his niggardly medium pace, just short of a length, always taxing and testing, and Worcestershire crumbled. At lunch, they were 88 for six, the game seemingly over.

At 104 for seven, the Warwickshire bowlers had only a not very strong tail to mop up, but, inexplicably, Bob Barber, a leg-spin bowler of Test class, bowled innocuous seam up, and Gifford and Brain relished it. The last six overs of the innings realised 43 runs, and at least Worcestershire were not disgraced, finishing with 155 for eight from 60 overs.

This did not present Warwickshire with too formidable a target, and, without risks and without sparkle, they reached 44 before Ibdalla fell to Gifford. At 130 for two, Warwickshire were cruising to victory, but three wickets fell for eight runs, and the complexion of the game changed. Had Graveney caught A. C. Smith before he had scored, as he should have done, Worcestershire might have snatched a sensational victory. As it was, Smith hit a six and three fours and scored all of the last 21 runs needed while his colleagues hesitated nervously. Victory came with 20 balls to spare.

On the Saturday evening, Worcestershire could reflect that two days earlier they had had hopes of a double, but they had ended with neither trophy. They had, however, continued to earn respect and admiration for the way in which they played the game. In an age when there was much dross, they had given glimpses of gold.

There was a first-round exit the following year, to Sussex by two wickets at New Road, and there was never a serious challenge for the Championship as youngsters filled more and more places in the side. Worcestershire finished fifth in the table. In the last six years under Kenyon, they were only once out of the top five, but, inevitably, something of a spark had gone from their game.

Flavell was injured for much of the summer, as was Coldwell, and retired at the end of the season to begin life as a successful restaurant owner. When Flavell went, Worcestershire lost one of their greatest bowlers.

Standen and Richardson, too, announced their official retirements, and 1967 was Don Kenyon's last in first-class cricket.

He reached his 1,000 runs in Championship matches and, at New Road, in July, he gave all something to remember. Essex set

Worcestershire the task of making 229 in 135 minutes. The County reached the target with five balls to spare, thanks to Kenyon. He hit 21 off six deliveries to end the match. His 121 not out was his 70th and last century for Worcestershire.

On 1 September, he led the County for the last time and hit 67 not out in 75 minutes out of 112 to give his side hope of victory over Glamorgan at Colwyn Bay. The Welshmen just held out for a draw. The Kenyon era was over.

In March 1968, a copper beech was planted at the County Ground to commemorate Don Kenyon's career, but he had left a legacy that can never be erased and that had no need of symbol. He had been seen as a 'promising bat' for Stourbridge in the Birmingham League at the age of 15, and on 3 August 1940 he hit his first hundred in the League, 103 against Aston Unity. The 'teenage prodigy' had sharpened his technique on the League bowlers before his first appearances for Worcestershire in 1946, but from the time he was at school his off-side play had been encouraged, and he batted in a manner that was free and flowing. If you walk round the ground at Worcester or Kidderminster today and chat to those who have been watching the County for half a century or more, they will tell you that of the great batsmen who have donned the green cap, Don Kenyon is the greatest.

As a captain, he brought wisdom and authority to Worcestershire cricket. He was quick to assess any situation, accurate in his judgment of men and pitches and he made decisions and acted with a crispness that excited admiration. He achieved unity through respect and success through being positive. He believed that those who were afraid to lose a match did not deserve to win one. In joyous aggression he led Worcestershire cricket into a new era.

It is no coincidence that when Worcestershire cricket moved into another golden age in the 1980s Booth, Fearnley, D'Oliveira and Kenyon himself, members of that great side of the 1960s, held senior administrative or directive positions in the Club.

RISE AND FALL

KENYON HAD BEEN ASKED ONLY a fortnight before the season began in 1960 to succeed Peter Richardson as captain; Tom Graveney had ample warning that he was to take over from Kenyon and knew only too well how difficult the task would be. Not only was he following one of the greatest of county captains, he was also inheriting a side which was about to enter a period of great transition at a time when cricket itself was in a state of flux.

Graveney was a mature player with experience of captaincy when he came to Worcestershire, yet he moulded well into the Worcester

The majesty of Tom Graveney.

scene. His flowing cover drive, healthy aspect and dedication to practice were perfectly suited to the beautiful ground with its cathedral backdrop. There are not too many players in the whole history of the game who have scored so many runs in such an exquisite manner as Tom Graveney. He was always grateful for the warmth and kindness with which he was treated when he moved down the road to Worcester, and he was thrilled to be part of the success to which he made no small contribution.

When he became captain he asked supporters to be patient for he knew that the team was being reshaped, that young players had to be blooded and that results, initially at least, might prove disappointing. In his second season as captain, 1969, at the age of 42, he had to contend with a third competition, the John Player Sunday League.

Kenyon's last year as captain had seen Hemsley, Bayliss, Barker, Carter, Griffith and Yardley, none of them regular players before that season, appear in the side more frequently. Graveney's first year saw the arrival of Vanburn Holder and Glenn Turner.

Holder had played against Graveney in the West Indies, and the new Worcester captain was so impressed with him that he persuaded the County to sign him in April 1968, under the new rule applicable from that year onward that counties were allowed to sign one overseas player on immediate registration.

Compared to some of the signings by other counties, Sobers at Nottinghamshire, Kanhai at Warwickshire, Engineer at Lancashire, Holder was a little known talent. He soon proved himself. A tall, lean, fast-medium bowler, sometimes deceptively very quick, and a batsman who could uncoil in West Indian fashion and smite with great power, he found himself in the West Indian party to tour England in 1969 and was to become the first Worcestershire player to take 100 wickets in Test cricket. Glenn Turner was a very different case.

Turner became obsessed with cricket at school and met, and was deeply influenced by, Billy Ibadulla, the Warwickshire and Pakistan all-rounder who coached in New Zealand. Ibadulla was impressed by Turner's ability and dedication and suggested that the young man would succeed in county cricket. Accordingly, he arranged for Turner to have a trial with Warwickshire.

For a year Turner worked on the night-shift at a bakery in Dunedin in order to raise the fare to England. However, shortly before he was due to leave New Zealand he received a telephone call from Mike Smith, the Warwickshire captain, saying that one of the Warwickshire committee had almost certainly engaged another overseas player which meant that Warwickshire had their full quota of overseas players and would not be able to engage Turner, although they would still honour the two-month trial contract that they had offered him.

Turner was in a quandary, but he decided to come to England as planned. He found Mike Smith and Warwickshire kind and helpful. They provided him with money and kit and arranged trials with other counties. He went first to Worcestershire, Warwickshire's near neighbours, and spent two days in the nets watched by Graveney and Kenyon. He was offered a contract worth £650.

He spent his qualification period in 1967 playing for Stourbridge in the Birmingham League without breaking records as some of his predecessors had done, and he played his first game for Worcestershire against the Pakistan tourists in August of the same year. The following season, Graveney's first as captain, he hit 1,000 runs, as did Ormrod and Headley, and Worcestershire, who won eight matches and finished sixth, had a better season than many had anticipated.

Worcestershire had begun the season with Headley and Fearnley as

Len Coldwell spins the coin before his benefit match against Warwickshire. He is flanked by Tom Graveney and A. C. Smith.

the opening pair, but in July Ormrod was pushed up to open the innings, and Fearnley lost his place and left the County at the end of the season.

Duncan Fearnley's only first-class century had come against Derbyshire at Kidderminster in 1966, but if he was never quite to find in the first team the most able form he consistently produced in the second, he was to prove one of the County's most astute signings, a man totally dedicated to the Worcestershire cause. Born in Pudsey, he joined Worcestershire in 1961, but, as soon as he left school, he learned the batmaker's craft at a one-man shop in Bradford. It was a craft he never abandoned, and at the end of his career with Worcestershire, he was given a small corner in a shop of fishing tackle makers run by a friend and Worcestershire supporter, Fred Poole. At A. Poole and Son, makers of flies for fishing, Duncan Fearnley's cricket bats came into being. In 1970 came the famous logo, a perspective view of a set of bails and wickets, which has become recognised throughout the world as a mark of quality on cricket equipment. He was well supported by his former colleagues, but he has supported them well in his turn. On leaving first-class cricket, he played for Lincolnshire, but, in 1972, he returned to captain Worcestershire Second Eleven, and he is now a dynamic chairman of the Club. It was a good day for Worcestershire cricket when Duncan Fearnley arrived from Yorkshire.

Although Glenn Turner scored more than 1,000 runs in his first full season, it should not be imagined that he was, in 1967, the free-flowing batsman that he became on occasions later in his career. He did not arrive at Worcester as a ready-made player in the mould of Sobers, Kanhai, Hadlee, Rice or Border; rather he came to learn the game. There was more than one county player and official who, seeing him in his first seasons with Worcestershire, described Turner as 'the strokeless wonder', and one needs to remember this, for the New Zealander was to achieve much and win many honours, but his cricket was shaped by and learned at Worcestershire.

Turner was available for only nine Championship matches in 1969 because he was with the New Zealand touring party, but Worcestershire lacked more than Turner that season. The splendid Roy Booth had retired and was replaced by Rodney Cass, formerly with Essex, a useful batsman and wicket-keeper, but one who found it hard to fill Booth's place as anyone would have done. On top of Booth's departure came the retirement, in mid-season, of Len Coldwell, who left cricket to take up a business appointment with Whitbread's in his native Devon. The abrupt departure of Coldwell may have caused a surprise, but he was 36 and had suffered several injuries to legs and back, and it was obviously time for him to accept an appointment outside cricket when a suitable one was offered. His smooth, economical approach to the wicket and his nagging accuracy were to be much missed, but he had given Worcestershire wonderful service.

The absence of Coldwell and of Holder, who was with the West Indian party for half the season, gave greater opportunity to Bob Carter, the bespectacled former teacher and outstanding coach, and to Brian Brain. Brain, in particular, responded well and took 66 Championship wickets. He was a fine professional, always ready to bowl and a glutton for work. Tall and wiry, he seemed as fresh at the end of a long stint of bowling as at the beginning.

Jim Standen came out of his retirement to play in a dozen matches and in some of the Sunday games, and Ted Hemsley, pugnacious on the off side and excellent in the field, an area in which the County fell below former standards, scored a maiden first-class century and batted aggressively and impressively before returning to soccer.

Nothing, however, could deny that 1969 was a bad year for Worcestershire. The instability of the team, the poor early season results, the inevitable, but frightening, drop in the number of people coming to watch the Championship matches, injuries and the weather, all combined to make life very difficult. The County Ground was flooded in May, and, at short notice, the game with Middlesex at the end of May and beginning of June had to be transferred to Dudley, and even there only one day's play was possible. Joe Lister was quoted as saying, 'I doubt whether we have ever had a more disastrous season financially.'

Losing crowds is the reverse of losing weight. They are easier to lose than to reclaim even if a few more people did drift back in Graveney's last year of first-class cricket. He hit 1,000 Championship runs in farewell, including, against Yorkshire at Worcester in August, his 122nd, and last, first-class century. He left the game after the final match against Warwickshire at New Road in September, and cricket lost a thing of beauty. Those who saw him bat will remain eternally grateful for the privilege.

At the sadness of his departure, there was speculation that a new star had risen, that New Road was again the home of greatness. Glenn Turner suddenly put stodginess behind him, hit over 2,000 runs, a record ten centuries for the County, and blossomed as an exciting batsman of true world class. The majority of his runs and centuries came in the last two months of the season when he appeared to throw off his shackles and inhibitions. Had only he been able to show more urgency earlier in the year and had Worcestershire been able to show more urgency in their first innings at all times, the County may well have prospered more than they did and finished higher than a commendable sixth.

Headley, the left-handed Yardley, D'Oliveira, when free from Test calls, and Ormrod all batted well, and there was the sense that a new, young side was coming into being.

Alan Ormrod, like Gifford a Lancastrian, worked hard at his game. From Kenyon and Graveney, he learned that success is based on sound technique, and, from the start, he showed a calm that was to stand him in good stead. Like Kenyon and Graveney, he was powerful and attractive in his off-side play, and he was never overshadowed by those with whom he played and whom he played against, some of whom gained honours that might well have come his way with better fortune.

If the batting was looking sound, however, the bowling was giving cause for concern. Brain was often out of the game through injury and the whole-hearted Carter could not find consistency. Slade's opportunities were limited by the presence of Gifford, who bore the brunt of work in attack and proved that he would be a capable successor to Graveney on the occasions when he was asked to lead the side.

Holder, like Gifford, worked manfully, but he was still a little raw in spite of his Test experience and was desperately in need of a partner with powers of penetration to assist him in the new ball attack. Jim Standen played more regularly than before his 'retirement', but 1970 was to be his last season.

In the John Player League in 1970, Worcestershire enjoyed a run of six victories in succession, but *Wisden* wrote that 'the side did not have all the resources needed for the one-day game. It is in the Championship that their best hopes rest now'. Gifford's first season of leadership proved quite the opposite.

In 1971, only Glamorgan and Derbyshire finished below Worcestershire in the Championship, yet the County had much to be pleased about, for this was achieved alongside a series of unfortunate mishaps that marred their season. Cass sustained a back injury at the start of the year, and Wilcock kept wicket for most of the season and proved most capable. Turner was also out with injury for several matches, as was D'Oliveira, and Gifford broke a thumb playing for England and missed the last month of the season. This brought a rota of captains, the most successful of whom was Ron Headley.

The series of injuries gave young players the chance to prove their worth, and, like Wilcock, several did. Griffith, off-breaks, Wilkinson, left-arm seam, and Stimpson, opening batsman, made impressive contributions although the bowling was carried almost entirely by Holder and Carter after Brain had announced his retirement through injury early in the season. Yardley, too, came to the fore and reached 1,000 runs in all matches for the first time. He also hit a maiden first-class century.

Yardley's century came in the match against the strong Indian touring side in September. Gavaskar and Wadekar shared a second wicket stand of 327 on the opening day, but Worcestershire came close to victory when, seeking 286 in three and a half hours, they finished on 250 for five with Yardley 104 not out. In the Worcestershire first innings, John Parker hit 91 on the occasion of his first-class debut.

Parker had followed a path trodden by his countryman Glenn Turner, giving up a teaching career in New Zealand to try his luck in county cricket. Like Turner, he was initially strokeless, but he developed into a Test cricketer.

Whatever the reassurances from the younger players, however, it was the John Player Sunday League which aroused interest and excitement. The County had made an early exit from the Gillette Cup, but seven of the first eight John Player League games were won in fine style. Unfortunately, Essex, too, had won seven of their first eight, and they edged ahead in the table when Worcestershire lost three games in succession in July and August. This was all the more unfortunate as Worcestershire had gained a resounding win over Essex at New Road on 18 July.

A crowd of 7,000, the biggest that Worcestershire had had at that time in the Sunday league, saw Holder, Carter and Gifford restrict Essex to 54 for two from their first twenty overs, and when the later batsmen tried to accelerate they fell to Ted Hemsley whose medium pace brought him four for 42 in his eight overs. Chasing a target of 125, the home side had no difficulties, and with Headley hitting 57 not out, they romped to victory with 19 balls to spare.

Worcestershire ended their lean spell with a narrow win over Somerset who were title contenders until this match at New Road, and the next Sunday, 22 August, they travelled to Old Trafford. Lancashire had just won five games in succession to go top of the league with 40 points. Victory over Worcestershire would have given them the title which they had won in the first two years of the competition's existence. Unfortunately, rain prevented any play until 5.00 pm, and the game was reduced to a ten-over thrash. In the days before fielding circles, captains were able to deploy their men around the outfield, and this is what Bond did, but Ron Headley played a masterly innings, hit 36, and Worcestershire made 77 for three. No Lancashire batsman could play a comparable innings as Brain, who had made himself available for one-day cricket although retiring from the first-class game, and Holder exerted a firm grip. Lancashire lost seven wickets, and Worcestershire won by ten runs, the issue never in doubt. On the same day, Essex completed their programme with a win over Warwickshire and, with 44 points, were top of the table.

Lancashire and Worcestershire, both on 40 points, had one game remaining, Lancashire on 12 September, Worcestershire a week earlier. It seemed certain that run-rate would decide the championship, and, in this area, Worcestershire were lagging.

Worcestershire's concluding match was, as chance would have it, against their arch rivals Warwickshire at Dudley. There was a crowd of 10,000 to see the match, more than the ground could hold and a Sunday League record for Worcestershire. As Les Hatton, a great connoisseur and critic of his county's standard of beer, remarked: 'There was one Guinness left after four o'clock.'

Warwickshire batted first on a true wicket with a fast outfield. They began confidently, but they were wrecked by Basil D'Oliveira, who sent back the formidable trio of Whitehouse, Kanhai and Amiss in the space of seven balls. From 51 for one, Warwickshire had descended to 54 for four. Mike Smith and Abberley effected a rescue act, but Brain and Holder ended all hope of a late revival when they took the last four wickets for nine runs and denied Warwickshire three overs of their quota.

Worcestershire were now confronted, not simply by the problem of winning, which seemed easy enough, but of scoring the runs at a rate quick enough to take them ahead of Essex's 4.519 for the season. As it transpired, they needed to score 127 in 17.5 overs, an asking rate of more than seven an over.

Fast scoring had not been their forte for most of the season. Indeed, their success had been founded largely on the bowling of Holder, 32 wickets, and Carter, 20. Both bowlers had taken four wickets in an innings on two occasions to claim a share of the prize money available. Holder's 32 wickets at 12.18 placed him second to Underwood in the Sunday averages, and only Boyce of Essex and Williams of Glamorgan, each with 33, took more John Player League wickets.

Of the batsmen, Ron Headley stood head and shoulders above the rest. He led by example in the closing stages of the season when he captained the side in Gifford's absence, and only Sobers and Mike Buss scored more runs than he while only Gordon Barker, who played five innings less, had a better average. It was Headley who again set the example in the vital match with Warwickshire after early shocks.

Headley struck the ball hard and true from the start, but in the first two overs he lost Stimpson and Yardley. Basil D'Oliveira was in electric form, but the crucial stand was between Headley and Ormrod who added 55 off 30 balls. Holder went without addition, and wickets were lost in the scramble for runs so that two of the least experienced members of the side, Griffith and Wilkinson, found themselves at the crease with four still needed off as many deliveries. They kept their heads and got the runs with two balls to spare.

Headley's 58 came in under an hour, but what was most commendable about the batting of Headley, D'Oliveira and Ormrod

Vanburn Holder.

was, as Tony Pawson wrote 'They kept the rate to over seven runs an over not by indiscriminate slogging, but clean and well judged hitting. At the crucial moment Ormrod accelerated the scoring with strokes of classical purity.'

Worcestershire could still be deprived of the title if Lancashire beat Glamorgan at Old Trafford the following Sunday. A capacity crowd of 30,000 arrived at the Manchester ground to hail their favourites, but Glamorgan won by 34 runs and Worcestershire were the champions. It could hardly have been closer.

	P	W	L	Pts	Run Rate
Worcestershire	16	11	5	44	4.522
Essex	16	11	5	44	4.519
Lancashire	16	10	6	40	4.575
Leicestershire	16	10	6	40	4.335

JOHN PLAYER LEAGUE
WORCESTERSHIRE *v* WARWICKSHIRE

Played at Tipton Road, Dudley on 5 September 1971

WORCESTERSHIRE WON BY 3 WICKETS

WARWICKSHIRE

J. Whitehouse	b D'Oliveira	19
J. A. Jameson	c Ormrod b Carter	20
R. B. Kanhai	c and b D'Oliveira	11
D. L. Amiss	b D'Oliveira	0
*M. J. K. Smith	c Griffith b Wilkinson	15
R. N. Abberley	c Griffith b Brain	26
K. Ibadulla	lbw b Brain	6
N. M. McVicker	b Carter	12
S. J. Rouse	lbw b Holder	0
L. R. Gibbs	b Holder	3
†B. J. Flick	not out	3
Extras	b 2, lb 6, nb 3	11
Total (37 overs)		126

Fall: 1-32, 2-51, 3-51, 4-54, 5-89, 6-100, 7-117, 8-120, 9-120

BOWLING	O	M	R	W
Holder	7	1	16	2
Carter	8	0	33	2
Wilkinson	8	1	36	1
D'Oliveira	8	2	19	3
Brain	6	2	11	2

WORCESTERSHIRE

*R. G. A. Headley	c Smith b Gibbs	58
P. J. Stimpson	c Ibadulla b McVicker	0
T. J. Yardley	run out	1
B. L. D'Oliveira	b McVicker	23
J. A. Ormrod	b Rouse	27
V. A. Holder	run out	0
†H. G. Wilcock	b Gibbs	2
K. Griffith	not out	9
K. Wilkinson	not out	1
B. M. Brain		
R. G. M. Carter		
Extras	b 4, lb 2	6
Total (17.3 overs)	(for 7 wkts)	127

Fall: 1-5, 2-10, 3-42, 4-97, 5-97, 6-104, 7-123

BOWLING	O	M	R	W
McVicker	6.3	0	43	2
Rouse	8	0	60	1
Gibbs	3	0	18	2

Umpires: H. D. Bird and E. J. Rowe

Worcestershire's first limited-over trophy was won with this victory.

*Captain; †Wicket-keeper

Ron Headley—
a family tradition.
(Ken Kelly)

Ironically, the season that saw Worcestershire's pulsating John Player League victory at Dudley was the last season in which a first-class match was played at the ground. Sunday League matches were to continue until 1977 by which time the ground was considered unsafe because of subsidence caused by the limestone mines beneath.

The season of 1977 also saw the end of Joe Lister's period as secretary of the Club, for he left to take up a similar position with Yorkshire, the county of his birth. He had done much for the Club and had led the Second Eleven with vigour until Henry Horton returned to the county for whom he had briefly played and took up the position of coach, bringing on the youngsters with much success. Lister was in the great tradition of Worcestershire secretaries like Foley and Green, and he was succeeded by a man of equal stature, Mike Vockins.

A graduate of the University College of Wales, Aberystwyth, Mike Vockins had nursed passion for farming and later for agricultural research, but, as well as carrying out his work as a research bio-chemist, he took on the job of secretary of the Shropshire Cricket Association. He devised and helped develop the new game of indoor cricket so that the winter months as well as the summer ones became full of the game. It was this full-time commitment to cricket which persuaded him to turn his back on agricultural science at the age of 27 and seek a new career in cricket administration. It was to prove to be an inspired appointment by the County committee, for not only did Vockins confirm that he was a first-rate administrator, but he also showed himself to be a man of tact, firmness, humour and wisdom with a flair for public relations and an appetite for hard work. They are qualities which have served him, and the Club, well and which are admirably suited to his other vocation, the church, for he took holy orders in 1988. To help him ease into his job there was, of course, Grace Fuller (née Cook), who remains a pillar of the Club after 42 years of service.

Mike Vockins was brought face to face with the fickleness of support in his first season, for as Worcestershire slid down the John Player League table, gate receipts fell by £1,500. Bad weather hit the Club hard in 1972, and, although they played steadily and encouragingly in the County Championship, the side paid dearly for failing to reach the final stages of the newly instigated Benson and Hedges Cup and for their crushing defeat at Edgbaston in the semi-final of the Gillette Cup.

Turner was the outstanding player of the season, hitting nearly 700 runs more than any other Worcestershire batsman in Championship matches and playing with 'stroke play of immense vision'. At Edgbaston, at the beginning of July, he hit a century in each innings and hit 108 in the John Player League game which punctuated the match, yet Worcestershire won neither game.

There was some swashbuckling batting from Ted Hemsley before football reclaimed him, and another soccer player, Jim Cumbes, joined the Worcestershire ranks and bowled with vigour. Jim had already been with Lancashire, twice, and Surrey, and he was to appear a few times for Warwickshire later, but the main part of his career as a medium-pace bowler with a somewhat flailing action was enjoyed with Worcestershire. One uses the word 'enjoyed', for Jim Cumbes has a zest for life that is infectious, and there has been no more popular player in the game among those who played with and against him. Another pace bowler to make an unobtrusive debut in 1972 was Paul Pridgeon. He was 18-years-old and another who had sharpened his teeth with the Stourbridge Club.

The bowling, for the time being at least, still relied heavily on Gifford and Holder, for Slade had gone and was to give good service to Shropshire, but help was on the way.

Although deprived of the assistance of Parker, who had showed a great advance in 1972, and Turner for much of the 1973 season because of their commitments to the New Zealand touring side, Worcestershire had a most encouraging year. Turner covered himself in glory with 1,000 runs before the end of May for the New Zealanders, and, on his return to Worcestershire in July, hit 1,036 for the County in nine matches. As he returned so Worcestershire lost Headley, who was called up by the West Indies and played in what were to be his only two Test matches. It was believed that the West Indies had wanted him four years earlier, but had been unable to come to an agreement with Worcestershire. Headley had been upset by this and was to leave the County rather abruptly, and with much good cricket still left in him, at the end of the 1974 season.

With such absentees as these and Holder, and on two occasions Gifford with the England side, it was hardly likely that Worcestershire would sustain a challenge for the Championship or the John Player League, and so it proved, but in the knock-out tournaments they fought strongly.

Brian Brain had thrown off his injury problems and returned to first-class cricket with immense success to take 84 Championship wickets, and John Inchmore had arrived from Northumberland to bowl a brisk medium pace with accuracy and to provide some hefty hitting in the late order. Imran Khan also played most successfully after the term at Oxford.

Imran had come to England with the Pakistan side of 1971, 18-years-old, raw and wild. He played in one Test and did nothing, took only 112 wickets on the tour and failed to score a 50. At the end of the tour, he went to play second eleven cricket for Worcestershire, hit a sparkling century and generally impressed. He was found a place at Worcester Royal Grammar School where, in 1972, he excelled, and he again did well for the County Second Eleven. The following year, his pace bowling was a great asset to the County with whom his disagreements lay three years in the future.

Imran was in the Oxford University side that competed in the Benson and Hedges Cup in 1973 and played in the same zone, the Midland, in which Worcestershire found themselves. The County lost their opening game to Leicestershire, but victories over Warwickshire, Northamptonshire and Oxford took them into the quarter-finals. Nottinghamshire could not recover from losing Hassan, Harris, Randall and Smedley for 18 runs at New Road, and with Gifford having Sobers caught by Yardley for 36, Worcestershire cruised into the semi-final with an 89-run victory.

The semi-final, against Lancashire at Manchester, was a wonderful game of cricket. Put in to bat, Lancashire had a torrid time against the relentlessly accurate new-ball bowling of Brain and Cumbes, and when David Lloyd was bowled by Brain in the ninth over the score was only 11. Hemsley and D'Oliveira maintained the stranglehold on the batsmen, and as they tried to break loose, despite a violent 36 by Engineer, they succumbed to Gifford who bowled five men and took the Gold Award.

Dismissed for 159, Lancashire fought back. Peter Lever bowled Headley in the opening over, and Lee accounted for Hemsley in the third. At 55 for five, Worcestershire looked beaten, but D'Oliveira and Johnson, a left-handed batsman and left-arm spinner from Bahamas, put on 58, and Cass, now the regular wicket-keeper, Gifford and Brain hit lustily. The last over arrived with two wickets standing and nine runs needed. Brain fell to Lee, but Jim Cumbes was in at the death and with one run needed off the last ball to level the scores and make Worcestershire victors by virtue of having lost fewer wickets, Cumbes swatted and went through for a single with his arms high in the air in triumph.

Once again Worcestershire were to be disappointed at Lord's. Again Brain and Cumbes bowled a splendid opening spell, and after 20 overs Kent were 34 for two. Luckhurst and Asif Iqbal changed the tenor of the game with a stand of 116 in 29 overs. They ran between the wickets excitingly, but it was D'Oliveira's throw from long-off which broke the stand. Gifford bowled Asif, but Kent plundered 53 from the last eight overs to reach 225 for seven in their 55 overs.

Graham and Asif contained Headley and Turner almost as much as Brain and Cumbes had contained the Kent pair, and Hemsley, Cass and Ormrod all became tied down. Gifford promoted himself in the order and went down the wicket to the medium-pace bowlers, driving and pulling them with gusto. He and D'Oliveira put on 70 in

12 overs, but D'Oliveira was caught on the boundary and Gifford bowled, and eventually Worcestershire failed by 39 runs. There was still the Gillette Cup.

Some fine bowling by Brain and a controlled spell under fire by Johnson gave the County victory over Warwickshire, and Leicestershire were beaten in the quarter-final by 56 runs.

A crowd of 8,500 saw the semi-final against Gloucestershire, further evidence of the power and economic necessity of one-day cricket, and the New Road faithful were once more to go home bitterly disappointed as, for the second year in succession, Worcestershire were to lose at the penultimate stage of the competition.

It all began so well with Gloucestershire 32 for two, but Procter was dropped off the first ball that the magnificent Brain bowled to him and Sadiq was put down a few balls later. Procter went on to score 101, and Gloucestershire made 243 for eight. Turner batted brilliantly for his 109, and he and Headley gave Worcestershire just the start that they wanted, 123, but the scoring rate lapsed. Nevertheless, with six overs left and six wickets standing, Worcestershire needed only 41 to win, but Procter sent back Turner, Gifford and Cass, and Gloucestershire were victors by five runs.

However great the disappointments of 1973, there was a conviction that Worcestershire once more had a strong and reasonably balanced side with depth and jostling for first team places.

Nothing was seen of Imran in 1974 because of his commitments at university and to the Pakistan touring side. Cumbes and Hemsley still had their football careers extending into the summer, but, apart from the breakdown of Cass with a back injury and occasional absences by Turner, Headley and D'Oliveira with minor ailments, Worcestershire were able to field a stable side for most of the season.

By the end of July, the County had lost six matches in the John Player League and had lost in the quarter-finals of the Benson and Hedges Cup so that efforts could be concentrated on the other two competitions.

A D'Oliveira century helped overwhelm Sussex in the Gillette Cup, and a narrow victory over Notts, with the young left-handed opener Wilkinson replacing the injured Headley and hitting 95, took them into the semi-final for the third year in succession. It proved to be the third semi-final defeat in a row as Worcestershire never fully recovered from the opening stand of 123 between Lancashire's David Lloyd and Barry Wood. This left only the Championship.

It was a wretched summer, but in the end the bad weather was to play a vital part in the destination of the title. From the start, Worcestershire were challenging strongly, winning seven of their first ten matches. They did not meet with defeat until they travelled to

Northampton on 24, 25 and 26 July when, set to score 280 in four hours, they lost their way and were beaten by 105 runs.

This was followed by another defeat when Leicestershire won in two days at New Road. 'On a pitch so well grassed that it could hardly be distinguished from the rest of the square', Worcestershire were put in to bat, lost three wickets in seven overs, but reached 181, thanks to a brave 50 from Parker. A thrilling century in two hours by Davison took Leicestershire to a six-run lead and, with Davison again in fine form, the visitors eventually won by four wickets.

Well as Worcestershire had started, Hampshire, who had lost their opening match of the season at Lord's, were sixteen points ahead of them on 12 July even though Worcestershire were, at that time, unbeaten. Surrey, too, were challenging strongly, but they began to fall out of the race in late July, and by the end of the first week in August when Worcestershire had regained their form with an innings victory at Cheltenham, Hampshire led Worcestershire by 19 points and Surrey were nine points further adrift, having played two games more than the two leaders. At this juncture, Worcestershire and Hampshire met at Portsmouth in a vital match.

Gifford chose to bat first on a well grassed pitch and must have fretted at his decision when his side was bowled out by the Hampshire seamers for 94, Worcestershire's lowest score of the season. Hampshire batted aggressively and were well served by skipper Gilliat and left-hander David Turner so that they moved to a first innings lead of 142. It proved to be ample as the Hampshire seamers again got to work. Glenn Turner was absent injured, but Ormrod and Parker put on 48 for the second wicket, after which the remaining wickets fell for 48 runs, and Worcestershire, 98, were beaten by an innings and 44 runs. Hampshire took 16 points, Worcestershire four, and the Championship seemed to have been decided.

Both sides drew the next match, but Hampshire took six points to Worcestershire's four against Somerset and so edged further ahead. Their lead was now 33 points, and only four matches remained. Suddenly, all went wrong for Hampshire, and everything went right for Worcestershire.

At Cardiff, Hampshire met Glamorgan who were vying for bottom place with Derbyshire and who had only one victory to their credit all season. Hampshire hit 234, and a devastating spell of fast bowling from Andy Roberts, eight for 47, the best of that magnificent career, shot out Glamorgan for 90. Hampshire batted lackadaisically in their second innings, but their 137 still left Glamorgan to make 282, a formidable task. They had no time worries and set about the job in cautious, but determined manner. Len Hill batted five and three quarter hours for 90, and he and Eifion Jones put on 106 for the fourth wicket. Glamorgan won a totally unexpected victory by five wickets.

Meanwhile, Worcestershire were beating Essex by ten wickets at New Road. There had seemed nothing extraordinary about this match at the outset when Essex, having lost five wickets for 78, were rallied by Ray East and Neil Smith and made 264. The home side lost Headley and Ormrod and had Turner retire hurt so sent in John Inchmore as night-watchman. He had been an immense asset to the attack with his fast-medium bowling, but his highest score remained the 30 he had hit against Gloucestershire the previous season, and his highest score in 1974 was ten. That was soon left well behind as he and John Parker put on 266. Both men reached centuries, Inchmore's coming with a six off Acfield, and his 113, the only three-figured innings of his career, occupying four hours. Worcestershire reached 404 for eight and went on to win by ten wickets so reducing the gap between them and Hampshire.

There followed a wonderful game at Newark. Headley and Ormrod went quickly, and Turner, on 59, retired with an elbow injury. Parker and D'Oliveira batted spiritedly, but five wickets fell for 23 runs, and it took the return of Turner to take Worcestershire past 300 and to four batting points. Fine bowling by Vanburn Holder gave the County a first innings lead of 130, but Worcestershire batted poorly in their second innings, and Notts needed 300 to win. Splendid knocks by Harris, Sobers and White meant that the home county reached the last twenty overs with three wickets in hand and 58 needed, but Brain bowled Taylor when five runs separated the sides to give Worcestershire victory and maximum points.

Hampshire were thwarted by Glamorgan and the weather at Southampton. They hit 393 for eight declared and captured two wickets on the first day, but there was little play on the second, and they were left to take 17 wickets on the final day. They managed 15, and the game was drawn. Only 11 points now separated the two title aspirants.

Worcestershire's last home game was against Glamorgan, who had done so much to damage Hampshire's chances. Brain and Holder took 14 wickets in the match, and, although they failed to reach a fourth batting pont, Worcestershire won by ten wickets. Turner hit 130, and Jim Yardley made an invaluable 56 in the first innings.

At Bournemouth, having dismissed Somerset for 264, Hampshire reached 405 for nine with contributions right down the order. Somerset were 90 for four at the end of the second day, and Hampshire looked poised for victory and the title, but rain prevented any play on the last day.

The final round of matches began, Worcestershire against Essex at Chelmsford and Hampshire against Yorkshire at Bournemouth, with the south coast county two points in the lead.

Rain delayed the start at Chelmsford, but when the sun came out Gifford, winning the toss, asked Essex to bat first on a drying wicket and played a major part in the events that followed. Hardie and McEwan opened the Essex innings and put on 42. Then Gifford joined the attack. He sent back both openers, and, in a spell of 14 overs, seven of them maidens, he took seven wickets for 15 runs. As batsmen played forward to smother the spin the ball would rear awkwardly at them, and Ormrod snapped up three catches at short-leg. Essex lost ten wickets for 42 runs and were all out for 84. Worcestershire had claimed the maximum four bowling points. Turner and Headley opened the innings with a stand of 57. Turner was 68 not out when Parker was caught at short-leg by Ray East off Stuart Turner to end the day with Worcestershire 126 for three.

It was also the end of the season. There was no play on the second and third days, and, at Bournemouth, where rain had washed out the first two days, they planned to start at 3.00 pm on the third when the rain returned and the match was abandoned. On a soggy afternoon at Chelmsford before a handful of people, Worcestershire had won the County Championship for the third time.

Norman Gifford receives the Championship Trophy from HRH the Duke of Edinburgh, 1974.

If the win lacked the sparkle of the earlier successes, it was just as hard-earned. A Championship is played over a season, not the last four days. Turner and Headley had again shown themselves to be batsmen of the highest quality. Holder, Gifford and Brain, who enjoyed a wonderful season and whose thoughts of retirement through injury were in the past, were a fine trio of bowlers; D'Oliveira, one of the best all-rounders in the country; and Inchmore and Cumbes excellent support bowlers. Wilcock, replacing the injured Cass, excelled behind the stumps, setting a bubbling example to the side.

Most importantly, when runs or wickets were needed, somebody, Ormrod, Yardley, Parker, Hemsley, had provided them. At Hull, on a dubious wicket, on which Yorkshire were bowled out for 101, Basil D'Oliveira had hit 227, an innings which epitomised the fighting spirit of the side.

Perhaps in every triumph there is the seed of decline, but few could have expected the upheavals that were to follow the two-point Championship victory of 1974. Gifford had enjoyed not only leading Worcestershire to the title, but had taken a fine benefit in spite of the weather. The following year D'Oliveira received a record benefit of £27,000, but the Club had a troubled time.

Headley had retired prematurely and surprisingly at the end of the 1974 season. He had suggested playing in one-day matches, but this was not an acceptable proposition to the Club. He did, in fact, play two seasons of Sunday League with Derbyshire after he had left Worcestershire. It was apparent that he did not part amicably with Worcestershire, but the breach has been healed, and it now seems possible that his son Dean, educated at Worcester Royal Grammar School, will join the Club and keep alive the link between Worcestershire and a great cricketing family.

Headley was not alone in feeling somewhat disenchanted, and there were rumours of dressing room unrest. To put the events that followed into context, it must be realised that these were restless times in cricket. They were the years before the Packer revolution and improvement in players' wages. Sponsorship, executive membership, hospitality tents and boxes were still in embryo form, and it was possible to walk into the first three days of a Lord's Test without buying a ticket in advance. There was, however, a growing feeling that the game was not being marketed as it should be, that there were untapped resources which could be used to benefit the game and all connected with it.

For Worcestershire, 1975 began disastrously. They lost all four zonal matches in the Benson and Hedges Cup, including the one against Oxford and Cambridge at New Road, when Imran Khan took four for 4 in 8.3 overs. There was a second-round exit in the

Gillette Cup, and the County were soon out of touch in the Championship and never looked like retaining their title. Only in the John Player League, which brought more money to Worcestershire than when they won the title in 1971, did the side do itself justice.

They had won eight and lost three matches when they entertained Derbyshire at New Road on 3 August. Worcestershire batted first and began with a partnership of 114 in 56 minutes between Ormrod and Turner. Later, Imran Khan reached 50 in 17 minutes, and 110 runs came from ten overs, Parker scoring 29 of them.

In 38 overs, Worcestershire made 307 for four, the first time that a side had reached 300 in a Sunday League game. This total was beaten by Essex at Southend eight years later, but, by then, the fielding circles and their attendant restrictions were in operation, and the Worcestershire score will remain a record for the pre-circle days. Turner hit 86, Ormrod 63, Yardley 64, Parker 29, Imran Khan 51 not out, Wilkinson 3 not out, and there were 11 extras. Derbyshire could manage only 189, but they lost only one wicket, and Ron Headley hit 87 not out against his old colleagues.

The following week, at Old Trafford, Lancashire made 146, and Worcestershire were 143 with four balls to go when Lee bowled Ormrod. A young Phil Neale and his skipper Norman Gifford could manage only three off the remaining deliveries, and the match was tied. That tie was to cost Worcestershire the title, for they won their four remaining matches, but finished two points behind Hampshire.

The excitement and pleasure at this stirring finish in the Sunday League was soon forgotten when it was learned after the final Championship defeat (in two days at the hands of Hampshire) that the players had presented a round-robin letter to the committee expressing a lack of confidence in various members of the administration and with the pay structure that they were being offered.

The situation was further exacerbated when Jack Bannister, secretary of the Players' Association, who had discussed the players' proposals with them, was quoted in the *Worcester Evening News* as saying that a member of the County committee had helped draft the round-robin which expressed no confidence in the administration.

On 17 September, the committee met and refuted the criticisms of officials. A statement was issued: 'The committee unanimously expressed its complete confidence in the officers of the club.' Also, at this meeting, the list of players to be retained for 1976 was decided upon. This list was not published for a week, but the news that two capped players, Brain and Yardley, were not to be retained was leaked to the press before then.

The dismissal of Brain was the great shock. He had had three very successful seasons after returning from injury which had threatened his career. He had been the new-ball bowler in 1975 although again he had been troubled by injury, and with Holder almost certain to be with the West Indian side in 1976, Worcestershire members wondered and asked who would do the bowling for their county.

When the list of retained players was announced it was learned that not only had Yardley and Brain been sacked, but Cass, who had hit 172 not out at Leicester earlier in the year, Wilkinson and Roberts were also not to be re-engaged. On top of this, John Inchmore had talked of resigning and Johnson had left cricket to follow a career as a journalist.

The reaction to these dismissals was strong, and the Supporters' Association and an action group urged that a special meeting should be called so that those concerned with the welfare of the Club could learn exactly what was happening. A meeting was called at Worcester Guildhall in October at which the committee were prepared to face their critics, but the hall could not accommodate all those who wanted to attend and the meeting was abandoned in chaos with some 1,000 people unable to gain admission and to hear the debate. The meeting was reconvened in Malvern on 10 November.

There was a sad and unfortunate clash between Norman Gifford and Dick Howorth, chairman of the cricket committee, at this second meeting, which was a stormy affair lasting two hours. When the heat died down certain things became clear. Mike Vockins explained the reason for the committee's decision not to re-engage five players, underlining three points:

1. The aim was to bring better results.
2. To allow room to bring in promising youngsters so that they could play alongside mature players rather than wait for a time when all the older players might retire and leave the side short of experience and the younger players bereft of guidance.
3. There was the need to budget sensibly in the face of deficit.

For their part, the committee agreed to a three-point proposal that they should examine their own structure, that they should improve communications with players and that dressing-room rumours should be brought into the open so that appropriate decisions could be made.

Brain joined Gloucestershire and continued to live in Worcester. He bore no malice against the County Club who, he said, 'thought I was too old'. He was 35 and prone to injury so that, anxious to give more work to Pridgeon, one can understand Worcestershire's reasoning. Yardley joined Northants, and Cass, who had left Essex in similar circumstances a few years earlier, left the game, as did Wilkinson and Roberts.

John Inchmore decided to continue with his career, but there were more shocks in store for Worcestershire. Imran had been assisting the County during his vacations from Oxford, but, having come down from university, his status would change. In October 1975, Worcestershire requested that he be registered for the following season, but they were told that, as Imran was no longer at an educational establishment, he was now considered as an overseas player. As the County already had its full quota of overseas players, Turner, Holder and Parker, they would not be allowed to register him. The registration committee's decision was unanimous, but, in January 1976, Worcestershire appealed to the Cricket Council, the game's highest authority, who overturned the decision on the grounds that Imran had resided in Worcester since 1971, a fact unknown to the registration committee.

So Imran played a full season for Worcestershire in 1976 and took 65 wickets and scored 1,062 runs in what was a heartening season for all concerned. The young players justified the confidence that the committee had shown in them. Phil Neale, with an Honours Degree in Russian from the University of Leeds and a Fourth Division Championship medal with Lincoln City, hit 90 against Kent in May and took a maiden century off the West Indian tourists in August. Dipak Patel scored 107 against Surrey in July to become, at the age of 17, the youngest Worcestershire century-maker, since Frank Chester.

If his off-breaks were yet barely used Patel promised, like Neale, to become a fine cricketer. Pridgeon, too, although expensive, showed great potential as the third seamer, for Inchmore generally shared the new ball with Imran and did wonderfully well. Senghera's off-breaks were a little disappointing, and Wilcock's wicket-keeping strangely erratic, but Boyns emerged in mid-season as a good all-round prospect and brilliant fielder while the senior members of the side, Gifford, Turner, Ormrod and D'Oliveira gave the youngsters the guidance and authority that was needed.

It was D'Oliveira who was the season's hero. Worcestershire were beaten in the first round of the Gillette Cup and mounted no challenge in the John Player League, but they reached the knock-out stage of the Benson and Hedges Cup. In the quarter-final, at Worcester, they gave a glorious display to beat Leicestershire by five wickets after being asked to make a formidable 269. Ormrod and D'Oliveira played magnificently in adding 104 for the second wicket at five an over. Later, when 68 were needed from the last ten overs, Imran and Neale took Worcestershire to victory with two balls to spare.

The semi-final, at Edgbaston, produced an equally fine game. Turner hit 143 not out, Imran 72, and Worcestershire reached 281 for four. Warwickshire died bravely, failing by 12 runs, but Pridgeon

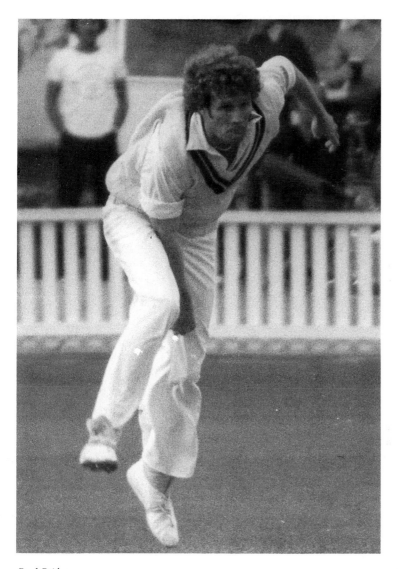

Paul Pridgeon.

made a vital contribution when he took a stunning catch off his own bowling to dismiss the dangerous Kanhai. Worcestershire were in their fourth final.

Gifford won the toss and asked Kent to bat first. It did not seem a wise decision when Johnson and Woolmer became the first opening pair to share a century stand in a Lord's final, Benson and Hedges or Gillette. Johnson started uncertainly, but Woolmer drove powerfully from the start with a sense of adventure which marked his play in the

195

one-day game, although not outside it. The advent of D'Oliveira slowed the run rate, but Woolmer, anxious not to become bogged down, launched an attack on the Worcestershire all-rounder and hit him for 15 in one over. Shortly after, D'Oliveira chased a wild throw from the outfield in an attempt to stop overthrows and, in doing so, tore a hamstring. He was helped from the field, and Worcestershire were denied the aid of their most economical one-day bowler and most aggressive batsman.

Having scored 61 in 30 overs, Woolmer was caught at deep mid-on. Gifford posted his men far and wide, and Kent did not score a boundary for 16 overs, but Asif and Ealham kept the score moving after Johnson was bowled by Boyns in the 44th over. They relied mainly on brisk running between the wickets, and Kent reached 236 for seven.

Basil D'Oliveira had only reached the dressing room with assitance. His leg was packed in ice, and doctors said that the injury was too severe for him to be allowed to bat.

Ormrod and Turner began soundly for Worcestershire, scoring at three runs an over. Then Woolmer and Shepherd took over the attack, and, in the 13th over, Shepherd had Turner taken low down behind the wicket. Neale, promoted in the order because of D'Oliveira's injury, was tied down before offering a catch to cover. Ormrod, Imran and Hemsley hit well, but each fell to a catch on the boundary by Johnson whose four catches and fine innings brought him the Gold Award.

Suddenly, to a roar of appreciation, D'Oliveira came down the pavilion steps with Turner to act as his runner. The score was 90 for 4. He had insisted that he would bat if needed, and he was. The whole of his left leg was strapped in an attempt to cut off feeling, even from the toes. He could only stand firm-footed at the crease and had to rely on powerful short-arm jabs. He explained later that he decided to get as far over to the off as he could and hit to leg. For Underwood, he stood firm and tried to carve the ball over extra cover. His left leg was giving him agony so that he could only play off the back foot: 'I kept my left foot slightly off the ground and hit through the line of the ball whenever it came near me. My power and the fact that I was a back-foot player obviously helped me.' He and Boyns added 35 and increased the run rate. The limping hero hit a succession of fours and straight drove into the pavilion for six. Worcestershire needed 75 from the last ten overs, and while D'Oliveira remained there was hope, but in the 47th over he was bowled by Jarvis having hit 50 out of 75 in 14 overs. So Worcestershire lost the fourth of their four cup finals, but none will forget D'Oliveira's brave innings.

The Worcestershire committee had done what was requested of

them and undergone a period of self-examination. As a result, the County committee was reduced in size and restructured. Much work had been carried out on the County Ground, none violating its essential character. The Ladies Pavilion had been opened in 1956 and was soon to win renown among those with the game at heart for the quality of its teas. These teas are the work of the voluntary ladies group, and anyone who has not tasted them has yet to enjoy cricket to the full. Initially, the late Lillian Buller was one of the main organisers, and she has been succeeded by Joyce Booth, so maintaining the Yorkshire-born Worcestershire wicket-keeper connection.

A covered stand was erected between the press box and the secretary's office in 1973–74, and in 1976, the Supporters' Association supplied most of the money that was needed for the Club to buy the ground from the Dean and Chapter of Worcester Cathedral, who had long been benevolent and kindly landlords. It was a momentous step. Tasteful improvements have taken place at the ground in the years since.

Having done so well with their blend of youth and experience, the Worcestershire Committee were bewildered and angry at the end of the 1976 season when Imran announced that he did not want to play for the County any more. The Committee were convinced that he had been offered large sums of money to move elsewhere, and allegations and rumour were rife. The whole affair has never been explained to the satisfaction of all. Imran said he found Worcester boring, that he missed Oxford and that all his friends had moved to London. Mike Vockins said it would be quite in order for him to live in London and travel to Worcester for his cricket. Imran rejected the idea. He accused Worcestershire of failing to provide him with adequate accommodation. It was generally believed that the County had paid for his education, finding him a place at Worcester Royal Grammar School and helping him through Oxford. Imran hotly denied this, but none could deny that Worcestershire had made it possible for him to play county cricket and had greatly assisted in the development of his game.

The County felt aggrieved. They had engaged Imran when he was a cricketer of unproven ability. He had been welcomed when few others took notice of him, and Worcestershire had gone to a great deal of trouble to have him recognised as eligible for county cricket and had provided him with the necessary residential qualification. They had invested much in Imran and were to receive nothing for their investment. They had a right to feel aggrieved, for, with Holder, D'Oliveira and, it was believed, Gifford, nearing the end of their careers, Imran, at 24, represented their future.

Worcestershire opposed his move vehemently, and there were few who supported him. The Professional Cricketers' Association deplored his transfer to Sussex. Imran was a great player, who always knew his own worth, but he did not prove the easiest of county cricketers, and it would be wrong to suggest that the followers of Worcestershire cricket have ever forgiven him.

His departure left Worcestershire with a void, and for two years they continued their policy of youthful rebuilding. There were to be no serious challenges for titles, but there was to be some good, honest, entertaining cricket. Turner, D'Oliveira and Ormrod were still in full flow. Henderson and Humphries arrived. Neither was quite to fulfil the hopes held for him. Jim Cumbes became more regularly available and, to the delight of all, was awarded his County cap in 1978.

Neale was capped the same year which, in many ways, was rather a disappointing one. The County did not win a Championship match at New Road and slipped to 15th in the table. The Australian all-rounder Greg Watson had a moderate season and Holder played in only four Championship matches although he appeared regularly in the Sunday League.

It was in the Sunday League that Worcestershire showed their best form. The opening John Player match was abandoned, but there was victory at Taunton, and a crowd of 5,000 paid £3,200 to see Warwickshire beaten at New Road. The win at Taunton began a run in which ten out of twelve matches ended in victory, and when Worcestershire went to Eastbourne on 6 August they led the table by six points. That match was lost and was followed by defeat at home to Kent and defeat at Trent Bridge. Lancashire were beaten in the last game of the season, but fourth position was rather disappointing after early season promise.

That promise came nearer to fulfilment in 1979 when Worcestershire enjoyed a successful, if bizarre, season. To begin with the County signed Younis Ahmed, who was released by Surrey. There is an automatic wistful shake of the head every time one thinks of Younis. Here was a glorious left-handed batsman, sound in technique and fluent of shot. He could so dwarf those around him as to suggest greatness, but as Surrey had found, and Worcestershire and Glamorgan were to find, he had the fatal flaw of a tragic hero and was his own worst enemy. In his first season with Worcestershire, however, he thrilled and entertained and scored 1,508 Championship runs alone at an average approaching 70.

The County had also expected to sign Garth le Roux. Holder was near the end of his career, as was D'Oliveira, who was bowling less and less, and Watson had been disappointing so that a bowler to open the attack was the obvious requirement. Le Roux had played for Sussex against the New Zealanders in 1978 and for Sussex Second Eleven.

Worcestershire, 1979. Standing (l to r): B. J. R. Jones, C. N. Boyns,
G. G. Watson, J. Cumbes, A. P. Pridgeon, D. N. Patel, P. A. Neale, Younis
Ahmed, D. J. Humphries. Seated: V. A. Holder, E. J. O. Hemsley,
G. M. Turner, N. Gifford (capt.), B. L. d'Oliveira, J. A. Ormrod,
J. D. Inchmore.

They offered him a contract, but he was later approached by Worcestershire whom he informed that he had no commitment to any other county. At the beginning of July, he declined an offer made to him by Lancashire and spoke again to Worcestershire. The County were of the opinion that he had agreed terms with them on 20 July, and two days later, at noon, he shook hands with three leading officials who believed he would take the field at 2.00 pm that afternoon. At 1.30 pm, he phoned Worcestershire to say that he was joining Sussex. Investigations revealed that both Sussex and Worcestershire had behaved perfectly well, and there was no animosity between them, but the TCCB deferred le Roux's registration until 1980.

To match the eccentricities off the field there were those on it. The opening match of the season welcomed Somerset to New Road. The weather was not welcoming. It was bitterly cold and there was rain, sleet and hail. As if these were not enough to contend with, while preparing the pitch the groundstaff rolled over the starting handle from the heavy roller, which had fallen off, and crushed it into the pitch. Another strip had to be prepared two yards away, and the start of the match was delayed.

In the Benson and Hedges Cup, Worcestershire lost their opening match at Cardiff. They beat Gloucestershire and Minor Counties (South), but cherished little hope of reaching the quarter-finals when Somerset arrived for the last game in the zonal matches while Glamorgan, with two victories, were due to play, and expected to beat, the Minor Counties side.

If Worcestershire beat Somerset, the two sides would be level on nine points each, which Glamorgan wee also expected to achieve. In the case of sides finishing level on points, strike rates by bowlers would decide the issue. Somerset were ahead on this count.

There was no play possible on 23 May, and the game at New Road was played on the following day before approximately 100 people who had braved the poor weather. Somerset batted first and Holder bowled to Rose, the Somerset captain. The first over produced one run, a no-ball, and then Rose declared. After the ten-minute interval Turner and Ormrod came out. Turner took a single off Dredge's first over and another single off Jennings' fourth ball. The match was over in under 20 minutes after 16 deliveries. Worcestershire were not pleased and refunded money to the paying spectators. Geoffrey Lampard, the chairman, who had done much to see the county through a difficult period, commented: 'It is a great pity when the supreme game of cricket is brought down to this level.' Rose had preserved the Somerset strike rate, but he had lost a few friends. Somerset were later disqualified from the competition although, in fairness, they had broken no written rules.

In spite of a brilliant 107 out of 178, with three sixes and seven fours, by Younis against his old club, Surrey, Worcestershire were beaten by five wickets in the quarter-final. In their first match in the Gillette Cup, they were swamped by Leicestershire.

The County's trials and tribulations were not over. The match against Northamptonshire at Worcester at the beginning of June provided another bizarre incident. There was no play on the first day, and Northants were bowled out for 294 on the second. Worcestershire reached 146 for six, and Gifford declared in an attempt to keep the match alive and believing that, as his side were 148 in arrears, they had avoided the follow-on. With the loss of the first day, however, the match was now a two-day affair, and the follow-on could be enforced when a side was 100 or more behind. Watts promptly enforced the follow-on, and Gifford, much embarrassed, saw his side draw.

Worcestershire did well in the Championship although they could not avoid their brushes with the Laws. At Derby, in mid-August, after stoppages throughout the three days, Gifford and Patel bowled out

Derbyshire in the nineteenth over of the last hour. Gifford believed that Worcestershire had four overs in which to make 25 to win. After two overs, however, with Worcestershire on 17 for one, the umpires, Halfyard and Spencer, removed the bails and the match was drawn. Gifford phoned Lord's and was highly critical of the way in which he had been misled, but his request to have the last ten minutes replayed was refused. On that same day, Essex won the Championship, and Worcestershire were to finish second.

Worcestershire had not challenged until August by which time Essex were far ahead in the Championship race and had, in fact, accumulated enough points by the end of July to win the title which was finally theirs by a margin of 77 points. As well as Younis, Turner, Neale, Ormrod and Hemsley batted consistently; Gifford, Cumbes and Inchmore carried most work in attack, while Patel was developing into a fine all-rounder.

The advance of the younger players was highly satisfactory, and the results in the John Player league were as encouraging as those in the Championship. Worcestershire finished third, eight points behind the leaders, but, not aided by three abandonments, they never looked likely to take the title. Younis added to his lustre in the Championship matches by scoring 668 runs in John Player League matches, more than any one else in the country.

The one discordant note for the County, in spite of their good form, was a decline in support, and there was a concern that an apathy had gripped the public in the City of Worcester in particular. For this reason, the County took a match to Stourport-on-Severn in July 1980, in an attempt to stimulate interest in the north of the county where traditionally, support has been strong.

Worcestershire batted first in this match and hit 387 with David Humphries, a pugnacious left-handed batsman, hitting 108 not out. He and Hartley Alleyne, the West Indian pace bowler who had been engaged to succeed Vanburn Holder, put on 146 in 96 minutes for the seventh wicket. Alleyne hit five sixes and six fours in his 72, which turned out to be his highest score for Worcestershire. Rain over the weekend turned a good wicket into a sticky one, and, after a blank Monday, Lancashire, Worcestershire's opponents, were bowled out twice in under four and a half hours. Gifford turned the ball prodigiously and had match figures of ten for 40.

The match was symbolic of the changing times in that it was sponsored by Parsons Controls Holdings Limited who owned the ground. Sadly, the recession the following year prevented Parsons from staging further matches at the ground.

The innings victory over Lancashire at Stourport-on-Severn was one of Worcestershire's few successes in 1980. The County did reach the semi-final of the Benson and Hedges Cup only to lose a soggy match spread over three days, and they were quarter-finalists in the Gillette Cup, but rain marred much of the summer and results generally were disappointing.

Turner, Ormrod, so good and so under-rated a player, and Younis scored well. Neale and Hemsley now gave themselves more fully to cricket, and Alleyne, Gifford and Pridgeon, awarded his County cap, had days of success. Alleyne, injury-prone, proved to be no real successor to Holder and played only 38 matches in three seasons with Worcestershire.

For Holder and D'Oliveira, 1980 was the final season. Of D'Oliveira we have said much, and his life with the Club was to continue on a full-time basis, for he was appointed coach, a post for which, it proved, he was admirably suited and in which he has had the greatest success. He will always be remembered as one of the brightest flowers in the garden of Worcestershire cricket.

Holder has never had the acclaim of some of his West Indian contemporaries like Holding and Roberts. Perhaps, the lean gentle giant was too self-effacing, but 109 Test wickets and a place in the first World Cup winning side are testimony to a very fine player. No man could have given more to Worcestershire where he is still looked upon as 'one of us' rather than as an overseas visitor.

Gifford decided to make 1980 his last year as captain and handed over to Glenn Turner, and new names like Curtis, Weston and Fisher began to appear on the score-card.

Paul Fisher, a wicket-keeper signed from Middlesex, had 27 dismissals in seven matches at the end of 1980 and was so successful that he resigned his post as a master at Marlborough College. His career with the County was to last only one more season, however, for Humphries, the better batsman, was preferred in 1981 and capped, and Fisher returned to teaching at Prior Park in Bath. He remembers his days with Worcestershire with pleasure, but believes that the County were in a state of flux at the time, as yet unable to come to terms with the more demanding pattern of the modern game.

Certainly, there was little to enthuse about in 1981. Turner invariably asked the other side to bat first when he won the toss, believing his team was better at chasing a target than bowling opponents out. In this, he was probably right, although Gifford, Pridgeon and Patel worked very hard in the absence of Alleyne and Inchmore for much of the time through injury. Turner himself continued to score with a panache that made the 'strokeless wonder' of 14 years earlier seem the dimmest of memories. He was never a muscular player, but relied on certainty of timing and uncanny placing for his runs. His fellow countryman, Richard Hadlee, described him as a run-a-ball man, but in his last years at Worcester, he was more like a four-a-ball man so eager was he to score runs, so adept at scoring them. In 1981, he again passed 2,000 runs. Nine times he reached three figures, and against both Northamptonshire at Stourbridge, the last time the County played at the ground, and against Warwickshire at Worcester, he hit a century in each innings.

Younis, Neale and Mark Scott, an impressive newcomer from the Lord's ground staff who opened the innings after Alan Ormrod had his arm broken when playing against Essex in June, gave Turner fine support, and Patel regained the all-round form which had deserted him the previous season. Worcestershire began disastrously and finished strongly, but there was a scent of change in the air. Holder had gone and so had D'Oliveira. Birkenshaw's brief, late career with the Club ended after one season, and Cumbes and Henderson had also departed.

Turner did not play when the Australians came to New Road in July, and the team was led for the first time in a first-class match by Phil Neale. The Australians won by seven wickets, but Neale hit 145 not out in the County's second innings. It was a knock of rare quality, and the 27-year-old Neale's leadership drew favourable comment. Worcestershire cricket was about to move into a new age.

TOWARDS THE SUMMIT

PHIL NEALE BECAME WORCESTERSHIRE'S third captain in three years in 1982. It was not an easy time to take over, but he had proved himself a man totally fitted for the job. In the summer of 1978, he had returned from his football commitments with Lincoln City later than had been agreed upon by the County. He was disciplined and accepted the punishment without argument. A man who is to give orders and exert discipline and control must know also how to take them. He had proved himself a capable batsman, an intelligent cricketer, willing to listen to advice, and a man who combined the qualities of tact and firmness, strength and consideration. In many ways he was in the Kenyon mould.

There were two problems that confronted him initially. The first was his early season absences because he was still trying to help Lincoln City win promotion; the second was the fact that, under the new TCCB ruling, Turner and Alleyne would not be able to appear in the

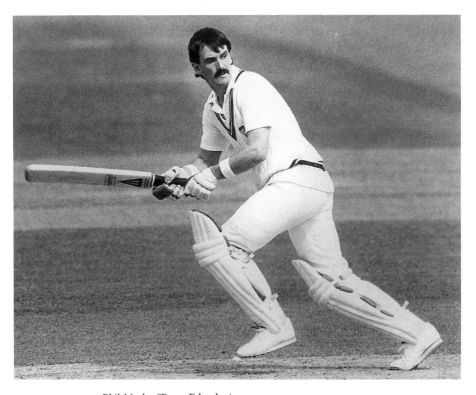

Phil Neale. (Tony Edenden)

side together as only one overseas player was now allowed. The great problem that emerged as the season progressed was that Neale did not have an attack at his disposal which was capable of bowling the other side out twice in three days.

An early exit from the Benson and Hedges Cup and failure to mount a challenge in the early stages of the John Player League were compensated for by the performance of Glenn Turner. In the first match of the season, against Oxford University in The Parks, he hit 239 not out, at the time of the highest score of his career. Neale

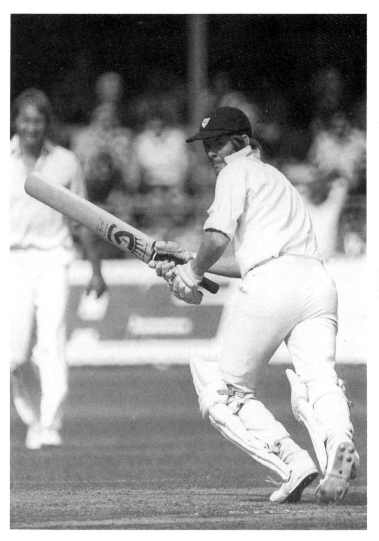

Glenn Turner.

declared at 401 for two, but it is significant that Worcestershire failed to win the match for, having been dismissed for 211 in their first innings, the University hit 202 for three in their second.

The innings against Oxford was the 99th century of Turner's career. He followed it with 4 and 27 against Derbyshire, 4 and 0 against Gloucestershire, and 6 and 4 against Somerset. This was a very bad run by Turner's standards, and it seemed it must be only a matter of time before he found his form again. Warwickshire were the visitors to New Road for the Bank Holiday game beginning on 29 May.

Neale won the toss, and Worcestershire batted. By 12.55 pm, after 115 minutes' batting, they were 148 without loss, and Turner had reached 102. At 3.03 pm, with Ormrod just out for 79, Worcestershire were 296 off 65 overs and Turner was 201. At 5.35 pm, he reached the first triple century in county cricket since Jack Robertson's 331 on the same ground in 1949. He had become the 19th batsman to score 100 hundreds in first-class cricket, and the first non-English player after Don Bradman to accomplish the feat. In all, he batted for 343 minutes and hit two sixes and 39 fours. Neale declared at 5.43 pm.

Kallicharran hit the highest score of his career on the second day, and the match was drawn.

Steve Perryman, medium-pace right-arm bowler, had come from Warwickshire in 'exchange' for Jim Cumbes, but he was to have little success in his two seasons with Worcestershire. More importantly, 1982 saw the debut of Richard Illingworth, a slow left-arm bowler from Yorkshire. His native county refused even to guarantee him a second-team game while Worcestershire offered him a contract. It proved to be one of their wisest of moves. Another to make an appearance in 1982 was Basil D'Oliveira's son, Damian. Other young men like Newport, Ellcock, Warner and Webster also pushed for first-team recognition. Tim Curtis had an extended run in the side.

Turner missed a couple of games through injury, and then he hit centuries against Lancashire, Yorkshire and Kent in successive Championship matches. The match against Kent was played at Hereford. First-class cricket had returned to the Race Course ground in 1981 when the game with Glamorgan was staged there to mark the formation of the County of Hereford and Worcester. That match was drawn as was the game in 1982, which marked Glen Turner's 284th appearance and last Championship match for Worcestershire. He hit 118 and 66. Appendicitis followed, and an operation ended the season which he said would be his last for the County. He remained top of the first-class averages with 1,171 runs, average 90.07. His 72 centuries for Worcestershire remain a record for the County.

His self-imposed exile from Test cricket for a period tended to

WORCESTERSHIRE *v* WARWICKSHIRE

Played at New Road, Worcester on 29 and 31 May and 1 June 1982

MATCH DRAWN

WORCESTERSHIRE	FIRST INNINGS		SECOND INNINGS	
G. M. Turner	not out	311	c and b Small	32
J. A. Ormrod	c Cumbes b Lethbridge	79	c Humpage b Lethbridge	43
D. N. Patel	not out	88	b Lethbridge	22
Younis Ahmed			c Willis b Sutcliffe	10
*P. A. Neale			not out	17
†D. J. Humphries			c and b Kallicharran	5
A. P. Pridgeon			b Sutcliffe	12
N. Gifford			not out	14
E. J. O. Hemsley				
R. K. Illingworth				
S. P. Perryman				
Extras	b 1, lb 19, nb 3	23	b 2, lb 4, nb 6	12
Total	(for 1 wkt dec)	501	(for 6 wkts dec)	167

BOWLING	O	M	R	W	O	M	R	W
Willis	12	0	76	0	5	1	17	0
Small	7	0	54	0	8	3	33	1
Cumbes	9	0	58	0				
Lethbridge	20	1	94	1	11	5	26	2
Sutcliffe	40	5	127	0	16	3	60	2
Asif Din	10	1	29	0				
Lloyd	7	1	22	0				
Kallicharran	7	0	18	0	7	1	19	1

1st inns: 1-291
2nd inns: 1-50, 2-103, 3-106, 4-124, 5-129, 6-152

WARWICKSHIRE	FIRST INNINGS		SECOND INNINGS	
D. L. Amiss	run out	64	c Humphries b Gifford	21
T. A. Lloyd	c Ormrod b Pridgeon	0	c Turner b Gifford	3
A. I. Kallicharran	c Perryman b Patel	235	b Patel	35
†G. W. Humpage	c Patel b Illingsworth	15	c Patel b Illingworth	23
K. D. Smith	c Pridgeon b Gifford	31	not out	62
M. Asif Din	c Humpage b Illingworth	12	c Turner b Illingworth	39
C. Lethbridge	c Neale b Illingworth	0	not out	2
G. C. Small	c Gifford b Patel	0		
*R. G. D. Willis	c Humphries b Illingworth	7		
S. P. Sutcliffe	not out	1		
J. Cumbes	not out	4		
Extras	b 2, lb 8, nb 1	11	b 1, lb 9, nb 2	12
Total	(for 9 wkts dec)	380	(for 5 wkts dec)	197

BOWLING	O	M	R	W	O	M	R	W
Pridgeon	15	2	54	1	7	2	15	0
Perryman	10	0	20	0	4	1	9	0
Gifford	41	11	100	1	20	1	59	2
Illingworth	37	9	85	4	19	7	42	2
Patel	40	8	110	2	13	3	60	1

1st inns: 1-4, 2-168, 3-217, 4-283, 5-326, 6-346, 7-347, 8-364, 9-372
2nd inns: 1-34, 2-35, 3-81, 4-101, 5-188

Umpires: W. L. Budd and C. Cook

Turner's 100th first-class century.

*Captain; †Wicket-keeper

diminish Turner's achievements in some quarters, but the final record at Test and county level speaks for itself. He had total application, searched for the art of pure technique and then imposed upon it some creations of his own. He was essentially his own man, something of an enigma, even a cricketing Bohemian, but he was a very great player.

With Younis, Neale, Patel, Ormrod and Curtis consistent, Worcestershire had no problem in scoring runs, even without Turner, and Weston, too, played some fine knocks, notably an innings against the Pakistan tourists. In the last hour and a quarter on the second day, the Sunday evening, he shared an opening partnership of 94, of which he scored 86 with 16 boundaries. In spite of moments like this, the ever-pressing problem of how to bowl people out tended to overshadow the joys of the batting.

At the end of the year, it was decided not to re-engage Norman Gifford. He was 42 and had been with Worcestershire for 22 years, and the County felt it was unfair to hold back the promising Richard Illingsworth who, with Newport and the other young players, had played an important part in Worcestershire winning the Second Eleven Championship under Basil D'Oliveira's tutelage.

Gifford was to enjoy an Indian summer with Warwickshire, but it was with Worcestershire that he spent by far the greater part of his fine career. He had a comparatively flat delivery and was accurate and economical, but he could also spin the ball appreciably and was devastating on a wicket that gave him a hint of assistance. Moreover, his career spanned the introduction of the one-day game (he was the individual award winner in the first Gillette Cup Final, remember) and he was one of the first to respond to the bowler's need for adaptation and flexibility now that he was confronted by so many different styles of cricket. He took more than 200 wickets for Worcestershire in the John Player League. He had been a thoughtful and strong captain for Worcestershire and had done much to encourage young players. He could be trenchant, as David Graveney recalled in his introduction to Brian Brain's book. Graveney survived against Holder and Brain late one evening in 1973, and Gifford's message to Brain was clear: 'If that lanky so-and-so gets another ball pitched in his half of the wicket, that's the last bloody game you'll play for Worcestershire.' He did not get another one. Brain had him caught behind off a lifter. Gifford was firm and fair, liked and respected. He played through good and bad times with Worcestershire and contributed so much and was a fine ambassador for the game.

Turner was gone and Gifford was gone, but an exciting young second eleven were champions, and there was a feeling of optimism. Ted Hemsley, too, had departed, and Hartley Alleyne had been released, but Terry Alderman had been contracted to play for one year

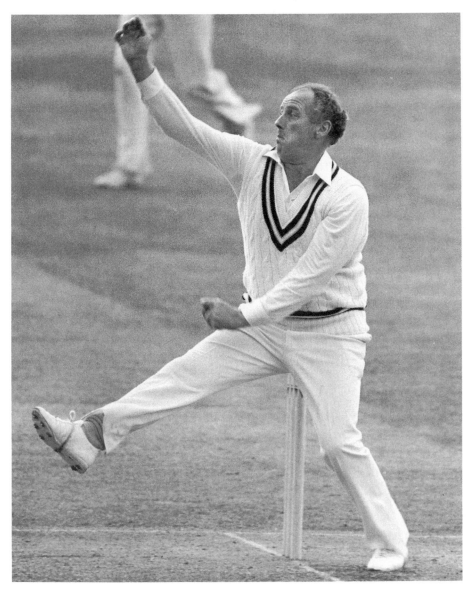

Norman Gifford. (George Herringshaw)

at least. Then, in November, 1982, at Perth, Alderman rugby tackled a
lout who had invaded the pitch during the first Test match and
dislocated his right shoulder. The injury did not heal, and a few weeks
before the start of the 1983 season Worcestershire were informed that
Alderman would not be joining them on medical advice.

This was not the end of the County's troubles. Younis Ahmed hit 10 not out in the opening match of the season against Yorkshire in which, because of rain, only 32 overs were possible. He followed this with 35 not out against Somerset at Taunton where so much time was lost to rain that each side had just one innings. The innings at Taunton proved to be the last Younis would play for the County. Worcestershire were due to play Leicestershire in a John Player League match on 8 May. The game, in fact, was rained off, and it was learned that Younis had placed a bet on Leicestershire to beat his own county in a match in which he was due to play. Such conduct was, of course, totally unacceptable, and Younis's days with Worcestershire were over.

The County engaged Collis King at short notice, but his commitments in the Lancashire League limited his appearances, and, in truth, he was never a man to shine fully in seven-day-a-week cricket. He did have the flair for the spectacular, however, and on the occasion of his debut, against Somerset at New Road, he hit 123 with six sixes and 12 fours.

This was typical of Worcestershire's season, moments of individual success, but very disappointing results as a team. Career-best performances tumbled over each other. Paul Pridgeon, offered his release at the end of the 1982 season, took 72 first-class wickets and became the spearhead of the attack. Weston, Damian D'Oliveira, McEvoy, who had joined the County from Essex, and David Banks all hit maiden centuries. For Banks, it came on the occasion of his first-class debut against Oxford University in The Parks. Neale and Patel batted splendidly, and Richard Illingworth was voted the Supporters' Association 'Uncapped Player of the Year'.

The Club had warned at the outset of the season that the financial position was not good and dreadful weather did not help to improve it. Nevertheless, for a side that finished second to bottom in the Championship and fifth from bottom in the John Player League, being engaged in three tied matches in succession at one time, they received most encouraging support. In an age when it was becoming fashionable only to follow a winning side, the people of Worcestershire were showing patience and understanding, and some excellent young cricketers were to remain grateful for it.

The only hint of anger from supporters came at the end of the season when the County announced that Perryman, Watkins, Webster, who had been hard hit by illness, Slater and Scott were not to be re-engaged. It was the dismissal of Scott which caused the resentment, but he was to return in a coaching capacity and play a distinguished part in the Club's later successes.

Joining the County in 1984 were David Smith, the hard-hitting left-hander from Surrey, and the great Indian all-rounder Kapil Dev.

There was also a young man who had been brought with the Zimbabwe side for the Prudential World Cup in 1983 in order to gain experience and who returned in 1984 to play in the Birmingham League and for Worcestershire Second Eleven. He was 18 years old, and his name was Graeme Hick.

It seemed that Worcestershire's fortunes with overseas players were continuing as they had always done when Kapil Dev could not begin his career with the County because of a knee operation, and he did not take his place in the side until 9 June when he hit a violent 95 in the first innings against Hampshire. As well as Kapil Dev's belated debut, there was injury to Smith (who nevertheless completed 1,000 runs and hit a career-best 189 not out against Kent) and the departure of Alan Ormrod to his native Lancashire where he was to take up a coaching and management post.

Kapil Dev was to play only two seasons for Worcestershire, and not more than a dozen matches in either. He performed well, being both a leading batsman and a leading bowler in each season, yet he did not make a significant mark on Worcestershire cricket if one judges by playing record alone, for his appearances were too few. However he did leave some happy memories. He began the 1985 season with 100 at Lord's. The weather was cold, with snow later in the day, but he warmed it with his hundred off 78 balls in 75 minutes. His first eight scoring shots were fours, of which he hit sixteen in all, and he also hit two sixes, one of them, a straight drive off Cowans into the pavilion, to bring up his hundred.

What Kapil Dev did contribute, and is not measured by the record book, was a warmth of personality and a helpfulness and kindliness which were of immeasurable help to young players.

The patient blooding of young players began to show signs of reward in 1984 as the County climbed the table in both Championship and John Player League. A victory over Sussex in two days was a heartening beginning to the season which ended with wins over Gloucestershire, Somerset and Northamptonshire in successive matches at New Road, the first time in seven years that Worcestershire had won three Championship matches in succession.

The last of the three wins was achieved in spectacular style, for, set to make 301 in 63 overs, Worcestershire reached their target with two balls to spare. The hero of the victory was Martin Weston who hit a career best 145 not out in 229 minutes with 18 fours.

Weston had formed an exciting opening partnership with Tim Curtis, and both players scored 1,000 runs. Curtis filled the position vacated by Ormrod with great success and confirmed that he had made a considerable advance technically and temperamentally in a brief period. He suggested that he had the right qualities for an opener.

He was calm, initially cautious, yet capable of authority when settled. He showed, too, that he had a quiet charm and a gentle humour befitting a student of English Literature that made him an excellent team man. He was also an integral part of a smart fielding side that was giving reminders of past standards.

Neale and Patel scored heavily, and Patel's value as an all-round cricketer, an off-spinner and attractive batsman, was engaging the interest of the press, who saw him as a future England cricketer. Against Cambridge University at New Road in June, he and Curtis shared a second wicket partnership of 226 in 192 minutes, and Patel hit a career best 197. He also returned match bowling figures of nine for 84.

Paul Pridgeon once more had an outstanding season and John Inchmore was as willing as ever. Newport was quietly edging his way into the side, and Illingworth's process of maturation continued. It was as if a jigsaw puzzle were being formed, and more and more pieces were easing into shape.

The last match of the season was at The Oval, and Worcestershire included Hick in their side for the first time. His stay in England had been made possible by a Zimbabwe Cricket Union scholarship, and he had performed thrillingly in the Birmingham League. For Kidderminster, he created two new records, 1,234 runs and an innings of 182 not out against Moseley, the highest score in the League for 44 years. When Hick was at the wicket there was excitement in the air.

He did not bat in the first innings against Surrey, and, in a match that had been killed by rain, he came in at number nine in the second innings and hit 82 not out against a weakened attack. It was not an innings of great import statistically, but it impressed in the minds of those who saw it that the lad was rather a good batsman. That view was confirmed the following season when he began Zimbabwe's short tour of England with an innings of 230 against Oxford University and followed it with 192 against Glamorgan. Returning to Worcestershire, he scored 664 Championship runs, including 174 not out against Somerset and 128 against Northants in the last three matches.

In the final game, the one against Northants, Hick and David Smith, who hit 104 not out, celebrated what had been an outstanding season for them both, for the upright Smith, strong in attack and particularly sound against pace, won a place in the England party to tour the West Indies. These were not the only successes in a season in which excitement mounted and triumph seemed close at hand.

The County leapt to fifth in the Championship and topped their zonal group in the Benson and Hedges Cup only to be beaten on a technicality in the quarter-final. They made 230 in 54 overs, and Middlesex were 45 for 1 off 13 when rain finally ended any further prospects of play. Middlesex were awarded the tie by virtue of having a superior striking rate in the zonal matches.

The jigsaw was getting closer to completion. Lancashire had engaged Neal Radford, a fast-medium bowler born in what was then Northern Rhodesia and is now Zambia, and, having kept him until he had served an apprenticeship and become qualified as an England player, they discarded him. Worcestershire engaged him, and in his first season, 1985, he took 100 Championship wickets alone. No other bowler in the country took 100 wickets.

Worcestershire had also been looking for a wicket-keeper. Advances had been made to Brassington, but he had decided to remain with Gloucestershire, and the County signed Steven Rhodes, a 21-year-old from Yorkshire and son of a former Nottinghamshire professional. He was immediately preferred to Humphries and at the end of his first season was chosen for the England 'B' tour of Sri Lanka where he won the highest praise.

The Yorkshire-born Worcestershire wicket-keeper was a tried and tested custom, but few could have anticipated the success of Radford. His advent was particularly welcome, and meritorious, in that Pridgeon, the spearhead of the attack the previous season, could play in only one first-class match because of operations to his shoulder. Phil Newport seized the extra opportunities given him, and Inchmore and young McEwan also bowled well.

In the batting, Neale, Curtis, Patel and D'Oliveira each made 1,000 runs and, with Smith and Hick or Kapil Dev constituted a formidable and attractive batting line-up. Weston asked to drop down the order as he was being asked to bowl his medium pace on many occasions. One felt it was not a wise move, for he and Curtis had formed an admirably contrasting and effective pair, but Damian D'Oliveira moved up to open with Curtis and did the job well. He also hit his first John Player League century, against Surrey at Worcester, and so emulated his distinguished father, whose only John Player League century had been against Surrey at Byfleet 12 years earlier. It is the only instance of a father and son both scoring centuries in the League.

Worcestershire's great disappointment in 1985 was their failure in the semi-final of the NatWest Bank Trophy at New Road. Hertfordshire, Lancashire (with Smith getting a fine century, Kapil Dev taking five wickets, Worcestershire getting their highest total, 312 for five, and Clive Lloyd being given the individual award) and Glamorgan, with Smith again in excellent form, were beaten on the way to the semi-final against Nottinghamshire, which went into a second day.

Worcestershire made a controversial decision in their selection for the match. Kapil Dev had left to lead the Indian side in Sri Lanka after

Neal Radford. (Steve Lindsell)

playing with considerable success in the earlier rounds. Hick was now playing regularly in the Championship side, but it was decided to call up Collis King for the semi-final as it was felt that an all-rounder was essential. It proved to be a bad decision, but that is with the value of hindsight, and it must be emphasised that Hick was party to the decision and agreed with it, and that King had a fine record as a one-day cricketer.

Neale elected to bat first when he won the toss, but D'Oliveira was lbw in Hadlee's first over and Curtis was put down off a simple chance at slip in the New Zealander's next over. Smith was in the powerful form he had shown all summer, and he and Curtis added 112 in 38 overs. It was a wonderful platform from which to assault the bowling, but the pitch was sluggish, and after Smith was bowled by Rice for 57, nothing went quite as Worcestershire might have hoped. King, seemingly out of practise, fretted, swung and ran himself out after hitting 11 off 23 balls. Curtis, who played so well, advanced down the wicket and skied a catch to the bowler, Pick. Neale and Patel were asked for too much too soon, and the total of 232 for eight was below expectations.

The score began to look bigger when the low bounce accounted for Broad and Randall, both lbw. Rice played quietly and 59 were added before he was caught behind off Inchmore. Johnson, happier against pace than spin, attempted to cut Patel and was bowled. Hadlee stayed with Robinson, 75 not out, until the close when Nottinghamshire were 137 for four off 46 overs. This meant that they needed 96 off 14 overs with their main line batsmen, Robinson apart, gone, and the odds were in favour of Worcestershire.

Hadlee could not find his attacking form and was caught and bowled by Patel for 18 at 175. Nottinghamshire needed seven runs an over, but with French pushing singles and giving Robinson the strike, this seemed no great problem. Robinson was in majestic form, and the Worcestershire support bowling suddenly seemed to have limitations. From the last five overs, Nottinghamshire needed 28. On the last ball of the 59th over, French swung Radford high to square-leg where D'Oliveira put down a straightforward catch, but, as the batsmen contemplated a second run, he gathered the ball and threw down Robinson's wicket. The Nottinghamshire and England opener had hit 139 off 173 balls. The last over was bowled by Newport, and the second ball, a delivery of full length, found the edge of Hemmings's bat and skidded off to the boundary for four and a Nottinghamshire victory.

If the defeat by Nottinghamshire was a disappointment, 1986 was to provide a double disappointment. There was no advance in the Championship, and the County again finished second to bottom in the

John Player League. Moreover, the Worcestershire faithful suffered two semi-final agonies. Yet if this record seems to suggest a year of stagnation and frustration, that was far from the case. There was a buoyant feeling that Worcestershire cricket was on the verge of momentous achievement. The side was now respected by all and frightened of none.

Neal Radford proved that he was no one-year wonder as some critics had suggested. He took 81 first-class wickets, played twice for England and, against Somerset at New Road, he took a career best nine for 70, the best return by a Worcestershire bowler for 40 years. Vigorous and accurate, able to move the ball late, and always hustling the batsman, Radford had no superior as a county bowler, yet failed to do himself justice at Test level where, it seemed, he did not play his natural game and strove for too much pace.

In his last season, the powerful and loyal John Inchmore reached 500 wickets for the County, and Paul Pridgeon confirmed a return to full fitness with 59 inexpensive wickets. Steve McEwan underlined the policy of strength in depth, and, above all, there was the leap forward of Phil Newport, a genuine all-rounder.

Newport was now 24, his geography degree studies at Portsmouth Polytechnic behind him, and his right-arm fast medium bowling, sharpened on second eleven success, a lethal weapon. His 85 wickets in the season nearly doubled his best return of previous years, and, like Weston, Illingworth, Rhodes and Hick, he was awarded his County cap.

This was Hick's first full season in first-class cricket, and he made the important decision to withdraw from the Zimbabwe side for the ICC Trophy so that he could qualify as an England player. While, in a few years time, we shall celebrate this most heartily, we should never forget that debt that the cricketing world owes to the Zimbabwe Cricket Union in their nurturing of Hick's extraordinary talent.

In his batting with Kidderminster and for Worcestershire in his limited appearances in 1985, Hick had been recognised as something exceptional by those who followed cricket in the Midlands. In July 1986, he became a player of national renown. When Nottinghamshire came to New Road on 5 July they were challenging strongly for the Championship. They took command of the game and bowled out Worcestershire for 192, Hadlee and Saxelby each taking four wickets. By the end of the second day, Nottinghamshire appeared to be heading for victory, for Worcestershire finished on 154 for three, a lead of 36. Hick, however, was 76 not out.

On the final day, he launched a blistering attack on the Nottinghamshire bowling. He played an innings of awesome power, hitting Hemmings for five sixes, three over the pavilion, one into the

New caps at New Road: Illingworth, Weston, Neale and Hick, 1987.

road. He also hit 31 fours and faced 303 balls for his 227 not out which occupied 288 minutes.

Worcestershire's next Championship match was at Neath. Glamorgan declared at 268 for eight, and Worcestershire lost D'Oliveira at 13. Hick then joined Curtis, and, in 172 minutes, they added 287, which broke Worcestershire's existing second wicket record stand set up by Gibbons and the Nawab of Pataudi 53 years earlier. Hick's contribution to this stand was 219; Curtis hit 66. Hick hit eight sixes and 24 fours, faced only 146 balls and became the first batsman in the country to reach 1,000 runs. It was the highest score made on the Neath ground. Between lunch and tea on the second day, he hit 188. The superlatives had been exhausted, but Graeme Hick's part in the match had not.

Neale declared at 301 for one, and eventually Worcestershire had to make 225 in 33 overs to win the match. They lost D'Oliveira quickly, but Hick hit 52 off 22 balls in 24 minutes with three sixes and six fours. Worcestershire won with nine balls to spare, Neale and Curtis batting splendidly. A thought should be spared for Curtis who hit 66 and 63 in

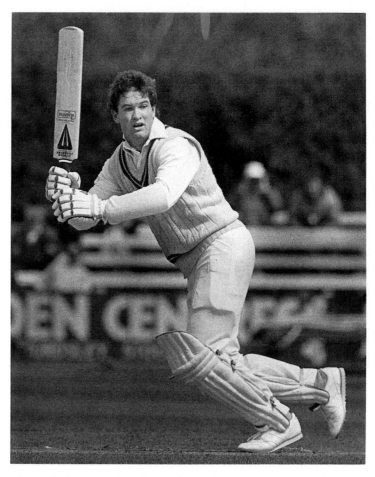

Graeme Hick. (George Herringshaw)

this match without being dismissed and whose part in Worcestershire triumphs has so often been overshadowed by Hick's brilliance. Curtis brought to the Worcestershire batting the solidity and consistency it had lacked, and much of what has been achieved was founded on his stability.

It was Hick, however, who was to steal the season's final headline when Glamorgan came to New Road for the return match in September. Glamorgan hit 399 for 7 declared, and, with David Smith hitting 100 in what proved to be his last game for the County, Neale was able to declare the Worcestershire innings at 304 for five. Morris asked Worcestershire to make 302 in 52 overs. Curtis was forced to retire hurt, and Hick went to the wicket needing 103 to complete

Tim Curtis. (Steve Lindsell)

2,000 runs for the season. He hit 107 off 121 balls in 147 minutes to become, at the age of 20, the youngest player to score 2,000 in a season. Worcestershire won by seven wickets with three balls to spare.

Amid these glories, there were disappointments. The semi-final of the Benson and Hedges Cup brought Kent to New Road. Neale asked the visitors to bat first, and Hinks and Benson, in an uncertain manner, put on 56 in 19 overs before Benson charged at Patel and was stumped. Hinks was lbw to the economic Weston seven runs later, but Tavaré and Taylor added 139 in under 26 overs to lay the foundation for a good score. Baptiste hit well, and Kent made 252 for eight.

Worcestershire began disastrously, losing D'Oliveira, Patel and Smith with only 38 scored. Hick and Neale began cautiously, but accelerated to add 118 in 32 overs. Both men batted excitingly, but both perished as the need for quick runs became more urgent. Neale was brilliantly run out by Chris Cowdrey, and Hick was lbw when he tried to steer Ellison to third man. Neale made 53, Hick 72. Weston, Radford and Inchmore batted bravely, but the task was too great. From the last ten overs, 91 were needed; 54 off the last five. Kent won by 11 runs.

There was still the NatWest Trophy, and Oxfordshire, Hampshire and Warwickshire had been brushed aside to bring a semi-final against Sussex at New Road. It was not a happy affair. The pitch had been under water earlier in the week, and a helicopter was used to dry out the ground. Only 32 balls were possible on the first day when Worcestershire reached 20 for no wicket. Play did not begin until 2.30 pm on the second day, and, at tea, after 33 overs, the score was 82 for two, a good total in prospect. Optimism was quickly dispelled by Imran, not well received by the crowd, who took three for 6 in five overs as Worcestershire lost six wickets for 17 runs in ten overs. Their final score of 125 was hardly likely to be a winning one, and Sussex won by five wickets on the third morning. Worcestershire had now lost three semi-finals in succession.

David Smith returned to Surrey at the end of the season after three fruitful seasons with Worcestershire. His career has had its turbulent moments and has not been without controversy, but he played some entertaining cricket in the Midlands, and he became an England player.

Dipak Patel also departed, electing to settle in New Zealand. He was still a very young man with many years of good cricket in him as was evidenced by his recognition at Test level by the New Zealanders. Quiet and unassuming, he was a graceful, attractive batsman, a brilliant fielder, and an off-spin bowler who did not quite reach the level of attainment that seemed possible. He was a very good team man and much missed.

Two surprising additions to the staff came shortly before the start of the 1987 season: Graham Dilley and Ian Botham. Few players have moved to another county in such a fanfare of publicity. Both men had their reasons for wanting a change; both settled on Worcestershire for their new cricketing home. The moves were not universally approved, but then Botham, in particular, has always excited debate, but they were to have a profound effect upon the future of Worcestershire cricket.

Both, of course, were Test cricketers of long standing. Dilley was a fast bowler who had a reputation of being prone to injury, and Botham, on his Test record, was the greatest all-rounder since W. G. Grace. Like Grace, he was a cricket Colossus. Importantly for Worcestershire, both men had tasted success whereas no-one else in the side had the experience of winning a competition. They brought to Worcestershire a new dimension, and Botham, in particular, brought the quality of self-belief.

Crowds flocked to New Road to see the opening match of the 1987 season when Kent, Dilley's old county, were the visitors. Dilley dismissed Taylor and Hinks in his second over, but Benson and Tavaré put on 285, and Kent controlled most of the match until Hick, Rhodes, Newport, Radford and Illingworth batted excitingly in the closing stages to give Worcestershire victory with 13 balls to spare.

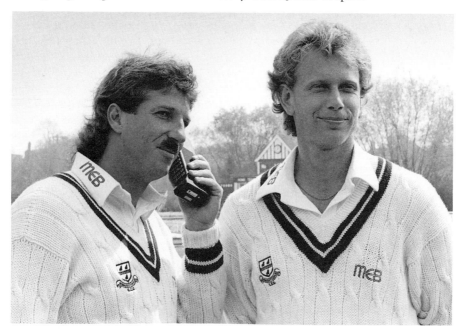

Ian Botham and Graham Dilley arrive at Worcester, April 1987. (Allsport)

Illingworth's batting was one of the surprises of the summer, and, going in as night-watchman against Warwickshire in July, he carried his bat for 120, the first century of his career. This could not disguise the fact that the departure of Smith and Patel had left Worcestershire with some holes in their batting line-up. Lord, lacking only in the confidence to match his undoubted ability, began to settle as Curtis's opening partner, but Weston took long to find his form and was rarely used as a bowler.

Botham played in only eleven Championship matches, being absent on Test duty for much of the summer, and Dilley, who showed great fire, missed the last part of the season through injury. Botham's one century, inevitably, came against Somerset at Taunton in what was a dour war of attrition, yet his influence on the side was to be significant.

It was apparent that, in spite of the continued brilliance of Hick, the consistency of Curtis and the exceptional bowling of Neal Radford who, for the second time in three seasons, took more than 100 wickets and was the leading bowler in the country, Worcestershire would not be serious challengers for the Championship. Also, for the first time in three years, they failed to reach the sem-final of either of the knock-out competitions.

Having scored 233 for eight in the Benson and Hedges quarter-final at The Oval, they fell victims of a violent assault by their former colleague David Smith, 110 not out, and Trevor Jesty, 85 not out, who put on 159 and took Surrey to victory with eight balls to spare.

In the first round of the NatWest Bank Trophy against Devon at Worcester, the County established a remarkable record for one-day cricket anywhere in the world by scoring 404 for three off their 60 overs. Botham and Curtis began with a stand of 152 of which Botham hit 101 off 92 balls. He hit three sixes and ten fours and was out before lunch. Hick then joined Curtis, and the pair added 127 before Curtis was out for 79. Hick reached his hundred off 81 balls, and his 172 not out, the highest score by a Worcestershire batsman in limited-over cricket, came off 111 deliveries. He hit eight sixes, four in succession in one over, and 13 fours. However weak the opposition and good the wicket, this was heady stuff.

Unfortunately, in the second round, at Chelmsford, Essex exploited a wicket that aided the seamers and won by 15 runs. Botham was caught behind first ball, and, in spite of a majestic 55 by Hick who was disdainful of the moving ball and late bravery from Radford and Dilley, Worcestershire never looked likely to match Essex's 194 for nine.

By this time, however, Botham had been converted most successfully into an opening batsman in limited-overs cricket, and he and Curtis blended into an ideal partnership. It is something of a

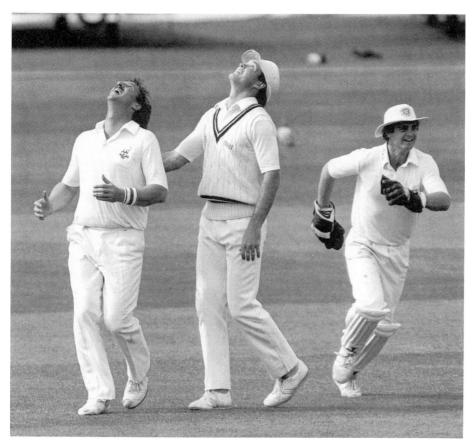

Success at The Oval, Benson and Hedges Cup Quarter-Final, 1987. Botham catches Lynch for o. Hick and Rhodes join in the celebrations, but the match was to end in disappointment for Worcestershire. (Allsport)

mystery why Botham had never been pushed higher up the order in one-day matches earlier in his career. It seems such a waste to have one of the world's most gifted attacking batsmen coming in with only a handful of overs remaining when he is capable of turning the course of any game. Neale recognised this, and asked Botham to open which he was glad to do. The move had its greatest reward in the Sunday League, sponsored for the first time by Refuge Assurance.

Two defeats in the first three matches hardly augured well for Worcestershire in this competition, but at the end of May, Essex came to New Road and made 202 for 6 in their 40 overs. Worcestershire lost Curtis at 58 in the 13th over after which Botham and Hick put on 145 in 18 overs and took their side to victory with 8.3 overs to spare. Botham scored 125 not out with two sixes and 16 fours. His hundred came off 106 balls. Wins over Leicestershire and Middlesex were followed by defeat at Trent Bridge and then an abandoned match at Gloucester where Botham took five for 27, his best Sunday bowling performance.

By the end of July, with Nottinghamshire two points ahead of Derbyshire at the top of the table, there was little thought of Worcestershire as serious contenders for the Refuge Assurance League, but victories over Sussex and Glamorgan suddenly changed the picture.

At Swansea, Curtis and Botham began Worcestershire's innings with a partnership of 104, and the following week, when Yorkshire were beaten at New Road, the same pair put on 119 in 16 overs and Worcestershire moved level with Nottinghamshire at the top of the table. Two matches remained.

On 30 August, Nottinghamshire suffered a surprisingly large defeat at the hands of Derbyshire while Worcestershire crushed Surrey at Hereford. Facing a target of 155, Curtis and Botham put on 130 for the first wicket. Worcestershire won by nine wickets. Botham hit 80 off 74 balls.

This meant that Worcestershire led Derbyshire by two points, with Nottinghamshire four points behind the leaders but with a game in hand. Rain came to Worcestershire's aid, for Nottinghamshire's game with Essex was abandoned so that Worcestershire had only to win their last game to become the first Refuge Assurance League Champions.

At Worcester, on Sunday, 13 September 1987, the gates were closed on a capacity crowd long before the start. Neale, whose quiet, intelligent captaincy had done much to bring Worcestershire to this brink of success, won the toss and asked Northamptonshire to bat. He was soon rewarded with the wickets of Bailey, Larkins, Lamb and Capel for only 28 runs. There was resistance from Roger Harper and Richard Williams who put on 85, but the visitors were bowled out in the last over for 168.

Curtis and Botham began Worcestershire's reply amid excitement greater than any that had been seen at New Road for many years. They put on 108 before Botham was bowled by Nick Cook for 61. It was the fourth time in succession that they had begun the Worcestershire innings in the Sunday League with a century partnership, a record. Hick joined Curtis, who finished with 69, and Worcestershire won by nine wickets with two overs to spare. There was great rejoicing, for the County had won their first trophy for 13 years.

In spite of the remarkable cricket played by Botham and Curtis, this was essentially a team achievement and was recognised as such. As well as being the leading wicket-taker in first-class cricket, Radford was the leading wicket-taker is the League, and he was ably supported by Botham, Newport, Pridgeon and latterly Hick. The batting had been consistently good.

If one may dwell on Botham's contribution, it was not simply his 707 runs and 27 wickets in one-day cricket that made him of such value, but his constant encouragement of his colleagues in the dressing room. He was ever telling them that they could and would win the title, and belief in oneself is so important in any field of human activity.

What was important about the Refuge Assurance League triumph was that it was, for the still young Worcestershire side, like running the first four-minute mile had been in athletics; now it had been achieved, anything was possible. There was a new-found confidence and an appetite for success.

Worcestershire seemed to grow in strength and entered the 1988 season fancied to win at least one of the five titles now on offer, yet there was early dismay when Botham, so much an inspiration the previous season, failed to find form and was discovered to be suffering from an injury to the back which necessitated surgery and which would end his season almost before it had begun. Dilley, on the other hand, was fit, but he was to be taken by England for much of the summer.

There were two notable additions to the staff, David Leatherdale, a Yorkshireman, and Steve O'Shaughnessy from Lancashire, one of those invaluable 'bits and pieces' players.

The County could hardly have hoped for a better start to the season. In the opening Championship match at Old Trafford, a four-day game, Graeme Hick hit 212 in 345 minutes. His innings included four sixes and 25 fours, and he and Phil Neale, who played the supporting role with 40 in four and a half hours, put on 202 for the fourth wicket. This was accomplished in conditions which were assisting the bowlers. Richard Illingworth had match figures of ten for 153, Hick took five wickets with his off-breaks, and Worcestershire won by ten wickets.

The success continued when Nottinghamshire, the reigning champions, were beaten at New Road. Dilley bowled at a lively pace and had a fine match, taking nine for 117. The next Championship match was against Somerset at Taunton, 5 to 9 May.

Worcestershire batted first and were soon in trouble. They had slipped to 132 for five when Rhodes joined Hick, but by the close the score was 312, with Hick 179 not out. The following morning, HIck and Rhodes continued their stand and extended it to 265, a County record for the sixth wicket, before Rhodes fell to Dredge for 56, made in 311 minutes off 274 balls. At lunch, Worcestershire were 427 for six, Hick 257, Newport 15.

Newport kept pace with Hick in the overs after the break until he was bowled by Marks for 27. Hick now cut loose. He reached his 300 with two sixes in three balls off medium-pacer Rose, and he moved from 300 to 400 in another 58 balls. On 379, he hit his eighth and ninth sixes, and his tenth took him to 398. A single brought him to 399, and then he pulled Dredge over mid-wicket for his eleventh six. He had also hit 35 fours. Neale declared, leaving Hick on 405 not out, the second highest score ever recorded in first-class cricket in England, beaten only by Archie MacLaren's 424 scored on the same ground 93 years earlier. Hick's innings had lasted for 552 minutes, and he had faced 469 balls. His runs were made out of 550 scored while he was at the wicket, and the last 137 had been scored in an eighth-wicket partnership of 177 with Illingworth in 106 minutes. This was also a County record. Hick now had scored 815 runs in the season, for he had batted well in the MCC–Championship County match at Lord's.

Somerset's woe was compounded when they lost Roebuck to the second ball of their innings, but they held out until the Monday when Worcestershire, with Phil Newport taking ten for 109, completed an innings victory.

Remarkably, a fortnight later, Somerset, who had had a dreadful start to the season, won at Worcester and brought the County back to earth with a crash.

Meanwhile, Worcestershire had qualified for the quarter-finals of the Benson and Hedges Cup and, in doing so, had shown great resilience. Their match against Minor Counties had been washed out so that they had been at a disadvantage to the other counties in their group, Yorkshire, Northamptonshire and Nottinghamshire. The chances of Worcestershire qualifying became very slim when Nottinghamshire came to New Road, and, in a game that went into a second day, won by one wicket. Put in to bat on a dubious wicket, Worcestershire suffered the early loss of Hick and Curtis, and, at 104 for six, they were in deep trouble. Rhodes batted with good sense, D'Oliveira played some brave shots, and a late flurry by Radford and Dilley raised them to a commendable 198 for nine.

A second wicket stand of 74 between Broad and Randall gave substance to the Nottinghamshire innings, but when bad light ended play they were 124 for three, still needing 75 from 18.2 overs. Worcestershire fought like tigers on the second day, and tight bowling and keen fielding reduced Nottinghamshire to 169 for eight. Hemmings found a good partner in Cooper, and when Botham came to bowl the last over only five were needed. Three were scrambled before Cooper was bowled. Pick, batting with a broken hand, snicked a single off the fifth ball to level the scores, and Hemmings clubbed the last ball of the match to the boundary.

SOMERSET *v* WORCESTERSHIRE

Played at Taunton on 5, 6, 7 and 9 May 1988

WORCESTERSHIRE WON BY AN INNINGS AND 214 RUNS

WORCESTERSHIRE FIRST INNINGS

T. S. Curtis	b Rose	27
G. J. Lord	c Mallender b Dredge	49
G. A. Hick	not out	405
D. B. D'Oliveira	c Roebuck b Rose	0
*P. A. Neale	c Marks b Mallender	0
I. T. Botham	b Rose	7
†S. J. Rhodes	c Felton b Dredge	56
P. J. Newport	b Marks	27
R. K. Illingworth	not out	31
N. V. Radford		
G. R. Dilley		
Extras	b 6, lb 16, nb 4	26
Total	(for 7 wkts dec)	628

BOWLING	O	M	R	W
Jones	32	4	97	0
Mallender	32	9	86	1
Marks	50	6	141	1
Rose	31	8	101	3
Dredge	34.5	8	133	2
Roebuck	10	0	48	0

Fall: 1-78, 2-112, 3-112, 4-119, 5-132, 6-397, 7-451

SOMERSET FIRST INNINGS / SECOND INNINGS

	FIRST INNINGS		SECOND INNINGS	
N. A. Felton	c Radford b Hick	24	c Rhodes b Newport	36
*P. M. Roebuck	lbw b Radford	0	lbw b Radford	17
J. J. E. Hardy	c Rhodes b Radford	39	b Newport	0
M. D. Crowe	c Rhodes b Newport	28	c Lord b Radford	53
R. J. Harden	lbw b Hick	2	lbw b Newport	3
V. J. Marks	c Botham b Newport	42	c Hick b Newport	7
†N. D. Burns	c Botham b Radford	32	c Illingworth b Hick	11
G. D. Rose	c Curtis b Newport	12	c Rhodes b Newport	30
N. A. Mallender	c Rhodes b Newport	3	lbw b Radford	1
C. H. Dredge	b Radford	16	c Curtis b Newport	17
A. N. Jones	not out	8	not out	3
Extras	lb 6, nb 10	16	b 2, lb 1, nb 11	14
Total		222		192

BOWLING	O	M	R	W	O	M	R	W
Dilley	12	0	40	0	14	2	40	0
Radford	23.5	1	77	4	17	6	39	3
Newport	17	4	59	4	15.3	3	50	6
Hick	8	3	18	2	11	4	15	1
Illingworth	1	0	4	0	11	4	20	0
Botham	9	3	18	0	6	2	25	0

1st inns: 1-1, 2-70, 3-70, 4-75, 5-147, 6-152, 7-166, 8-173, 9-203
2nd inns: 1-49, 2-59, 3-62, 4-74, 5-90, 6-111, 7-154, 8-167, 9-185

Umpires: R. Julian and R. Palmer

Graeme Hick's record-breaking innings.

*Captain; †Wicket-keeper

Worcestershire won at Northampton and then entertained Yorkshire, knowing that they had to win to qualify. At 41 for three, their
chances looked very slim, but Phil Neale played a splendid innings of
91, adding a record 121 for the sixth wicket with Rhodes, so that
Worcestershire reached 227. This proved too much for Yorkshire who
were out for 172. Ian Botham took five wickets and became the sixth
man to take 100 wickets in Benson and Hedges Cup games.

Worcestershire's dream of a Lord's final ended in the quarter-final
when, on a spiteful wicket in uncertain weather, they lost to
Hampshire by three wickets. Put in to bat, Worcestershire ended the
truncated day on 111 for five from 42 overs. Spirited batting from
Weston and Rhodes took them to 169 next morning, which looked
unlikely to be sufficient to win the match, but they fought
magnificently. Hampshire plunged to 84 for six against some inspired
bowling and briliant fielding, but a memorable innings from Robin
Smith won Hampshire the match with 11 balls to spare.

The interest now switched to the match against the West Indian
tourists on 28, 29 and 30 May. Hick began the game needing 153 to
reach his 1,000 runs for the season. He was soon at the wicket, for Lord
was bowled by Ambrose for nought. The pitch was not easy and the
bowling, inevitably, was sharp, and he worked hard for his runs. He
and Curtis put on 284, and Hick hit 22 fours in his innings of 172 which
meant that he became the eighth player in the history of the game to
score 1,000 runs before the end of May.

In the County Championship, Worcestershire had lost ground to
Middlesex who had started the season in majestic form and were
leading the table when they entertained Worcestershire at Lord's at the
beginning of June. There was no play on the first day, and Curtis
scored a patient 100 in six hours on the second. Each side forfeited an
innings which left Middlesex to score on the last day what
Worcestershire had scored on the second, 333. They never looked like
achieving the target. They were 15 for four and, finally, 124 all out on
a pitch which was never over-helpful to the bowlers. Phil Newport
was magnificent, constantly attacking the batsman, moving the ball
away late and bowling with fire and enthusiasm. He took a career-best
eight for 52, and Worcestershire were top of the table.

This lead was consolidated when maximum points were taken in
the game against Hampshire at New Road. Hick and Curtis scored
centuries of contrasting style, and Botham's helicopter, taking the
great man for convalescence, dipped in salute over the ground on the
first afternoon.

There now followed a lapse as three draws and defeat at Trent
Bridge coincided with Kent's winning streak. The loss at Trent Bridge
was unexpected, for Worcestershire had a first innings lead of 24 and
set Nottinghamshire to make 224 on the last day on a wicket which

was treacherous; but Tim Robinson hit a century and Nottinghamshire won by six wickets.

The Worcestershire challenge was reasserted with a thrilling victory over Yorkshire at Worcester in the third week in July. Graeme Hick drove, cut and pulled his way to 198 off 227 balls, and Neale was able to declare in the 99th over with 356 for seven on the board. Hick was splendidly supported by Phil Newport who hit 77 not out in a record seventh-wicket stand of 205. Yorkshire, without suggesting the same flair, made 302 for six on the second day. With the onus on Worcestershire to try to force a victory, Lord and Bent, substituting for Curtis on Test duty, batted enterprisingly in an opening partnership of 102, and Neale set Yorkshire to make 270 in 68 overs. Illingworth, whose form in the last month of the season played a significant part in Worcestershire's success, bowled a long and intelligent spell and took four wickets. The fourth was when he ran to mid-on to take a skier from Hartley. In the previous over, Radford had dismissed both Carrick and Sidebottom, and when Swallow was run out Worcestershire were victors by 21 runs with 13 balls to spare.

Sadly, the top of the table confrontation with Kent at Folkestone was ruined by rain, but Kent slumped badly at home to Somerset while Worcestershire engaged in another of those eccentricities which so often colour their matches with Northamptonshire. Another Hick century dominated the first day, and Neale declared after six overs on Monday. Some superb bowling by Radford, seven for 73, tumbled out Northamptonshire in 65.1 overs. Both sides then took the field, Geoff Cook insisting that he had not been informed that his side was to follow on. An altercation took place, and a ruling was sought from the TCCB by which time many valuable overs had been lost. Eventually Northamptonshire did follow on, but batted grimly through the last day.

With Kent and Essex, who were now challenging strongly, idle, Worcestershire moved into second place 11 points behind Kent with a resounding win over Sussex at Kidderminster. Phil Newport again bowled splendidly and Sussex were all out shortly after lunch on the Saturday, and the home side were well in the lead by the evening. Neale and Weston took their fifth wicket stand to 181 before Weston, on 94, edged leg-spinner Clarke to the 'keeper. Neale reached the highest score of his career, 167, and his side's 370 gave them a first innings lead of 224. Although Radford was suffering from a thigh strain, Sussex again fell to Newport, and Worcestershire won by nine wickets after 75 minutes on the third morning.

The interest now switched to the semi-final of the NatWest Bank Trophy. Worcestershire had beaten Cumberland and Nottinghamshire in a rain-ruined match at Trent Bridge where Curtis, 120, and Hick, 105, shared a stand of 186 in 36 overs of vintage batting.

Worcestershire's 283 for five left them winners on the faster run rate. The quarter-final victory over Gloucestershire was a tense affair. Gloucestershire made 185, and Worcestershire were 86 for four before Neale and Weston put on 74. Neale hit 45 and handled his bowling with such intelligence as to make him the obvious recipient of the Man-of-the-Match award as his side won by four wickets with 13 balls to spare.

The semi-final opponents were Hampshire, who had thwarted Worcestershire earlier in the season. Mark Nicholas's decision to field first was nullified when Curtis and O'Shaughnessy put on 148 in 40 overs, but Worcestershire lost seven wickets in 25 balls for the addition of 24 runs at the close of their innings. Nevertheless, they still reached a formidable 268. Hampshire were in contention until they lost three wickets in ten balls, including the wicket of Robin Smith, and they were beaten by 29 runs in light that was closer to night than day.

Worcestershire had now regained their early season momentum and, with Kent held at Chesterfield, they went to the top of the Championship table with a breathtaking win at Abergavenny. Neale declared Worcestershire's innings 98 behind Glamorgan's 298, offered the home side some friendly bowling and was rewarded with a target of 341 in 72 overs. Many counties would have ignored such a demand, but, after the early loss of Lord, Hick and Curtis batted with great purpose. They added 192 in 49 overs, and Hick became the first player in the country to reach 2,000 runs. Neale hit cleanly, and he and Hick put on 100 in 49 minutes. Both were out, Hick for 159, and although 72 were needed from the last ten overs, Weston hit 13 in the penultimate over of the match to make a memorable victory certain.

At The Oval, bad weather and some mediocre batting cost Worcestershire their Championship lead. At this point of the season, Neale showed his authority. Quiet he may be, but he accepted the role of leadership with understanding of its good and bad moments. He closed the door of the dressing room at the end of the first day's play at The Oval and was strong and clear in what he wanted of his team in the closing weeks of the season. He was always ready to give praise where it was due; he was equally ready to deliver a salvo of condemnation when he thought it was required. After an uncertain start to the season, his own batting had given the middle order the substance it had required. He led by example, and it was an example that many would do well to follow. On the last morning, Hick hit the fastest century of the season, 79 balls, but the rain came.

In the crucial top-of-the-tale clash with Essex, played in miserable conditions and poor light, Worcestershire were beaten by 77 runs in spite of fine bowling by Newport, who had just heard of his deserved selection for the England side.

Although losing to Essex in the Championship match, Worcester-shire won the Sunday League game by 18 runs. The Refuge Assurance League had, of course, been running parallel to the Britannic Assurance County Championship. Worcestershire had started indifferently in defence of their title, but had always kept in touch with the top four who would contest the new Refuge Assurance Cup. Defeat by Middlesex, the early pacemakers, at Lord's had been followed by a run of nine matches without defeat, one abandoned, the rest won, and the victory over Essex, the ninth in the sequence, had taken Worcestershire to the top of the table where, if they won their last match, they would stay.

The final match of the season was, inevitably it seems, against Warwickshire at New Road. Again there was a capacity crowd and television cameras, but there was a different kind of excitement from that provided by thrilling victories. Radford and the rest of the Worcestershire attack kept a stranglehold on the limp Warwickshire batting, and in 36 overs, the visitors were bowled out for 82. Totally professional application by Curtis and O'Shaughnessy saw the runs scored without loss in 27.1 overs. Worcestershire had won the Refuge Assurance League for the second year in succession, but celebrations were muted for they still had interest in the other three competitions that remained to be decided.

The Championship match with Warwickshire was ruined by rain, with Worcestershire in a strong position, but Kent surprisingly lost to Sussex at Maidstone. For the time being, however, attention switched to the NatWest Bank Trophy Final at Lord's.

Worcestershire C.C.C., 1988. County Champions, Refuge Assurance League Champions, Runners-Up NatWest Bank Trophy, Runners-Up Refuge Assurance Cup, Quarter-Finalists Benson and Hedges Cup. (Allsport)

It was Worcestershire's fifth appearance in a Lord's final, and they had lost the previous four. The day threatened rain which never came, but Gatting was pleased to win a toss which allowed him to ask Worcestrshire to bat first at 10.30 am on a damp pitch under lowering cloud. It proved to be a decisive toss to win.

Fraser bowled Curtis with a magnificent ball which pitched on leg stump and knocked back the off. O'Shaughnessy edged a widish ball to Downton, and Hick, after one classical cover drive, misjudged a straight ball. The first 12 overs produced only four scoring strokes, and Worcestershire were 9 for three.

Leatherdale, a highly confident and capable young man who had proved himself a fine acquisition, batted with bravery and determination as he tried to resuscitate the Worcestershire innings. Middlesex raced through their overs in an attempt to keep the pressure on Worcestershire, and Leatherdale and Neale were confronted by the problem of evaporating overs and approaching lunch. Feeling the urge to score runs, Leatherdale, who had batted with sense and aggression, hit at Needham in the last over before lunch and was bowled. The break came at 71 for four off 42 overs, Middlesex very much on top.

Weston, who had been an excellent substitute for Botham since early season and who had recaptured the zest of his game, helped Neale to add 66 before falling to the impressive Fraser, and Neale's courageous and exemplary innings was ended by Hughes who profited as batsmen swung for quick runs.

Middlesex could have had little fear about making 162 to win on a day which was now fine and warm, but Dilley was fast and fierce and menacing. He moved a ball away from Carr and forced both Slack and Needham to nudge into their stumps. There was a bonus for Worcestershire when Gatting was run out without facing a ball. Slack drove to mid-off and the former England skipper trotted gently down the pitch, bat in air, and arrived after the ball. At 28 for four, Middlesex were embarrassed, and Worcestershire had sight of the improbable.

Butcher stroked the ball elegantly, but he charged down the wicket when Ramprakash stayed put and was run out, 64 for five, and the game in the balance. It quickly tilted in Middlesex's favour as Ramprakash, graceful and powerful, and the purposeful Emburey added 85 in 24 overs and took the game out of Worcestershire's reach.

Dilley returned to bowl Emburey and have Ramprakash taken at long-leg. It was an outstanding bowling performance by Dilley, and had Worcestershire scored 20 or so runs more, it might have been a match-winning one, but Downton was able to stroke his side to victory with five overs to spare.

Four days later, the sides met again in the semi-final of the Refuge

Assurance Cup. It was a dour game on a sluggish wicket which troubled the batsmen. Worcestershire, eager for revenge, bowled well, none better than Radford and Illingworth, and restrained Middlesex to 146 for nine in their 40 overs, an unfinished last wicket stand of 36 between Cowans and Downton bolstering the score.

Worcestershire soon lost Rhodes, and Curtis top-edged to square-leg after a defensive vigil. Leatherdale then mocked the careworn attitude of the earlier batsmen with an innings of 41 in a partnership of 66 in 11 overs with Hick. By the time he was bowled, Worcestershire were only six runs short of victory. Hick took the individual award for his durable 74 not out on an untrustworthy pitch. It was an innings out of character to his usual exuberant stroke-making, but it proved the man's flexibilty and resolution.

Middlesex's part in Worcestershire's season was not yet over. In the penultimate round of Championship matches, they, and the weather, denied Kent at Lord's while, with Hick and Neale hitting centuries and Illingworth taking ten wickets, Worcestershire trounced Gloucestershire at Bristol.

This meant that Worcestershire began their last Championship match of the season just one point ahead of Kent and knew that if they won and took maximum points, the title was theirs for the first time in 14 years and for only the fourth time in their history. Kent did all that they could and beat Surrey by an innings early on the third day so that, briefly, they were top of the table. Worcestershire were opposed by Glamorgan, the wooden spoonists elect, and the Welshmen batted doggedly enough on the opening day. Their suspect middle order was never likely to deny the avid Worcestershire attack, however, and the home side duly collected their four bowling points. There was a little uncertainty at the start of the Worcestershire innings, and Hick was dropped at slip when 41. He is not a man who offers two chances, and he proceeded to bat in regal manner, reaching his tenth century of the summer, so equalling Turner's record. He was out for 197 and was not needed again, so 'Doc' Gibbons record number of runs in a season for the County remained intact by 39 runs.

Glamorgan began their second innings just before lunch on the third day of what was scheduled as a four-day match. The game had begun late that day because of an insane attempt on the part of someone whose knowledge of cricket was limited to vandalise the pitch. The groundstaff worked hard to remove deposits of industrial soap, and play began an hour late. It was to matter little, and it seemed to disturb Glamorgan more than it frustrated Worcestershire. The Glamorgan second innings lasted less than 36 overs and when Bastien skied Illingworth to Leatherdale and the catch was gleefully accepted Worcestershire were champions by one point.

The season was not quite at an end for there was still the final of the new Refuge Assurance Cup and there was a full house at Edgbaston to see Worcestershire play Lancashire. Neale won the toss and asked Lancashire to bat. Weston bowled Mendis with the second legitimate ball of the match and had Hayhurst stumped so that Lancashire were 4 for two in the third over. Fowler and Fairbrother repaired the damage cautiously, and they added 65, but it was Jesty, who should have been run out when he was one, and Watkinson who brought Lancashire back into the game with 81 in nine overs. For the first time in the season, Worcestershire's bowling looked a little jaded and the fielding erred. Lancashire made 201 for five.

O'Shaughnessy was well caught by Mendis, and Hick was bowled by Watkinson when he tried to cut a ball too close to him after a frustratingly barren period. Curtis was caught behind when he tried to force the pace, but Leatherdale and Neale breathed hope. Leatherdale was bowled when the wily Simmons forced him onto the back foot, and Neale, after some fine shots, was caught at deep mid-wicket by Watkinson. Rhodes promised briefly to lift the innings, but he was caught off a widish ball from Hayhurst and Radford fell the same way first ball. It was Lancashire's day. Another year it would have been a more bitter disappointment than it was, but Worcestershire could hardly complain about a season which had seen them win two of the five competitions, finish runners-up in two others and quarter-finalists in the fifth. No other county can claim a comparable record.

It seemed a long cry from the time before Don Kenyon became captain and said: 'We knew we were never going to win anything so we just enjoyed it.' The joy is still there, as is apparent to all those who have watched the County in recent seasons, but the winning has come too.

In spite of the praise rightfully lavished on Hick, the success has been based on team work and on the philosophy of strength in depth. This allowed Weston to play such an important part when Botham was injured, for Leatherdale to find his feet when D'Oliveira was injured and lost form, and for Pridgeon, O'Shaughnessy, Bent, McEwan and Ellcock to make significant contributions at various parts of the season.

Hick topped the national batting averages. Curtis, Dilley and Newport (93 wickets at 19.82 runs each in all matches) played for England. The two Yorkshiremen, Rhodes and Illingworth, enhanced their claims for a Test cap, and Neal Radford, in the England squad for the Texaco Trophy matches, remained among the most prolific wicket-takers in county cricket.

Initially, there had seemed to be a middle-order weakness, but Rhodes, who hit a maiden first-class hundred, and Neale rectified the fault. Neale, unobtrusively, but always positively, saved several difficult situations and enjoyed a splendid season. He led the side

WORCESTERSHIRE *v* GLAMORGAN

Played at New Road, Worcester on 14, 15 and 16 September 1988

WORCESTERSHIRE WON BY AN INNINGS AND 76 RUNS

GLAMORGAN	FIRST INNINGS		SECOND INNINGS	
*A. R. Butcher	b Newport	35	c Illingworth b Dilley	9
P. A. Cottey	c Illingworth b Weston	13	lbw b Radford	5
P. G. P. Roebuck	c Rhodes b Newport	13	c Illingworth b Dilley	1
M. P. Maynard	c Newport b Illingworth	69	(7) st Rhodes b Illingworth	19
G. C. Holmes	b Radford	6	(4) c Hick b Newport	33
M. J. Cann	st Rhodes b Illingworth	28	(5) c Rhodes b Newport	9
J. G. Thomas	b Radford	40	(6) c Neale b Newport	0
J. Derrick	not out	21	c Curtis b Newport	0
†C. P. Metson	b Radford	1	c and b Newport	0
S. L. Watkin	c Illingworth b Radford	1	not out	13
S. Bastien	c Curtis b Illingworth	5	c Leatherdale b Illingworth	10
Extras	b 2, lb 4, nb 6	12	b 1, lb 1, w 2	4
Total		244		103

BOWLING	O	M	R	W	O	M	R	W
Dilley	21	4	54	0	8	3	30	2
Radford	28	5	84	4	8	2	16	1
Newport	15	2	53	2	10	2	23	5
Weston	7	2	16	1	5	1	14	0
Illingworth	25	14	31	3	4.2	1	18	2

1st inns: 1-32, 2-62, 3-63, 4-77, 5-153, 6-178, 7-225, 8-227, 9-231
2nd inns: 1-14, 2-14, 3-24, 4-58, 5-58, 6-72, 7-72, 8-80, 8-80

WORCESTERSHIRE	FIRST INNINGS	
T. S. Curtis	b Thomas	8
G. J. Lord	b Derrick	42
G. A. Hick	c sub b Thomas	197
D. A. Leatherdale	c Metson b Bastien	4
*P. A. Neale	c Roebuck b Cann	29
M. J. Weston	c Bastien b Cann	2
†S. J. Rhodes	c Thomas b Watkin	46
P. J. Newport	c Metson b Thomas	30
R. K. Illingworth	c sub b Derrick	16
N. V. Radford	not out	10
G. R. Dilley	b Derrick	5
Extras	b 5, lb 21, w 2, nb 6	34
Total		423

BOWLING	O	M	R	W
Thomas	36	4	130	3
Watkin	34	8	91	1
Derrick	32	7	91	3
Bastien	25	5	65	1
Cann	8	2	20	2

Fall: 1-8, 2-101, 3-110, 4-253, 5-263, 6-342, 7-383, 8-386, 9-417

Umpires: B. Dudleston and B. Leadbeater

The victory which won Worcestershire their fourth County Championship.

*Captain; †Wicket-keeper

calmly and shrewdly and celebrated his benefit year as few men have ever been able to.

Rhodes and Illingworth have said that the joy they have had in coming to Worcestershire is that the pressure is less than it was at Yorkshire where there was a constant hassle to succeed. They feel that they have been allowed to develop their games at the correct pace. It says much for those who administer the Club and who have never lost sight of the joy of cricket and of the leaner days.

Whatever is celebrated today and whatever the ambitions for the future (to win a cup final?), it must never be forgotten that without Foley, the Fosters, Root, Perks, the Lytteltons, the Coventrys, Major Jewell and the rest, there would be no Worcestershire cricket. From the very outset they knew that there was a beauty in the game at Worcester under the gaze of the cathedral that there is nowhere else and which must be kept alive. It imposes a tranquillity which transcends winning or losing and which is the very essence of the game. Arlott knew it, and so do those who watch their cricket at New Road.

Like rattle of dry peas in pods,
The warm crowd faintly clapped,
The boys who came to watch their gods,
The tired old men who napped.
The members sat in their strong deck-chairs
And sometimes glanced at the play,
They smoked, and talked of stocks and shares,
And the bar stayed open all day.'

STATISTICAL SECTION

BIOGRAPHICAL DETAILS
OF WORCESTERSHIRE PLAYERS

NAME AND EXTENT OF Career	BIRTHPLACE	DATE OF BIRTH	DATE OF DEATH
J. D. Abbott 1919–1920	unknown	unknown	unknown
George Edmond Brackenbury Abel 1923–1939	Worcester	22. 6.1904	
Frank Hand Adshead 1927	Dudley	9. 2.1894	22.11.1977
William Ewart Adshead 1922–1928 (later known as Barnie-Adshead)	Dudley	10. 4.1901	26. 1.1951
Frank Douglas Ahl 1931–1933	Potchefstroom, South Africa	24.11.1908	3. 5.1967
Joe Ainley 1905–11906	Huddersfield, Yorkshire	28.10.1878	18.11.1907
Michael Lionel Yeoward Ainsworth 1948–1950	Hooton, Cheshire	13. 5.1922	28. 8.1978
Keith John Aldridge 1956–1960	Evesham	13. 3.1935	
Thomas Allchurch 1919–1920	Stourbridge	1883	23.10.1934
Hartley Leroy Alleyne 1980–1982	Bridgetown, Barbados	28. 2.1957	
John Hamish Hugh Anton 1950	Kidderminster	19. 9.1926	
Alfred German Archer 1900–1901	Richmond, Surrey	6.12.1871	15. 7.1935
E. Argent 1928		6. 2.1902	
Edward George Arnold 1899–1913	Exmouth, Devon	7.11.1876	25.10.1942
John Robert Ashman 1953–1954	Rotherham, Yorks	20. 5.1926	
Gilbert Ashton 1922–1936	Bromley, Kent	29. 9.1896	6. 8.1981
Harry Austin 1928	Moseley, Birmingham	17. 4.1892	29. 8.1968
Harold Godfrey Bache 1907–1910	Churchill	20. 8.1889	15. 2.1916
Edward Stanley Baker 1933–1934	Moseley, Birmingham	9.11.1910	
Harold Frank Baker 1911	Walsall, Staffs	4. 5.1884	4. 5.1954
W. Baker 1920			
Ernest William Bale 1908–1920	Mitcham, Surrey	18. 9.1878	6. 7.1952
David Andrew Banks 1983–1985	Brierley Hill, Staffs	11. 1.1961	
Arthur Frederick Bannister 1900–1902	Birmingham	15. 6.1874	1933
Anthony Royston Paul Barker 1967–1969	Newcastle-under-Lyme, Staffs	30. 5.1947	
Jack Charles Barley 1909	Eton, Bucks	4.12.1887	1960
Brian Joseph Barrett 1985	Auckland, N.Z.	16.11.1966	
Keith Rodney Baylis 1966–1967	Redditch	5.11.1947	
Edward George Bayliss 1939	Worcester	5. 1.1918	
Enoch Harvey Bennett 1925	Dudley	21.12.1894	
Hugh Frederic Bennett 1901	Pershore	10.11.1862	26. 7.1943
M. Bennett 1946			
Paul Bent 1985–1988	Worcester	1. 5.1965	
Robert George Wilmot Berkeley 1919–1922	Romford, Essex	23. 4.1898	28. 8.1969
Robert Berry 1955–1958	Manchester	29. 1.1926	

Albert Bird *1899–1909*	Moseley, Birmingham	17. 8.1867	17. 6.1927
Ronald Ernest Bird *1946–1954*	Quarry Bank, Staffs	4. 4.1915	20. 2.1985
Jack Birkenshaw *1981*	Rothwell, Yorks	13.11.1940	
George Matthew Blakey *1939*	Fylde, Lancs	1907	1968
Charles Percy Blewitt *1912*	Dudley	1877	15.12.1937
Leonard Blunt *1946–1948*	Worcester	29. 3.1921	
Roy Booth *1956–1970*	Marsden, Yorks	1.10.1926	
Ian Terence Botham *1987–1988*	Heswall, Cheshire	24.11.1955	
John Jesse Bowles *1926–1928*	Lower Slaughter, Glos	3. 4.1890	27.11.1971
Frederick Lloyd Bowley *1899–1923*	Brecon, Wales	9.11.1873	31. 5.1943
Cedric Nigel Boyns *1976–1979*	Harrogate, Yorks	14. 8.1954	
Michael Ewart Bradley *1951–1952*	Halesowen	29. 3.1934	
Brian Maurice Brain *1959–1975*	Worcester	13. 9.1940	
Percival Robert Brinton *1904*	Kidderminster	5. 2.1873	14. 5.1958
Ronald Lewis Brinton *1924*	Kidderminster	26. 2.1903	19. 4.1980
Reginald Seymour Brinton *1903–1909*	Lower Mitton	15.12.1869	23. 2.1942
Robert Gillespie Broadbent *1950–1963*	Beckenham, Kent	21. 6.1984	
Eliot George Bromley-Martin *1899–1900*	St. Cloud, Worcester	8.10.1866	23. 1.1946
Granville Edward Bromley-Martin *1899–1904*	Callow End, Worcester	18.10.1875	31. 5.1941
George Wilfred Brook *1930–1935*	Mirfield, Yorks	30. 8.1888	24. 7.1966
Alan Brown *1979*	Darwen, Lancs	23.12.1957	
Eric Lindsay Douglas Brownell *1908*	Hobart, Tasmania	7.11.1876	22.10.1945
Edwin Harvey Bryant *1923–1925*	Bromsgrove	12. 9.1886	24.10.1948
Charles Harry Bull *1931–1939*	Lewisham, Kent	29. 3.1909	28. 5.1939
John Sydney Buller *1935–1946*	Bramley, Yorks	23. 8.1909	7. 8.1970
Mark Bullock *1900*	Dudley	1872	1925
Percy George Bullock *1921*	Birmingham	28. 8.1893	1.12.1986
Edward Lancelot Bunting *1922*	Tillington, Staffs	10.12.1883	26. 2..1962
Arthur Temple Burlton *1922*	Coimbatore, India	10. 3.1900	10. 2.1980
William Beaumont Burns *1903–1913*	Rugeley, Staffs	29. 8.1883	7. 7.1916
Frederick Bonham Burr *1911*	Hastings, Sussex	2. 8.1887	12. 3.1915
Robert Dixon Burrows *1899–1919*	Eastwood, Notts	6. 6.1871	12. 2.1943
Sydney Edmund Busher *1908–1910*	Solihull, Warwicks	19.12.1882	6.1953
George Robert Byrne *1914–1921*	Northfield, Birmingham	28. 5.1892	23. 6.1973
William Somerville Caldwell *1901–1904*	Altrincham, Cheshire	26. 2.1878	14. 1.1964
Evelyn George Massey Carmichael (of Carmichael) *1903*	Worcester	3. 4.1871	14. 7.1959
Austin Michael Carr *1921–1925*	Chester	29. 9.1898	20.12.1946
Robert George Mallaby Carter *1961–1973*	Horden, Co. Durham	11. 7.1939	
George Rodney Cass *1969–1975*	Overton, Yorks	23. 4.1940	
Rupert Ashley Cave-Rogers *1919*	Cannock, Staffs	27. 5.1902	2. 5.1976
John Etheridge Chadd *1955–1956*	Whitestone, Hereford	27.10.1933	

Charles Henry Chatham *1934*	Tewkesbury, Glos	18. 6.1910	
Frank Chester *1912–1914*	Bushey, Herts	20. 1.1895	8. 4.1957
George Herbert Chesterton *1950–1957*	Chirbury, Salop	15. 7.1922	
Thomas Clare *1920–1925*	Stourbridge	1883	6. 5.1940
Alfred Talbot Cliff *1912–1920*	Glanford Brigg, Lincs	27.10.1878	25. 1.1966
John Cavendish Cobham *1924–1925* (9th Viscount) formerly Lyttelton	Hagley Hall	23.10.1881	31. 7.1949
Leonard John Coldwell *1955–1969*	Newton Abbot, Devon	10. 1.1933	
Christopher George Arthur Collier *1910–1914*	Banff, Scotland	23. 8.1886	25. 8.1916
John Collinson *1946*	Sotterley, Suffolk	2.10.1911	29. 8.1979
Arthur Joseph Conway *1910–1919*	Stirchley	1. 4.1885	29.10.1954
Edwin Cooper *1936–1951*	Bacup, Lancs	30.11.1915	29.10.1968
Frederick Cooper *1947–1950*	Bacup, Lancs	18. 4.1921	22.12.1986
Percival Thomas Corbett *1922–1923*	Droitwich	1900	26. 6.1944
Charles Frederic Corden *1900–1903*	Croydon, Surrey	30.12.1874	26. 2.1924
John Bonynge Coventry *1919–1935*	London	9. 1.1903	4. 7.1969
Gilbert Clifford Cox *1935*	Stroud, Glos	5. 7.1908	31. 3.1974
Leonard George Crawley *1922–1923*	Nacton, Suffolk	26. 7.1903	9. 7.1981
Robert James Crisp *1939*	Calcutta, India	28. 5.1911	
George Lawson Crowe *1906–1913*	Worcester	8. 1.1885	23. 6.1976
John Alexander Cuffe *1903–1914*	Toowoomba, Queensland, Australia	26. 6.1880	16. 5.1931
James Cumbes *1972–1981*	East Didsbury, Manchester	4. 5.1944	
Timothy Stephen Curtis *1979–1988*	Chislehurst, Kent	15. 1.1960	
Geoffrey Charlton Darks *1946–1950*	Bewdley	28. 6.1926	
Guy Mortimer Coleridge Davidge *1911*	Woolwich, Kent	2. 3.1878	17. 2.1956
Trefor E. Davies *1955–1961*	Stourbridge	14. 3.1939	
John Percy Davis *1922*	Lye	26. 1.1884	16. 2.1951
Major Davis *1911*	Lye	1882	27. 4.1959
John Edward Days *1900–1907*	Pershore	1872	1947
Louis Norman Devereux *1950–1955*	Heavitree, Exeter, Devon	20.10.1931	
Richard Jaynes Devereux *1963*	Castle Bromwich, Warwickshire	24.12.1938	
George Dews *1946–1961*	Ossett, Yorks	5. 6.1921	
Graham Roy Dilley *1987–1988*	Dartford, Kent	18. 5.1959	
Basil Lewis D'Oliveira *1964–1980*	Cape Town, S. Africa	4.10.1931	
Damian Basil D'Oliveira *1982–1988*	Cape Town, S. Africa	19.10.1960	
Philip George Dorrell *1946*	Worcester	6.12.1914	
Alan Robert Duff *1960–1961*	Kinver, Staffs	12. 1.1938	
E. Eden *1923*		unknown	
Herbert Charles Edwards *1946*	Colley Gate, Staffs	3.12.1913	

Ricardo McDonald Ellcock *1982–1988*	Bridgetown, Barbados, W.I.	17. 6.1956
John William Elliott *1959–1965*	Worcester	12. 2.1942
P. S. Evans *1928*		unknown
William Henry Brereton Evans *1901*	South Africa	29. 1.1883 7. 8.1913
Russell Stanley Everitt *1901*	Kings Heath, Birmingham	8. 9.1881 11. 5.1973
Ralph Denis Mark Evers *1936–1938*	Stourbridge	11. 8.1913
Percy Hamilton Farnfield *1925*	Guildford, Surrey	16. 6.1881 19. 8.1962
Charles Leslie Dinsdale Fawcus *1925*	Bromley, Kent	8.12.1898 8.12.1967
Charles Duncan Fearnley *1962–1968*	Pudsey, Yorks	12. 4.1940
John Benjamin Fereday *1899–1901*	Dudley	24.11.1873 1. 1.1958
Charles Anderson Fiddian Green *1931–1934*	Handsworth, Birmingham	22.12.1898 5. 9.1976
Frank Field *1928–1931*	Langley, Worcs	29. 2.1908 25. 4.1981
Paul Bernard Fisher *1980–1981*	Edmonton, Middlesex	19.12.1954
John Alfred Flavell *1949–1967*	Wall Heath, Staffs	15. 5.1929
Henry Thomas Hamilton Foley *1925*	Hereford	25. 4.1905 13.12.1959
Basil Samuel Foster *1902–1911*	Malvern	12. 2.1882 28. 9.1959
Christopher Knollys Foster *1927*	Ledbury	27. 9.1904 4.12.1971
Geoffrey Norman Foster *1903–1914*	Malvern	16.10.1884 11. 8.1971
Henry Knollys Foster *1899–1925*	Malvern	30.10.1873 23. 6.1950
Maurice Kirshaw Foster *1908–1934*	Malvern	1. 1.1889 3.12.1940
Neville John Acland Foster *1914–1923*	Malvern	28. 9.1890 8. 1.1978
Reginald Erskine Foster *1899–1912*	Malvern	16. 4.1878 13. 5.1914
Wilfred Lionel Foster *1899–1911*	Malvern	2.12.1874 22. 3.1958
Richard Harold Fowler *1921*	Islington, Middlesex	5. 3.1887 27.10.1970
John Fox *1929–1933*	Northfield, Birmingham	7. 9.1904 15.11.1961
William Victor Fox *1923–1932*	Middlesbrough, Yorkshire	8. 1.1898 17. 2.1949
Percy Thomas Francis *1901–1902*	Suffolk	1875 8. 9.1964
Herbert Angus Fulton *1914*	Bangalore, India	3.10.1872 23.12.1951
Leslie Edward Gale *1923–1928*	Solihull, Warwickshire	11.11.1904 22. 1.1982
Humphry Stone Garratt *1925–1928*	Kingston-on-Thames, Surrey	12. 1.1898 1. 9.1974
George Warrington Gaukrodger *1900–1910*	Belfast, N. Ireland	1877 13.12.1937
William Roy Genders *1947–1948*	Dore, Derbyshire	21. 1.1913 28. 9.1985
Stanley John Gethin *1900–1901*	Kidderminster	1875 17. 2.1950
William George Gethin *1921*	Kidderminster	1877 4.11.1939
Harold Harry Ian Gibbons *1927–1946*	Devonport, Devon	10.10.1904 16. 2.1973
Norman Gifford *1960–1982*	Ulverston, Lancs	30. 3.1940
Humphrey Adam Gilbert *1921–1930*	Bombay, India	2. 6.1886 19. 7.1960
Dennis Cunliffe Good *1946*	Leeds, Yorks	29. 8.1926
William Arthur Goodreds *1952*	Pensnett	3.11.1920
Herbert Pritchard Gordon *1923–1924*	Bridgnorth, Salop	13. 9.1898 17.10.1965

Name	Place	Born	Died
Thomas William Graveney *1961–1970*	Riding Mill, Northumberland	16. 6.1927	
John Wilfred Greenstock *1924–1927*	Malvern	15. 5.1905	
William Greenstock *1899–1919*	Keiskama Hoek, Cape Province, S.A.	15. 1.1865	13.11.1944
Leonard Warwick Greenwood *1922–1926*	Liverpool	25. 3.1899	20. 7.1982
Geoffrey George Fenner Greig 1920–1985	Blything, Suffolk	15. 8.1897	24.10.1960
Kevin Griffith *1967–1972*	Warrington, Lancs	17. 1.1950	
Gordon Craven Griffiths *1932–1935*	Birmingham	19. 6.1905	
Vernon Grimshaw *1936–1938*	Leeds, Yorks	15. 4.1916	
Frederick Henry Grisewood *1908*	Daylesford	11. 4.1888	15.11.1972
Charles William Grove *1954*	Birmingham	16.12.1912	15. 2.1982
Brian Charles Hall *1956–1957*	Marylebone, London	2. 3.1934	
William Marcus Hampton *1925–1926*	Bromsgrove	20. 1.1903	7. 4.1964
John Harber *1914*	Worcestershire	1889	11. 8.1962
Donald Peter Harkness *1954*	Sydney, Australia	13. 2.1931	
Herbert Harper *1920*	Birmingham	1. 2.1889	6. 8.1983
George Cecil Harris *1925*	Droitwich	1906	
Cyril Stanley Harrison *1934–1935*	Droitwich	11.11.1915	
Frank Harry *1919–1920*	Torquay, Devon	22.12.1876	27.10.1925
William Norman Hartill *1935*	Dudley	13.12.1911	3. 3.1971
Ronald George Alphonso Headley *1958–1974*	Kingston, Jamaica, W.I.	29. 6.1939	
Edward John Orton Hemsley *1963–1982*	Norton, Stoke-on-Trent, Staffs	1. 9.1943	
Stephen Peter Henderson *1977–1981*	Oxford	24. 9.1958	
Graeme Ashley HIck *1984–1988*	Salisbury, Rhodesia	23. 5.1966	
William Henry Hickton *1909*	Lower Broughton, Lancashire	28. 8.1885	8. 4.1942
Harry Leslie Higgins *1920–1927*	Bournville	24. 2.1894	19. 9.1979
John Bernard Higgins *1912–1930*	Harborne, Warwicks	31.12.1885	3. 1.1970
J. D. Higginson *1912*	Worcester	1.1885	9.1940
James Arthur Higgs-Walker *1913–1919*	Clent, Worcs.	31. 7.1892	3. 9.1979
Denys Vivian Hill *1927–1929*	Edmonton, Middlesex	13. 4.1896	15. 5.1971
W. H. Hill *1900*		unknown	unknown
Vanburn Alonza Holder *1968–1980*	Bridgetown, Barbados, W.I.	8.10.1945	
Ronald Hubert Holyoake *1924*	Droitwich	1894	8.11.1966
Herbert Oxley Hopkins *1921–1931*	Australia	6. 7.1895	23. 2.1972
Henry Horton *1946–1949*	Colwall, Herefordshire	18. 4.1923	
Joseph Horton *1934–1938*	Colwall, Herefordshire	12. 8.1916	
Martin John Horton *1952–1966*	Worcester	21. 4.1934	
Joseph Howard *1900–1901*	Epsom, Surrey	12. 1.1871	25. 1.1951
Richard Howarth *1933–1951*	Bacup, Lancs	26. 4.1909	2. 4.1980
Noel Hughes *1953–1954*	Sydney, Australia	6. 4.1929	

Name	Birthplace	Born	Died
Richard Clive Hughes *1950–1951*	Watford, Herts	30. 9.1926	
Roger Henry Charles Human *1934–1939*	Newcastle-on-Tyne	11. 5.1909	21.11.1942
Victor William Humpherson *1921–1923*	Bewdley	15. 7.1896	19.10.1978
Cedric Alfred Humphries *1934–1935*	Kidderminster	26.12.1914	18.11.1944
David John Humphries *1977–1985*	Alveley, Salop	6. 8.1953	
Gerald Harvey Humphries *1932–1934*	Kidderminster	8.12.1908	3. 2.1983
Norman Hampton Humphries *1946*	Kidderminster	19. 5.1917	
Frederick Hunt Hunt *1900–1922*	Aldworth, Berks	13. 9.1875	31. 3.1967
Mehriyar Hussain *1985*	South Shields, Co. Durham	17.10.1963	
William Edward Colebrooke Hutchings *1905–1906*	Southborough, Kent	31. 5.1879	8. 3.1948
Richard Keith Illingworth *1982–1988*	Bradford, Yorks	23. 8.1963	
Imran Khan Niazi *1971–1976*	Lahore, Pakistan	25.11.1952	
John Darling Inchmore *1973–1986*	Ashington, Northumberland	22. 2.1949	
Arthur Whitmore Isaac *1899–1911*	Powick	4.10.1873	7. 7.1916
Herbert Whitmore Isaac *1919*	Worcester	11.12.1899	26. 4.1962
John Edmund Valentine Isaac *1907*	Upton	14. 2.1880	9. 5.1915
Derek Isles *1967*	Bradford, Yorks	14.10.1943	
John Frederick Cecil Jackson *1907*	North Aylesford, Kent	1880	1968
Percy Frederick Jackson *1929–1950*	Aberfeldy, Perthshire	11. 5.1911	
Samuel Thornton Jagger *1922–1923*	Llangollen, Denbigh	30. 6.1904	30. 5.1964
Enoch Percy Jeavons *1924*	Dudley	1893	1967
Roland Oliver Jenkins *1938–1959*	Worcester	24.11.1918	
Arthur North Jewell *1919–1920*	Iquique, Chile	1888	8. 9.1922
John Mark Herbert Jewell *1939*	Bloemfontein, South Africa	1917	29.10.1946
Maurice Francis Stewart Jewell *1909–1933*	Iquique, Chile	15. 9.1885	28. 5.1978
Edward Percy Jobson *1900–1903*	Wall Heath, Staffs	20. 3.1855	20. 4.1909
Ivan Nicholas Johnson *1972–1975*	Nassau, Bahamas	27. 6.1953	
Norman William Jolly *1907*	Adelaide, Australia	5. 8.1882	5.1954
Barry John Richardson Jones *1976–1980*	Shrewsbury, Salop	2.11.1955	
Ronald Jones *1955*	Wolverhampton, Staffs	9. 9.1938	
Ramlal Nikhanj Kapil Dev *1984–1985*	Chandigarh, India	6. 1.1959	
John William Keene *1903–1905*	Mitcham, Surrey	25. 4.1873	3. 1.1931
Donald Kenyon *1946–1967*	Wordsley, Staffs	15. 5.1924	
Simon Julian Spencer Kimber *1985*	Ormskirk, Lancs	6.10.1963	
Roger Charles Macdonald Kimpton *1937–1949*	Toorak, Melbourne, Australia	21. 9.1916	
Benjamin Philip King *1935–1939*	Leeds, Yorks	22. 4.1915	31. 3.1970
Collis Llewellyn King *1983*	Christchurch, Barbados, W.I.	11. 6.1951	

John William King *1927–1928*	Leicester	21. 1.1908	25. 3.1953
Brian Egbert Krikken *1969*	Horwich, Lancs	26. 8.1946	
Stuart Richard Lampitt *1985–1987*	Wolverhampton, Staffs	29. 7.1965	
Robert John Lanchbury *1973–1974*	Evesham	11. 2.1950	
Albert Frederick Lane *1914–1932*	Rowley Regis, Staffs	29. 8.1885	29. 1.1948
S. M. Lang *1923–1924*	unknown	unknown	unknown
William Trevor Larkham *1952*	Kidderminster	10.11.1929	
David Anthony Leatherdale *1988*	Bradford, Yorks	26.11.1967	
Patrick George Leeson *1936*	Darjeeling, India	17. 7.1915	
Antony Ronald Legard *1935*	Sialkot, India	17. 1.1912	
Joseph Lister *1954–1959*	Thirsk, Yorks	14. 5.1930	
Kenneth Lobban *1952–1954*	Jamaica, W.I.	9. 5.1924	
Gordon John Lord *1987–1988*	Edgbaston, Birmingham	25. 4.1961	
William Walter Lowe *1899–1911*	Stamford, Lincs	17.11.1873	26. 5.1945
Charles Frederick Lyttelton *1906–1910*	London	26. 1.1887	3.10.1931
Charles John Lyttelton *1932–39* (*succeeded as 10th Viscount Cobham in 1949*)	London	8. 8.1909	20. 3.1977
Michael Stephen Anthony McEvoy *1983–1984*	Jorhat, Asam, India	25. 1.1956	
Steven Michael McEwan *1985–1988*	Worcester	5. 5.1962	
John Francis Maclean *1922–1924*	Alnwick, Northumberland	1. 3.1901	9. 3.1986
William Horace Mann *1924*	Melksham, Wiltshire	28. 7.1878	24. 2.1938
Evelyn George Martin *1903–1907*	Upton on Severn	22. 3.1881	27. 4.1945
Sidney Hugh Martin *1931–1939*	Durban, South Africa	11. 1.1909	
Cecil Reginald Napp Maxwell *1948–1951*	London	21. 5.1913	25. 9.1973
George Thomas Mills *1953*	Redditch	12. 9.1923	15. 9.1983
Kenneth James Mitchell *1946*	Old Hill, Staffs	5.12.1924	
Peter Moores *1983–1984*	Macclesfield, Cheshire	18.12.1962	
P. J. Morris *1914*	unknown	unknown	unknown
Ray Morris *1958*	Hartlebury	20. 6.1929	
Harry Mortimer *1904*	Sculcoates, Yorks	1872	1953
Reginald Heber Moss *1925*	Huyton, Lancs	24. 2.1868	19. 3.1956
Harry George Moule *1952*	Kidderminster	23.12.1921	
Reginald George Munn *1900*	Madresfield, Worcs	20. 8.1869	12. 4.1947
Peter Earnshaw Murray-Willis *1935–1936*	Aston, Birmingham	17. 7.1910	
James Rupert Naden *1922*	Tipton, Staffs	13. 7.1889	14. 6.1963
Phillip Anthony Neale *1975–1988*	Scunthorpe, Lincolnshire	5. 6.1954	
Arnold Stearns Nesbitt *1914*	Chertsey, Surrey	16.10.1878	17.11.1914
Edward Roy Nesfield *1919–1920*	Armthorpe, Yorks	7. 3.1900	
Bernard Philip Nevile *1913*	Wellingore, Lincolnshire	1. 8.1888	11. 2.1916

Philip John Newport *1982–1988* — High Wycombe, Bucks 11.10.1962

Maurice Nichol *1928–1934* — Hetton, Co. Durham 10. 9.1904 21. 5.1934

John Ernest Nichols *1902–1904* — Acle, Norwich 20. 4.1878 29. 2.1952

Ernest Willmott Norton *1922–1923* — Birmingham 19. 6.1889 1972

Leonard Oakley *1935–1948* — Stourbridge 11. 1.1916

Joseph Alan Ormrod *1962–1983* — Ramsbottom, Lancs 22.12.1942

Steven Joseph O'Shaughnessy *1988* — Bury, Lancs 9. 9.1961

Ladislaw Outschoorn *1946–1959* — Colombo, Ceylon 26. 9.1918

Cecil Howard Palmer *1904* — Eastbourne, Sussex 14. 7.1873 26. 7.1915

Charles Henry Palmer *1938–1949* — Old Hill, Staffs 15. 5.1919

John Morton Parker *1971–1975* — Dannevirke, Hawke's Bay, New Zealand 21. 2.1951

Michael Francis William Passey *1953* — Crossway Green, Worcs 6. 6.1937

Nawab of Pataudi *1932–1938* (*Iftikhar Ali Khan*) — New Delhi, India 16. 3.1910 5. 1.1952

Dipak Narshibhai Patel *1976–1986* — Nairobi, Kenya 25.10.1958

Harshad Vallabhbhia Patel *1985* — Nairobi, Kenya 29. 1.1966

Albert Guy Pawson *1908* — Bramley, Yorks 30. 5.1888 25. 2.1985

Derek Brooke Pearson *1954–1961* — Stourbridge 29. 3.1937

Frederick Albert Perason *1900–1936* — Brixton, London 23. 9.1880 10.11.1963

Reginald Thomas David Perks *1930–1955* — Hereford 4.10.1911 22.11.1977

Ernest Harvey Perry *1933–1946* — Chaddesley Corbett 16. 1.1908

Harry Perry *1927–1928* — Stourbridge 1895 28. 2.1961

Stephen Peter Perryman *1982–1983* — Yardley, Birmingham 22.10.1955

Peter Horsley Phelps *1931–1932* — Malvern 5. 2.1909

Cecil Brabazon Ponsonby *1911–1928* — London 26.12.1892 11. 5.1945

Stanley Clive Porthouse *1934–1935* — Redditch 14. 8.1910

Albert James Powell *1921* — Presteigne, Radnor, Wales 8.12.1893 15. 2.1979

Horatio James Powys-Keck *1903–1907* — Switzerland 7. 3.1873 30. 1.1952

David Pratt *1959* — Watford, Herts 20. 7.1938

Charles Richard Preece *1920–1929* — Broadheath, Worcs 15.12.1887 5. 2.197?

John Price *1927–1929* — Worcester 6. 7.1908

William Harry Price *1923* — Worcester 28. 5.1900 15. 4.1982

Walter Longsdon Price *1904* — Toxeth Park, Liverpool 2. 2.1886 26.12.1943

Alan Paul Pridgeon *1972–1988* — Wall Heath, Staffs 22. 2.1954

Cecil Douglas Ayrton Pullan *1935–1938* — Mahoba, India 26. 7.1910 24. 6.1910

Bernard William Quaife *1928–1937* — Olton, Warwickshire 24.11.1899 28.11.1984

Neal Victor Radford *1985–1988* — Luanshya, Northn Rhodesia 7. 6.1957

Steven John Rhodes 1985–1988	Bradford, Yorks	17. 6.1964	
Derek Walter Richardson 1952–1967	Hereford	3.11.1934	
Peter Edward Richardson 1949–1958	Hereford	4. 7.1931	
William Ethelbert Richardson 1920–1928	St Helens, Lancs	23.12.1894	5.11.1971
Edward Grantham Righton (sen) 1911–1913	Evesham	23.11.1885	3. 1.1964
Edward Grantham Righton (jun) 1934–1936	Evesham	24. 9.1912	2. 5.1986
Jack Riley 1953	Accrington, Lancs	27. 4.1927	
Christopher Paul Roberts 1974	Cleethorpes, Lincs	12.10.1951	9. 6.1977
Edward Stanley Roberts 1925	Oswestry, Salop	6. 5.1890	9.1964
A. W. Robinson 1920–1926	unknown	unknown	unknown
Peter James Robinson 1963–1964	Worcester	9. 2.1943	
Clayton Graeme Wynne Robson 1921	Bareilly, India	3. 7.1901	
Harry Oliver Rogers 1923–1928	Hednesford, Staffs	21. 1.1889	4. 7.1956
Francis William Romney 1900	Tewkesbury, Glos	25.11.1873	28. 1.1963
Charles Frederick Root 1921–1932	Somercotes, Derbyshire	16. 4.1890	20. 1.1954
Thomas Ginnever Rose 1922	Ilkeston, Derbyshire	16. 3.1901	8. 8.1979
Lloyd Maurice Rudge 1952	Walsall, Staffs	11. 2.1934	
Frederick Edward Rumsey 1960–1962	Stepney, London	4.12.1935	
Ian Alexander Rutherford 1976	Dunedin, N. Zealand	30. 6.1957	
Henry George Sale 1921–1925	Shipston-on-Stour, Warwickshire	26. 3.1889	30. 8.1975
Gerald Barry Sanderson 1901	Toxeth Park, Liverpool	13. 5.1881	3.10.1964
John Frank Eden Santall 1930	King's Heath, Birmingham	3.12.1907	5.1986
Martyn Saunders 1980	Worcester	16. 5.1958	
John Colin Scholey 1952–1953	Leeds, Yorks	28. 9.1930	
Michael Graham Scothern 1985	Skipton, Yorks	9. 3.1961	
Mark Stephen Scott 1981–1983	Muswell Hill, Middlesex	10. 3.1959	
John Brian Sedgley 1959–1961	West Bromwich, Staffs	17. 2.1939	
Gerald Henry Seeley 1921	Port Blair, Andaman Islands	9. 5.1903	23. 7.1941
Ravindera Senghera 1974–1976	Delhi, India	25. 1.1947	
Louis Roy Serrurier 1927	Cape Town, South Africa	7. 2.1905	
William Harold Nelson Shakespeare 1919–1931	Worcester	24. 8.1893	10. 7.1976
Sydney George Shepherd 1936	York	23. 8.1908	20.12.1987
Geoffrey Allan Sheppard 1919		18.12.1890	22. 5.1940
Thomas Winter Sheppard 1909	Havant, Hampshire	4. 3.1873	7. 6.1954
Wilfred Lionel Shorting 1922–1926	Tenbury	12. 3.1904	10.10.1982
Albert Shutt 1972	Stockton-on-Tees, Co. Durham	21. 9.1952	
George Hayward Thomas Simpson-Hayward 1899–1914	Stoneleigh, Warwickshire	7. 6.1875	2.10.1936
Alexander Parkinson Singleton 1934–1946	Repton, Derbyshire	5. 8.1914	

George Michael Singleton *1946*	Repton, Derbyshire	12. 5.1913	
Douglas Norman Frank Slade *1958–1971*	Feckenham	24. 8.1940	
Douglas James Smith *1901–1904*	Batley, Yorks	29. 5.1873	16. 8.1949
David Mark Smith *1984–1986*	Balham, London	9. 1.1956	
James Crosbie Smith *1923–1925*	Ledbury, Herefordshire	26. 9.1894	19. 2.1980
Lawrence Kilner Smith *1985–1987*	Mirfield, Yorks	6. 1.1964	
Edward Walter Solly *1903–1907*	Eastry, Kent	7. 5.1882	12. 2.1966
Arthur Herbert Tennyson, Lord Somers *1923–1925*	Isle of Wight	20. 3.1887	14. 7.1944
Ernest Somers-Smith *1921*	Sheffield, Yorks	1895	1950
H. Southall *1907*	unknown	unknown	unknown
Alan Horace Spencer *1957–1961*	Lee Green, London	4. 7.1936	
Harry Norman Ernest Spencer *1927*	Shipston-on-Stour, Warwickshire	1.10.1901	13. 8.1954
John William Edward Spilsbury *1952*	Worcester	27.10.1933	
James Alfred Standen *1959–1970*	Edmonton, London	30. 5.1935	
John Stanning *1939–1946*	Nairobi, Kenya	24. 6..1919	
John William Arthur Stephenson *1947*	Hong Kong	1. 8.1907	20. 5.1982
Bertie Grosvenor Stevens *1905–1914*	Thingoe, Suffolk	9. 4.1886	3.1943
David Ernest Robertson Stewart *1970–1973*	Bombay, India	22. 5.1948	
Peter John Stimpson *1971–1972*	Aberfan, Glamorgan	25. 5.1947	
Thomas Straw *1899–1907*	Hucknall Torkard, Notts	1. 9.1870	5. 9.1959
Thomas Stringer *1909*	Yorkshire	1874	unknown
Sidney William Styler *1929–1931*	Cotteridge, Warwickshire	26. 8.1908	1980
Ernest Suckling *1923–1924*	Birmingham	27. 3.1890	24. 2.1962
Douglas Walter Levi Summers *1930*	Smethwick, Staffs	12.10.1911	
Francis Theodore Summers *1921–1928*	Alcester, Warwicks	25. 1.1887	27.10.1967
John Alan Sutor *1928*	Tenbury	7.1909	12.1966
Reginald Sawdon Swalwell *1907–1920*	York	25. 6.1873	20. 9.1930
Charles Victor Tarbox *1921–1929*	Hemel Hempstead, Herts	2. 7.1891	15. 6.1978
Alfred George Ernest Tasker *1956*	Southwark, London	16. 6.1934	
Robert Joseph Taylor *1900*	Liverpool	1.11.1873	unknown
William Herbert Taylor *1909–1925*	Sale, Cheshire	23. 6.1885	27. 5.1959
William Richard Keay Thomas *1981*	Redditch	22. 7.1960	
Guy Mytton Thornycroft *1947*	Ulverston, Lancs	1. 4.1917	
Philip Thorp *1935*	Kidderminster	6. 5.1911	
John Hunt Thursfield *1922–1925*	Alvechurch	16. 6.1892	26. 4.1951
Edgar Tinkler *1953*	Burnley, Lancs	11. 3.1921	
Benjamin Claude Cecil Tipper *1919*	Birmingham	7. 7.1896	11. 7.1970
Francis Martin Tomkinson *1902*	Kidderminster	21.10.1883	24.11.1963
Geoffrey Stewart Tomkinson *1903–1926*	Kidderminster	7.11.1881	8. 2.1963
Charles Graham Toppin *1927–1928*	Upton	17. 4.1906	20. 5.1972
John Fallowfield Townsend Toppin *1920*	Malvern	25. 2.1900	22.11.1969
Glenn Maitland Turner *1967–1982*	Dunedin, New Zealand	26. 5.1947	

James William Cecil Turner 1911–1921	Bromley, Kent	2.10.1886	29.11.1968
Richard Ernest Turner 1909–1922	Mitcham, Surrey	4. 5.1888	16. 3.1967
Louis Phillippus Vorster 1988	Potchefstroom, South Africa	2.11.1966	
Percy Harold Wakefield 1922	Pill, Somerset	3. 9.1888	20.12.1973
Edwin Wakelin 1910	Oxford	1880	1925
John Erskine Scott Walford 1923–1930	Hanbury, Worcs	14. 8.1899	22. 8.1961
Charles William Wallace 1921–1922	Sunderland	24.11.1884	5. 9.1946
Cyril Frederick Walters 1928–1935	Bedlinog, Glamorgan	28. 8.1908	
Frank Belmont Warne 1934–1938	North Carlton, Victoria, Australia	3.10.1906	
Alan Esmond Warner 1982–1984	Birmingham	12. 5.1957	
Stephen George Watkins 1983	Hereford	23. 3.1959	
Gregory George Watson 1978–1979	Mudgee, New South Wales, Australia	29. 1.1955	
Andrew John Webster 1981–1982	Burton-on-Trent, Staffs	5. 3.1959	
Thomas Umfrey Wells 1950	Panmure, New Zealand	6. 2.1927	
Martin John Weston 1979–1988	Worcester	8. 4.1959	
George Frederick Wheldon 1899–1906	Langley Green, Worcs	1.11.1869	13. 1.1924
Philip John Whitcombe 1949–1952	Worcester	11.11.1928	
Allan Frederick Tinsdale White 1939–1949	Coventry, Warwicks	5. 9.1915	
Montague Eric White 1931–1934	London	21. 1.1908	21. 6.1970
John Parkin Whitehead 1953–1955	Upper Mill, Yorks	3. 9.1925	
Norman Harry Whiting 1947–1952	Wollaston, Stourbridge	2.10.1920	
Howard Gordon Wilcock 1971–1978	New Malden, Surrey	26. 2.1950	
Alexander John Wilkes 1925–1927	Kidderminster	1900	12. 7.1937
William Harry Walters Wilkes 1899–1902	Aston, Birmingham	1866	18. 2.1940
John William Wilkinson 1927	Dudley	1892	3. 8.1967
Keith William Wilkinson 1969–1975	Fenton, Stoke-on-Trent, Staffs	15. 1.1950	
H. Williams 1927	unknown	unknown	unknown
Richard Harry Williams 1923–1932	Brockmoor, Staffs	23. 4.1901	19.12.1982
George Alfred Wilson 1899–1906	Amersham, Bucks	5. 4..1877	3. 3.1962
George Clifford Wilson 1924–1926	Kidderminster	27. 7.1902	1957
Grenville Thomas Owen Wilson 1951–1953	Elmley Lovett, Worcs	9. 4.1932	
Harry Wilson 1901–1906	Yorkshire	1873	13. 8.1906
John Francis Sartorius Winnington 1908	Martley, Worcs	17. 9.1876	22. 9.1918
Thomas Lawson Winwood 1930–1934	Dudley	7. 2.1910	
Leslie Wright 1925–1933	Durham	20. 1.1903	6. 1.1956

Robert Elliott Storey Wyatt *1946–1951*	Milford, Surrey	2. 5.1901	
Alick Wyers *1927*	Droitwich	15.12.1907	28.11.1980
Thomas James Yardley *1967–1975*	Chaddesley Corbet	27.10.1946	
Henry Yarnold *1938–1955*	Worcester	6. 7.1917	13. 8.1974
Douglas Martin Young *1946–1948*	Coalville, Leics	15. 4.1924	
Mohammad Younis Ahmed *1979–1982*	Jullunder, India	20.10.1947	

CAREER RECORDS OF
WORCESTERSHIRE PLAYERS, 1899–1988

	Inns	NO	Runs	HS	Avge	100s	Runs	Wkts	Avge	Best	5WI
Abbott, J. D.	5	0	63	42	12.60	—					
Abell, G. E. B.	58	7	1290	131	25.29	2	4	0	—	—	—
Adshead, F. H.	3	0	26	14	8.66	—					
Adshead, W. E.	22	1	244	51	11.61	—					
Ahl, F. D.	53	3	592	43	11.84	—	384	13	29.53	4/44	—
Ainslet, J.	25	16	64	13	7.11	—					
Ainsworth, M. L. Y.	28	1	854	100	31.62	1	15	0	—	—	—
Aldridge, K. J.	100	30	459	24*	6.55	—	5519	241	22.90	6/26	7
Allchurch, T.	6	0	74	51	12.33	—	280	10	28.00	5/70	1
Alleyne, H. L.	41	8	398	72	12.06	—	3222	119	27.07	8/43	5
Anton, J. H. H.	7	0	74	26	10.57	—					
Archer, A. G.	8	0	34	12	4.25	—					
Argent, E.	4	1	22	19	7.33	—	63	0	—	—	—
Arnold, E. G.	527	54	14825	215	31.34	24	21411	902	23.73	9/64	56
Ashman, J. R.	40	14	149	24	5.73	—	2430	57	42.63	7/111	3
Ashton, G.	44	0	773	125	17.56	1	43	1	43.00	1/39	—
Austin, H.	4	0	22	9	5.50	—	56	1	56.00	1/41	—
Bache, H. G.	25	1	222	36	9.25	—	33	3	11.00	2/4	—
Baker, E. S.	44	19	160	21*	6.40	—					
Baker, H. F.	4	1	21	8*	7.00	—	66	0	—	—	—
Baker, W.	4	0	24	7	6.00	—	38	1	38.00	1/38	—
Bale, E. W.	217	79	1096	43	7.94	—	217	8	27.12	3/46	—
Banks, D. A.	29	3	691	100	26.57	1	17	0	—	—	—
Bannister, A. F.	62	16	354	44	7.69	—	2175	92	23.64	7/29	5
Barker, A. R. P.	43	3	544	67	13.60	—					
Barley, J. C.	2	1	1	1*	1.00	—					
Barrett, B. J.			did not bat				40	1	40.00	1/40	—
Baylis, K. R.	7	1	89	26	14.83	—	495	14	35.35	4/112	—
Bayliss, E. G.	2	0	0		0.00	—					
Bennett, E. H.	6	0	24	10	4.00	—					
Bennett, H. F.	3	1	63	31*	31.50	—					
Bennett, M.	2	0	10	8	5.00	—					
Bent, P.	7	1	125	50	20.83	—					
Berkeley, R. G. W.	7	0	37	16	5.28	—					
Berry, R.	118	40	601	32	7.70	—	6263	250	25.05	6/37	13
Bird, A.	225	63	1951	64*	12.04	—	7393	292	25.31	7/41	20
Bird, R. E.	317	31	7442	158*	26.02	7	1110	23	48.26	3/26	—
Birkenshaw, J.	10	0	165	54	16.50	—	644	11	58.54	3/131	—
Blakey, G. M.	4	1	46	42	15.33	—	87	0	—	—	—
Blewitt, C. P.	2	0	7	4	3.50	—					
Blunt, L.	19	5	109	18	7.78	—	885	33	26.81	5/60	1
Booth, R.	594	107	9360	113*	19.21	2	3	0	—	—	—
Botham, I. T.	18	1	384	126*	22.58	1	575	15	38.33	3/51	—
Bowles, J. J.	102	14	1155	73	13.12	—	2999	72	41.65	5/56	1
Bowley, F. L.	722	24	20751	276	29.72	38	101	4	25.25	1/6	—
Boyns, C. N.	46	7	778	95	19.94	—	1617	36	44.91	3/24	—
Bradley, M. E.	9	7	9	6*	4.50	—	867	23	37.69	6/162	1
Brain, B. M.	157	41	807	38	6.95	—	12298	508	24.20	8/55	20

	Inns	NO	Runs	HS	Avge	100s	Runs	Wkts	Avge	Best	5WI
Brinton, P. R.	1	0	1	1	1.00	—					
Brinton, R. L.	4	0	22	10	5.50	—	22	0	—	—	—
Brinton, R. S.	24	7	332	72*	19.52	—	13	0	—	—	—
Broadbent, R. G.	520	56	12800	155	27.58	13	382	4	95.50	1/16	—
Bromley-Martin, E. G.	13	1	171	39	14.25	—	274	10	37.40	4/33	—
Bromey-Martin, G. E.	56	0	1106	129	19.75	1	72	1	72.00	1/11	—
Brook, G. W.	218	17	1877	56	9.33	—	12841	461	27.85	7/50	23
Brown, A.			did not bat								
Brownell, E. L. D.	2	0	28	21	14.00	—					
Bryant, E. H.	30	0	329	63	10.96	—					
Bull, C. H.	302	20	6768	161	24.00	5	56	0	—	—	—
Buller, J. S.	168	43	1732	64	13.85	—					
Bullock, M.	6	0	59	27	9.83	—					
Bullock, P. G.	5	0	11	9	2.20	—					
Bunting, E. L.	2	0	1	1	0.50	—					
Burlton, A. T.	10	1	114	35*	12.66	—	38	0	—	—	—
Burns, W. B.	335	20	8688	196	27.58	12	5752	187	30.75	6/41	5
Burr, F. B.	2	1	46	39	46.00	—					
Burrows, R. D.	436	65	5223	112	14.07	2	23604	894	26.40	8/48	57
Busher, S. E.	7	1	32	18*	5.33	—	288	19	15.15	6/63	3
Byrne, G. R.	8	0	28	18	3.50	—	155	1	155.00	1/86	—
Caldwell, W. S.	33	1	673	133	21.03	2	40	2	20.00	2/23	—
Carmichael, E. G. M.	2	0	6	5	3.00	—					
Carr, A. M.	10	0	150	82	15.00	—	10	0	—	—	—
Carter, R. G. M.	163	94	317	23	4.59	—	13630	521	26.16	7/61	17
Cass, G. R.	144	22	2572	172*	21.08	1					
Cave-Rogers, R. A.	1	0	3	3	3.00	—	25	0	—	—	—
Chadd, J. E.	1	0	4	4	4.00	—	98	2	49.00	2/84	—
Chatham, C. H.	2	0	12	8	6.00	—	65	1	65.00	1/49	—
Chester, F.	90	17	1768	178*	24.21	4	2493	80	31.16	6/43	2
Chesterton, G. H.	69	21	353	23	7/35	—	4339	168	25.82	6/56	11
Clare, T.	4	0	63	34	15.75	—					
Cliff, A. T.	74	2	986	81*	13.69	—	410	8	51.25	1/4	—
Cobham, 9th Viscount	6	1	63	30	12.60	—					
Coldwell, L. W.	333	92	1446	37	6.00	—	21490	1029	20.88	8/38	57
Collier, C. G. A.	85	8	982	72	12.75	—	341	7	48.71	3/51	—
Collinson, J.	2	0	24	23	12.00	—					
Conway, A. J.	49	14	157	20*	4.48	—	1904	53	35.92	9/38	2
Cooper, E.	442	28	13213	216*	31.91	18	44	0	—	—	—
Cooper, F.	74	11	1204	113*	19.11	1	30	0	—	—	—
Corbett, P. T.	13	3	57	20	5.70	—	77	0	—	—	—
Corden, C. F.	33	4	479	64	16.51	—					
Coventry, J. B.	133	13	1774	86	14.78	—	733	16	45.81	2/18	—
Cox, G. C.	4	0	28	19	7.00	—					
Crawley, L. G.	9	0	602	161	66.88	2					
Crisp, R. J.	13	3	107	29	10.70	—	993	42	23.64	7/82	5
Crowe, G. L.	38	2	584	78	16.22	—	35	2	17.50	1/6	—
Cliffe, J. A.	357	32	7404	145	22.78	4	18273	716	25.52	9/38	31
Cumbes, J.	92	43	384	43	7.83	—	7902	246	32.12	6/24	8
Curtis, T. S.	241	33	8004	153	38.48	12	218	4	54.50	2/72	—
Darks, G. C.	8	3	89	39	17.80	—	452	13	34.76	5/49	1

	Inns	NO	Runs	HS	Avge	100s	Runs	Wkts	Avge	Best	5WI
Davidge, G. M. C.	1	0	0	0	0.00	—					
Davies, T. E.	30	5	481	76	19.24	—	169	6	28.16	2/22	—
Davis, J. P.	8	1	48	38*	6.85	—	45	0	—	—	—
Davis, M.	2	0	35	29	17.50	—					
Days, J. E.	3	0	8	5	2.66	—	42	2	21.00	2/42	—
Devereux, L. N.	129	21	2070	81*	16.17	—	4497	106	42.42	4/103	—
Devereux, R. J.	16	3	216	55*	16.61	—	581	13	44.69	3/44	—
Dews, G.	638	53	16671	145	28.49	20	202	2	101.00	1/31	—
Dilly. G. R.	12	2	129	36	12.90	—	1124	55	20.43	6/43	5
D'Oliveira, B. L.	435	65	14120	227	38.16	31	11103	445	24.95	6/29	17
D'Oliveira, D. B.	213	16	5408	146*	27.45	6	923	23	40.13	2/17	—
Dorrell, P. G.	1	0	1	1	1.00	—					
Duff, A. R.	8	2	79	50*	13.16	—	284	14	20.28	4/24	—
Eden, E.	2	1	27	18*	27.00	—					
Edwards, H. C.	2	0	11	10	5.50	—					
Ellcock, R. M.	35	11	335	45*	13.95	—	2391	71	33.67	4/34	—
Elliott, J. W.	11	3	66	18*	8.25	—					
Evans, P. S.	9	3	15	5	2.50	—	199	3	66.33	3/84	—
Evans, W. H. B.	9	2	217	107	31.00	1	185	3	61.66	1/21	—
Everitt, R. S.	2	1	6	6*	6.00	—					
Evers, R. D. M.	26	1	3.83	60*	15.32	—					
Farnfield, P. H.	1	0	0	0	0.00	—					
Fawcus, C. L. D.	2	0	47	43	23.50	—	6	0	—	—	—
Fearnley, C. D.	174	14	3294	112	20.58	1	37	1	37.00	1/37	—
Fereday, J. B.	19	0	211	37	11.10	—	103	2	51.50	1/27	—
Fiddian-Green, C. A. F.	36	0	956	108	26.55	1	20	0	—	—	—
Field, F.	4	2	26	12	13.00	—	116	4	29.00	4/60	—
Fisher, P. B.	18	8	114	28*	11.40	—					
Flavell, J. A.	444	138	1984	54	6.48	—	32120	1507	21.31	9/30	86
Foley, H. T. H.	2	1	6	6	6.00	—					
Foster, B. S.	11	0	94	36	8.54	—	29	0	—	—	—
Foster, C. K.	5	2	34	16*	11.33	—					
Foster, G. N.	144	13	4114	175	31.40	7	48	2	34.00	2/21	—
Foster, H. K.	441	15	15053	216	35.33	28	349	11	31.72	3/16	—
Foster, M. K.	276	8	7876	158	29.38	12	256	3	85.33	2/17	—
Foster, N. J. A.	14	4	219	40*	21.90	—					
Foster, R. E.	136	9	5699	246*	44.87	13	1004	21	47.80	3/54	—
Foster, W. L.	51	2	1600	172*	32.65	3	13	0	—	—	—
Fowler, R. H.	7	1	72	35	12.00	—	105	7	15.00	5/33	1
Fox, J.	159	16	2438	73	17.04	—	1285	31	41.45	4/77	—
Fox, W. V.	281	31	6654	198	26.61	11	137	2	68.50	1/13	—
Francis, P. T.	5	1	95	66	23.75	—					
Fulton, H. A.	1	1	2	2*	—	—					
Gale, L. E.	26	6	155	19	7.75	—	394	10	39.40	5/49	1
Garratt, H. S.	9	0	111	39	12.33	—					
Gaukrodger, G. W.	177	45	2230	91	16.89	—					
Genders, W. R.	9	3	154	55*	25.66	—	70	3	23.33	2/43	—
Gethin, S. J.	7	0	86	41	12.28	—	49	1	49.00	1/25	—
Gethin, W. G.	2	0	20	19	10.00	—					
Gibbons, H. H. I.	666	57	918	212*	34.34	44	737	7	105.28	2/27	—

	Inns	NO	Runs	HS	Avge	100s	Runs	Wkts	Avge	Best	5WI
Gifford, N.	619	189	5848	89	13.60	—	36071	1615	22.33	8/28	76
Gilbert, H. A.	111	35	538	31*	7.07	—	6973	249	28.00	7/60	17
Good, D. C.	2	1	7	6*	7.00	—	75	1	75.00	1/60	—
Goodreds, W. A.	1	1	4	4*	—	—	48	0	—	—	—
Gordon, H. P.	13	1	157	68*	13.08	—					
Graveney, T. W.	347	62	13160	166	46.17	27	182	4	45.50	2/10	—
Greenstock, J. W.	22	4	124	23*	6.88	—	875	23	38.04	4/69	—
Greenstock, W.	7	0	86	33	12.28	—	26	0	—	—	—
Greenwood, L. W.	4	0	33	25	8.25	—					
Greig, G. G. F.	34	8	215	37	8.26	—	1220	31	39.35	7/86	1
Griffith, K.	61	8	795	59	15.00	—	1753	50	35.06	7/41	1
Griffiths, G. C.	10	0	42	16	4.20	—					
Grimshaw, V.	32	2	4.18	103	13.93	1	46	2	23.00	1/2	—
Grisewood, F. H.	2	1	7	6*	7.00	—					
Grove, C. W.	20	1	180	25	9.47	—	1275	42	30.35	8/66	2
Hall, B. C.	4	1	34	21	11.33	—	97	3	32.33	2/11	—
Hampton, W. M.	24	1	298	57	12.95	—	13	1	13.00	1/11	—
Harber, J.	2	0	3	3	1.50	—	46	3	15.33	2/24	—
Harkness, D. P.	19	0	488	163	25.68	1	274	6	45.66	3/29	—
Harper, H.	2	0	10	7	5.00	—					
Harris, G. C.	8	3	6	4	1.20	—	120	2	60.00	3/40	—
Harrison, C. S.	29	2	166	28	6.14	—	1043	25	41.72	7/51	1
Harry, F.	11	2	77	14*	8.55	—	294	8	36.75	3/60	—
Hartill, W. N.	1	0	2	2	2.00	—					
Headley, R. G. A.	725	60	20712	187	31.14	32	568	12	47.33	4/40	—
Hemsley, E. J. O.	389	57	9740	176*	29.33	8	2497	70	35.67	3/5	—
Henderson, S. P.	36	4	467	64	14.59	—	46	0	—	—	—
Hick, G. A.	127	12	7247	405*	63.01	26	2085	54	38.61	4/31	—
Hickton, W. H.	9	0	41	17	4.55	—	104	2	52.00	1/9	—
Higgins, H. L.	181	13	3437	137*	20.45	4					
Higgins, J. B.	204	10	3837	123	19.77	3	28	47.82	5/72	1	
Higginson, J. D.	1	1	0	—	—	—	20	0	—	—	—
Higgs-Walker, J. A.	3	1	44	44	22.00	—	89	1	89.00	1/69	—
Hill, D. V.	46	7	405	38	10.38	—	2321	78	29.75	6/59	4
Hill, W. H.	4	1	46	13*	15.33	—					
Holder, V. A.	196	51	1553	52	10.71	—	13530	586	23.08	7/40	28
Holyoake, R. H.	6	0	47	22	7.83	—					
Hopkins, H. O.	114	5	2257	137	20.70	2	190	4	47.50	2/23	—
Horton, H.	19	3	129	21	8.06	—	32	0	—	—	—
Horton, J.	103	12	1258	70	13.82	—	362	5	72.40	2/3	—
Horton, M. J.	665	47	17974	233	29.04	22	20381	774	26.33	9/56	38
Howard, J.	10	0	85	28	8.50	—					
Howorth, R.	571	50	10538	114	20.22	3	27218	1274	21.36	7/18	71
Hughes, N.	32	6	651	95	25.03	—	317	10	31.70	4/19	—
Hughes, R. C.	10	2	47	21	5.87	—	695	15	46.26	3/38	—
Human, R. H. C.	62	4	1540	81	26.55	—	601	10	60.10	2/51	—
Humpherson, V. W.	25	5	154	16	7.70	—	500	16	31.25	5/50	1
Humphries, C. A.	24	3	328	44	15.61	—					
Humphries, D. J.	243	43	4969	133*	24.84	4					
Humphries, G. H.	3	0	66	36	22.00	—	13	0	—	—	—
Humphries, N. H.	11	1	137	22	13.70	—	52	0	—	—	—

253

	Inns	NO	Runs	HS	Avge	100s	Runs	Wkts	Avge	Best	5WI
Hunt, F. H.	87	18	774	40★	11.21	—	1463	44	33.25	4/36	—
Hussain, M.	1	0	4	4	4.00	—					
Hutchings, W. E. C.	39	3	814	85	22.61	—					
Illingworth, R. K.	147	44	2018	120★	19.59	1	9585	279	34.35	7/50	10
Imran Khan	67	6	1518	166	24.88	4	3150	128	24.60	7/53	7
Inchmore, J. D.	243	53	3137	113	16.51	1	14546	503	29.91	8/58	18
Isaac, A. W.	87	5	1106	60	13.48	—					
Isaac, H. W.	3	0	32	23	10.66	—	32	0	—	—	—
Isaac, J. E. V.	3	0	19	10	6.33	—					
Isles, D.	1	1	17	17★	—	—					
Jackson, J. F. C.	2	0	6	6	3.00	—					
Jackson, P. F.	546	208	2044	40	6.04	—	30209	1139	26.52	9/45	58
Jagger, S. T.	9	0	74	41	8.22	—	196	7	28.00	3/25	—
Jeavons, E. P.	2	1	1	1★	1.00	—					
Jenkins, R. O.	530	109	9215	109	21.88	1	27240	1148	23.72	8/62	80
Jewell, A. N.	43	0	864	128	20.09	3					
Jewell, J. M. H.	4	0	30	24	7.50						
Jewell, M. F. S.	220	14	3906	125	18.96	2	3217	98	32.82	7/56	2
Jobson, E. P.	12	0	162	26	13.50	—	8	0	—	—	—
Johnson, I. N.	43	10	716	69	21.69	1533	37	43	5.74	5/74	1
Jolly, N. W.	2	1	9	8	9.00	—					
Jones, B. J. R.	81	3	1076	65	13.79	—					
Jones, R.	2	0	25	23	12.50	—					
Kapil, D. E. V.	40	6	1456	100	42.82	1	1624	72	22.55	5/30	2
Keene, J. W.	32	9	107	12	4.65	—	1312	62	21.16	6/22	5
Kenyon, D.	1060	51	34490	259	34.18	70	178	1	178.00	1/8	—
Kimber, S. J. S.	1	1	14	14★	—	—	72	3	24.00	3/40	—
Kimpton, R. C. M.	25	1	695	106	28.95	1	71	2	35.50	2/20	—
King, B. P.	140	6	2619	124	19.54	4	4	0	—	—	—
King, C. L.	3	0	158	123	52.66	1	39	1	39.00	1/26	—
King, J. W.	73	12	1015	91	16.63	—					
Krikken, B. E.	1	0	4	4	4.00	—					
Lampitt, S. R.	16	4	122	24	10.16	—	295	3	98.33	2/37	—
Lanchbury, R. J.	13	3	245	50★	24.50	—					
Lane, A. F.	76	8	1163	76	17.10	—	1218	23	52.95	3/41	—
Lang, J. M.	14	8	27	9★	4.50	—	412	8	51.50	2/21	—
Larkham, T. W.	2	0	13	13	6.50	—	64	1	64.00	1/64	—
Leatherdale, D. A.	15	1	255	34★	18.21	—	20	1	30.00	1/12	—
Leeson, P. G.	2	0	7	7	3.50	—					
Legard, A. R.	2	0	22	18	11.0	—	31	0	—	—	—
Lister, J.	37	4	750	99	22.72	—					
Lobban, K.	23	11	81	18	6.75	1	1452	47	30.89	6/51	4
Lord, G. J.	52	4	1215	101	25.31	1	24	0	—	—	—
Lowe, W. W.	65	5	1328	154	22.13	4	950	28	33.92	3/76	—
Lyttelton, C. F.	12	2	67	18★	6.70	—	510	19	26.84	3/60	—
Lyttelton, C. J.	152	14	2708	162	19.62	1	1250	32	39.06	4/83	—
McEvoy, M. S. A.	39	1	757	103	19.92	1					
McEwan, S. M.	14	8	45	13★	7.50	—	1881	49	38.38	4/34	—
Maclean, J. F.	79	7	1163	121	16.15	1					
Mann, W. H.	2	0	7	4	3.50	—					
Martin, E. G.	5	1	35	18★	8.75	—	136	2	68.00	2/73	—

254

	Inns	NO	Runs	HS	Avge	100s	Runs	Wkts	Avge	Best	5WI
Martin, S. H.	405	26	9993	191*	26.36	13	13358	458	29.10	8/24	18
Maxwell, C. R. N.	9	0	138	31	15.33	—					
Mills, G. T.	4	0	46	23	11.50	—					
Mitchell, K. J.	2	0	10	10	5.00	—					
Moores, P.	15	3	215	45	17.91	—					
Morris, P. J.	2	0	74	71	37.00	—	13	0	—	—	—
Morris, R.	3	0	7	7	2.33	—					
Mortimer, H.	2	0	11	7	5.50	—					
Moss, R. H.	2	0	2	2	1.00	—	5	1	5.00	1/5	—
Moule, H. G.	2	0	102	57	56.00	—					
Munn, R. G.	1	0	2	2	2.00	—					
Murray-Willis, P. G.	12	0	80	20	6.66	—					
Naden, J. R.	3	2	23	16*	23.00	—	136	2	68.00	2/111	—
Neale, P. A.	480	68	14928	167	36.23	26	275	1	275.00	1/15	—
Nesbitt, A. S.	2	1	5	3	5.00	—					
Nesfield, E. R.	4	0	37	16	6.75	—	10	0	—	—	—
Neville, B. P.	9	2	61	17*	8.71	—	148	7	21.14	4/53	—
Newport, P. J.	112	41	1875	77*	16.74	—	7924	289	27.41	8/52	16
Nichol, M.	233	16	7480	262*	34.47	17	1281	21	61.00	3/6	—
Nichols, J. E.	9	1	39	13	4.87	—	13	0	—	—	—
Norton, E. W.	10	3	82	23	11.71	—	338	7	48.28	3/74	—
Oakley, L.	13	4	43	11	4.77	—	393	12	32.75	6/64	1
Ormrod, J. A.	789	91	31753	204*	31.16	31	1064	25	42.56	5/27	1
O'Shaughnessy, S. J.	18	1	142	44	8.36	—	161	4	40.25	2/55	—
Outschoorn, L.	586	53	15257	215*	28.62	35	1961	33	59.42	2/15	—
Palmer, Cecil, H.	2	1	116	75*	116.00	—					
Palmer, Charles, H.	114	7	3252	177	30.39	6	1844	49	37.63	4/50	—
Parker, J. M.	103	9	3315	140	35.36	6	188	4	47.00	1/14	—
Passey, M. F. W.	1	0	1	1	1.00	—	57	1	57.00	1/57	—
Pataudi, Nawab, of (snr)	64	7	2860	231*	50.17	8	239	2	119.50	1/19	—
Patel, D. N.	364	31	9734	197	29.23	16	13089	357	36.66	7/46	12
Patel, H. V.	1	0	39	39	39.00	—					
Pawson, A. G.	2	1	12	12	12.00	—					
Pearson, D. B.	104	21	712	49	8.57	—	5347	202	26.47	6/70	9
Pearson, F. A.	794	37	18496	167	24.43	22	24208	815	29.70	8/42	35
Perks, R. T. D.	841	142	8485	75	12.13	—	50857	2143	23.73	9/40	140
Perry, E. H.	16	0	148	46	9.25	—	732	22	33.27	5/42	1
Perry, H.	8	1	109	40	15.57	—	46	1	46.00	1/38	—
Perryman, S. P.	33	16	127	22	7.47	—	1966	49	40.12	6/49	3
Phelps, P. H.	4	0	25	11	6.25	—					
Ponsonby, C. B.	127	26	784	50*	7.76	—					
Porthouse, S. C.	8	1	70	27	10.00	—	4	0	—	—	—
Powell, A. J.	2	0	10	9	5.00	—	8	0	—	—	—
Powys-Keck, H. J.	5	1	32	25	8.00	—	149	4	37.25	2/65	—
Pratt, D.	12	6	10	3*	1.66	—	546	13	42.00	5/54	1
Preece, C. R.	160	23	1575	69	11.49	—	4037	135	29.90	7/35	5
Price, J.	18	4	81	33	5.78	—	611	12	50.91	2/35	—
Price, W. H.	1	1	0	0*	—	—	12	0	—	—	—
Price, W. L.	3	0	12	7	4.00	—	284	8	35.50	4/86	—
Pridgeon, A. P.	216	83	1164	67	8.75	—	17218	526	32.73	7/35	10

	Inns	NO	Runs	HS	Avge	100s	Runs	Wkts	Avge	Best	5WI
Pullan, C. D. A.	43	6	768	84	20.75	—	192	5	38.40	2/26	—
Quaife. B. W.	447	42	8498	136*	20.98	3	231	5	46.20	2/5	—
Radford, N. V.	74	19	868	65	15.78	—	8477	359	23.61	9/70	21
Rhodes, S. J.	125	40	2188	108	25.74	1					
Richardson, D. W.	638	61	15843	169	27.45	16	322	8	40.25	2/11	—
Richardson, P. E.	286	20	9118	185	34.27	15	178	1	178.00	1/19	—
Richardson, W. E.	57	17	269	24	6.72	—	1865	44	42.38	6/48	1
Righton, E. G. (snr)	4	0	60	48	15.00	—	21	1	21.00	1/21	—
Righton, E. G. (jun)	7	0	27	19	3.5	—					
Riley, J.	1	0	1	1	1.00	—	48	3	16.00	3/25	—
Roberts, C. P.	1	1	0	0*	—	—	40	1	40.00	1/34	
Roberts, E. S.	6	0	23	12	3.83	—					
Robinson, A. W.	11	1	95	37	9.50	—					
Robinson, P. J.	5	0	49	37	9.80	—	132	6	22.00	2/12	—
Robson, C. G. W.	4	0	103	46	25.75	—					
Rogers, H. O.	146	31	1683	118*	14.63	1	3705	138	26.84	8/85	5
Romney, F. W.	7	3	39	20*	9.75	—					
Root, C. F.	470	38	6772	107	15.67	1	28465	1387	20.52	9/23	121
Rose, T. G.	10	1	47	15	5.22	—	219	7	31.28	3/68	—
Rudge, L. M.	1	0	1	1	1.00	—	36	0	—	—	—
Rumsey, F. E.	16	2	166	43	11.85	—	661	31	21.32	7/50	2
Rutherford, I. A.	3	0	9	8	3.00	—	15	1	15.00	1/15	—
Sale, H. G.	8	3	74	28*	14.80	—					
Sanderson, G. B.	1	0	16	16	16.00	—					
Santall, J. F. E.	13	1	117	36*	9.75	—	124	2	63.00	2/29	—
Saunders, M.	2	0	12	12	6.00	—	212	6	35.33	3/47	—
Scholey, J. C.	7	2	32	16	6.40	—	42	1	42.00	1/42	—
Scothern, M. G.			did not bat								
Scott, M. S.	60	3	1383	109	24.26	1	37	0	—	—	—
Sedgley, J. B.	27	2	389	95	15.58	—					
Seeley, G. H.	1	0	7	7	7.00	—					
Senghera, R.	25	7	281	36*	15.61	—	2179	57	38.22	5/81	1
Serrurier, L. R.	10	2	279	110	34.87	1	267	7	38.14	2/31	—
Shakespeare, W. H. N.	44	4	789	67*	19.72	—	8	0	—	—	—
Shepherd, S. G.	2	0	9	9	4.50	—	4	0	—	—	—
Sheppard, G. A.	4	0	18	11	4.50	—					
Sheppard, T. W.	2	0	36	22	18.00	—					
Shorting, W. L.	17	1	165	27	10.31	—					
Shutt, A.			did not bat				181	2	90.50	1/36	—
Simpson-Hayward, G. H. T.	253	24	4335	130	18.93	3	8099	362	22.37	7/54	24
Singleton, A. P.	100	11	2848	164	32.00	4	2614	70	37.34	4/30	—
Singleton, G. M.	4	0	31	23	7.75	—	91	4	22.75	1/1	—
Slade, D. N. F.	376	98	5021	125	18.06	1	10761	469	22.94	7/47	12
Smith, D. J.	15	0	114	29	7.60	—					
Smith, D. M.	87	13	3247	189*	43.87	8	57	3	19.00	2/35	—
Smith, J. C.	27	1	313	70	12.03	—	10	0	—	—	—
Smith, L. K.	7	1	62	28	10.33	—	20	1	20.00	1/20	—
Solly, E. W.	10	1	78	43	8.66	—	665	14	47.50	3/25	—
Somers, Lord A. H. T.	28	1	377	52	13.96	—	4	0	—	—	—
Somers-Smith, E.	4	0	33	22	8.25	—					

	Inns	NO	Runs	HS	Avge	100s	Runs	Wkts	Avge	Best	5WI
Southall, H.	1	0	11	11	11.00	—					
Spencer, A. H.	52	1	934	85	18.31	—	23	0	—	—	—
Spencer, H. N. E.	2	0	28	26	14.00	—	68	2	34.00	1/34	—
Spilsbury, J. W. E.	1	0	16	16	126.00	—	86	0	—	—	—
Standen, J. A.	175	29	2096	92★	14.35	—	7934	313	25.34	7/30	13
Stanning, J.	11	1	127	56★	12.70	—					
Stephenson, J. W. A.	2	0	20	12	10.00	—	66	1	66.00	1/51	—
Stevens, B. G.	31	2	364	41	12.55	—	18	0	—	—	—
Stewart, D. E. R.	35	3	578	69	18.06	—	72	0	—	—	—
Stimpson, P. J.	54	3	1327	103	26.01	1	19	0	—	—	—
Straw, T.	94	38	600	32	10.71	—					
Stringer, T.	2	1	0	0★	0.00	—	103	1	103.00	1/103	—
Styler, S. W.	31	6	134	24	5.36	—					
Suckling, E.	5	1	85	58	21.25	—	100	4	25.00	4/71	—
Summers, D. W. L.	1	0	4	4	4.00	—	11	0	—	—	—
Summers, F. T.	91	27	409	36	6.39	—					
Sutor, J. A.	2	0	3	2	1.50	—					
Swalwell, R. S.	30	1	409	57	14.10	—	35	0	—	—	—
Tarbox, C. V.	398	31	5824	109	15.86	2	13256	375	35.34	7/55	11
Tasker, A. G. E.			did not bat								
Taylor, R. J.	2	0	1	1	0.50	—	41	0	—	—	—
Taylor, W. H.	189	39	1733	59★	11.55	—	5673	159	35.67	7/64	5
Thomas, W. R. K.	2	1	57	44	57.00	—	54	0	—	—	—
Thornycroft, G. M.	2	0	3	3	1.50	—					
Thorp, P.	4	0	19	11	4.75	—					
Thursfield, J. H.	6	0	70	35	11.66	—					
Tinkler, E.	2	0	8	7	4.00	—					
Tipper, B. C. C.	10	1	137	43	15.22	—	80	4	20.00	2/0	—
Tomkinson, F. M.	1	0	0	0	0.00	—					
Tomkinson, G. S.	3	0	12	10	4.00	—					
Toppin, C. G.	5	0	17	10	3.40	—					
Toppin, J. F. T.	2	0	8	6	4.00	—	5	0	—	—	—
Turner, G. M.	493	65	22298	311★	52.09	72	114	5	22.80	3/18	—
Turner, J. W. C.	87	3	1215	106	14.46	1	32	2	16.00	1/14	—
Turner, R. E.	96	8	1010	66	11.47	—	225	4	56.25	3/7	—
Vorster, L. P.	1	1	16	16★	—	—					
Wakefield, P. H.	2	0	8	8	4.00	—	13	0	—	—	—
Wakelin, E.	1	0	6	6	6.00	—					
Walford, J. E. S.	12	0	145	31	12.08	—	67	1	67.00	1/1	—
Wallace, C. W.	7	1	66	39★	11.00	—					
Walters, C. F.	237	20	8193	226	37.75	18	335	5	67.00	2/22	—
Warne, F. B.	141	12	2670	115	20.69	2	3481	96	36.26	6/51	3
Warner, A. E.	39	9	480	67	16.00	—	1947	61	31.91	5/27	1
Watkins, S. G.	2	0	105	77	52.50	—					
Watson, G. G.	35	6	341	38	11.75	—	2360	70	33.71	6/45	1
Webster, A. J.	11	5	81	25	13.50	—	734	15	48.93	5/87	1
Wells, T. U.	2	0	9	9	4.50	—					
Weston, M. J.	207	16	4716	145★	24.69	3	2559	65	39.36	4/24	—
Wheldon, G. F.	244	25	4938	112	22.54	3	77	0	—	—	—
Whitcombe, P. J.	10	3	241	89★	34.42	—					
White, A. F. T.	188	12	3745	95	21.27	—	26	0	—	—	—

	Inns	NO	Runs	HS	Avge	100s	Runs	Wkts	Avge	Best	5WI
White, M. E.	46	12	238	37	7.00	—	2076	66	31.45	5/34	1
Whitehead, J. P.	46	9	741	71	20.02	—	1384	35	39.54	5/89	1
Whiting, N. H.	96	11	1583	118	18.62	2	657	13	50.53	2/27	—
Wilcock, H. G.	137	31	1697	74	16.01	—	3	0	—	—	—
Wilkes, A. J.	22	2	113	25	5.65	—					
Wilkes, W. H. W.	25	1	419	109	17.45	1					
Wilkinson, J. W.	2	2	4	4★	—	—	45	1	45.00	1/45	—
Wilkinson, K. W.	77	11	1657	141	25.10	2	1551	48	32.31	5/60	1
Williams, H.	6	3	7	4	2.33	—	185	2	92.50	1/13	—
Williams, R. H.	68	4	713	81	11.14	—					
Wilson, G. A.	229	37	2202	78	11.46	—	17129	719	23.82	9/75	58
Wilson, G. C.	119	34	609	40	7.16	—	4049	150	26.99	8/81	8
Wilson, G. T. O.	16	7	10	4★	1.11	—	1000	18	55.55	3/42	—
Wilson, H.	11	3	64	21	8.00	—	373	13	28.69	6/86	1
Winnington, J. F. S.	2	0	20	20	10.00	—					
Winwood, T. L.	30	4	404	104	15.53	1	10	0	—	—	—
Wright, L.	348	18	6593	134	19.97	5	3649	76	48.01	3/6	—
Wyatt, R. E. S.	138	13	4233	166★	33.86	6	2387	62	38.50	5/43	1
Wyers, A.	1	0	3	3	3.00	—					
Yardley, T. J.	232	40	4865	135	25.33	4	14	0	—	—	—
Yarnold, H.	409	68	3620	64	10.61	—					
Young, D. M.	47	7	766	90	19.15	—	0	0	—	—	—
Younis Ahmed	133	30	5486	221★	53.26	13	521	12	43.41	3/33	—

RESULTS OF ALL INTER-COUNTY FIRST-CLASS MATCHES 1899–1988

	DY	EX	GM	GS	HA	KT	LA	LE	MX	NR	NT	SM	SY	SX	WA	YO	P	W	L	D	Tie	Pos
1899	WD				DL		WL							DL	LD	LD	12	2	5	5	—	12
1900	DL		LW	DW	LL	LL	WD	DD					LD	DL	LD	DL	22	3	10	9	—	12
1901	WW			WD	DW	DW	LL	LW				AW	LL	DL	LL	LL	21	7	10	4	—	11
1902	DD			DW	DW	LL	DL	LW				DW	DD	DL	WD	DL	22	5	6	11	—	9
1903				WL	WW	DL	LD	DW				WL	DL	WL	WW	DD	20	8	6	6	—	6
1904					DL	WW	LL	LL	DL			LW	DL		DD	DD	18	3	8	7	—	13
1905				WL	DW	DD	DL	WW				DW	DL		DD	LL	18	5	5	8	—	8
1906					DL	DL	DL	DW	DL		LW	DD	DL		DD	LL	20	2	8	10	—	14
1907						WW	DW	DL	WD			DW	DD	DW	LD	WW	18	8	2	8	—	2=
1908						WW	WD	DL	WD			DW	LL	DL	DW	LD	18	6	5	7	—	6
1909				WD	LL	LW	LW				LW	DW	LL	DL	DW	WW	20	8	8	4	—	8=
1910		DW			LL	WL	LL	DL			DD	DW	WL	WD	DD	DL	22	5	8	9	—	13
1911		LL		WL	WL	LL	LL	WW	WL		WW	WW	WW	WW	WD	LL	24	12	11	1	—	9
1912				LD	LL	LL	DL	DW	DL			DD	DL		LD	DL	20	1	10	9	—	16
1913				WL	LL	LD	WW	LL	DW			WW	DD		DL	LL	20	6	9	5	—	12
1914	LL	DL		DW	DL	LL	DL	LL				LW	DL	DL	LD		22	2	13	7	—	14
1919				DD								DL			DD		6	0	1	5	—	
1920		LL		LW	LL	LL	LL					LL		DL	LL	LL	18	1	16	1	—	15
1921	LW	DL	WL	WL	LL	LL	LL			LL	WL	LW		LD			22	5	15	2	—	14
1922	DL	DL	DW	DL	LL	LL	LD			LL	LL	DD		DL	LL	LD	26	1	16	9	—	17
1923	DD	LW	WD	LL	LL	LL	DL			WD	LL	LL		WL	WL	LL	26	5	16	5	—	15
1924	WD	WL	DW	LL	LL	DL	DD			DW	DL	LL			DL	LD	24	4	11	9	—	14
1925	LL	DL	WW	LL	WD		LL		LL	LL	LL	LD		LW	LW	LL	26	5	18	3	—	16
1926	LL	DD	LD	LD	DL		LD	LW	LD	LW	LD	DD		LW	DL	DL	28	3	13	12	—	17
1927	DD	LL	DD	LL	AL	LL	LD	LD	WD	LL	LD			LL	DD	DL	29	1	17	11	—	17
1928	LL	DL	DL	LL	DD	DL	DD	LL	LL	LL	LD	LL		LL	DD	DL	30	0	19	11	—	17
1929	LL	DW	WD	LL	DL		LL	LD	DL	LL	DL	DD		LL	DD	LD	28	2	15	11	—	16
1930	WL	DD	DL	DD	DL	DD	DL	DD	WW	LW	DD	LL		WL	DL	DD	28	5	9	14	—	10
1931	DL	WL	DL	WL	WD	WD	DL	DD	DW	LL			DL	DD	LD	LD	28	5	10	13	—	14
1932	DD	DD	DD	WL	LD	DL	LL	LD	DL			LL	DD	DD	LL	DL	28	1	12	15	—	17
1933	DL	DL	WL	DL	DD	DL	DL	WD	DD	DL	DD	LD		LL	LL	DL	30	2	13	15	—	15
1934	LD	DD	DD	DD	WL	LL	LL	DD		DW	DD	WL		LL	DL	LL	28	3	12	13	—	16
1935	WD	LL	DD	LW	WW	DD	LL	LL	LL	WW		WW	LL	LL	LW	LL	30	9	16	5	—	12
1936	LL	WD	DW	DW	DD	LW	DD	DD	LL	WW		LL	DL		DD	WL	28	7	9	12	—	12
1937	WL	LL	WL	WL	WL	LL	DD	DW	LL	WW	LD	LL		LL	DW	LL	30	8	17	5	—	15
1938	DL	LW	DW	LL	DW	DL	DW	DL	DW	WW	DL	WL	DW	WL	DD	LD	32	9	11	12	—	11
1939	DL	DL	WD	WL	WW	LW	LL	DW		DW	WD	TL	WL	WL	DD	WL	30	11	10	8	1	7
1946	WA	DW	LW	WW	-L	L-	-L	LD	L-	DW	WL	LL	D-	LL	WW	-L	25	9	12	4	—	8=
1947	LL	LW	WD	LL	D-	-L	D-	WL	-L	WL	DD	DL	-D	DW	WW	L-	26	7	11	8	—	7=
1948	D-	WL	L-	LD	DD	DL	D-	-D	WL	DW	-D	LW	WW	L-	DD	DL	26	6	8	12	—	10
1949	-W	WD	-L	DD	WW	WW	D-	D-	LL	DW	D-	WL	WL	-W	WL	LW	26	12	7	7	—	3
1950	WL	DD	D-	LD	WW	DD	-L	DW	DL	WD	-D	LD	LL	DW	LW	L-	28	7	9	12	—	6
1951	DW	DD	-L	WL	DL	WL	D-	WL	WD	DD	W-	DW	DL	WD	DL	-W	28	9	7	12	—	4
1952	LL	DD	DW	-D	D-	LL	DD	LL	-L	DD	WW	L-	WD	WW	LL	D-	28	6	11	11	—	14
1953	DL	DL	DL	DD	D-	-L	DL	LL	LW	D-	WL	WW	-L	WL	DD	DL	28	5	12	11	—	15
1954	WL	DD	D-	DL	DW	DL	D-	WD	LL	DL	-L	DW	LL	LL	LW	-D	28	5	12	11	—	11=
1955	LL	DW	-L	WL	DL	WW	-L	DL	LL	LD	W-	DL	LL	LL	LD	L-	28	5	17	6	—	15
1956	WD	DD	WD	WL	-D	D-	DD	WD	DD	-D	DL	WW	D-	DL	WD	WL	28	8	4	16	—	9=
1957	WD	DD	DL	DW	D-	-L	LL	WD	LW	D-	DL	LD	-L	DD	DD	LD	28	4	9	15	—	16
1958	WD	WL	D-	WW	DL	WD	D-	LW	DD	WL	-D	LL	LW	DD	WD	-A	27	9	7	11	—	9
1959	LL	LD	-L	WW	DD	DL	-D	WW	DD	DD	D-	DD	WL	DW	LD	L-	28	6	8	14	—	14
1960	DL	DD	WL	LW	DA	LL	LD	DD	LD	WL	WW	LW	DL	WW	LD	DL	31	8	12	11	—	13
1961	WW	WW	WW	DD	LD	LD	LW	WL	WL	WW	WL	WL	WD	LW	WD	LL	32	16	9	7	—	4
1962	WD	DW	DW	WL	WD	WD	WD	DD	DW	LW	WW	WW	DD	WD	LD	DD	32	14	3	15	—	2
1963	WD	DL	LL	DD	-D	D-	DD	DL	LD	-W	LL	WD	D-	LD	DD	WD	28	4	8	16	—	14
1964	WW	DW	WW	WW	L-	-W	WW	WW	WW	D-	WW	LW	-D	DD	DW	DL	28	18	3	7	—	1
1965	WW	DL	W-	DW	DW	WL	W-	WD	LD	WD	-D	WL	WD	WW	DD	-D	28	13	4	11	—	1
1966	WD	DW	-W	WD	DD	WL	-W	LW	DW	DW	D-	LW	WD	LD	LW	D-	28	13	5	10	—	2

Note: Worcs did not enter the County Championship in 1919 but played friendlies (First-Class) only.

	DY	EX	GM	GS	HA	KT	LA	LE	MX	NR	NT	SM	SY	SX	WA	YO	P	W	L	D	Tie	Pos
1967	DD	WD	DD	DW	D–	–L	WD	DL	LD	W–	DD	WD	–L	WD	DD	LL	28	6	6	16	—	5
1968	LL	DD	DD	DW	–W	L–	DW	WL	DL	–D	DD	LD	D–	WW	DW	WL	28	8	7	13	—	7
1969	AD	DD	LL	LL	L–	W–	–D	–W	D–	D–	–W	DW	DD	DD	LW	–L	23	5	7	11	—	12=
1970	LD	WD	DW	DD	–D	–D	D–	D–	D–	–W	W–	WD	DW	DW	DD	D–	24	7	1	16	—	6
1971	–D	DW	DL	LD	D–	DD	DL	LD	D–	D–	–D	–L	–L	D–	WL	DW	24	3	7	14	—	15
1972	W–	LD	WD	DL	–L	L–	D–	W–	D–	–D	–W	D–	–D	–D	DD	–D	20	4	4	12	—	7
1973	–W	DW	DD	WL	L–	–D	–D	–W	–D	L–	W–	–D	D–	W–	LD	D–	20	6	4	10	—	6
1974	W–	WD	WW	WW	–L	W–	D–	L–	D–	–L	–W	D–	–D	–W	DW	–W	20	11	3	6	—	1
1975	–D	LW	LD	WW	L–	–L	–D	–D	–D	L–	W–	–W	L–	D–	DD	D–	20	5	6	9	—	10
1976	W–	–D	DW	LA	–W	L–	W–	D–	D–	–L	–W	DD	D–	–W	DD	–D	19	6	3	10	—	11
1977	–L	L–	LD	LL	L–	–W	WD	–D	–L	L–	LW	DD	–D	–L	WD	W–	22	5	10	7	—	13
1978	D–	–D	DD	DL	–D	L–	DL	D–	D–	–D	DW	DL	D–	–W	DD	–L	22	2	5	15	—	15
1979	–D	W–	WD	LD	D–	–D	WL	–D	–W	D–	DW	DL	–W	D–	LA	W–	21	7	4	10	—	2
1980	D–	–D	DA	DL	–L	D–	WL	D–	D–	–D	DW	LL	L–	–D	LW	–D	21	3	7	11	—	11
1981	–L	W–	DW	LD	L–	–D	LL	–D	–D	D–	LL	DL	–L	D–	WW	W–	22	5	9	8	—	11
1982	D–	–D	DD	DW	–W	D–	WD	D–	L–	–D	DL	LL	D–	–L	DD	–D	22	3	5	14	—	14
1983	–L	–L	LD	WD	LL	–D	WD	L–	L–	–L	L–	DD	LL	DD	DD	D–	24	2	11	11	—	16
1984	D–	DL	LD	WD	W–	D–	–D	LD	–L	WD	DL	WD	–D	W–	DD	–D	24	5	5	14	—	10
1985	LD	D–	DD	LL	–D	WW	W–	–D	LL	L–	–D	WD	D–	–D	DW	DD	24	5	6	13	—	5
1986	–D	W–	WD	LD	WD	–D	LD	W–	W–	–D	D–	WL	DD	DL	DW	D–	24	7	5	12	—	5
1987	D–	DW	DL	DW	L–	W–	–L	DD	–D	WD	WD	DD	–D	L–	DD	–D	24	5	4	15	—	9
1988	–D	L–	WW	DW	W–	–D	DW	–D	–W	D–	WL	LW	–D	W–	DD	W–	22	10	3	9	—	1

RESULTS OF ALL SUNDAY LEAGUE MATCHES 1969–1988

	DY	EX	GM	GS	HA	KT	LA	LE	MX	NR	NT	SM	SY	SX	WA	YO	P	W	L	ND	Tie	Pos
1969	L	W	W	L	L	W	W	L	W	L	W	A	L	ND	A	L	14	6	7	1	—	12
1970	L	L	W	W	W	L	L	W	L	L	W	W	ND	W	L	W	16	8	7	1	—	6
1971	W	W	L	W	W	W	W	L	W	L	L	W	W	W	W	L	16	11	5	—	—	1
1972	A	L	W	W	L	L	L	L	W	W	W	L	L	W	L	W	15	7	8	—	—	11
1973	W	W	W	ND	L	L	ND	L	L	L	L	L	T	L	L	W	16	4	9	2	1	15
1974	W	W	L	A	L	W	ND	L	W	L	W	L	W	L	L	W	15	7	7	1	—	8
1975	W	W	W	L	W	W	T	W	W	W	L	W	W	W	W	L	16	12	3	—	1	2
1976	L	L	W	W	L	L	W	L	L	W	L	W	W	L	W	W	16	8	8	—	—	8=
1977	W	L	W	A	W	L	W	L	L	L	W	ND	L	L	L	L	15	5	9	1	—	13=
1978	W	W	A	W	L	L	W	W	W	W	L	W	W	L	W	L	15	10	5	—	—	4
1979	L	L	W	L	W	W	W	ND	W	L	A	W	W	W	A		14	9	4	1	—	3
1980	L	L	W	L	W	W	ND	W	L	L	W	L	W	L	W	W	16	8	7	1	—	6=
1981	L	L	W	W	W	W	L	W	L	W	L	W	L	L	L	L	16	7	9	—	—	10=
1982	L	L	L	L	W	L	L	L	L	L	W	L	W	W	ND	W	16	5	10	1	—	15
1983	L	W	L	A	L	L	T	A	L	W	T	W	L	W	T	L	14	4	7	—	3	11=
1984	W	L	ND	W	W	W	L	L	W	L	W	W	W	L	A	W	15	9	5	1	—	5=
1985	L	L	L	L	L	L	A	W	W	W	L	ND	W	L	W	L	15	5	9	1	—	16
1986	L	L	W	W	L	L	W	L	L	L	L	L	W	W	L		16	5	11	—	—	16
1987	L	W	W	ND	W	L	W	W	L	W	L	L	W	W	W	W	16	11	4	1	—	1
1988	W	W	W	A	W	W	L	W	L	W	L	W	L	W	W	W	15	12	3	—	—	1

RESULTS OF ALL NATWEST TROPHY/GILLETTE CUP MATCHES 1963–1988

1963 *1st Round*: beat Surrey; *Q/Final*: beat Glamorgan; *S/Final*: beat Lancashire; *Final*: lost to Sussex

1964 *1st Round*: lost to Glamorgan

1965 *1st Round*: bye; *2nd Round*: lost to Sussex

1966 *1st Round*: bye; *2nd Round*: beat Nottinghamshire; *Q/Final*: beat Essex; *S/Final*: beat Hampshire; *Final*: lost to Warwickshire

1967 *1st Round*: lost to Sussex

1968 *1st Round*: beat Durham; *2nd Round*: lost to Nottinghamshire

1969 *1st Round*: bye; *2nd Round*: lost to Derbyshire

1970 *1st Round*: beat Oxfordshire; *2nd Round*: lost to Kent

1971 *1st Round*: bye; *2nd Round*: lost to Lancashire

1972 *1st Round*: beat Sussex; *2nd Round*: beat Derbyshire; *Q/Final*: beat Surrey; *S/Final*: lost to Warwickshire

1973 *1st Round*: bye; *2nd Round*: beat Warwickshire; *Q/Final*: beat Leicestershire; *S/Final*: lost to Gloucestershire

1974 *1st Round*: bye; *2nd Round*: beat Sussex; *Q/Final*: beat Nottinghamshire; *S/Final*: lost to Lancashire

1975 *1st Round*: bye; *2nd Round*: beat Essex; *Q/Final*: lost to Middlesex

1976 *1st Round*: lost to Gloucestershire

1977 *1st Round*: bye; *2nd Round*: lost to Glamorgan

1978 *1st Round*: lost to Derbyshire

1979 *1st Round*: bye; *2nd Round*: lost to Leicestershire

1980 *1st Round*: beat Somerset; *2nd Round*: beat Lancashire; *Q/Final*: lost to Middlesex

1981 *1st Round*: bye; *2nd Round*: lost to Derbyshire

1982 *1st Round*: bye; *2nd Round*: lost to Yorkshire

1983 *1st Round*: lost to Nottinghamshire

1984 *1st Round*: beat Suffolk; *2nd Round*: lost to Northamptonshire

1985 *1st Round*: beat Hertfordshire; *2nd Round*: beat Lancashire; *Q/Final*: beat Glamorgan; *S/Final*: lost to Nottinghamshire

1986 *1st Round*: beat Oxfordshire; *2nd Round*: beat Hampshire; *Q/Final*: beat Warwickshire; *S/Final*: lost to Sussex

1987 *1st Round*: beat Devon; *2nd Round*: lost to Essex

1988 *1st Round*: beat Cumberland; *2nd Round*: beat Nottinghamshire; *Q/Final*: beat Gloucestershire; *S/Final*: beat Hampshire; *Final*: lost to Middlesex

RESULTS IN
BENSON AND HEDGES
CUP COMPETITION
1972–1988

1972   Third in Group Midlands
1973   Second in Group Midlands; *Q/Final*: beat Nottinghamshire; *S/Final*: beat Lancashire; *Final*: lost to Kent
1974   First in Group Midlands; *Q/Final*: lost to Lancashire
1975   Fifth in Group Midlands
1976   Second in Group B; *Q/Final*: beat Leicestershire; *S/Final*: beat Warwickshire; *Final*: lost to Kent
1977   Fourth in Group B
1978   Fourth in Group B
1979   Second in Group A; *Q/Final*: lost to Surrey
1980   Second in Group B; *Q/Final*: beat Lancashire; *S/Final*: lost to Essex
1981   Fifth in Group A
1982   Third in Group A
1983   Fourth in Group A
1984   Fourth in Group B
1985   First in Group B; *Q/Final*: lost to Middlesex
1986   First in Group B; *Q/Final*: beat Northamptonshire; *S/Final*: lost to Kent
1987   Second in Group B; *Q/Final*: lost to Surrey
1988   First in Group B; *Q/Final*: lost to Hampshire

RESULTS OF
REFUGE ASSURANCE CUP MATCHES

1988   Beat Middlesex in the Semi-Final; lost to Lancashire in the Final

GROUNDS USED
BY WORCESTERSHIRE 1899–1988

FIRST-CLASS RECORD

Ground	First	Last	P	W	L	D	
New Road, Worcester	1899	1988	871	218	260	391	(1 tied)
Amblecote, Stourbridge	1905	1981	61	16	28	17	
Tipton Road, Dudley	1911	1971	88	16	30	42	
Chester Road North, Kidderminster	1921	1988	49	19	17	12	(1 tied)
Bournville	1910	1911	2	1	0	1	
The Racecourse, Hereford	1919	1983	5	0	3	2	
Evesham	1951	1951	1	1	0	0	
Halesowen	1964	1969	2	2	0	0	
Stourport-on-Severn	1980	1980	1	1	0	0	

TEAM RECORDS

(1) HIGHEST AND LOWEST SCORE FOR WORCESTERSHIRE AGAINST EACH COUNTY

Opponents	Highest	Year	Lowest	Year
Derbyshire	557 at Worcester	1899	46 at Derby	1922
Essex	515 at Chelmsford	1934	49 at Leyton	1922
Glamorgan	506-5 at Worcester	1934	63 at Swansea	1921
Gloucestershire	529-4 at Worcester	1913	35 at Cheltenham	1928
Hampshire	547 at Southampton	1903	68 at Dudley	1961
Kent	627-9 at Worcester	1905	25 at Tunbridge Wells	1960
Lancashire	492 at Old Trafford	1906	41 at Old Trafford	1912
Leicestershire	561 at Leicester	1901	40 (2 absent hurt) at Worcester	1971
Middlesex	436-9 at Worcester	1951	62 at Worcester	1960
Northants	546-6 at Dudley	1939	63 at Kidderminster	1973
Nottinghamshire	486 at Dudley	1947	53 at Trent Bridge	1922
Somerset	628-7 at Taunton	1988	42 at Bath	1965
Surrey	446-7 at Guildford	1979	25 at The Oval	1954
Sussex	458-5 at Worcester	1947	57 at Horsham	1984
Warwickshire	633 at Worcester	1906	71 at Edgbaston	1903 and 1949
Yorkshire	456-8 at Worcester	1904	24 at Huddersfield	1903

(2) HIGHEST AND LOWEST SCORE AGAINST WORCESTERSHIRE BY EACH COUNTY

Opponents	Highest	Year	Lowest	Year
Derbyshire	513-8 at Chesterfield	1933	54 at Worcester	1935
Essex	560.-5 at Leyton	1931	65 at Chelmsford	1947
Glamorgan	506-8 at Swansea	1929	61 at Neath	1936
Gloucestershire	625-6 at Dudley	1934	55 at Worcester	1908
Hampshire	481-7 at Worcester	1923	30 at Worcester	1903
Kent	602-7 at Dudley	1938	50 at Dover	1955
Lancashire	592-4 at Worcester	1929	55 at Worcester	1965
Leicestershire	701-4 at Worcester	1906	52 at Worcester	1965
Middlesex	623-5 at Worcester	1949	54 at Lords	1964
Northants	527 at Kidderminster	1946	50 at Northampton	1946
Nottinghamshire	540 at Worksop	1934	73 at Trent Bridge	1962
Somerset	545 at Taunton	1906	56 at Wells	1935
Surrey	544 at Worcester	1904	57 at The Oval	1958
Sussex	539 at Hove	1920	47 at Worcester	1903
Warwickshire	645-7 at Dudley	1914	66 at Edgbaston	1950
Yorkshire	560-6 at Worcester	1928	62 at Bradford	1907

HIGHEST AND LOWEST SCORES IN LIMITED OVERS COMPETITIONS

HIGHEST FOR WORCESTERSHIRE

Sunday League　　　　　307-4　　　　*v* Derbyshire *at* Worcester, 1975
　　　　　　　　　　　　(38 overs)
Benson and Hedges Cup　314-5　　　　*v* Lancashire *at* Old Trafford, 1980
NatWest/Gillette Cup　　404-3　　　　*v* Devon *at* Worcester, 1987
　　　　　　　　　　　　(312-5　　　　*v* Lancashire *at* Old Trafford, 1985, is the highest score
　　　　　　　　　　　　against first-class opposition)

HIGHEST AGAINST WORCESTERSHIRE

Sunday League　　　　　293-4　　　　*by* Sussex *at* Horsham, 1980
Benson and Hedges Cup　284-6　　　　*by* Derbyshire *at* Worcester, 1979
NatWest/Gillette Cup　　326-6　　　　*by* Leicestershire *at* Leicester, 1979

LOWEST FOR WORCESTERSHIRE

Sunday League　　　　　86　　　　　　*v* Yorkshire *at* Headingley, 1969
　　　　　　　　　　　　(32.4 overs)
Benson and Hedges Cup　81　　　　　　*v* Leicestershire *at* Worcester, 1983
　　　　　　　　　　　　(34.4 overs)
NatWest/Gillette Cup　　98　　　　　　*v* Durham *at* Chester-le-Street, 1968
　　　　　　　　　　　　(56.2 overs)

LOWEST AGAINST WORCESTERSHIRE

Sunday League　　　　　56　　　　　　*by* Middlesex *at* Kidderminster, 1969
　　　　　　　　　　　　(27.1 overs)
Benson and Hedges Cup　94　　　　　　*by* Minor Counties (South) *at* High Wycombe, 1979
　　　　　　　　　　　　(42.5 overs)
NatWest/Gillette Cup　　59　　　　　　*by* Lancashire *at* Worcester, 1963
　　　　　　　　　　　　(31.1 overs)

INDIVIDUAL BATTING RECORDS

(1) DOUBLE-CENTURIES IN FIRST-CLASS MATCHES

Score	Batsman	Opponents	Venue	Year
405*	G. A. Hick	Somerset	Taunton	1988
311*	G. M. Turner	Warwickshire	Worcester	1982
276	F. L. Bowley	Hampshire	Dudley	1914
262*	M. Nichol	Hampshire	Bournemouth	1930
259	D. Kenyon	Yorkshire	Kidderminster	1956
253*	D. Kenyon	Leicestershire	Worcester	1954
246*	R. E. Foster	Kent	Worcester	1905
239*	G. M. Turner	Oxford U	Oxford	1982
238*	D. Kenyon	Yorkshire	Worcester	1953
233	M. J. Horton	Somerset	Worcester	1962
231*	Nawab of Pataudi	Essex	Worcester	1933
229	D. Kenyon	Hampshire	Portsmouth	1959
228*	G. M. Turner	Gloucestershire	Worcester	1980
227*	G. A. Hick	Nottinghamshire	Worcester	1986
227	B. L. D'Oliveira	Yorkshire	Hull	1974
226	C. F. Walters	Kent	Gravesend	1933
224*	Nawab of Pataudi	Kent	Worcester	1933
222	Nawab of Pataudi	Somerset	Weston-super-Mare	1933
221*	Younis Ahmed	Nottinghamshire	Trent Bridge	1979
219*	G. A. Hick	Glamorgan	Neath	1986
217	F. L. Bowley	Leicestershire	Stourbridge	1905
216*	E. Cooper	Warwickshire	Dudley	1939
216	H. K. Foster	Somerset	Worcester	1903
215*	L. Outschoorn	Northants	Worcester	1949
215	H. K. Foster	Warwickshire	Worcester	1908
215	E. G. Arnold	Oxford	Oxford	1910
214*	Nawab of Pataudi	Glamorgan	Worcester	1934
214*	G. M. Turner	Oxford U	Worcester	1975
212*	H. H. I. Gibbons	Northamptonshire	Dudley	1939
212	M. J. Horton	Essex	Leyton	1959
212	G. A. Hick	Lancashire	Old Trafford	1988
204*	J. A. Ormrod	Kent	Dartford	1973
202*	D. Kenyon	Hampshire	Portsmouth	1954
202*	G. M. Turner	Cambridge U	Cambridge	1974
202*	G. M. Turner	Warwickshire	Edgbaston	1978
201	F. L. Bowley	Gloucestershire	Worcester	1913
201	D. Kenyon	Glamorgan	Stourbridge	1960
200*	E. G. Arnold	Warwickshire	Edgbaston	1909
200*	H. H. I. Gibbons	West Indies	Worcester	1928
200*	L. Outschoorn	Scotland	Dundee	1951
200*	D. Kenyon	Nottinghamshire	Worcester	1957
200*	J. A. Ormrod	Gloucestershire	Worcester	1982

(2) CENTURIES IN LIMITED-OVERS MATCHES

(a) Sunday League (John Player/Refuge Assurance)

Score	Batsman	Opponents	Venue	Year
147	G. M. Turner	Sussex	Horsham	1980
129★	G. M. Turner	Glamorgan	Worcester	1973
127	C. L. King	Surrey	Guildford	1983
125★	I. T. Botham	Essex	Worcester	1987
125	D. N. Patel	Hampshire	Southampton	1982
121	G. M. Turner	Sussex	Dudley	1972
113	Younis Ahmed	Middlesex	Lord's	1979
112★	R. G. A. Headley	Kent	Worcester	1974
111	G. A. Hick	Yorkshire	Worcester	1988
110★	J. A. Ormrod	Kent	Canterbury	1975
109	M. J. Weston	Somerset	Taunton	1982
108	G. M. Turner	Warwickshire	Edgbaston	1972
103	D. B. D'Oliveira	Surrey	Worcester	1985
102	P. A. Neale	Northamptonshire	Luton	1982
102	T. S. Curtis	Glamorgan	Worcester	1986
101★	C. L. King	Nottinghamshire	Worcester	1984
100	B. L. D'Oliveira	Surrey	Byfleet	1973
100	Younis Ahmed	Leicestershire	Leicester	1979

(b) Benson and Hedges Cup

Score	Player	Opponents	Venue	Year
143★	G. M. Turner	Warwickshire	Edgbaston	1976
132	R. G. A. Headley	Oxford	Worcester	1973
128	P. A. Neale	Lancashire	Old Trafford	1980
126	D. M. Smith	Warwickshire	Worcester	1985
124★	J. A. Ormrod	Gloucestershire	Worcester	1976
122	G. M. Turner	Lancashire	Old Trafford	1980
115	Younis Ahmed	Yorkshire	Worcester	1980
107	Younis Ahmed	Surrey	Worcester	1979
103★	G. A. Hick	Nottinghamshire	Worcester	1986
103★	G. A. Hick	Northamptonshire	Worcester	1986

(c) NatWest Trophy/Gillette Cup

Score	Player	Opponents	Venue	Year
172★	G. A. Hick	Devon	Worcester	1987
138	G. A. Hick	Cumberland	Worcester	1988
120	T. S. Curtis	Nottinghamshire	Trent Bridge	1988
117★	G. M. Turner	Lancashire	Worcester	1971
115	G. M. Turner	Lancashire	Worcester	1980
114	M. J. Horton	Hampshire	Worcester	1966
109	D. M. Smith	Lancashire	Old Trafford	1985
109	G. M. Turner	Gloucestershire	Worcester	1973
107	J. M. Parker	Middlesex	Worcester	1975
105	G. M. Turner	Yorkshire	Headingley	1982
105	G. A. Hick	Nottinghamshire	Trent Bridge	1988
102	B. L. D'Oliveira	Sussex	Hove	1974
101★	G. M. Turner	Derbyshire	Derby	1972
101	I. T. Botham	Devon	Worcester	1987

(3) CARRYING BAT THROUGH A COMPLETED FIRST-CLASS INNINGS

The following opening batsmen have batted throughout a completed innings in which all ten of their partners have been dismissed.

Batsman	Score	Total	Opponents	Venue	Year
F. L. Bowley	104*	(267)	Middlesex	Lord's	1911
F. A. Pearson	154*	(342)	Surrey	Dudley	1912
F. A. Pearson	67*	(152)	Sussex	Eastbourne	1914
F. A. Pearson	151*	(275)	Warwickshire	Worcester	1921
F. A. Pearson	68*	(123)	Hampshire	Southampton	1923
B. W. Quaife	31*	(112)	Kent	Stourbridge	1931
H. H. I. Gibbons	70*	(165)	Warwickshire	Kidderminster	1934
C. H. Bull	57*	(150)	Lancashire (1st inns)	Kidderminster	1935
H. H. I. Gibbons	83*	(148)	Lancashire (2nd inns)	Kidderminster	1935
F. B. T. Warne	43*	(153)	Middlesex	Lord's	1937
E. Cooper	104*	(273)	Lancashire	Old Trafford	1939
E. Cooper	69*	(154)	Warwickshire	Dudley	1951
P. E. Richardson	91*	(155)	Hampshire	Worcester	1955
D. Kenyon	103*	(215)	Hampshire	Bournemouth	1955
M. J. Horton	53*	(91)	Lancashire	Old Trafford	1966
G. M. Turner	88*	(202)	Somerset	Worcester	1972
J. A. Ormrod	66*	(187)	Essex	Chelmsford	1975
J. A. Ormrod	36*	(73)	Sussex	Worcester	1977
G. M. Turner	141*	(169)	Glamorgan	Swansea	1977
(World record of 83.43 per cent of the total)					
J. A. Ormrod	126*	(219)	Hampshire	Bournemouth	1980
J. A. Ormrod	63*	(136)	Derbyshire	Derby	1983

(4) CARRYING BAT THROUGH A COMPLETED LIMITED-OVERS INNINGS

(a) Sunday League (John Player and Refuge Assurance)

Batsman	Score	Total	Opponents	Venue	Year
G. M. Turner	129*	(229-3)	Glamorgan		1973
R. G. A. Headley	112*	(216-5)	Kent	Worcester	1974
J. A. Ormrod	110*	(231-4)	Kent	Canterbury	1975
G. M. Turner	81*	(163-6)	Kent		1979
J. A. Ormrod	92*	(236-1)	Hampshire	Southampton	1982

(b) NatWest Trophy/Gillette Cup

Batsman	Score	Total	Opponents	Venue	Year
G. M. Turner	117*	(215-6)	Lancashire	Worcester	1971

(b) Benson and Hedges Cup

Batsman	Score	Total	Opponents	Venue	Year
G. M. Turner	143*	(281-4)	Warwickshire	Edgbaston	1976

(5) CENTURY IN EACH INNINGS OF A FIRST-CLASS MATCH

(b) NatWest Trophy/Gillette Cup

Batsman	Scores	Opponents	Venue	Year
R. E. Foster	134*, 101	Hampshire	Worcester	1899
W. L. Foster	140, 172*	Hampshire	Worcester	1899

(The first time two batsmen had scored two separate hundreds in the same match)

E. G. Arnold	101*, 128	Cambridge U	Cambridge	1903
M. K. Foster	141, 106	Hampshire	Worcester	1926
H. H. I. Gibbons	111*, 100*	Hampshire	Worcester	1939
E. Cooper	191, 106*	Northamptonshire	Kidderminster	1946
R. G. A. Headley	187, 108	Northamptonshire	Worcester	1971
G. M. Turner	122, 128*	Warwickshire	Edgbaston	1972

(In between these innings he scored 108 v Warwickshire, also at Edgbaston, in the Sunday League)

J. A. Ormrod	101, 131*	Somerset	Worcester	1980
G. M. Turner	161, 101	Northamptonshire	Stourbridge	1981
G. M. Turner	147*, 139	Warwickshire	Worcester	1981

(6) CENTURY ON FIRST-CLASS DEBUT FOR WORCESTERSHIRE

Batsman	Score	Opponents	Venue	Year
M. Nichol	104	West Indies	Worcester	1928
*C. A. F. Fiddian-Green	108	Essex	Worcester	1931
D. A. Banks	100	Oxford U	Oxford	1983
*C. L. King	123	Somerset	Worcester	1983

Both had previously played First-Class cricket before these innings

(7) 2,000 RUNS IN A SEASON FOR WORCESTERSHIRE

Batsman	Inns	NO	Runs	HS	Avge	100s	Year
H. H. I. Gibbons	57	6	2,654	157	52.03	8	1934
G. A. Hick	35	2	2,615	405*	79.24	10	1988
D. Kenyon	50	6	2,430	253*	55.22	6	1954
G. M. Turner	46	7	2,379	154*	61.00	10	1970
T. W. Graveney	50	7	2,375	164	55.23	5	1964
G. F. Walters	47	4	2,292	226	53.30	9	1933
D. Kenyon	48	2	2,278	258*	49.52	6	1953
D. Kenyon	50	2	2,174	163	45.29	6	1950
D. Kenyon	58	3	2,160	200*	39.27	6	1957
M. Nichol	54	5	2,154	165*	43.95	8	1933
D. Kenyon	57	6	2,133	145	41.82	6	1951
D. Kenyon	54	2	2,126	171	40.88	6	1952
M. J. Horton	51	3	2,123	212	44.22	4	1959
H. H. I. Gibbons	55	6	2,120	178	43.26	6	1938
G. M. Turner	42	4	2,101	168	55.28	9	1981
P. E. Richardson	55	3	2,029	171	39.01	3	1953
R. G. A. Headley	67	5	2,026	150*	32.67	4	1961
H. H. I. Gibbons	57	4	2,008	155	37.88	4	1933
G. A. Hick	37	6	2,004	227*	64.64	6	1986

INDIVIDUAL BOWLING RECORDS

(1) HAT-TRICKS IN FIRST-CLASS MATCHES

Bowler	Opponents	Venue	Year
G. A. Wilson	London County	Worcester	1900
G. A. Wilson	Surrey	Worcester	1901
G. A. Wilson	Australians	Worcester	1905
J. A. Cuffe	Hampshire	Bournemouth	1910
W. B. Burns	Gloucestershire	Worcester	1913
(Having scored 102★ in Worcestershire innings)			
F. A. Pearson	Surrey	Worcester	1914
C. R. Preece	Warwickshire	Edgbaston	1924
R. T. D. Perks	Kent	Stourbridge	1931
R. T. D. Perks	Warwickshire	Edgbaston	1933
P. F. Jackson	Glamorgan	Neath	1936
R. O. Jenkins	Surrey	Oval	1948
R. O. Jenkins	Surrey	Worcester	1949
R. O. Jenkins	Surrey	Worcester	1949
(Only fourth time of two hat-tricks in the same County Championship match)			
R. Howorth	Warwickshire	Edgbaston	1950
J. A. Flavell	Kent	Kidderminster	1951
J. A. Flavell	Cambridge U	Cambridge	1953
M. J. Horton	Somerset	Bath	1956
L. J. Coldwell	Leicestershire	Stourbridge	1957
J. A. Flavell	Lancashire	Old Trafford	1963
(All lbw, given by F. C. Gardner)			
L. J. Coldwell	Essex	Brentwood	1965
R. G. M. Carter	Lancashire	Worcester	1965
N. Gifford	Derbyshire	Chesterfield	1965
J. Cumbes	Northamptonshire	Worcester	1977
H. L. Alleyne	Middlesex	Lord's	1981
(Last two balls of first innings and first ball of second)			

Note: There are no limited-overs hat-tricks for Worcestershire.

(2) NINE WICKETS IN AN INNINGS FOR WORCESTERSHIRE

Bowler	Analysis	Opponents	Venue	Year
C. F. Root	9-23	Lancashire	Worcester	1931
J. A. Flavell	9-30	Kent	Dover	1955
J. A. Cuffe	9-38	Yorkshire	Bradford	1907
A. J. Conway	9-38	Gloucestershire	Moreton-in-Marsh	1914
C. F. Root	9-40	Essex	Worcester	1924
R. T. D. Perks	9-40	Glamorgan	Stourbridge	1939
R. T. D. Perks	9-42	Gloucestershire	Cheltenham	1946
P. F. Jackson	9-45	Somerset	Dudley	1935
M. J. Horton	9-56	South Africans	Worcester	1955

J. A. Flavell	9-56	Middlesex	Kidderminster	1964
E. G. Arnold	9-64	Oxford U	Oxford	1905
N. V. Radford	9-70	Somerset	Worcester	1986
G. A. Wilson	9-75	Oxford U	Oxford	1904
C. F. Root	9-81	Kent	Tunbridge Wells	1930
J. A. Flavell	9-122	Sussex	Hastings	1954

(3) 14 WICKETS IN A MATCH FOR WORCESTERSHIRE

Bowler	Analysis	Opponents	Venue	Year
A. J. Conway	15-87	Gloucestershire	Moreton-in-Marsh	1914
R. T. D. Perks	15-106	Essex	Worcester	1937
R. O. Jenkins	15-122	Sussex	Dudley	1953
G. A. Wilson	15-142	Somerset	Taunton	1905
N. Gifford	14-76	Cambridge U	Cambridge	1972
R. T. D. Perks	14-96	Gloucestershire	Cheltenham	1946
S. H. Martin	14-107	Kent	Gillingham	1939
A. Bird	14-109	Hampshire	Southampton	1901
S. H. Martin	14-110	Somerset	Bath	1937
J. A. Cuffe	14-115	Gloucestershire	Dudley	1911

(4) SIX WICKETS IN A LIMITED OVERS INNINGS

(a) Sunday League (John Player/Refuge Assurance)

Bowler	Analysis	Opponents	Venue	Year
A. P. Pridgeon	6-26	Surrey	Worcester	1978
V. A. Holder	6-33	Middlesex	Lord's	1972

(b) Benson and Hedges Cup

Bowler	Analysis	Opponents	Venue	Year
N. Gifford	6-8	Minor Counties (South)	High Wycombe	1979
J. D. Inchmore	6-29	Lancashire	Old Trafford	1984

(c) NatWest Trophy/Gillette Cup

Bowler	Analysis	Opponents	Venue	Year
J. A. Flavell	6-14	Lancashire	Worcester	1963

(4) 125 WICKETS IN A SEASON FOR COUNTY (100 since 1969)

Bowler	Runs	Wkts	Avge	Best	5WI	Year
C. F. Root	3,627	207	17.52	8-56	27	1925
C. F. Root	3,402	168	20.25	8-75	16	1923
R. O. Jenkins	3,314	159	20.84	7-38	15	1949
J. A. Flavell	2,720	158	17.21	8-43	10	1961
R. T. D. Perks	2,901	154	18.83	9-40	15	1939

C. F. Root	2,435	152	16.01	9-40	15	1934
C. F. Root	3,266	148	22.06	8-118	11	1929
C. F. Root	2,597	145	17.91	8-25	15	1927
J. A. Flavell	2,100	142	14.78	8-74	11	1965
L. J. Coldwell	2,696	140	19.25	8-41	10	1961
R. T. D. Perks	2,863	139	20.59	8-63	8	1937
L. J. Coldwell	2,499	139	17.97	8-64	11	1962
R. Howorth	2,221	138	16.09	7-50	11	1947
R. O. Jenkins	3,218	138	23.31	7-81	10	1951
R. T. D. Perks	3,261	136	23.97	7-58	8	1938
J. A. Flavell	1,891	135	14.00	7-36	9	1966
R. T. D. Perks	2,471	134	18.44	8-43	10	1936
N. Gifford	2,616	133	19.66	7-37	6	1961
G. W. Brook	2,889	132	21.88	7-50	12	1930
C. F. Root	2,963	131	22.61	9-81	7	1930
R. Howorth	2,473	127	19.47	7-58	8	1936
C. F. Root	2,020	126	16.03	9-23	9	1931
R. T. D. Perks	2,778	126	22.04	8-44	8	1935
J. A. Flavell	2,528	126	20.06	6-50	8	1960
E. G. Arnold	2,149	125	17.19	7-48	10	1903
R. Howorth	2,452	125	19.61	7-54	12	1935
N. Gifford	2,092	105	19.92	6-43	7	1970
N. V. Radford	2,493	101	24.68	6-45	4	1985
N. V. Radford	2,269	109	20.81	8-55	8	1987

RECORD WICKET PARTNERSHIPS

(1) IN FIRST-CLASS MATCHES

First Wicket (Qualification 250)

309	H. K. Foster *and* F. L. Bowley *v* Derbyshire *at* Derby	1901
306	F. L. Bowley *and* F. A. Pearson *v* Gloucestershire *at* Worcester	1913
291	G. M. Turner *and* J. A. Ormrod *v* Warwickshire *at* Worcester	1982
290	D. Kenyon *and* P. E. Richardson *v* Gloucestershire *at* Dudley	1953
279	C. F. Walters *and* H. H. I. Gibbons *v* Essex *at* Chelmsford	1934
278★	C. F. Walters *and* H. H. I. Gibbons *v* Leicestershire *at* Worcester	1934
277	D. Kenyon *and* L. Outschoorn *v* Kent *at* Gravesend	1954
274	H. K. Foster *and* F. L. Bowley *v* Hampshire *at* Portsmouth	1907
259	R. G. A. Headley *and* G. M. Turner *v* Warwickshire *at* Worcester	1972
254	G. M. Turner *and* J. A. Ormrod *v* Surrey *at* Worcester	1978

Second Wicket (Qualification 250)

287★	T. S. Curtis *and* G. A. Hick *v* Glamorgan *at* Neath	1986
284	T. S. Curtis *and* G. A. Hick *v* West Indies *at* Worcester	1988
276	T. S. Curtis *and* G. A. Hick *v* Hampshire *at* Worcester	1988
274	H. H. I. Gibbons *and* Nawab of Pataudi *v* Kent *at* Worcester	1933
258	T. S. Curtis *and* G. A. Hick *v* Middlesex *at* Lords	1987
250	F. L. Bowley *and* H. K. Foster *v* Somerset *at* Worcester	1903

Third Wicket (Qualification 250)

314	M. J. Horton *and* T. W. Graveney *v* Somerset *at* Worcester	1962
306	L. G. Crawley *and* W. V. Fox *v* Northamptonshire *at* Worcester	1923
303	H. K. Foster *and* R. E. Foster *v* Kent *at* Worcester	1907
279	H. H. I. Gibbons *and* S. H. Martin *v* Northamptonshire *at* Stourbridge	1934
278	J. A. Ormrod *and* Imran Khan *v* Warwickshire *at* Worcester	1976
277★	G. R. Cass *and* T. J. Yardley *v* Leicestershire *at* Leicester	1975
266	J. D. Inchmore *and* J. M. Parker *v* Essex *at* Worcester	1974
250	C. H. Bull *and* H. H. I. Gibbons *v* Northamptonshire *at* Kidderminster	1937

Fourth Wicket (Qualification 250)

281	J. A. Ormrod *and* Younis Ahmed *v* Nottinghamshire *at* Trent Bridge	1979
277	H. H. I. Gibbons *and* B. W. Quaife *v* Middlesex *at* Worcester	1931
271	T. W. Graveney *and* B. L. D'Oliveira *v* Essex *at* Worcester	1966
260	C. F. Walters *and* C. H. Bull *v* Kent *at* Gravesend	1933
256	C. F. Walters *and* M. Nichol *v* Hampshire *at* Bournemouth	1933
254	F. Chester *and* G. N. Foster *v* Middlesex *at* Lord's	1913
250	H. H. I. Gibbons *and* M. Nicholl *v* Warwickshire *at* Dudley	1929

Fifth Wicket (Qualification 200)

393	E. G. Arnold *and* W. B. Burns *v* Warwicks *at* Edgbaston	1909
261	H. H. I. Gibbons *and* C. H. Palmer *v* Northamptonshire *at* Dudley	1939
227	T. S. Curtis *and* M. J. Weston *v* Surrey *at* Worcester	1985
207★	H. H. I. Gibbons *and* S. H. Martin *v* Hampshire *at* Worcester	1939
203	M. J. Horton *and* G. Dews *v* Essex *at* Leyton	1959

Sixth Wicket (Qualification 200)

265	G. A. Hick *and* S. J. Rhodes *v* Somerset *at* Taunton	1988
227	E. J. O. Hemsley *and* D. N. Patel *v* Oxford U *at* Oxford	1976
206	P. A. Neale *and* S. J. Rhodes *v* Derbyshire *at* Derby	1988
195	G. N. Foster *and* J. A. Cuffe *v* Leicestershire *at* Worcester	1913
191★	D. N. Patel *and* S. J. Rhodes *v* Surrey *at* The Oval	1986

Seventh Wicket (Qualification 150)

205	G. A. Hick *and* P. J. Newport *v* Yorkshire *at* Worcester	1988
197	H. H. I. Gibbons *and* R. Howorth *v* Surrey *at* The Oval	1938
190	R. E. S. Wyatt *and* R. O. Jenkins *v* Leicestershire *at* Worcester	1949
181	G. N. Foster *and* W. B. Burns *v* Hampshire *at* Worcester	1905

Eighth Wicket (Qualification 100)

177★	G. A. Hick *and* R. K. Illingworth *v* Somerset *at* Taunton	1988
145★	F. Chester *and* W. H. Taylor *v* Essex *at* Worcester	1914
133★	P. A. Neale *and* G. A. Hick *v* Surrey *at* The Oval	1984

Ninth Wicket (Qualification 100)

181	J. A. Cuffe *and* R. D. Burrows *v* Gloucester *at* Worcester	1907
141	W. V. Fox *and* C. V. Tarbox *v* Warwicks *at* Edgbaston	1929
127	Imran Khan *and* N. Gifford *v* Northamptonshire *at* Northampton	1976

Tenth Wicket (Qualification 100)

119	W. B. Burns *and* G. A. Wilson *v* Somerset *at* Worcester	1906
94	R. D. Burrows *and* E. W. Bale *v* Yorkshire *at* Worcester	1910
93	C. F. Root *and* R. T. D. Perks *v* Derbyshire *at* Kidderminster	1930

IN LIMITED-OVERS MATCHES

(a) Sunday League

First Wicket (Qualification 175)

224	J. A. Ormrod *and* D. N. Patel *v* Hampshire *at* Southampton	1982
182	R. G. A. Headley *and* G. M. Turner *v* Warwickshire *at* Edgbaston	1972
177	G. M. Turner *and* J. M. Parker *v* Glamorgan *at* Worcester	1973
175*	G. M. Turner *and* J. A. Ormrod *v* Surrey *at* Worcester	1976

Second Wicket (Qualification 140)

149	G. M. Turner *and* Younis Ahmed *v* Leicestershire	1979
145*	I. T. Botham *and* G. A. Hick *v* Essex *at* Worcester	1987
140	G. M. Turner *and* Younis Ahmed *v* Hampshire *at* Worcester	1979

Third Wicket (Qualification 125)

132	G. A. Hick *and* D. N. Patel *v* Gloucestershire *at* Moreton-in-Marsh	1985
125	Younis Ahmed *and* E. J. O. Hemsley *v* Glamorgan *at* Cardiff	1979

Fourth Wicket (Qualification 110)

121	E. J. O. Hemsley *and* J. A. Ormrod *v* Nottinghamshire *at* Trent Bridge	1969
118	G. A. Hick *and* P. A. Neale *v* Northamptonshire *at* Worcester	1985
117	K. W. Wilkinson *and* T. J. Yardley *v* Sussex *at* Worcester	1973
110*	D. A. Leatherdale *and* P. A. Neale *v* Kent *at* Folkestone	1988

Fifth Wicket (Qualification 99)

123	P. A. Neale *and* M. J. Weston *v* Derbyshire *at* Knypersley	1988
99	D. M. Smith *and* M. J. Weston *v* Warwickshire *at* Edgbaston	1986

Sixth Wicket

62	C. L. King *and* D. J. Humphries *v* Surrey *at* Guildford	1983

Seventh Wicket

79	P. A. Neale *and* D. J. Humphries *v* Northamptonshire *at* Luton	1982

Eighth Wicket

80	G. R. Cass *and* J. D. Inchmore *v* Essex *at* Chelmsford	1975

Ninth Wicket

68	P. A. Neale *and* N. Gifford *v* Gloucestershire *at* Bristol	1980

Tenth Wicket

45* J. D. Inchmore *and* A. P. Pridgeon *v* Essex *at* Dudley　　　　　　　　1976

(b) BENSON AND HEDGES CUP

First Wicket (Qualification 125)

191	J. A. Ormrod *and* G. M. Turner *v* Gloucestershire *at* Worcester	1976
125	G. M. Turner *and* J. A. Ormrod *v* Minor Counties *at* Wellington, Shropshire	1982

Second Wicket (Qualification 150)

191	G. M. Turner *and* P. A. Neale *v* Lancashire *at* Old Trafford	1980
174	T. S. Curtis *and* D. M. Smith *v* Warwickshire *at* Worcester	1985
166	J. A. Ormrod *and* Younis Ahmed *v* Yorkshire *at* Worcester	1980
155	R. G. A. Headley *and* E. J. O. Hemsley *v* Oxford U *at* Worcester	1973

Third Wicket (Qualification 125)

190*	D. M. Smith *and* G. A. Hick *v* Nottinghamshire *at* Trent Bridge	1986
179*	D. M. Smith *and* G. A. Hick *v* Northamptonshire *at* Worcester	1986
128	G. M. Turner *and* Imran Khan *v* Warwickshire *at* Edgbaston	1976

Fourth Wicket

118	G. A. Hick *and* P. A. Neale *v* Kent *at* Worcester	1986

Fifth Wicket

131	J. M. Parker *and* T. J. Yardley *v* Leicestershire *at* Worcester	1975
105	P. A. Neale *and* D. N. Patel *v* Lancashire *at* Worcester	1986

Sixth Wicket

121	P. A. Neale *and* S. J. Rhodes *v* Yorkshire *at* Worcester	1988

Seventh Wicket

44*	S. J. Rhodes *and* N. V. Radford *v* Warwickshire *at* Edgbaston	1987

Eighth Wicket

47	J. D. Inchmore *and* R. Senghera *v* Somerset *at* Taunton	1976

Ninth Wicket

42	N. V. Radford *and* G. R. Dilley *v* Nottinghamshire *at* Worcester	1988

Tenth Wicket

22	N. Gifford *and* A. P. Pridgeon *v* Gloucestershire *at* Worcester	1981

NATWEST TROPHY/GILLETTE CUP

First Wicket (Qualification 120)

152	T. S. Curtis *and* I. T. Botham *v* Devon *at* Worcester	1987
123	R. G. A. Headley *and* G. M. Turner *v* Gloucestershire *at* Worcester	1973

Second Wicket (Qualification 125)

186	T. S. Curtis *and* G. A. Hick *v* Nottinghamshire *at* Trent Bridge	1988
127	T. S. Curtis *and* G. A. Hick *v* Devon *at* Worcester	1987

Third Wicket (Qualification 145)

153	D. M. Smith *and* P. A. Neale *v* Lancashire *at* Old Trafford	1985
145	R. G. A. Headley *and* T. W. Graveney *v* Surrey *at* Worcester	1963

Fourth Wicket

152	G. A. Hick *and* P. A. Neale *v* Cumberland *at* Worcester	1988

Fifth Wicket

116	R. G. Broadbent *and* T. W. Graveney *v* Glamorgan *at* Neath	1963

Sixth Wicket

94	B. L. D'Oliveira *and* G. R. Cass *v* Sussex *at* Hove	1974

Seventh Wicket

86★	G. R. Cass *and* T. W. Graveney *v* Derbyshire *at* Derby	1969

Eighth Wicket

50	B. M. Brain *and* N. Gifford *v* Warwickshire *at* Lord's	1966

Ninth Wicket

37★	J. A. Ormrod *and* A. P. Pridgeon *v* Somerset *at* Taunton	1980

Tenth Wicket

21	R. Booth *and* R. G. M. Carter *v* Sussex *at* Lord's	1963

WICKET-KEEPING RECORDS

(1) SIX DISMISSALS IN AN INNINGS

Keeper	Total	Ct	St	Opponents and Venue	Year
H. Yarnold	7	1	6	Scotland at Broughty Ferry, Dundee	1951
G. W. Gaukrodger	6	4	2	Kent at Tunbridge Wells	1907
E. W. Bale	6	2	4	Australians at Worcester	1909
H. Yarnold	6	3	3	Hampshire at Worcester	1949
G. R. Cass	6	6	0	Essex at Worcester	1973
H. G. Wilcock	6	6	0	Hampshire at Portsmouth	1974
S. J. Rhodes	6	6	0	Sussex at Kidderminster	1988

(2) EIGHT DISMISSALS IN A MATCH

Keeper	Total	Ct	St	Opponents and Venue	Year
H. Yarnold	9	5	4	Hampshire at Worcester	1949
S. J. Rhodes	9	9	0	Sussex at Kidderminster	1988
E. W. Bale	8	7	1	Gloucestershire at Cheltenham	1913
H. Yarnold	8	4	4	Kent at Dover	1949
H. Yarnold	8	3	5	Cambridge at Worcester	1950
H. Yarnold	8	1	7	Scotland at Broughty Ferry, Dundee	1951
R. Booth	8	8	0	Essex at Romford	1962
D. J. Humphries	8	7	1	Derbyshire at Derby	1979

(3) 60 DISMISSALS IN A SEASON

Keeper	Total	Ct	St	Year
H. Yarnold	104	59	45	1949
R. Booth	101	85	16	1960
R. Booth	100	90	10	1964
R. Booth	97	83	14	1962
H. Yarnold	95	59	36	1951
H. Yarnold	94	62	32	1950
R. Booth	90	74	16	1961
R. Booth	88	83	5	1959
R. Booth	78	59	19	1957
S. J. Rhodes	78	70	8	1988
R. Booth	72	64	8	1966
R. Booth	69	61	8	1965
R. Booth	68	62	6	1958
J. S. Buller	67	49	18	1938
H. Yarnold	67	42	25	1948
S. J. Rhodes	66	58	8	1986
H. Yarnold	65	52	13	1955
J. S. Buller	62	44	18	1937
R. Booth	62	43	19	1956

(4) 200 DISMISSALS IN A CAREER

Keeper	Total	Ct	St	Career
R. Booth	1,015	868	147	1956–1970
H. Yarnold	684	458	226	1938–1955
D. J. Humphries	345	286	59	1977–1985
E. W. Bale	319	234	85	1908–1920
S. J. Rhodes	257	232	25	1985–1988
J. S. Buller	247	176	71	1935–1946
G. W. Gaukrodger	229	169	60	1900–1910
G. R. Cass	205	183	22	1969–1975

FIELDING RECORDS

(1) FIVE CATCHES IN AN INNINGS

Fielder	Opponents	Venue	Year
R. G. Broadbent (6)	Glamorgan	Stourbridge	1960
G. N. Foster	Hampshire	Southampton	1911
L. Outschoorn	Derbyshire	Kidderminster	1948
R. G. A. Headley	Kent	Dartford	1964
R. G. A. Headley	Gloucestershire	Cheltenham	1967

(2) SEVEN CATCHES IN A MATCH

Fielder	Opponents	Venue	Year
W. B. Burns (8)	Yorkshire	Bradford	1907
R. G. Broadbent	Glamorgan	Stourbridge	1960

(3) 40 CATCHES IN A SEASON

Fielder	Total	Year
D. W. Richardson	65	1961
L. Outschoorn	55	1949
D. W. Richardson	51	1964
R. G. A. Headley	49	1964
L. Outschoorn	43	1951
D. W. Richardson	42	1962
D. W. Richardson	41	1963

(4) 250 CATCHES IN A CAREER

Fielder	Total	Career
D. W. Richardson	414	1952–1967
J. A. Ormrod	384	1962–1983
G. Dews	353	1946–1961

R. G. A. Headley	343	1958–1974
D. Kenyon	306	1946–1967
R. G. Broadbent	297	1950–1963
L. Outschoorn	276	1946–1959
N. Gifford	259	1960–1982

ALL-ROUND CRICKET RECORDS

[1] ALMOST 100 RUNS AND 10 WICKETS IN A MATCH

Player	Batting	Bowling	Opponents and Venue	Year
E. G. Arnold	200*	3-70, 7-44	Warwickshire *at* Edgbaston	1909
C. F. Root	62, 37	7-37, 5-67	Derbyshire *at* Worcester	1924
Imran Khan	111*	7-53, 6-45	Lancashire *at* Worcester	1976

(2) 1,000 RUNS AND 100 WICKETS IN A SEASON

Player	Runs	Avge	Wkts	Avge	Year
E. G. Arnold	1,040	31.51	125	17.19	1903
J. A. Cuffe	1,054	25.70	110	23.56	1911
F. A. Pearson	1,052	25.04	111	22.89	1923
C. F. Root	1,044	20.88	118	29.26	1928
S. H. Martin	1,130	21.73	114	20.25	1937
R. Howorth	1,019	21.22	100	24.34	1939
S. H. Martin	1,262	25.24	106	25.00	1939
R. Howorth	1,050	22.82	104	20.18	1946
R. Howorth	1,172	24.93	138	16.09	1947
M. J. Horton	1,808	29.16	101	21.12	1961

TEST CAREER RECORDS OF PLAYERS WHO HAVE PLAYED FIRST-CLASS CRICKET FOR WORCESTERSHIRE

Name	Country	M	Runs	Avge	Wkts	Avge
A. G. Archer	England	1	31	31.00		
E. G. Arnold	England	10	160	13.33	31	25.41
R. Berry	England	2	6	3.00	9	25.33
J. Birkenshaw	England	5	148	21.14	13	36.07
I. T. Botham	England	94	5,057	34.87	373	37.86
L. J. Coldwell	England	7	9	4.50	22	27.72
R. J. Crisp	South Africa	9	123	10.25	20	37.35
T. S. Curtis	England	2	69	17.25		
G. R. Dilley	England	39	479	12.94	133	28.48
B. L. D'Oliveira	England	44	2,484	40.06	47	39.55
J. A. Flavell	England	4	31	7.75	7	52.42
R. E. Foster	England	8	602	46.30		
N. Gifford	England	15	179	16.27	33	31.09
T. W. Graveney	England	79	4,882	44.38	1	167.00
R. G. A. Headley	West Indies	2	62	15.50		
V. A. Holder	West Indies	40	682	14.20	109	33.27
M. J. Horton	England	2	60	30.00	2	29.50
R. Howorth	England	5	145	18.12	19	33.42
Imran Khan	Pakistan	73	2,860	32.50	334	21.91
R. O. Jenkins	England	9	198	18.00	32	34.31
Kapil Dev	India	92	3,889	32.14	319	29.63
D. Kenyon	England	8	192	12.80		
C. L. King	West Indies	9	418	32.15	3	94.00
P. J. Newport	England	1	26	26.00	7	23.42
C. H. Palmer	England	1	22	11.00		
J. M. Parker	New Zealand	36	1,498	24.55	1	24.00
Nawab of Pataudi	England/India	6	199	19.90		
D. N. Patel	New Zealand	6	265	22.08		
R. T. D. Perks	England	2	3	—	11	32.27
N. V. Radford	England	3	21	7.00	4	87.75
D. W. Richardson	England	1	33	33.00		
P. E. Richardson	England	34	2,061	37.47	3	16.00
C. F. Root	England	3	—	—	8	24.25
F. E. Rumsey	England	5	30	15.00	17	27.11
G. H. T. Simpson-Hayward	England	5	105	15.00	23	18.26
D. M. Smith	England	2	80	20.00		
G. M. Turner	New Zealand	41	2,991	44.64		
C. F. Walters	England	11	784	52.26		
R. E. S. Wyatt	England	40	1,839	31.70	18	35.66
Younis Ahmed	Pakistan	4	177	29.50		

CAPTAINS OF WORCESTERSHIRE

1899–1900	H. K. Foster
1901	R. E. Foster
1902–1910	H. K. Foster
1911–1912	G. H. T. Simpson-Hayward
1913	H. K. Foster
1914–1919	W. H. Taylor
1920–1921	M. F. S. Jewell
1922	W. H. Taylor
1923–1925	M. K. Foster
1926	M. F. S. Jewell
1927	C. B. Ponsonby
1928–1929	M. F. S. Jewell
1929–1930	J. B. Coventry
1931–1935	C. F. Walters
1936–1939	C. J. Lyttelton
1946	A. P. Singleton
1947–1948	A. F. T. White
1949	A. F. T. White and R. E. S. Wyatt
1950–1951	R. E. S. Wyatt
1952–1954	R. E. Bird
1955	R. T. D. Perks
1956–1958	P. E. Richardson
1959–1967	D. Kenyon
1968–1970	T. W. Graveney
1971–1980	N. Gifford
1981	G. M. Turner
1982–1988	P. A. Neale

WORCESTERSHIRE CRICKETERS TO BE AWARDED A BLUE

AT OXFORD

G. E. B. Abell 1924, 1926, 1927
E. G. Bromley-Martin 1897, 1898
G. H. Chesterson 1949
A. R. Duff 1960–1961
W. H. B. Evans 1902–1905
P. B. Fisher 1975–1978
G. N. Foster 1905–1908
H. K. Foster 1894–1896
R. E. Foster 1897–1900
H. A. Gilbert 1907–1909
J. W. Greenstock 1925–1927

H. O. Hopkins 1923
Imran Khan 1973–1975
R. C. M. Kimpton 1935, 1937, 1938
A. R. Legard 1932–1935
E. G.Martin 1903–1906
R. H. Moss 1889
Nawab of Pataudi Snr 1929–1931
A. G. Pawson 1908–1911
A. P. Singleton 1934–1937
J. Stanning 1939
P. J. Whitcombe 1951–1952

AT CAMBRIDGE

G. Ashton 1919, 1920, 1921
L. G. Crowley 1923, 1924, 1925
T. S. Curtis 1983
C. A. F. Fiddian Green 1921–1922
S. P. Henderson 1982–1983
R. H. C. Human 1930–1931

S. T. Jagger 1925–1926
W. W. Lowe 1895
C. F. Lyttelton 1908–1909
T. U. Wells 1950
A. F. T. White 1936

SELECT BIBLIOGRAPHY

P. Bailey, P. Thorn and P.Wynne-Thomas: *Who's Who of Cricketers* (Newnes Books, Feltham, 1984)

Wisden Cricketers' Almanak (various editions)

Fred Root: *A Cricket Pro's Lot* (Edward Arnold, London, 1937)

Roy Genders: *Worcestershire* (Convoy, London, 1952)

W. R. Chignell: *A History of the Worcestershire County Cricket Club* (Littlebury, Worcester, 1951)

W. R. Chignell: *Worcestershire Cricket 1950 to 1968* (Littlebury, Worcester, 1969)

Les Hatton: *John Player Special League Record Book, 1969 to 1986* Association of Cricket Statisticians, Nottingham, 1969)

M. D. Vockins: *Worcestershire—A Pictorial History* (Worcestershire County Cricket Club, 1980)

Les Hatton: *Cricket Grounds of Worcestershire* (Association of Cricket Statisticians, Nottingham, 1984)

Alex E. Davis: *First in the Field, A History of the Birmingham League* (K. and F. Brewin, Studley, 1988)

ACKNOWLEDGEMENTS

The author would like to thank the President, Chairman, Committee and Staff of Worcestershire County Cricket Club for their help and encouragement in the preparation of this work.

Special thanks are due to John Arlott for his kindness, to Brian Croudy for his help and to Les Hatton, a devotee of Worcestershire cricket, without whose encouragement this book would not have been possible.

The Statistical Section was compiled by Les Hatton and the first-class records conform to the recommendations of the Association of Cricket Statisticians, as laid out in the series of *Guides to First-Class Cricket*, published by the Association. Les Hatton has not only provided the statistics, but has given advice and information at all stages.

INDEX

Obviously in work of this nature, not every reference to a player or county can be listed in the index. The page numbers refer to where details of a man's main performances or contributions can be found.

Abell, G. E. B. 74
Ahl, F. 83
Aldridge 141–2
All England XI 8
Alleyne, H. L. 201
Amphlett, R. 59
Archer, A. G. 27
Arlott, J. 236
Arnold, E. G. 17–19, 23, 26, 27, 31–2, 41, 43, 44, 46, 52–3
Australians 13, 41, 54, 80, 91, 101, 115–6, 132

Bale, E. 55
Bannister, A. 36
Benson & Hedges Cup
1973 185–7
1988 226–8
Berry, R. 134
Bird, A. 24, 41
Bird, R. E. 132
Booth, R. 136, 142, 143–5
Botham, I. T. 221–3
Boughton Park 9
Bowley, F. L. 34, 36, 37, 38, 39, 41, 44, 46, 53, 67
Bowen, R. 19
Bradman, D. G. 80–1, 91, 101, 115–6
Brain, B. M. 158, 177, 180, 185
Brandt, D. 55
Brinten, R. 43
Broadbent, R. G. 124
Bromley, E. H. 83–4
Bromley-Martin, E. H. 24, 34
Bromley-Martin, G. E. 17, 23, 24
Bromsgrove School 11, 12
Brook, G. 81
Bull, C. 88, 101, 104
Buller, J. S. 92, 100, 104, 115
Burns, W. B. 41–3, 52–3
Burrows, R. D. 19, 24, 25, 38, 53, 57–8, 60

Caldicott, W. 12
Cardus, N. 164–5
Carter, R. G. 177
Chester, F. 54–6

Chesterton, G. H. 124
City of Worcester C.C. 8
Coldwell, L. 138, 145–6, 167, 176–7
Conway, J. A. 54
Cook, Grace (Mrs Fuller) 109, 184
Cooper, E. 102, 116, 132
Cooper, F. 113, 116
County Championship, entry to 14, 19–21
Coventry family 9–11, 73
Crawley, L. G. 67
Crisis, 1975 192–4
Crisp, R. J. 100
Cuffe, J. A. 42–3, 48, 53
Cumbes, J. 185
Curtis, Tim 211–2, 217–8, 222–3

Derbyshire v Worcestershire
1964 158–9
Dews, G. 124
Dilley, G. R. 221
D'Oliveira, Basil 165–6, 202
Doverdale, Lord 95
Dudley, Lord 41

Elgar, Sir Edward 7, 164–5
Essex v Worcestershire
1929 76–9
1934 91–2

Fearnley, Duncan 151, 172, 176
Financial Crises 50–1, 56–8, 59, 74, 83–4, 88–9
Fisher, P. 202
Flavell, J. 138, 142, 145
Foley, P. H. 13–17, 19–21, 28, 29, 41, 51, 57, 164
Formation of Club 9
Foster family 12, 19, 22, 23, 28–32, 38–54, 57–8
Rev. H. 12
H. K. 164–5
M. K. 67, 70–1, 93
R. E.'s death 54
Foster, F. R. 53
Fox, W. V. 67

Gaukrodger, G. 20, 39, 40, 55
Gibbons, H. H. I. 74, 93, 104, 109
Gilbert, H. A. 63, 83
Gifford, N. 142–4, 208
Gillette Cup, 1973 186–7
Glamorgan v Worcestershire
1988 233–5
Gloucestershire v Worcestershire
1964 161–3
Graveney, T. W. 148, 150, 161, 165–6, 173–4, 177
Green, M. A. 108, 112, 118, 131
Greenstock, W. 60
Grove, C. W. 132–3

Hagley 11
Hampshire v Worcestershire
1899 32–4
1903 43–5
1920 60–1
1965 168–9
1974 188
Hartlebury Common 8
Headley, R. G. A. 148, 191
Hick, G. A. 211–2, 216–7, 219–20
1000 runs before end of May 228
Higgins, H. L. 63, 82
Higgins, J. B. 82
Holder, V. A. 174, 202
Horton, J. 91
Horton, M. J. 132, 134–5, 150–1, 170
Howorth, R. 90, 95, 101–2, 111, 114–5, 129–30
Human, R. H. C. 91
Humphries, D. J. 201
Hunt, F. 19, 61, 94–5, 104, 108, 112

Ibadulla, Billy 174
Illingworth, R. K. 206
Imran Khan 185–6
Inchmore, J. D. 185, 189, 194, 216
Indian tourists 110, 179

Jackson, P. F. 88, 102, 114

Jenkins, R. 40, 105, 114–23, 136, 138
Jewell, A. N. 61–2
Jewell, M. F. S. 54, 60, 62, 71–3, 82–3
Jobson, E. B. 17
John Player League
1971 178–81

Kapil Dev, R. N. 210
Keene, J. A. 46
Kenyon, D. 111, 112–3, 125–6, 132, 133–4, 136–8, 141, 142, 145, 171–2
Kent v Worcestershire
1960 142–4
1976 (Benson & Hedges Cup Final) 195–6
King, Collis 210–1
King, P. 94, 109
Kimpton, R. C. M. 100

Lacey, F. E. 20
Lancashire v Worcestershire
1931 83–5
Lane, A. F. 100, 108
Lane, W. W. 34–5
Langland 7
Lawrence, D. H. 19
Le Roux, G. S. 198–9
Lister, Joe 134–5
Lyttelton family 8, 9, 11, 12, 14, 51
  C. J. 95–8, 101–2, 109

Malvern College 12, 14, 17, 35
Martin, S. H. 88, 101, 104
Maxwell, C. R. 115
Minor Counties 15–18
Middlesex v Worcestershire
NatWest Final 1988 232
Moss, Rev. R. H. 70

Neale, P. A. 194, 203–5, 230
Newport, P. J. 228
New Road Ground 18–20, 197
Nichol, M. 82, 87–9, 91

Nottinghamshire v Worcestershire
1950 126–8
1962 152–4
1985 NatWest 213–5

O'Connor, T. P. 7
Ormrod, J. A. 170, 178, 211
Outschoorn, L. 113, 116, 123, 128–9, 132

Palmer, C. H. 105, 113–4
Parker, J. M. 179, 185
Pataudi, Nawab of 86–7, 93
Patel, D. N. 220
Pawson, A. G. 55
Pearson, D. B. 141–2
Pearson, F. A. 20, 36, 38, 39, 53, 67–9
Pevsner, N. 7
Perks, R. T. D. 44, 78, 80–1, 86, 95, 104–5, 110–1, 113, 114, 134, 135–6
Pitchcroft 9
Ponsonby, Cecil 74
Powick 8
Preece, C. A. 61
Pridgeon, A. P. 185, 194–5, 216

Quaife, B. W. 75

Radford, N. V. 213
Raynor, S. 17
Refuge Assurance League
1987 223–5
Rhodes, S. J. 213, 216
Richardson, D. W. 135, 148
Richardson, P. E. 132, 136, 140
Root, F. 64, 69–70, 72–3, 84–6, 104

Shepherd, Don 112
Simpson-Hayward, G. 34, 52, 55
Singleton, A. P. 110
Smith, D. M. 210, 212, 220
Smith, C. G. 110
Somerset v Worcestershire
1939 105–7

1950 128–9
1962 150
1979 B & H 200
1988 225–7
South Africans 1955 134–5
Standen, J. 145
Straw, G. 27
Sussex v Worcestershire
1963 Gillette Cup Final 155–7
1965 169–70

Tarbox, C. V. 64
Taylor, W. H. 54, 65–6
Turner, G. M. 174, 176–7, 184–5, 202–3, 205, 208
  100th 100 206–7

Vockins, M. 184

Walters, C. F. 75, 89–90, 95
Warton, R. G. 10
Warwickshire v Worcestershire
1906 46–7
1909 52
1964 159–60
1966 Gillette Cup 170–1
1971 JP League 180–2
Weston, M. J. 208, 211
Wheldon, F. 23, 27–8, 43
White, A. F. T. 112–3
Wilks, W. H. W. 38
Wilmott, Bill 19
Wilson, G. A. 17, 23, 24, 39, 40, 44–6
Wyatt, R. E. S. 111–2, 116, 128–9

Yardley, J. T. 178–9
Yarnold, H. 115, 123
Yorkshire v Worcestershire
1899 22–4
1903 43
1907 47–8
1936 98–9
1956 136–8
Young, D. M. 110
Younis Ahmed 198, 210